D1358078

Social Learning
Psychological and Biological Perspectives

Social Learning
Psychological and Biological Perspectives

edited by

Thomas R. Zentall
UNIVERSITY OF KENTUCKY

Bennett G. Galef, Jr.
MCMASTER UNIVERSITY

LEA LAWRENCE ERLBAUM ASSOCIATES, PUBLISHERS
1988 Hillsdale, New Jersey   Hove and London

Lawrence Erlbaum Associates, Inc., Publishers
365 Broadway
Hillsdale, New Jersey 07642

Library of Congress Cataloging-in-Publication Data

Social learning.

Includes bibliographies and index.
1. Social behavior in animals.   2. Learning in
animals.   I. Zentall, Thomas R.   II. Galef, Bennett G.
[DNLM: 1. Learning.   2. Psychology, Social.   3. Social
QL775.S64   1987   591.5'1   87-22364
ISBN 0-89859-921-0
ISBN 0-8085-0104-9 (pbk.)

Printed in the United States of America
10   9   8   7   6   5   4   3   2   1

Contents

Preface

During the past decade there has been a marked increase in the number of North American and European laboratories engaged in the study of social learning. As a consequence, evidence is rapidly accumulating that in animals, as in humans, social interaction plays an important role in facilitating development of adaptive patterns of behavior.

In many cases, studies of social learning appear to have been initiated independently by researchers who began with an interest in individual acquisition of a particular behavioral capacity and only later recognized the importance of social learning in the development of that behavior. For example, research on the social basis of bird-song dialect learning grew out of a long tradition of research on the functions of bird vocalizations. Similarly, interest in the role of social cues in the development of feeding behavior arose from research on the involvement of individual learning in diet selection. Because investigations of social learning research have often started from very different research literatures and perspectives, it is not surprising that the study of social learning as a general phenomenon is highly segmented. Experimenters are isolated both by the phenomena they study and by the species with which they work. The process of creating a coherent field out of the diversity of current social learning research is likely to be both long and difficult. It is our hope, however, that the present volume may prove a useful first step in bringing order to a diverse field.

The idea for this book grew from the premise that researchers who study the role of social learning in the acquisition of one behavior could benefit from exposure to the methods and theories developed by others in their studies of social influences on behavioral development. The purpose of the present volume is, thus, both to initiate a rapprochement among researchers working on diverse problems in the general area of social learning and to serve as an introduction to current research and thinking about problems in social learning for outsiders to the field.

To assess interest in an integrative volume of this type, the editors organized a symposium at the meeting of the Midwestern Psychological Association held in Chicago in 1985. In addition to the organizers, David Hogan, Russ Mason, Sue Mineka, and Irene Pepperberg presented papers. After the symposium, participants expressed unanimous interest in development of an edited book that would serve as a forum both for the research of participants and for the work of others concerned with psychological and biological aspects of social learning.

We wanted to include both discussion of some of the methodological and theoretical issues involved in social learning research and descriptions of a wide range of research programs concerned with the role of social learning in the development of a variety of different behaviors. Methodological issues are presented in historical perspective in Galef's opening chapter (see also Zentall's chapter). Boyd and Richerson follow with a discussion of social learning within an evolutionary perspective.

In an effort to avoid the parochialism that has tended to fractionate social learning research by species and by problem within species, we have organized the book by topic. The chapter groupings reflect research problems that we felt had most in common or would benefit most from a comparison of findings. Following the first section of theoretical and methodological issues, is a section on social influences on avoidance learning. The section deals with fear conditioning of monkeys (Mineka & Cook), mobbing by jackdaws (Curio), and poison avoidance by blackbirds (Mason).

In the third section social influences in foraging and feeding behavior are discussed. This section includes chapters on socially influenced food preferences in both rats (Galef) and humans (Rosin), as well as social modification of foraging strategies of pigeons (Lefebvre & Palameta).

Chapters in the fourth section are concerned with effects of social modeling on the acquisition of arbitrary responses by rats (Zentall and Denny, Clos, & Bell), mice (Mainardi & Mainardi), and pigeons (Zentall, & Hogan).

The last section deals with social influences on communication. Petrinovich's chapter concerns social factors in bird song acquisition, Pepperberg's discusses the allospecific communication by an African Grey parrot (the renowned Alex), and chapters by Meltzoff and Masur deal with nonverbal social modeling by human infants.

We intend this volume as an introduction to some of the many roles that social learning can play in the ontogeny of animal behavior. We hope that it will stimulate interest in social learning research in general and will lead to an increased appreciation of the importance of social factors in the development of behavior.

PART I

Social Learning: Theoretical and Methodological Issues

Imitation in Animals: History, Definition, and Interpretation of Data from the Psychological Laboratory

Bennett G. Galef, Jr.
McMaster University

INTRODUCTION

Since the latter part of the 19th century, scientists have discussed the possibility that animals are capable of learning by imitation. Darwin (1871) explained difficulties in poisoning or trapping wild animals as the result of their ability "to learn caution by seeing their brethren trapped or poisoned" (p. 49). Wallace (1870) interpreted consistency from generation to generation in the structure of the nests of birds of the same species as the result of young observing and imitating the nest of their parents. Romanes (1884) treated imitation learning and subsequent biological inheritance of imitated behaviors as responsible for both continuity across generations in species-typical patterns of behavior and the perfection of instincts. During the early part of the present century, many of the major figures in the early history of experimental psychology (Hobhouse, 1901; Kohler, 1925; Lashley, 1913; McDougall, 1924; Morgan, 1900; Thorndike, 1911; Watson, 1908), as well as any number of less well remembered behavioral scientists, studied and speculated about the process of imitation learning (Berry, 1906, 1908; Cole, 1907; Davis, 1903; Haggarty, 1909; Kempf, 1916; Kinnaman, 1902; Porter, 1910; Sheperd, 1910, 1911, 1923; Small, 1900, 1901; Witmer, 1910).

In consequence, in discussing imitative learning in animals, one has to consider a long and venerable history that provides sources of both comfort and confusion: Comfort, in that study of learning by imitation in animals for more than a century suggests the topic of animal imitation is of intrinsic interest; confusion, in that historical diversity in approaches to study of imitative behavior has produced incompatible conceptual frameworks for analysis of imitative phenomena. One man's example of true learning by imitation is another's paradigmatic case of "pseudo-imitation" and each can cite historical precedent for treating phenomena of interest as he does.

Early work on imitation learning is not only of historical interest. The latter half of the 19th century saw the formulation of alternative approaches to the study of imitative phenomena that, even today, shape research in the area. The views of major figures in the behavioral biology and psychology of the last century, provide an important foundation for understanding the origins of much contemporary disagreement and confusion as well as a benchmark from which to measure a century's progress in the study of imitative behavior.

EARLY PERSPECTIVES ON LEARNING BY IMITATION

The major impetus for 19th-century discussion of imitation arose out of disagreement among leading scientific figures of the period concerning the origins of the higher mental faculties of man. Darwin and Wallace, co-formulators of evolutionary theory, differed profoundly over the possibility of employing the principle of evolution, of descent with modification, to understand the development of the human mind. As a contemporary, George Romanes (1884), stated the issue:

> . . . the great school of evolutionists is divided in two sects; according to one the mind of man has been slowly evolved from the lower types of psychical existence, and according to the other the mind of man, not having been thus evolved, stands apart, *sui generis* from all other types of existence. (p. 9)

The dispute was similar to modern debate over whether animals, like men, are capable of conscious thought, "for them to know, or think consciously about the eventual results of what they are doing" (Griffin, 1985, p. 480); the issue today, as in 1884, is the continuity of human and animal mind. In one way, the controversy at the end of the last century was more respectable than its modern counterpart; during the former debate, there was some consensus as to evidence that would decide the issue: indication that animals had humanlike emotions such as shame, remorse, jealousy, and benevolence, that they could use tools or act deceitfully, that they were able to solve complex problems or imitate complex acts.

G. J. Romanes

For both George Romanes, a staunch advocate of the Darwinian view, and for his opponents, demonstrations of imitative learning in animals were seen as providing important evidence of an evolutionary origin of the higher mental faculties of man. The capacity for imitation in animals was viewed as ancestral to the unique human faculty for culture.

Because of the view of phylogeny held by Romanes and many of his contemporaries, failure to find evidence of gradually increasing complexity in imitative behavior as one ascended the great chain of being would have disconfirmed the continuity position. Romanes did not share Darwin's conception of phylogeny as a branching process (Galef, 1986). Rather, Romanes's discussions of evolution have implicit within them the older Spencerian (1855) view (now discredited; Hodos & Campbell, 1969) that it is possible to trace a historically meaningful, linear development of mind across extant species. In consequence, Romanes believed the Darwinian notion of continuity required the presence in living animals of a graded series of primitive precursors of human mental and moral faculties.

Imitation learning was a particularly important test case for Romanes (1884, 1889) because he believed that the imitative faculty reached its highest levels of perfection, not in rational, adult, European man, but in slightly inferior forms: monkeys, children, savages, and idiots (Romanes, 1884, p. 225). Hence, imitation was a faculty one would expect to find, in at least rudimentary form, in species standing yet lower on the psychological scale. Seeking evidences of primitive imitative capacities in animals, Romanes was quick to find them. Romanes's (1884, 1889) classic texts provide many examples.

The first instance of imitation, and the one described by Romanes (1884) at greatest length, is an example of imitation by honeybees of a behavior exhibited by bumblebees.

> One morning for the first time, I[1] saw several humble-bees . . . visiting flowers [of the kidney bean], and I saw them in the act of cutting with their mandibles holes through the under side of the calyx, and thus sucking the nectar: all the flowers in the course of the day became perforated, and the humble-bees in their repeated visits of the flowers were thus saved much trouble in suckling. The very next day I found all the hive-bees, without exception, sucking through the holes which had been made by the humble-bees. How did the hive-bees find out that all the flowers were bored, and how did they so suddenly acquire the habit of using the holes? . . . I must think that the hive-bees either saw the humble-bees cutting the holes, and

---

[1]The "I" in this case is actually Charles Darwin. Romanes's 1884 text contains several quotes from an unpublished Darwin manuscript, originally intended as part of *Origin of Species*.

understood what they were doing and immediately profited by their labour; or that they merely imitated the humble-bees after they had cut the holes, and when sucking at them. (p. 220–221)

Romanes then briefly mentions a number of additional cases of imitative learning reported by other correspondents: (1) dogs in the Falkland islands that learned from one another the best way of attacking cattle, (2) chickens learning to respond to "the danger cries and signals employed by other species," (3) birds imitating the songs of different species, (4) birds of some species that "articulate words" or "songs having a proper musical notation," (5) dogs foster-reared by cats acquiring feline patterns of behavior such as face-washing, avoidance of water, and stalking mice, (6) juvenile birds taught by their elders to fly, (7) hawks taught by their parents "to more perfectly swoop upon their prey," and (8) newly hatched chicks learning to drink water by imitating their fellows.

Romanes (1884) justified treating this diverse collection of observations as exemplifying a single underlying process, imitation, by inferring that in each case "there must first be intelligent perception of the desirability of the modification on the part of certain individuals, who modify their actions accordingly" (p. 229).

In Romanes's view, modification of behavior as the result of interaction with others implied both intelligence and intentionality in the imitator. These inferences of intelligence and intentionality from evidences of imitation were both crucial to Romanes's main line of argument and a recurring problem in succeeding decades.

If imitation in animals results from psychological processes qualitatively different from those underlying imitation in man (presumed to be intentional and intelligent), then instances of apparent imitative learning in animals are not true precursors of the human faculty for culture; such examples of animal imitation would be, in modern terms, analogues rather than homologues of human imitation. In consequence, Romanes's use of evidence of imitation in animals to provide a bridge between the minds of animals and the minds of men required interpretation of instances of animal imitation as examples of the exercise of rudimentary versions of humanlike capacities for intelligent, intentional action. J. T. Bonner's (1980) recent tracing of the evolution of culture has a similar underlying philosophy.

C. L. Morgan

The need to determine whether a given instance of animal imitation depended on faculties of mind similar to those assumed to be employed in imitation learning by humans was recognized early in the history of behavioral biology. C. L. Morgan (1900) proposed that imitation may be of two basic types, either "instinctive," or "reflective"[2] and that it is only the latter type, "deliberate and intentional imitation . . . directed to a special end more or less clearly perceived as such" (p. 193), that should properly be considered imitation in the sense the term is used in describing the behavior of humans after infancy.

> A chick sounds the danger note; this is the stimulus under which another chick sounds a similar note. . . . Such a procedure may be described as imitative in its effects, but not imitative in its purpose. Only from the observer's standpoint does such instinctive behaviour differ from other modes of congenital procedure. It may be termed biological but not psychological imitation. And if it be held [as Romanes asserted] that the essence of imitation lies in the purpose so to imitate, we must find some other term under which to describe the facts. This does not seem necessary, however, if we are careful to qualify the term "imitation" by the adjective "instinctive" or "biological". And the retention of the term [imitation] serves to indicate that this is the stock on which deliberate imitation is eventually grafted (p. 190).

Thus, Morgan departs from Romanes in suggesting that changes in behavior, which to an outside observer appear to be the result of deliberate, conscious imitation, may rest on a different psychological process, instinctive imitation.

In addition to distinguishing instinctive from reflective imitation, Morgan (1900) introduced a further important concept, that of *intelligent imitation,* into discussions of imitative behavior. "Instinctive imitation introduces into the conscious situation certain modes of behavior, and if the development of the situation as a whole is pleasurable, there will be a tendency to its redevelopment under the guidance of intelligence on subsequent occasions" (p. 121).

As William James has proposed in 1892, "every instinctive act, in an animal with memory, must cease to be 'blind' after being once repeated" (James, 1961, p. 262). Either instinct or instinctive imitation may introduce behavioral elements into an individual's repertoire, but its subsequent maintenance, frequency of occurrence, and conditions of expression will reflect nonimitative learning processes, the action of intelligence. The distinction between processes leading to introduction of a pattern of behavior into an individual's repertoire and those influencing its subsequent expression, first suggested by James and Morgan, is one to which I return later in the present chapter.

E. L. Thorndike

Although both Romanes and Morgan were willing to infer occurrence of learning by imitation from observation of animals of unknown previous history in uncontrolled environments, Edward Thorndike (1911) was far more cautious in accept-

---

[2]The same distinction appears in the essays of the Scottish philosopher Thomas Reid (1764), though I do not know whether Morgan was aware of Reid's analysis of imitation learning.

ing evidence that animals could "from an act witnessed learn to do an act" (p. 79). Thorndike's unwillingness to accept anecdotal evidence of imitation in animals arose from his more general position that "the idea of a response is in and of itself unable to produce that response" (p. 257). If animals could learn to do acts simply by seeing those acts performed, clearly the idea of an act is sufficient impulse for its performance.

Thorndike's attempts to experimentally demonstrate imitation learning in chickens, cats, dogs, and monkeys failed to provide evidence of a capacity for imitation learning. The problem remaining was to explain purported instances of learning by imitation described by his contemporaries. It is in that explanation that Thorndike (1911) provided the conceptual basis for much subsequent experimental investigation of imitative phenomena.

> To the question, "Do animals imitate?" science has uniformly answered, "Yes." But so long as the question is left in this general form, no correct answer to it is possible. It will be seen, from the results of numerous experiments soon to be described, that imitation of a certain sort is not possible for animals, and before entering upon that description it will be helpful to differentiate this matter of imitation into several varieties or aspects. The presence of some sorts of imitation does not imply that of other sorts.
>
> There are, to begin with, the well-known phenomena presented by the imitative birds. The power is extended widely, ranging from the parrot who knows a hundred or more articulate sounds to the sparrow whom a patient shoemaker taught to get through a tune. Now, if a bird really gets a sound in his mind from hearing it and sets out forthwith to imitate it, as mocking birds are said at times to do, it is a mystery and deserves closest study. If a bird, out of a lot of random noises that it makes, chooses those for repetition which are like sounds that he has heard, it is again a mystery why, though not as in the previous case a mystery how, he does it. The important fact for our purpose is that, though the imitation of sounds is so habitual, there does not appear to be any marked general imitative tendency in these birds. There is no proof that parrots do muscular acts from having seen other parrots do them. But this should be studied. At any rate, until we know what sort of sounds birds imitate, what circumstances or emotional attitudes these are connected with, how they learn them and, above all, whether there is in birds which repeat sounds any tendency to imitate in other lines, we cannot, it seems to me, connect these phenomena with anything found in the mammals or use them to advantage in a discussion of animal imitation as the forerunner of human. In what follows they will be left out of account, will be regarded as a specialization removed from the general course of mental development, just as the feathers or right aortic arch of birds are particular specializations of no consequence for the physical development of mammals. For us, henceforth, imitation will mean imitation minus the phenomena of imitative birds.
>
> There are also certain pseudo-imitative or semi-imitative phenomena which ought to be considered by themselves. For example, the rapid loss of the fear of railroad trains or telegraph wires among birds, the rapid acquisition of arboreal habits among Australian rodents, the use of proper feeding grounds, etc., may be

held to be due to imitation. The young animal stays with or follows its mother from a specific instinct to keep near that particular object, to wit, its mother. It may thus learn to stay near trains, or scramble up trees, or feed at certain places and on certain plants. Actions due to following pure and simple may thus simulate imitation. Other groups of acts which now seem truly imitative may be indirect fruits of some one instinct. This must be kept in mind when one estimates the supposed imitation of parents by young. Further, it is certain that in the case of the chick, where early animal life has been carefully observed, instinct and individual experience between them rob imitation of practically all its supposed influence. Chicks get along without a mother very well. Yet no mother takes more care of her children than the hen. Care in other cases, then, need not mean instruction through imitation.

These considerations may prevent an unreserved acceptance of the common view that young animals get a great number of their useful habits from imitation, but I do not expect or desire them to lead to its summary rejection. I should not now myself reject it, though I think it quite possible that more investigation and experiment may finally reduce all the phenomena of so-called imitation of parents by young to the level of indirect results of instinctive acts.

Another special department of imitation may be at least vaguely marked off: namely, apparent imitation of certain limited sorts of acts which are somewhat frequent in the animal's life. An example will do better than further definition.

Some sheep were being driven on board ship one at a time. In the course of their progress they had to jump over a hurdle. On this being removed before all had passed it, the next sheep was seen to jump as if to get over a hurdle, and so on for five or six, apparently sure evidence that they imitated the action, each of the one in front. Now, it is again possible that among gregarious animals there may be elaborate connections in the nervous system which allow the sight of certain particular acts in another animal to arouse the innervation leading to those acts, but that these connections are limited. The reactions on this view are specific responses to definite signals, comparable to any other instinctive or associational reaction. The sheep jumps when he sees the other sheep jump, not because of a general ability to do what he sees done, but because he is furnished with the instinct to jump at such a sight, or because his experience of following the flock over boulders and brooks and walls has got him into the habit of jumping at the spot where he sees one ahead of him jump; and so he jumps even though no obstacle be in his way. If due to instinct, the only peculiarity of such a reaction would be that the sense-impression calling forth the act would be the same act as done by another. If due to experience, there would be an exact correspondence to the frequent acts called forth originally by several elements in a sense-impression, one of which is essential, and done afterwards when only the non-essentials are present. These two possibilities have not been sufficiently realized, yet they may contain the truth. On the other hand, these limited acts may be the primitive, sporadic beginnings of the general imitative faculty which we find in man. (p. 76–79)

Explicit in Thorndike's exposition are several ideas: First, acceptance of evidence that social interaction can result in increased similarity in the behavior of interactants; second, the novel view that a wide variety of psychological processes, not just one or two, can underlie socially induced similarities in behavior. Third, Thorndike is the first to offer a clear alternative to the view that the various types of "semi-imitative phenomena" he described are simpler forms of the "general imitative faculty which we find in man." Thorndike's distinction between pseudo-imitative and imitative behaviors suggests that the processes of social learning seen in man and in animals may be different in kind rather than in degree, that there is no single imitative capacity that appears in various guises in animals possessing nervous systems of varying complexity. Finally, because of the importance of demonstrations of true imitative learning to Thorndike's general theoretical position, the process of imitation was to be used as an explanation of last resort, only after alternative explanations had been excluded.

Summary

By the end of the 19th century the term imitation was being used in three very different senses. Romanes described all instances of socially induced changes in behavior as imitative, assuming that simpler forms were the homologous antecedents of more complex ones. Morgan, although maintaining the use of *imitation* as a generic, wished to distinguish between instinctive and reflective imitation, suggesting that two different psychological processes might underlie superficially similar acquisition process. Thorndike defined imitation in a more restrictive sense than either Morgan or Romanes, as learning to do an act from seeing it performed, and described a number of "pseudo-imitative" processes, qualitatively different from true imitation, that might result in what to the uncritical observer appeared to be true imitation learning, homologous to imitation in man.

TWENTIETH-CENTURY VIEWS ON IMITATION

Unfortunately, the 80 years and more since publication of Thorndike's (1898) monograph have seen no resolution of the conflicting usages of the term imitation already evident at the turn of the century (Morgan, 1900, p. 179). Some continue to use imitation to refer to any instance of social influence on behavior acquisition. Others employ a Morgan-like dichotomy between reflective and instinctive imitation, using the more modern terminology of *imitation* and *social facilitation*. Yet others (including the present author) treat imitation as did Thorndike, as an onerous concept to be employed only when no other explanation of an observed social influence on behavior is possible.

This ambiguity in relationship between labels and phenomena has become increasingly problematic as work on social learning has broadened and scientists with diverse backgrounds attempt to communicate across disciplinary boundaries. Indeed, during the present century, the problem has become more acute in that an elaborate terminology has developed referring to various instances of imitative learning. We now have available (in addition to imitation, intelligent imitation, reflective imitation, instinctive imitation, and pseudo-imitation), true imitation, allelomimetic behavior, mimesis, protoculture, tradition, contagious behavior, social facilitation, local enhancement, matched dependent behavior, stimulus enhancement, vicarious conditioning, observational conditioning, copying, modeling, social learning, social transmission, and observational learning. to mention but some of the more visible terms.

The superficial impression created by this vocabulary is that the old topic of imitation learning can be divided into distinct subtopics each reflecting different behavioral processes. Unfortunately, this is not the case. There is little agreement as to the proper descriptive to apply to various examples of imitative learning. In consequence, labeling phenomena neither increases understanding nor aids in communication. Although increased understanding can come only from further research, communication may be facilitated by calling attention to current chaos and suggesting ways to circumvent it.

The danger is that discussing terms will encourage reification of what are, generally, vague abstractions reflecting ignorance of the processes underlying social effects on behavior. Thorndike's failure either to provide labels for or attempt precise definitions of the "pseudo-imitative" behaviors he described reflected an appropriate caution in codifying poorly understood phenomena. Even today, the few experiments exploring necessary and sufficient conditions for occurrence of social effects on behavior do not provide an adequate empirical basis for meaningful classification. Yet, we have inherited a rich vocabulary for discussion of imitative phenomena and use of that vocabulary can surely be improved while avoiding both the Scylla of reification and the Charybdis of ambiguity.

In the present section, I discuss terms often found in the literature on imitative phenomena. My goals are (1) to review the vocabulary, (2) to point out contradictions in usage, and (3) in some cases, to make explicit assumptions concealed within the terms themselves that have interfered with analyses of instances of imitative behavior.

Some will surely object to my treatment of one or another of the terms in the lexicon of imitative learning. I can respond only that semantic issues are secondary. Regardless of the labels one attaches to phenomena, the task before us is unchanged, to understand the myriad ways in which social influences on learning and performance contribute to the development and expression of adaptive behavioral repertoires. I hope the following discussion will prove useful in that regard.

Description and Explanation

A recurring problem in discussions and definitions of imitative behaviors has been a failure to differentiate description of observed behaviors from explanation of the processes responsible for the occurrence of the behaviors observed. Too often the observation that social interaction is important in the acquisition of a behavior has been used to infer that a particular learning process (imitation, social facilitation, local enhancement, etc.) is responsible, without the necessary analytic investigations being carried out. Thus it seems to me that a necessary first step in discussion of the vocabulary of imitation is to clearly distinguish descriptive from explanatory terminology. In the present section, I first introduce and discuss three descriptive terms (*social learning, social enhancement,* and *social transmission*) and then proceed to consider terms referring to processes that might produce any given instance of social learning, social enhancement, or social transmission.

Descriptive Terms

Social Learning: Imitation, Observational Learning.   Morgan (1900) proposed *imitation* as a generic to refer to all cases in which social interaction functioned to modify the probability of a naive individual's exhibiting or acquiring some pattern of behavior exhibited by others. Although he was surely correct in suggesting that a generic would be useful, the term imitation has acquired too many meanings in intervening years to be unambiguous when used in that way. Hall (1963) suggested *observational learning* "to avoid the conundra associated with [use of] imitation" (p. 206) though, over the years, observational learning also has become subject to diverse usages.

H. O. Box (1984, p. 213) introduced *social learning* as a generic. It is theoretically neutral and suggests a dichotomy between learning that is influenced socially and instances of individual learning in which behavior acquisition is not influenced by interaction with others.

It should be kept in mind, however, that even the distinction between individual and social learning is not so clear as one might hope. It is obvious that in the final analysis it is always individuals that learn. As Morgan indicated, social interaction may facilitate introduction of a pattern of behavior into an individual's repertoire. However, if that pattern of behavior is maintained, such maintenance is the result of favorable consequences resulting from performance of the behavior. Thus, although social learning may play a role in facilitating acquisition of behavior, it may be misleading to refer to a behavior exhibited by an animal as socially learned.

Social Enhancement: Coaction, Social Facilitation.   Clayton (1978) has defined *social facilitation* as "an increase in the frequency or intensity of responses or the initiation of particular responses already in an animal's repertoire, when shown in the presence of others engaged in the same behavior at the same time" (p. 374). Zajonc (1964) used *coaction* to refer to the same effects. In defining social facilitation, Clayton emphasized a distinction between social effects on the performance of behaviors already in an animal's repertoire and social effects on acquisition processes. At a descriptive level, this distinction seems valuable.

Clayton specifically excluded from consideration as socially facilitated, instances of behavior in which simple presence of others increased performance of behaviors already in a subject's repertoire. Thus, in Clayton's usage, social facilitation has both descriptive and explanatory connotations. (Use of social facilitation as an explanatory term is discussed later.) Clearly, it is an empirical question whether socially induced enhanced performance is the result of the behavior of others or of their simple presence.

It would be useful to have available a generic to refer to all social influences on performance of established responses, independent of underlying mechanism, to provide a framework within which analytic investigations could be conducted. There is, so far as I know, no such term in the literature and I propose *social enhancement* for that purpose. The problem with *social facilitation* is that it, like *imitation,* has been defined in so many ways by so many authors that it no longer has any clear referent. (Compare, for example, Crawford, 1939; Clayton, 1978; Thorpe, 1963; Wechkin, 1970; and Zajonc, 1965.)

I would also include as instances of social enhancement, effects on performance resulting from the presence of residual traces others leave in a shared environment. It is, again, an empirical question whether, in any particular case, the presence or activity of others is necessary to produce social enhancement of performance. Even during periods of coaction, coactors may, for example, release chemicals that are responsible for any observed social enhancement of behavior.

Simple presence of others, presence of behaving others, or presence of residual cues emitted by others could each, at least in principle, enhance performance of responses already in an individual's repertoire. A generic such as *social enhancement* would be useful to refer to such effects as distinct from *social learning,* i.e., cases of social effects on acquisition and extinction processes.

Social Transmission: Protoculture, Subculture, Preculture, Tradition.   For historical as well as theoretical reasons, cases of social learning that result in increased homogeneity of behavior of interactants that extends beyond the period of their interaction are an important subset of socially learned or socially enhanced behaviors. I have proposed (Galef, 1976) calling such behaviors *socially transmitted,* in that social interaction increases the probability that one individual will come to independently exhibit a behavior initially in the repertoire of another.

I have suggested limiting use of the term socially transmitted to those instances of social learning or social enhancement in which (1) social interaction is not a necessary condition for the ontogeny of a pattern of behavior; (2) the change in behavior resulting from social interaction is increased homogeneity of the behavior of interactants; and (3) this increased homogeneity of behavior extends in time beyond the period of interaction between transmitter and recipient. These three criteria distinguish forms of social learning that might act to disseminate patterns of behavior through a population from those incapable of doing so.

There are many interesting social learning phenomena that are not instances of social transmission. For example, West, King, and Harrocks (1983) have shown that the song of male cowbirds is modified by interactions with conspecific males and females. Although social learning results from these interactions, they often do not produce increased homogeneity in the behavior of interactants. Harlow and Harlow's (1965) demonstrations of the necessary role of social interaction in the development of normal patterns of sexual and maternal behavior in rhesus monkeys would be an instance of social learning, but not social transmission. In this case, social interaction is obligate and not facultative for development of behavior. (See Galef, 1976, for futher discussion.)

The purpose of distinguishing social transmission from social learning is to differentiate social interactions that facilitate the spread of idiosyncratic behaviors through a population, that can produce protoculture (Count, 1973), preculture (Kawai, 1965), subculture (Kawamura, 1959) or tradition (Kummer, 1971), from those that can not.

Explanatory Terms

Selection of descriptive terms is not particularly contentious. Greater problems arise in choosing terms to refer to behavioral processes that support social enhancement, social learning, and social transmission. Existing explanatory terminology is extensive, contradictory, and vague, and, in my view, of little use in analysis of the behavioral phenomena to which it refers. Attaching explanatory labels to phenomena has frequently both served to hide ignorance of underlying process and interfered with further investigation, rather than clarified issues.

Careful experiment can determine whether social interaction plays a role in development of a behavior, can define necessary and sufficient conditions for social influence, can identify social stimuli that modify behavior, and so forth. However, in the absence of clearly defined, mutually exclusive categories, each reflecting a unique process underlying social learning or social enhancement, there is little to be gained by explaining instances of social learning as produced by one type of social learning rather than another.

During the period when general process theories of individual learning dominated experimental animal psychology, advance in study of social learning seemed to require identification of social learning analogues of such individual learning processes as operant and classical conditioning. If one could elucidate critical features of paradigmatic cases of social learning, then social learning could be studied at the same level of abstraction as individual learning (Jenkins, 1984).

However, study of social learning was, from its inception, more profoundly influenced by field observation than was study of individual learning. The need to discuss cases of "imitation" reported in the field literature required attention to a broad range of phenomena, the complexity of which defied simple categorical schemes. Perhaps in consequence, assimilation of the study of social learning into the methodological framework that dominated study of individual learning in the psychological laboratory did not occur.

Attempts at classification of instances of social learning according to underlying behavioral mechanisms, though failing to reach their primary goal, did
prove useful. Such attempts were heuristic in suggesting experimental approaches
to analysis of social learning phenomena. This heuristic value becomes evident if
one treats attempts at classification as extensions of Thorndike's (1898) list of
vaguely defined "pseudo-imitative" processes that can produce social learning,
rather than as formal classificatory schemes.

Local Enhancement and Stimulus Enhancement.   Probably the most frequently used
term in analyses of social learning is *local enhancement,* introduced by Thorpe
(1956) in his discussion of evidences of ideation in animals. Thorpe (1963)
defined local enhancement as "apparent imitation resulting from directing the
animal's attention to a particular object or to a particular part of the environment" (p. 134). The term has usually been used to refer to instances in which
animals directly interact, though this restriction seems to me unnecessary. If, for
example, rats mark foods they have eaten, thereby increasing the probability that
conspecifics will eat the same foods (Galef & Beck, 1985), or leave scent trails as
they move about the environment, inducing others to follow the same path
(Telle, 1966), the absence of the initiator of the pattern of feeding or movement
at the time of acquisition by a second individual does not seem to me to change
the nature of the basic process.

Thorpe's hypothesis that local enhancement is the result of increased attention to certain objects or places is also unnecessarily restrictive. Consider Thorndike's (1911) example of the rapid loss of fear of railroad trains among birds,
quoted above and interpreted by Thorndike as due to an inherent tendency to
follow or affiliate. It seems unlikely that birds lose their fear of trains as a result of
socially induced enhanced attention to them. Socially induced increased exposure
to trains and consequent habituation to the threatening stimuli that trains emit
seem a likely explanation of the observed social transmission of behavior.

A tendency on the part of naive individuals to approach conspecifics,
alterations conspecifics have made in the environment, or objects they have
contacted, can increase a naive individual's probability of exposure to one set of
stimuli rather than others. Enhanced exposure can lead to habituation, familiarity, perceptual learning. latent learning, increased probability of manipulation
of one portion of the environment, and so forth. All such socially initiated
alterations in behavior seem to me to be instances of local enhancement and, in
consequence, Thorpe's 1963 definition appears too narrow.

Use of the term local enhancement to describe an instance of social learning
should not be allowed to conceal the fact that we remain ignorant of many
important features of social interactions labeled in this way: the necessary and
sufficient conditions for one organism directing the behavior of another to some
portion of the environment, whether, in fact, changes in focus of "attention"
actually have anything to do with such phenomena (Davis, 1973).

Spence (1937) used the term *stimulus enhancement* to refer to "a change in stimulus conditions, the enhancement of the particular limited aspect of the total stimulus situation to which the response is to be made" (p. 821). Although Spence's term never achieved the frequency of usage of Thorpe's local enhancement, it is in my view preferable, both avoiding reference to unobservable attentional processes and broader in scope than is Thorpe's use of local enhancement. The notion of stimulus enhancement, as defined by Spence, extends the concept of local enhancement to include the entire class of objects sharing stimulus characteristics with an object a demonstrator manipulates, contacts, or marks.

Investigators employing the duplicate-cage method (Warden & Jackson, 1935), in which a demonstrator and observer are kept in separate enclosures and contact separate, identical manipulanda to receive reinforcement, have frequently not considered local enhancement as an explanation of observed social effects on learning (Suboski & Bartashunas, 1984; Warden & Jackson, 1935; Zentall & Levine, 1972). Given Thorpe's narrow definition of local enhancement they should not have. However, stimulus enhancement could play a role in facilitating learning in many situations in which local enhancement could not occur. Thus, use of Thorpe's narrow definition of the phenomenon of local enhancement can obscure possible explanations of social learning phenomena.

Social Facilitation.   Zajonc (1965, 1969) has suggested that the simple presence of others "energizes all responses made salient by the stimulus situation confronting the individual at the moment. Among those, the dominant responses (i.e., those most likely to be emitted) are assumed to derive the greatest benefit from the presence of others" (1969, p. 10). Experimental evidence of such "social facilitation" is surprisingly scant. In most cases described in the literature, the others present are engaged in the same behavior as the subject and there is no opportunity to observe the effects of pure social facilitation in Zajonc's sense. Some studies designed to separate the effects of the simple presence of others from the effects of others engaging in the target behavior (e.g., Galef, 1971; Strobel, 1972; Tolman & Wilson, 1965) have failed to find evidence of such social facilitation; other studies have found such effects, though they are generally not large (Levine & Zentall, 1974; Zentall & Hogan, 1976).

Clayton (1978) has proposed that in some studies in which behavior was alleged to increase in frequency in socially stimulated, as compared with isolate animals (e.g., Pishkin & Shurley, 1966; Tolman, 1967), social facilitation resulted from disinhibition of behavior by reduction of isolation-induced fear. Fear reduction or reduction in arousal resulting from the presence of conspecifics is known to have profound effects on behavior (e.g., Campbell & Raskin, 1978; Kaufman & Hinde, 1961; Randall & Campbell, 1976; Stamm, 1961) and, in consequence, it is difficult to determine whether, as Zajonc proposed, the simple presence of others also has energizing effects on behavior. Whether fear reduction or social facilitation is involved, it seems reasonable to suppose that members of some species are, for example, more likely to exhibit feeding behavior in an area that contains other individuals than in one that does not.

Although social facilitation in Zajonc's sense of the term is a form of social enhancement, it could play a role in social learning or social transmission via processes analogous to Morgan's intelligent imitation. For example, Sullivan (1984a) found that downy woodpeckers, when feeding in a mixed species flock, reduced the time they spent "looking-out" and increased the time they spent feeding. Contact calls of chickadees played through a loudspeaker also increased the time spent feeding by the downy woodpeckers (Sullivan, 1984b). Stimuli indicating the simple presence of chickadees rather than chickadee feeding behavior facilitated woodpecker feeding.

If woodpeckers are sensitive to the different foraging rates they exhibit when alone and when in mixed species flocks, flock-induced augmentation of feeding rate could be the proximate cause of flock joining. The tendency to join flocks of chickadees could modify choice of feeding patches by woodpeckers. Changes in patch selection could influence prey selection. Thus, although social facilitation cannot itself produce social transmission, in concert with individual learning, it too might play a role in social transmission processes.

Contagious Behavior: Mimesis, Allelomimetic Behavior, Instinctive Imitation, Social Facilitation.   Yet another long-recognized process that may result in social enhancement of behavior is that which Morgan (1900) and Washburn (1908) called instinctive imitation, Thorpe (1963) called both social facilitation and contagious behavior, Armstrong (1951) and Verplanck (1957) labeled mimesis, Scott (1958) allelomimesis, and both Mowrer (1960) and Humphrey (1921) called imitation. Because social facilitation and imitation have been widely used in other contexts, I prefer *contagious behavior* to refer to situations in which "the performance of a more or less instinctive pattern of behavior by one will tend to act as a releaser for the same behavior in others and so initiate the same line of action in the whole group" (Thorpe, 1963, p. 133). Yawning in humans (Thorpe, 1963), chorusing in roosters or dogs (Humphrey, 1921), maneuvering in flocks of birds or schools of fish, the "flying up" of partridge or quail (Armstrong, 1951; Scott, 1958) have all been discussed as exemplifying contagious behavior.

Processes other than instinctive response to releasing stimuli have been proposed to account for such contagious behaviors. Humphrey (1921), suggested the following hypothetical example:

> Suppose that a herd of cattle is feeding together and something occurs to startle them . . . all manifest signs of fear and run . . . Any individual, A, will as he runs, see his fellows running, and this will have always occurred whatever the stimulus. Hence the sight of a running fellow will act as a conditioned stimulus for the activity of running. (p. 4)

In this case, contagious behavior is seen as resulting from response to classically conditioned stimuli rather than unconditional releasers. (See also Church, 1959.)

Obviously, contagious behavior, though sufficient to produce social enhancement, is itself inadequate to produce social learning or social transmission. However, as Morgan indicated in his discussion of intelligent imitation, in combination with individual learning, contagious behavior may play an important role in both. (See, for example, Suboski & Bartashunas, 1984.)

Observational Conditioning: Vicarious Instigation, Pseudovicarious Instigation. Berger (1962, p. 450) introduced the term *vicarious instigation* to be employed "If an observer responds emotionally to a performer's unconditioned emotional response . . ." and distinguished true vicarious instigation from various forms of *pseudovicarious instigation.* Among the latter, Berger (1962) suggested that "a performer's unconditioned response [to a stimulus] may be an unconditioned stimulus which elicits an observer's emotional response; in this case the observer responds to the performer's unconditioned response [not to the performer's emotional response] so that the performer's unconditioned stimulus and unconditioned emotional response are superfluous" (p. 451). Thus, in Berger's view, vicarious instigation is not a form of emotional contagious behavior; vicarious instigation is dependent upon an observer's inference or perception of the emotional state of a performer. In vicarious instigation, a scream does not elicit fear in an observer; this would be a form of pseudovicarious instigation. In vicarious instigation perception of the fear of the screamer elicits fear in an observer.

Whether animal observers respond emotionally to the stimuli emitted by an emotionally aroused performer or respond emotionally to inferences as to the emotional state of performers arrived at by integrating contextual information with information in the display of the performer, the result would be similar. A response to an emotion-eliciting stimulus by one animal could elicit an emotional response in an observer. Stimuli experienced by the observer in temporal contiguity with its socially elicited emotional response might, in turn, acquire classically conditioned emotion-evoking capacity.

A number of interesting instances of social transmission of behavior discovered in recent years appear to be the result of processes of this type, labeled *observational conditioning* by Cook, Mineka, Wolkenstein, and Laitsch (1985). In discussion of learning in animals, I prefer *observational conditioning* to *vicarious instigation* unless and until there is reason to believe that animals make the complex inferences the latter term requires.

Curio, Enst, and Vieth (1978) have found that jackdaws exposed to an arbitrary stimulus while listening to mobbing calls of conspecifics subsequently give a mobbing call in response to presentation of the arbitrary stimulus. Mineka and coworkers' (1984, 1985) studies of the development of snake avoidance in rhesus monkeys have shown that observation of an adult exhibiting fear of a snake leads to avoidance of snakes in naive juveniles (Cook et al., 1985; Mineka, Davidson, Cook, & Keir, 1984).

The rapidity with which these conditioned responses are established suggests that, if they do depend on classical conditioning for their development, they may be instances of adaptively specialized learning processes analogous to that hypothesized to underlie taste-aversion learning in rats (Rozin & Kalat, 1971). Further, in natural circumstances, a naive conspecific observer of a fearful rhesus or mobbing jackdaw is likely to perceive the upset conspecific prior to detecting the stimulus to which it is reacting. Thus, if observational conditioning occurs in nature, experience of the US prior to the CS (e.g., backward conditioning) should not disrupt observational conditioning as it does other forms of Pavlovian learning.

Matched Dependent Behavior.   The process of operant conditioning, like that of classical conditioning, has been suggested as a mechanism for both social learning and social transmission of behavior. Miller and Dollard (1941) in their classic text *Social Learning and Imitation* introduced the term *matched dependent behavior* to refer to situations in which the application of external reinforcement leads organisms to match their own behavior to that of conspecifics. In matched dependent behavior, the behavior of one animal (the leader) serves as a discriminative stimulus for a second animal (the imitator), indicating those occasions on which the imitator will be reinforced for performing some behavior. For example, Miller and Dollard (1941) trained rats either to make the same choice as their leader at the junction of a T-maze or to make the opposite choice from the leader to receive food reinforcement. The choice by a leader of, for example, the left arm of the maze served in both cases as a discriminative stimulus, eliciting left or right turning in the follower depending on the reinforcement contingencies to which the follower had been exposed) Skinner (1953) has argued that appropriate contingencies for the development of matched dependent behavior often occur in nature. "Thus, if a pigeon is scratching in a leaf-strewn field, this is an occasion upon which another pigeon is likely to be reinforced for similar behavior" (p. 120).

Although the matched dependent process is sufficient to produce a degree of uniformity in the behavior of pairs of animals, once the leader (the discriminative stimulus) departs, those aspects of a follower's behavior dependent on the presence of the leader are lost. For the pattern of behavior initiated by the leader to become part of the behavioral repertoire of the follower, independent of the leader, the pattern of behavior must come under the control of stimuli not dependent on the presence of the leader.

Church (1957, 1968) has provided evidence that incidental learning can result in the transfer of stimulus control of behavior from a leader organism to other stimuli in the environment. Rats first trained to follow a leader into the left and right arms of a T-maze, then exposed to a number of trials in which they always followed the leader into the arm of the T-maze marked by a light, when subsequently tested without the leader, entered the lighted arm of the maze. Thus, matched dependent behavior, acting in concert with incidental learning, provides a mechanism for social transmission of behavior among conspecifics (Bayroff & Lard, 1944; Solomon & Coles, 1954; Stimbert, 1970).

Copying: "vocal imitation'.   Miller and Dollard (1941) distinguished *copying* from the *matched dependent behavior* described above in terms of whether an observer simply used its model's behavior as a discriminative stimulus for the occasion to exhibit the reinforced behavior or was sensitive to the relationship (same or different) between its own behavior and that of its model. In either case, one would observe the development of similar behavior in model and subject as the result of differential extrinsic reinforcement. However, the underlying process of behavior acquisition by the social learner would differ in the two cases.

According to Miller and Dollard (1941), in the initial stages of copying, an external agent both punishes responses of the subject that are different from those of its model and reinforces responses similar to those of its model. In time, Miller and Dollard propose, the copier comes to experience anxiety when producing responses differing from those of models and relief from anxiety when producing responses similar to those of models.

Early stages of the development of copying in Miller and Dollard's exposition seem to require action by an external agent consciously differentially reinforcing same and different responses. Such deliberate tuition has not been demonstrated in any species other than our own (Ewer, 1969). In consequence, copying, in Miller and Dollard's sense, seems unlikely to occur in animals and Miller and Dollard (1941) provide no examples of copying in nonhuman species.

Thorndike's (1911, p. 76–77) discussion of vocal imitation in birds, quoted in the first section of the present chapter, assumes a process similar to Dollard and Miller's copying, i.e. a sensitivity of the imitator to the degree of similarity of its vocal output to the auditory input it is imitating. Thorndike's model, however, rests on an assumed intrinsic motivation in some species of bird to experience as rewarding production of vocalizations similar to previously experienced auditory stimuli.

Thorndike (1911) saw such vocal imitation in birds as dependent on a specialized process not seen either in other species or in other instances of social learning by birds. In one sense, any vocal copying is unique in that the feedback from the copier's output is perceived via the same sensory modality that the signal to be copied was originally perceived (McDougall, 1924, p. 174). A talking or singing bird receives auditory feedback from its vocal output that can be matched with a stored representation of an auditory signal, the human speech or bird song the copier originally heard. Copying of motor outputs other than vocalizations requires the copier to make cross-modality comparisons between a models' behavior and its own and, therefore, seems intuitively less likely.

As Thorndike proposed, the ability of parrots and some other birds to reproduce human vocalizations and of some songbirds to learn dialects suggests an intrinsic motivation to respond differently to their own production of familiar and novel sounds, but other explanations are possible. Mowrer (1960) described a process, sufficient to produce copying of human vocalizations by birds, though insufficient to account for some results of studies of acquisition of dialect by birds (for example, those in which adult song is played to juveniles through loudspeakers; Marler & Tamura, 1964). On Mowrer's (1960) model, the necessary condition for vocal imitation of humans by birds is the formation of an emotional attachment to a human caretaker (see also Lashley, 1913; Pepperberg, 1985; West, Stroud, & King, 1983). According to Mowrer (1960), if the caretaker, a source of reinforcement, produces auditory signals in the presence of the subject, these sounds

> become positively conditioned, i.e. they become *good sounds;* and in the course of its own, at first largely random vocalizations, the bird will eventually make somewhat similar sounds. By the principle of generalization, some of the derived satisfaction or pleasure which has become attached to the trainer's sounds will now be experienced when the bird itself makes and hears like sounds; and when this begins to happen the stage is set for the bird's learning to "talk." (p. 79)

Recent studies (Baptista & Petrinovich, 1984; Petrinovich, 1985) indicating that important aspects of song acquisition differ between those white-crowned sparrows exposed to recorded song and those exposed to a live, interacting tutor suggest that social learning of the type Mowrer proposed may be important in some aspects of vocal learning by birds. (See Pepperberg, 1985, for discussion.)

Whether copying of the type to be seen in talking or singing birds should be considered true learning by imitation is, like any semantic issue, open to debate. Such copying lacks the goal directedness that is a central feature of many definitions of imitation and, at least in the models proposed by Dollard and Miller, Thorndike, and Mowrer, can be seen as an extension of operant or classical conditioning rather than as reflecting a capacity for imitative learning.

Imitation or Observational Learning

As mentioned in discussion of 19th-century work on imitation, early study of social learning in animals was largely motivated by the question of whether observed coincidence in the behavior of interacting organisms provided evidence of *reflective imitation* (Morgan, 1900) or *true imitation* (Thorpe, 1963) in Thorndike's (1898) sense of "learning to do an act from seeing it done." True reflective imitation requires that the sight of an act be sufficient instigation to the act. It suggests purposeful, goal-directed copying of the behavior of one animal by another. Demonstration of true imitation would require a far more cognitive approach to the study of animal behavior than has generally been pursued by laboratory investigators. Hence, convincing demonstrations of observational learning or imitation (which I treat as synonymous) would, as Thorndike implied, have profound consequences for our understanding of animal behavior.

The usual approach in such demonstrations, since the time of Thorndike, has been to conduct an experiment in which a control group learns some operant in social isolation and an experimental group learns the same operant after observing a conspecific exhibit it. More rapid acquisition of the operant by subjects in the experimental group provides evidence of social learning. If proper controls can be devised for the effects of all social learning processes other than imitation, one can infer that the observed social learning was the result of imitation. All serious discussions of social learning in animals have found relatively unconvincing the evidences of imitation learning provided by such experiments (see, for example, Davis, 1973; Hall, 1963; Roberts, 1941; Spence, 1937; Thorpe, 1963; Warden & Jackson, 1935).

Part of the problem is that adequately controlling for effects of stimulus enhancement, in the broad sense in which it is defined above, is difficult. For example, Chesler (1969), in a study widely cited as demonstrating imitation, found that kittens observing their mothers pressing a lever to obtain food acquired the lever-pressing response far more rapidly than those kittens observing a strange female pressing the lever, thus demonstrating either imitation by observation of the mother or better stimulus enhancement by the mother cats than by strange cats.

Similarly, in a recent, careful study of social transmission of food-finding techniques in pigeons, Palameta and Lefebvre (1985) found that observer pigeons that saw a trained bird piercing paper covering a food box and eating from it learned to feed from paper-covered food boxes faster than pigeons that either saw a model only eat, but not pierce, or only pierce, but not eat. Palameta and Lefebvre (1985) suggest "that copying was dependent upon observer recognition of the fact that the model was getting a food reward and that pigeons were capable of learning aspects of the piercing technique by observation" (p. 1). It is, of course, also possible that piercing-and-eating models are better stimulus enhancers than either eating models or piercing models and that differences in the stimulus-enhancing capacities of the various types of models were responsible for differences in rate of behavior acquisition by their observers. Data on the degree of match of piercing technique between observers and models might prove useful in determining whether imitation learning was, in fact, involved.

The list of studies with the terms observational learning or imitation in the title is long indeed, leading the unwary to conclude that these processes have been demonstrated many times in many species. My suspicion is that the strategy described above is so seriously flawed as to preclude the possibility of convincing demonstrations of imitation learning. It is simply too unwieldy to control for all alternative social learning processes.

An infrequently employed alternative strategy for the investigation of imitation requires observers to imitate different motor acts addressed by a demonstrator to a single manipulandum. Dawson and Foss (1965) permitted naive budgies to watch demonstrators using one of three motor patterns to remove the cover from a food dish. Those budgies that saw a demonstrator use its foot to remove the cover subsequently used their feet to remove the cover; those that observed a demonstrator use its bill to peck or pull the cover off did the same. Students in my laboratory have repeated the Dawson and Foss experiment (Galef, Manzig, & Field, 1986) and found weaker but similar effects. The Dawson and Foss procedure of requiring imitation of motor patterns, rather than imitation of the location in which an act is to be performed or the stimuli to which behavior is to be addressed, goes a long way toward solving problems of control for other types of social learning. Positive outcomes are, therefore, more clearly indicative of "true imitation," of "learning to do an act from seeing it done," than positive outcomes in more commonly employed procedures. Dawson and Foss's work with budgies seems among the most convincing of the scores of laboratory experiments on learning by imitation. I would encourage the adoption of their paradigm for use with other species and behaviors in future work on the question of the occurrence of true imitation in animals. (See also Denny & Clos, this volume.)

CONCLUSIONS

It is somewhat surprising that almost 100 years of study of social learning in animals has failed to produce a clear answer to the question of whether animals can in fact learn "to do an act from seeing it done," whether they can, in Thorndike's sense, truly imitate. Although a few studies of social learning (e.g., John, Chesler, Bartlett, & Victor, 1968; Herbert & Harsh, 1944) seem to provide unequivocal evidence of imitation learning, successful experiments have rarely been independently replicated and the majority of attempted demonstrations of imitation have failed to provide convincing evidence of the phenomenon.

There is still a pressing need for investigations that proceed beyond identification of an effect of social interaction on behavior acquisition to analysis of the conditions under which such social learning occurs. It is clear from information collected both in field and laboratory (Galef, 1976) that social interaction can play an important role in modifying the behavior of animals, both facilitating the acquisition of useful patterns of behavior and increasing the probability that behaviors already in an individual's repertoire will be performed. Although such observations may in themselves satisfy those interested in demonstrating functions of social interaction in the production of adaptive behavior, they represent a challenge to students of causation or mechanism. Analysis of the behavioral processes supporting social influences on behavior has not proceeded far beyond the listing of examples undertaken by Thorndike in 1898. Our vocabulary may be richer than Thorndike's but our level of understanding of the behavioral processes involved in social learning remains similar to his.

Study of social learning offers opportunities both for integration of functional and causal analyses of behavior and for synthesis of field and laboratory studies. As many of the chapters in the present volume make clear, those opportunities are beginning to be exploited and a data base is in process of development that should greatly expand our understanding of social learning in animals.

ACKNOWLEDGMENTS

Preparation of this chapter was greatly facilitated by grants from the Natural Sciences and Engineering Research Council of Canada and the McMaster University Research Board. I thank Tom Zentall, Antoinette Dyer, and Mertice Clark for their useful comments on earlier drafts.

REFERENCES

Armstrong, E. A. (1951). The nature and function of animal mimesis. *Bulletin of Animal Behaviour, 9,* 46–48.

Baptista, L. F., & Petrinovich, L. (1984). Social interaction, sensitive phases, and the song template hypothesis in the White-crowned sparrow. *Animal Behaviour, 32,* 172–181.

Bayroff, A. G., and Lard, K. E. (1944). Experimental social behavior of animals: III. Imitational learning of white rats. *Journal of Comparative and Physiological Psychology, 51,* 327–333.

Berger, S. M. (1962). Conditioning through vicarious instigation. *Psychological Review, 69,* 450–466.

Berry, C. S. (1906). The imitative tendency of white rats. *Journal of Comparative Neurology, 16,* 333–361.

Berry, C. S. (1908). An experimental study of imitation in cats. *Journal of Comparative Neurology, 18,* 1–26.

Bonner, J. T. (1980). *The evolution of culture in animals.* Princeton: Princeton University Press.

Box, H. O. (1984). *Primate behavior and social ecology.* London: Chapman & Hall.

Campbell, B. A., & Raskin, L. A. (1978). The ontogeny of behavioral arousal: Role of environmental stimuli. *Journal of Comparative and Physiological Psychology, 92,* 176–184.

Chesler, P. (1969). Maternal influence in learning by observation in kittens. *Science, 166,* 901–903.

Church, R. M. (1959). Emotional reaction of rats to the pain of others. *Journal of Comparative and Physiological Psychology, 52,* 132–134.

Church, R. M. (1968). Applications of behavior theory to social psychology. In E. C. Simmel, R. A. Hoppe, & G. D. Milton (Eds.), *Social facilitation and imitative behavior.* Boston: Allyn & Bacon.

Church, R. M. (1957). Two procedures for the establishment of imitative behavior. *Journal of Comparative and Physiological Psychology, 50,* 315–318.

Clayton, D. A. (1978). Socially facilitated behavior. *Quarterly Review of Biology, 53,* 373–391.

Cole, L. W. (1907). Concerning the intelligence of racoons. *Journal of Comparative Neurology, 17,* 211–261.

Cook, M., Mineka, S., Wolkenstein, B., & Laitsch, K. (1985). Observational conditioning of snake fear in unrelated rhesus monkeys. *Journal of Abnormal Psychology, 94,* 591–610.

Count, E. W. (1973). On the idea of protoculture. In E. W. Menzel (Ed.), *Precultural primate behavior.* Basel: S. Karger.

Crawford, M. P. (1939). Social facilitation. *Psychological Bulletin, 36,* 407–446.

Curio, E., Ernst, U., & Vieth, W. (1978). Cultural transmission of enemy recognition: One function of mobbing. *Science, 202,* 899–901.

Darwin, C. (1871). *The descent of man.* London: Murray.

Davis, H. B. (1903). The racoon: A study in animal intelligence. *American Journal of Psychology, 18,* 447–489.

Davis, J. M. (1973). Imitation: A review and critique. In P. P. G. Bateson & P. H. Klopfer (Eds.), *Perspectives in ethology.* New York: Plenum.

Dawson, B. V., & Foss, B. M. (1965). Observational learning in budgerigars. *Animal Behaviour, 13,* 470–474.

Ewer, R. F. (1969). The "instinct to teach." *Nature, 222,* 698.

Galef, B. G., Jr. (1971). Social effects in the weaning of domestic rat pups. *Journal of Comparative and Physiological Psychology, 75,* 358–362.

Galef, B. G., Jr. (1976). Social transmission of acquired behavior: A discussion of tradition and social learning in vertebrates. In J. S. Rosenblatt, R. A. Hinde, E. Shaw, & C. Beer (Eds.), *Advances in the study of behavior (Vol. 6,* pp. 77–100). New York: Academic Press.

Galef, B. G., Jr. (1986). Evolution and learning before Thorndike: A forgotten epoch in the history of behavioral research. In M. Becker & R. C. Bolles (Eds.), *Evolution and learning.* Hillsdale, NJ: Lawrence Erlbaum Associates.

Galef, B. G., Jr., & Beck, M. (1985). Aversive and attractive marking of toxic and safe foods by Norway rats. *Behavioral and Neural Biology, 43,* 298–310.

Galef, B. G., Jr., Manzig, L. A., & Field, R. M. (1986). Imitation learning in budgerigars: Dawson and Foss (1965) revisited. *Behavioral Processes, 13,* 191–202.

Griffin, D. R. (1985). The cognitive dimensions of animal communication. In B. Holldobler & M. Lindauer (Eds.), *Experimental behavioral ecology and sociobiology.* Sunderland, MA: Sinauer.

Haggarty, M. E. (1909). Imitation in monkeys. *Journal of Comparative Neurology, 19,* 337–455.

Hall, K. R. L. (1963). Observational learning in monkeys and apes. *British Journal of Psychology, 54,* 201–226.

Harlow, H. F., & Harlow, M. K. (1965). The affectional systems. In A. M. Sehrier, H. F., Harlow, & F. Stollaitz (Eds.), *Behavior of non-human primates (Vol. 2,* pp. 287–334). New York: Academic Press.

Herbert, M. J., & Harsh, C. M. (1944). Observational learning by cats. *Journal of Comparative Psychology, 37,* 81–95.

Hobhouse, L. T. (1936). *Mind in evolution* (3rd ed.). London: Macmillan.

Hodos, W., & Campbell, C. B. G. (1969). Scala naturae: Why there is no theory in comparative psychology. *Psychological Review, 76,* 337–350.

Humphrey, G. (1921). Imitation and the conditioned reflex. *Pedagogical Seminary, 28,* 1–21.

James, W. (1961). *Psychology: The briefer course.* New York: Harper.

Jenkins, H. M. (1984). The study of animal learning in the tradition of Pavlov and Thorndike. In P. Marler & H. S. Terrace (Eds.), *The biology of learning.* Berlin: Springer-Verlag.

John, E. R., Chesler, P., Bartlett, F., & Victor, I. (1968). Observation learning in cats. *Science, 159,* 1489–1491.

Kaufman, I. C., & Hinde, R. A. (1961). Factors influencing distress calling in chicks with special reference to temperature changes and social isolation. *Animal Behaviour, 9,* 197–204.

Kawai, M. (1965). Newly acquired pre-cultural behavior of the natural troop of Japanese monkeys on Koshima Inlet. *Primates, 6,* 1–30.

Kawamura, S. (1959). The process of sub-culture propagation among Japanese macaques. *Primates, 2,* 43–60.

Kempf, E. J. (1916). Two methods of subjective learning in the monkey *Macacus Rhesus. Journal of Animal Behavior, 6,* 256–265.

Kinnaman, A. J. (1902). Mental life of two Macacus Rhesus monkeys in captivity. *American Journal of Psychology, 13,* 98–148.

Kohler, W. (1925). *The mentality of apes.* London: Routledge & Kegan Paul.

Kummer, H. (1971). *Primate societies.* Chicago: Aldine.

Lashley, K. S. (1913). Reproduction of inarticulate sounds in the parrot. *Journal of Animal Behaviour, 3,* 361–366.

Levine, J. M., & Zentall, T. R. (1974). Effects of a conspecific's presence on deprived rats' performance: Social facilitation vs. distraction/imitation. *Animal Learning & Behavior, 2,* 119–122.

Marler, P., & Tamura, M. (1964). Culturally transmitted patterns of vocal behavior in sparrows. *Science, 146,* 1483–1486.

McDougall, W. (1924). *Outline of psychology.* New York: Scribner's.

Miller, N. E., & Dollard, J. (1941). *Social learning and imitation.* New Haven: Yale University Press.

Mineka, S., Davidson, M., Cook, M., & Keir, R. (1984). Observational conditioning of snake fear in rhesus monkeys. *Journal of Abnormal Psychology, 93,* 355–372.

Morgan, C. L. (1900). *Animal behaviour.* London: Arnold.

Mowrer, O. H. (1960). *Learning theory and the symbolic processes.* New York: Wiley.

Palameta, B., & Lefebvre, L. (1985). The social transmission of a food-finding technique in pigeons: What is learned? *Animal Behaviour, 33,* 892–896.

Pepperberg, I. M. (1985). Social modeling theory: A possible framework for understanding avian vocal learning. *Auk, 102,* 854–864.

Petrinovich, L. (1985). Factors influencing song development in the White-crowned Sparrow (Zonotrichia leucophrys). *Journal of Comparative Psychology, 99,* 15–29.

Pishkin, V., and Shurley, J. T. (1966). Social facilitation and sensory deprivation in operant behavior of rats. *Psychonomic Science, 6,* 335–336.

Porter, J. P. (1910). Intelligence and imitation in birds: A criterion of imitation. *American Journal of Psychology, 34,* 590–591.

Randall, P. K., & Campbell, B. A. (1976). Ontogeny of behavioral arousal in rats: Effect of maternal and sibling presence. *Journal of Comparative and Physiological Psychology, 90,* 453–459.

Reid, T. (1764). *An inquiry into the human mind, on the principles of common sense* (4th ed.). London: T. Cadell.

Roberts, D. (1941). Imitation and suggestion in animals. *Bulletin of Animal Behaviour, 1*, 11–19.

Romanes, G. J. (1884). *Mental evolution in animals*. New York: AMS Press.

Romanes, G. J. (1889). *Mental evolution in man*. New York: Appleton.

Rozin, P., & Kalat, J. W. (1971). Specific hungers and poison avoidance as adaptive specializations of learning. *Psychological Review, 78*, 459–486.

Scott, J. P. (1958). *Animal behavior*. Chicago: University of Chicago Press.

Sheperd, W. T. (1910). Some mental processes of the rhesus monkey. *Psychological Monographs, 12*, No. 5.

Sheperd, W. T. (1911). Imitation in racoons. *American Journal of Psychology, 22*, 583–585.

Sheperd, W. T. (1923). Some observations and experiments on the intelligence of the chimpanzee and ourang. *American Journal of Psychology, 34*, 590–591.

Skinner, B. F. (1953). *Science and human behavior*. New York: Macmillan.

Small, W. S. (1900). An experimental study of the mental processes of the rat. *American Journal of Psychology, 11*, 133–165.

Small, W. S. (1901). Study of the mental processes in rats: II. *American Journal of Psychology, 12*, 206–239.

Solomon, R. L., & Coles, M. R. (1954). A case of failure of generalization of imitation across drives and across situations. *Journal of Abnormal and Social Psychology, 49*, 7–13.

Spence, K. W. (1937). Experimental studies of learning and higher mental processes in infra-human primates. *Psychological Bulletin, 34*, 806–850.

Spencer, H. (1855). *Principles of psychology* (2 Vols.). New York: Appleton.

Stamm, J. S. (1961). Social facilitation in monkeys. *Psychological Reports, 8*, 479–484.

Stimbert, V. E. (1970). A comparison of learning based on social or nonsocial discriminative stimuli. *Psychonomic Science, 20*, 185–186.

Strobel, M. G. (1972). Social facilitation of operant behavior in satiated rats. *Journal of Comparative and Physiological Psychology, 80*, 502–508.

Suboski, M. D., & Bartashunas, C. (1984). Mechanisms for social transmission of pecking preferences to neonatal chicks. *Journal of Experimental Psychology: Animal Behaviour Processes, 10*, 182–194.

Sullivan, K. A. (1984a). The advantages of social foraging in downy woodpeckers. *Animal Behaviour, 32*, 16–21.

Sullivan, K. A. (1984b). Information exploitation by downy woodpeckers in mixed-species flocks. *Behaviour, 91*, 294–311.

Telle, H. J. (1966). Beitrag zur Kenntnis der Verhaltensweise von Ratten, vergleichand dargestellt bei *Rattus norvegicus* and *Rattus rattus*. *Zeitschrift fur Angewandte Zoologie, 53*, 179–196.

Thorndike, E. L. (1898). Animal intelligence: An experimental study of the associative process in animals. *Psychological Review Monographs, 2*, No. 8.

Thorndike, E. L. (1911). *Animal intelligence*. New York: Macmillan.

Thorpe, W. H. (1956). Learning and instinct in animals. London: Methuen.

Thorpe, W. H. (1963). *Learning and instinct in animals*. 2nd edition. London: Methuen.

Tolman, C. W. (1967). The effects of tapping sounds on feeding behaviour of domestic chicks. *Animal Behaviour, 15*, 145–148.

Tolman, C. W., & Wilson, G. F. (1965). Social feeding in the domestic chick. *Animal Behaviour, 13*, 134–142.

Verplanck, W. S. (1957). A glossary of some terms used in the objective science of behaviour. *Psychological Review, 6,* Supplement 64

Wallace, A. R. (1870). *Contributions to the theory of natural selection.* New York: AMS Press.

Warden, C. J., & Jackson, T. A. (1935). Imitative behavior in the rhesus monkey. *Journal of Genetic Psychology, 46,* 103–125.

Washburn, M. F. (1908). *The animal mind.* New York: Macmillan.

Watson, J. B. (1908). Imitation in monkeys. *Psychological Bulletin, 5,* 169–178.

Wechkin, S. (1970). Social relationships and social facilitation of object manipulation in *Macaca mulatta. Journal of Comparative and Physiological Psychology, 73,* 456–460.

West, M. J., King, A. P., & Harrocks, T. J. (1983). Cultural transmission of cowbird song (*Molothrus ater*): Measuring its development and outcome. *Journal of Comparative Psychology, 97,* 327–337.

West, M. J., Stroud, A. N., & King, A. P. (1983). Mimicry of the human voice by Eurasian starlings (*Sturnus vulgaris*): The role of social interaction. *Wilson Bulletin, 95,* 635–640.

Witmer, L. (1910). Intelligent imitation and curiosity in a monkey. *Psychological Clinic, 3,* 225–227.

Zajonc, R. B. (1965). Social facilitation. *Science, 149,* 269–274.

Zajonc, R. B. (1969). Coaction. In R. B. Zajonc (Ed.), *Animal social psychology.* New York: Wiley.

Zentall, T. R., & Hogan, D. E. (1976). Imitation and social facilitation in the pigeon. *Animal Learning & Behavior, 4,* 427–430.

Zentall, T. R., & Levine, J. M. (1972). Observational learning and social facilitation in the rat. *Science, 170,* 1220–1221.

An Evolutionary Model of Social Learning: The Effects of Spatial and Temporal Variation

Robert Boyd
*Emory University**

Peter J. Richerson
University of California—Davis

From an evolutionary perspective, both individual and social learning can be viewed as forms of phenotypic plasticity. Both modes of learning are developmental processes that cause organisms to acquire different behaviors in different environments. Phenotypic plasticity may be adaptive in temporally or spatially varying environments if the use of environmental cues enables organisms to acquire behavior that is adaptive in each local habitat. For example, by sampling novel foods and learning to avoid noxious food types, a cosmopolitan species like the rat can acquire an appropriate diet in a wide range of environments. Mechanisms of phenotypic plasticity may also have fitness costs. By sampling novel foods, the rat incurs risks that could be avoided by an animal with rigid genetically specified food preferences.

The ways in which individual learning and social learning allow organisms to adapt to different environments are, however, quite different. Behavioral variants acquired by individual learning are not transmitted from one generation to the next. This means that each individual's behavior develops independently based on the interaction of genetically inherited learning mechanisms and the local environment. Genetic variation underlying learning mechanisms may evolve, but the behavioral variants acquired by learning do not. Individual learn-

---

*Current address: Department of Anthropology, University of California, Los Angeles, CA 90024

ing is adaptive if it bestows some advantage on the individual. In contrast, behaviors acquired by the imitative and observational forms of social learning (Galef, this volume) are transmitted from one individual to another and thus from one generation to the next. From an evolutionary biologist's perspective social learning is interesting because it mixes aspects of a system of inheritance with aspects of ordinary phenotypic flexibility, creating a system for the inheritance of acquired variation. To understand the conditions under which social learning is adaptive we must understand how individual learning and social learning interact to determine the evolutionary dynamics of the behavioral variants themselves as well as the genes that underlie learning processes.

The evolutionary properties of the inheritance of acquired variation have received relatively little theoretical attention. This inattention may be due to the fact that evolutionary biologists have supposed that the inheritance of acquired variation is rare in nature, essentially restricted to human culture and a few unusual animal systems, such as the songs of some birds. Those biologists (e.g., Bonner, 1980) who have imagined that social learning is common in animals besides humans have not always taken proper account of the difficulty of demonstrating true imitation in the face of several processes that can mimic its effects (Galef, 1980; McGrew & Tutin, 1978). With a few exceptions (Boyd & Richerson, 1983, 1985; Pulliam & Dunford, 1980) recent theoretical work on cultural transmission (Cavalli-Sforza & Feldman, 1981; Lumsden & Wilson, 1981) has concentrated on explaining human culture rather than on the more general properties of social learning.

In this chapter, we consider the question, Under what circumstances should natural selection favor a growth of reliance on social learning at the expense of individual learning? The answer to this question is important because it seems likely that social learning originally evolved in species with extensive individual learning abilities. Our focus on the adaptive value of social learning does not imply that selection is the only important evolutionary process, or that all behavior is adaptive. We do believe, however, that understanding the conditions under which social learning is adaptive is an important first step in understanding its evolution and the conditions under which one would expect to find social learning in nature.

At first glance, it may seem that social learning will always be the superior form of phenotypic plasticity. Acquiring adaptive behavior by conditioning and other forms of individual learning is often an inefficient process. Learning trials divert time and energy from other fitness-enhancing activities, they may entail serious risks, and there may be substantial chance of not acquiring locally adaptive behavior. It thus seems much more efficient to acquire behaviors by social learning. Studies of humans suggest that social learning can be both rapid and accurate (Bandura, 1986; Rosenthal & Zimmerman, 1979). It is plausible that by simply copying the behavior of others, individuals can acquire locally adaptive behaviors without incurring the costs associated with individual learning.

This argument is problematical, however. It certainly makes sense to imitate others if the most common behavior among available models is adaptive in the local environment. The problem is that as individuals come increasingly to rely on social learning, models exhibiting locally adaptive behaviors might become uncommon. To see that this is the case, consider the very simple example in which there are two kinds of individuals in a population—*learners* who acquire their behavior by a process of individual learning that results in adaptive behavior, and *imitators* who depend completely on imitation. As long as imitators are rare, they are likely to copy the adaptive behavior of learners. Assuming that imitation is less costly than individual learning, imitation will be more adaptive. However, as imitators become more common, they are more and more likely to acquire their behavior by copying another imitator, who may have also copied an imitator and so on. In a variable environment, the most common behavior may not be the most adaptive behavior, and individual learning may be more adaptive than imitation.

In this chapter we present several simple mathematical models designed to clarify the conditions under which social learning is adaptive. We want to construct the simplest possible models that capture the basic nature of social and individual learning, and the interaction between the two systems. By downplaying the confusing detail of any real situation, we hope to be able to clearly understand the relation between the generic properties of social and individual learning.

The construction of such simple models is a basic part of the strategy of theory building in population biology. The reason that elementary general models are useful, despite their simplicity and unrealism, is that even the simplest evolutionary processes are hard to understand. Thus, simple models serve as an essential supplement to intuition, which is often misleading. In the case at hand, several quantitative variables, such as accuracy of individual learning, costs of achieving a given level of accuracy, and patterns of environmental variation, interact to affect the mixture of social and individual learning that selection would favor. Furthermore, the optimal mix of social and individual learning is affected by population-level properties of social learning; because behaviors can be spread from individual to individual by social learning, long-run outcomes over many generations are relevant to the problem. It is not trivial to keep all these interacting parts of the problem straight. Simple models can serve as a check on less formal methods of deductive reasoning, as a basis for constructing more realistic models, and as an unambiguous standard of comparison for purposes of discussion. (For a more extensive treatment of the strategy of using simple models see Boyd and Richerson, 1985, chap. 2, or Richerson and Boyd, 1987).

We begin by analyzing a model in which a population of organisms acquires behavior by a combination of individual and social learning in a uniform and constant environment. This model indicates that, on average, in constant environments reliance on social learning always leads to higher fitness than reliance on individual learning. We then add environmental variability to the model in two different ways. These models involving more complex environments show that there is an optimal mix of social and individual learning. The relative importance of social learning in the optimal mix is increased when (1) environments are predictable, and (2) individual learning is costly. We conclude from these models, and from related ones reported elsewhere, that conditions for evolution of a substantial dependence on social learning are not very restrictive. Difficulties of empirical demonstration aside, there is good theoretical reason to suppose that many animals should use social learning to acquire certain kinds of behavior, although the models also suggest that individual learning (and fixed instincts) are superior for development of other kinds of traits.

THE BASIC MODEL

We begin by addressing the question, When does social learning allow a more accurate tracking of the environment than individual learning? To answer this question, we want to construct a model that embodies the following assumptions about the interaction of social and individual learning:

1. A population of organisms is potentially confronted with a variable environment in which different behaviors are favored by selection in different habitats.

2. Individuals in the population can acquire their behavior by some mixture of social learning and individual learning, where

3. Social learning involves the faithful copying of the behavior of other individuals in the population (we intend the model to be general enough not to depend on the exact means by which social learning occurs, so long as some information about how to behave is acquired by the social learner at a smaller cost than learning the behavior by interacting independently with the environment), and

4. Individual learning allows an individual to acquire behavior that is adaptive in the local environment, but, at least occasionally, leads to errors.

5. All individuals pay any fitness costs associated with individual learning whether they ultimately acquire a behavior by social learning or by individual learning.

Consider a population that occupies an environment that can be in either of two distinct states, labeled habitat 1 and habitat 2. Each individual in the population will acquire one of two alternative behaviors, also labeled 1 and 2. As is shown in Table 2.1, each individual has a "baseline" fitness, W; individuals who acquire the behavior that is best in their environment achieve an increase in fitness, D. Thus, individuals that acquire behavior 1 have higher fitness in habitat 1 than individuals that acquire behavior 2. Similarly, behavior 2 yields higher fitness in habitat 2 than does behavior 1. Once an individual has acquired one of the two behaviors, it does not change, and an individual experiences only one of the two environmental states during its lifetime.

The adaptive problem that faces each individual is to determine which of the two habitats it is in. Individuals in the model have two sources of information available to help them solve this problem.

1. Each individual obtains evidence from its own experience. By this we mean any observations, learning trials, or other nonsocial information that can help determine the state of the environment. We assume the result of each individual's experience can be quantified in terms of a single normally distributed random variable, x. If the environment is in state 1, the mean value of x is M; if it is in state 2, the mean value of x is $-M$. In other words, the true state of the environment is either M or $-M$; individuals acquire an imperfect estimate of the state of the environment, x, from personal experience. The standard deviation of the distribution of x, S, is an inverse measure of the quality of the evidence available to the members of the population. The larger is S, the poorer the individual's estimate of M or $-M$. If $S \ll |M|$ then most individuals' experiences will clearly indicate the state of the environment. If $S \gg |M|$, the results of gathering direct evidence will usually not be decisive.

2. Assume that the population is structured into nonoverlapping cohorts. Individuals in one cohort can observe the behavior of individuals from the previous cohort that have already acquired either behavior 1 or behavior 2. Individuals in the previous cohort thus act as models for individuals in the next cohort.

We imagine that individuals in the population use information available to them to decide between the two alternatives in the following way: If the outcome

Table 2.1

	Fitness Associated with	
	Behavior 1	Behavior 2
Habitat 1	$W + D$	W
Habitat 2	W	$W + D$

of direct observation, x, is greater than a threshold value d $(d \geq 0)$, the individual acquires behavior 1; if x is less than $-d$, then it acquires behavior 2. This is our attempt to capture the essence of the processes of individual learning. Finally, if $-d \leq x \leq d$, then the individual imitates the behavior of one of the models available to him, chosen at random. The order in which the two kinds of learning occur is not crucial; the model applies equally well to a situation in which individuals begin by imitating others, and then adopt a new behavior only if confronted with decisive personal experience. We will say that individuals that acquire behavior by imitation utilize social learning.

The parameter d serves two functions. First, as is shown in Figure 2.1, it is analogous to a confidence interval. The larger the value of d that characterizes the population, the more decisive the evidence must be before it will affect the individual's decision. Second, the value of d simultaneously determines the relative importance of social learning and individual learning. We assume that when individuals are in doubt on the basis of their own experience, they utilize behaviors acquired by imitation. Let p_1 be the probability that $x > d$, let p_2 be the probability that $x < -d$. If d is large, then individuals attend to their own experience only if it provides compelling evidence of the state of the environment (i.e., $p_1, p_2 \approx 0$); for the most part they imitate another individual. If d is small, behavior is mainly determined by an individual's experience, and social learning has little importance (i.e., $p_1 + p_2 \approx 1$).

To predict the likelihood that an individual will acquire a particular behavior by social learning, we must know what behaviors characterize the models to which the individual is exposed. This situation is analogous to the dependence of an individual's expected genotype on the genotypes of the previous generation,

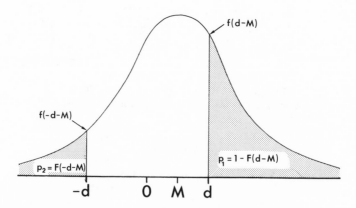

Figure 2.1. Illustrates the definition of p_1 and p_2, and their relationship to the parameter d assuming, that the population is in habitat 1. $F(x)$ is the cumulative normal distribution, and $f(x)$ is the normal density function.

and we can use the evolutionary biologist's formalism to model this part of the problem. Suppose that sets of models are random samples from the population as a whole. Further suppose that a fraction q_i of the models available to a naive individual in cohort t acquired behavior 1 in the previous time period. A fraction p_1 of the naive individuals in cohort t will acquire behavior 1 based on their own experience, and a fraction $q_t (1 - p_1 - p_2)$ acquire alternative 1 by imitation. Thus in cohort t the fraction (or "frequency") of individuals acquiring behavior 1, q_t', is

$$q_t' = q_t(1 - p_1 - p_2) + p_1 \tag{1}$$

Now suppose that these individuals then serve as models for individuals in the cohort $t + 1$. Then the frequency of behavior 1 amongst the models for cohort $t + 1$, q_{t+1}, is approximately:

$$q_{t+1} = q_t' \tag{2}$$

We say approximately because we have ignored the effect of natural selection. In environment 1, differential mortality will increase the frequency of behavior 1. Here we are assuming that the effect of learning on the relative frequencies of the two behaviors is so much greater than the effect of selection that selection can be safely ignored.

Suppose that this process is repeated many times. That is, members of a cohort acquire their behavior by a combination of social and individual learning, then serve as models for the next cohort, and this process is repeated for many successive cohorts. Eventually the fraction of each cohort acquiring behavior 1 would stabilize at the equilibrium value

$$\hat{q} = \frac{1}{1 + p_2/p_1} \tag{3}$$

Thus, the fraction of individuals acquiring behavior 1 at equilibrium depends only on the ratio of the probability that an individual will choose behavior 2 based on its own experience (p_2) to the probability that it will choose behavior 1 based on its own experience (p_1). If $p_2/p_1 > 1$, then the equilibrium frequency of individuals choosing alternative 1 is less than one half; if $p_2/p_1 < 1$, $\hat{q} > \frac{1}{2}$. The fraction choosing behavior 1 at equilibrium does not depend (directly) on the relative importance of social learning versus individual learning in determining the behavior of individuals (i.e., the magnitude of $1 - p_1 - p_2$). However, from Equation 1 we know that the rate at which the population converges to the equilibrium value depends crucially on the amount of social learning, because if there is little individual learning p_1 and p_2 will be very small and social learning will ensure that the population remains very similar from one generation to the next. Thus as individual learning becomes less important in determining individual behavior, the population will converge more slowly to equilibrium. This property is crucial to understanding the evolution of mixed systems of social and individual learning in variable environments, as we see below.

THE EVOLUTION OF SOCIAL LEARNING

We now consider the evolution of social learning. The relative importance of ordinary learning and social learning in determining phenotype is given by the parameter d. Suppose that d is affected by heritable genetic variation. Then natural selection will change d in the direction that increases average individual fitness, taking the frequency of behavior 1 and behavior 2 in the population as given. Thus, assuming both that there is suffcient genetic variation and that selection is more important than nonadaptive processes such as genetic drift, the equilibrium of d will be the value that maximizes average fitness. When the fitness maximizing value of d is very large, we will say that social learning is adaptive, because when d is large, most individuals will depend on social learning.

To calculate the fitness maximizing value of d, assume that the environment is in state 1. Then if the frequency of behavior 1 in the previous cohort is q_t, the expected fitness of an individual is

$$E(w) = W + D[\hat{q}(1 - p_1 - p_2) + p_1]   \qquad (4)$$

Differentiating Eqn. 4 with respect to d (regarding $\hat{q}$ as constant) shows that selection will lead to an increase in their value of d whenever

$$\frac{dp_1}{dd} p_2 - \frac{dp_2}{dd} p_1 > 0 \qquad (5)$$

It can be shown numerically that this expression is satisfied for all values of d. This means that the optimal value of d is as large as possible. In other words, in a constant, uniform environment natural selection always favors a heavier reliance on social learning, at least in the context of this model. The only evolutionary equilibrium is a population that relies entirely on social learning.

It is important to notice that this result was derived assuming that every individual in every cohort experienced habitat 1. This assumption of an invariant environment is crucial because, as we have seen, the equilibrium frequency of the superior variant does not depend on rate of social learning, but the rate of approach to that frequency does. It seems likely that in a variable environment the expected fitness of individuals in the population will depend on the rate at which the population can respond to changes as well as the eventual equilibrium. It is also important to remember that an invariant environment may favor a genetically transmitted invariant behavior pattern. We return to this latter issue in the discussion.

HETEROGENEOUS ENVIRONMENTS

Two qualitatively different kinds of environmental variation are possible. Different members of a single cohort might experience different environments, or alternatively, all the members of a given cohort could experience the same environment, but members of different cohorts might experience different environments. We refer to the first kind of environment as *heterogeneous* and the second kind as *fluctuating*. Fluctuating environments are the result of temporal change of various kinds; for example, climatic change may cause different cohorts to experience different environments. Heterogeneous environments might arise when a single population lives in a variety of different geographically distinct habitats, or exploits several distinct ecological niches. In this section we modify the basic model to allow for the effects of one simple kind of heterogeneous environment.

Suppose that one half of each cohort experiences state 1 of the environment and the other half of each cohort experiences state 2. (The assumption that the habitats are symmetric greatly simplifies the mathematical argument without altering the essential aspects of the problem.) Let p_{jk} be the probability that an individual's choice is based on direct experience and that it results in behavior k given that the state of the environment is j. Notice that because of the symmetry of the model

$$p_{11} = p_{22}$$
$$p_{12} = p_{21} \tag{6}$$

Heterogeneous environments are only interesting in an evolutionary context if events in one environment affect the other. A flow of cultural variants, adapted to one environment but flowing into the other by migration, is one major consequence of heterogeneous environments. To model this effect we suppose that there is a probability $1 - m$ that each model to whom a given individual is exposed experienced the same state of the environment that the given individual will experience, and therefore a probability m that the model experienced the other state of the environment. Thus, m measures the effective rate of migration of individuals from one habitat to the other. Let $q_{t,j}$ be the fraction of individuals that acquire behavior 1 within the population of individuals that experience environmental state j in cohort t. Then the state of the two populations after individual and social learning but before migration will be:

$$q'_{t,1} = (1 - p_{11} - p_{12})q_{t,1} + p_{11}$$
$$q'_{t,2} = (1 - p_{21} - p_{22})q_{t,2} + p_{21} \tag{7}$$

and the frequency of models exhibiting behavior 1 in habitat j during cohort $t + 1$ is

$$q_{t+1,1} = (1 - m)q'_{t,1} + mq'_{t,2}$$

$$q_{t+1,2} = (1 - m)q'_{t,2} + mq'_{t,1} \qquad (8)$$

if the migration rates to and from each environment are equal.

Once again let us suppose that this process is repeated until a stable equilibrium is reached. First, notice that due to the assumed symmetry of the model we know that

$$\hat{q}_1 = 1 - \hat{q}_2 \qquad (9)$$

where $\hat{q}_1$ is the fraction of individuals acquiring behavior 1 in environment 1, and $\hat{q}_2$ is the fraction of individuals acquiring behavior 1 in environment 2. Using this fact one can show that

$$\hat{q}_1 = \frac{(1 - 2m)p_{11} + m}{(1 - 2m)(p_{11} + p_{11}) + 2m} \qquad (10)$$

Notice that when $m = 0$, (10) reduces to the equilibrium derived in the model without any environmental variation. Also notice that if individuals are equally likely to imitate models drawn from both environments (i.e., $m = \frac{1}{2}$), then $\hat{q}_1 = \frac{1}{2}$. For intermediate values of m, $\hat{q}_1$ falls between these two extreme values.

These properties make sense. In a uniform environment the behavior that results in higher fitness will increase in frequency according to the simplified model of the previous section; individuals should depend entirely on social learning and not take a chance on trial and error learning. When $m = 0$, there is no contact between individuals who experience the different environments; the correct behavior becomes overwhelmingly common. Individual learning cannot do better than a perfected tradition, and it will frequently lead to errors. On the other hand, within-cohort environmental variation, represented now by the movement of individuals among groups exposed to different environments, causes individuals to be exposed to some immigrant models who are likely to have acquired the behavior favored by individual learning in the other environment. Therefore, the movement of models among groups in a heterogeneous environment causes social learning to be a less reliable method of acquiring one's behavior than it is in a homogeneous environment. When $m = \frac{1}{2}$ the frequency of the superior behavior is increased in each environment by the effects of individuals' experience, but the mixing of models from the two environments exactly erases the gains, and the individuals in the next cohort must start from scratch. In this case social learning is useless.

The most interesting cases are the ones at intermediate values of m where both social and individual learning are likely to be important. We will now compute the fitness maximizing amount of social learning in a heterogeneous environment for $0 < m < 1/2$. The expected individual fitness in the population at equilibrium is given by

$$E(w) = 1/2(W + D\hat{q}'_1) + 1/2(W = D(1 - \hat{q}'_2))$$
$$= W + D\hat{q}'_1 \qquad (11)$$

Thus increasing $\hat{q}'_1$ (and this $1 - \hat{q}'_2$) increases the expected fitness of individuals in the population.

By differentiating (11) with respect to d, the confidence-interval-like parameter that determines the relative importance of social and individual learning, and once again holding the frequency of behavior 1 constant, one can show that expected individual fitness will increase whenever

$$(1 - 2m)\left(\frac{dp_{11}}{dd}p_{12} - \frac{dp_{12}}{dd}p_{11}\right) + m\left(\frac{dp_{11}}{dd} - \frac{dp_{12}}{dd}\right) > 0 \qquad (12)$$

$$\text{term 1} \qquad\qquad \text{term 2}$$

First, let us consider how varying d affects the sign of the left-hand side of (12). We know from the models of a constant environment that term 1 is always positive (see Equation 5). It is clear from the definition of p_{11} and p_{12} (see Fig. 2.1) that term 2 is 0 when $d = 0$, and negative for all larger values of d. This means that when $d = 0$, the left-hand side of (12) will be positive and expected fitness can be increased by increasing d. Next notice that as d becomes large both

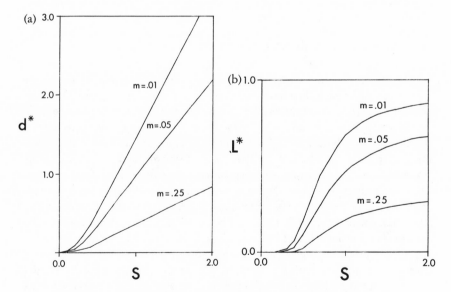

Figure 2.2. (a) Plots the evolutionary equilibrium value of d, d^*, as a function the quality of information available for individual learning, S, for three levels of environmental heterogeneity, measured by m. (b) Plots the fraction of the population acquiring behavior by social learning when d is at its equilibrium value, $L^* = (1 - p_1(d^*) - p_2(d^*))$, as a function of S and m.

p_{11} and p_{12} approach zero, and therefore for large enough values of d, the left-hand side of (12) is negative, and expected fitness can be increased by decreasing d. Taken together these facts mean that expected individual fitness is maximized for some amount of social learning intermediate between zero and one.

Although we have not been able to determine the optimal value of d by solving Eqn. (12) analytically, it is easy to solve numerically. The results, shown in Fig. 2.2, suggest that there is a wide combination of migration rates and degrees of quality of individual experience where it is optimal to employ a mixture of social and individual learning. There is a broad region with combinations of modest migration rates and moderate to low information quality where social learning should be much more important than individual learning in determining individual behavior. In Fig. 2.2a, the optimal value of d, d^*, is plotted as a function of the measure of the quality of the information available to individuals (S) and the probability that naive individuals are exposed to models who learned from the wrong environment (m). There are two things to notice about these results: first, as individual experience becomes less reliable (i.e., S becomes large) the optimal amount of social learning increases. Second, as the environment becomes less predictable (i.e., m increases) the optimal amount of social learning decreases. In Fig. 2.2b, we plot the probability that individuals rely on social learning ($L^* = 1 - p_{11}(d^*) - p_{12}(d^*)$) given that d equals its optimal value.

FLUCTUATING ENVIRONMENTS

Environments may also change through time, varying from one cohort to the next. We model such fluctuating environments in the following way: We suppose that there is a probability $1 - a$ that cohort $t + 1$ experiences the same environmental state as did cohort t, and a probability a that the environments experienced by cohorts t and $t + 1$ are different. Thus the parameter a plays a role similar to m in the model of a heterogeneous environment—it measures the extent to which the environment of an animal's models are likely to be different from its own environment. When $a = 0$, the model reduces to a constant environment; when $a = \frac{1}{2}$ the environment fluctuates completely unpredictably. At intermediate values of a, there will be a statistical resemblance between the environments of models and imitators.

It is shown in Appendix 1 that the necessary condition for d to be fitness maximizing in a fluctuating environment is exactly the same as the condition derived assuming a heterogeneous environment if $a = m$. There is an intermediate value of d (and therefore L) that maximizes fitness and this value responds to changes in S and a in the way shown in Figs. 2.2a and 2.2b with the substitution $m = a$. This result makes sense for the same reasons that the analogous result did in the case of a heterogeneous environment. When a is small, the chances are that the available models have acquired the superior alternative, because it is likely that they, and their models, and their models' models, and so on, all experienced the present environment. A strong emphasis on social learning yields the highest fitness. When $a \rightarrow \frac{1}{2}$, imitating a model is essentially choosing an alternative by flipping a coin. Any better than even chance of acquiring the superior alternative will lead to increased fitness on the average, so pure individual learning has the highest fitness. Once again, there seems to be a large range of moderately variable environments in which the model suggests that social learning should be as important or more important than individual learning.

VARYING THE QUALITY OF INDIVIDUAL LEARNING

To this point, we have assumed that the quality of the information on which individual learning is based (measured by S) is fixed. It seems plausible that in many circumstances selection might favor individuals that invest in obtaining better information. We have seen that as the quality of information increases, the optimal amount of social learning decreases in both heterogeneous and fluctuating environments. On the other hand, the effort invested in individual learning may be costly. Thus, as individual learning becomes more costly, the fitness-maximizing value of S should increase, and more social learning should result.

To formalize these ideas assume that expected individual fitness has the form

$$E(w) = W + D(q(1 - p_1 - p_2) + p_1) - C(S) \qquad (13)$$

where $C(S)$, the cost of learning, has the form shown in Figure 2.3, and q is either the equilibrium frequency of behavior 1 among models of individuals learning in environment 1 in a heterogeneous environment, or the expected frequency of behavior 1 among models given that the environment is in state 1 in a fluctuating environment. Thus increasing the quality of information is costly in the sense that it decreases fitness—of course decreasing S may also have compensating benefits in improved individual learning.

We have seen the fitness-maximizing value of d depends on the value of S. In general, we would expect that the reverse would also be true. We will assume that d is at its optimum value, d^* as defined by (Eqn. 12). Then it is shown in Appendix 2 that the optimum value of S must satisfy the following equation:

$$\frac{M}{S}\{(1 - q)f(d^* - M) + qf(-d^* - M)\} = -\frac{\partial C}{\partial S} \qquad (14)$$

The left-hand side of (14) gives the change in expected individual fitness (taking q as fixed) that results from the effect of a change in the value of d on the probability of acquiring the two behaviors (the "incremental benefits" of a small change in d). The right-hand side of (14) gives the incremental cost of changing

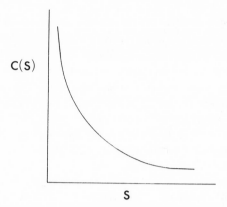

C(S)

S

Figure 2.3. Illustrates the assumed relationship between increasing the accuracy of individual learning and the cost of individual learning. This relationship is represented mathematically by the function $C(S)$, which gives the reduction in fitness associated with a change in S, the accuracy of social learning.

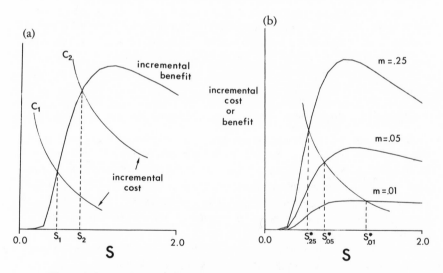

Figure 2.4. (a) Plots the incremental cost and benefit associated with a small change in the accuracy of learning, S, as a function of S, assuming that the relative importance of social learning (measured by d) is at its evolutionary equilibrium value, d^*. The intersections of the cost and benefit curves give the evolutionary equilibrium value of S, S^*. The figures illustrate that increasing the cost of learning leads to less accurate individual learning. This result together with the results shown in Figure 2.3 indicates that increasing the cost of information will increase the importance of social learning at evolutionary equilibrium. (b) Plots the same cost and benefit curves as in part (a) for three values of environmental heterogeneity. They illustrate that increasing environmental heterogeneity should favor more accurate individual learning, and, therefore, less social learning.

the value of d. In Figure 2.4a the incremental cost and benefit are plotted as a function of S. The optimum value of S occurs where these curves intersect. Notice that as the cost of information, $C(S)$, increases, the optimal value of S also increases. This means that as acquiring information becomes more costly it is better to be satisfied with lower quality information. In Fig. 2.4b the incremental benefit curve is plotted for three values of m. Notice that increasing the amount of environmental predictability (i.e., lowering the value of a or m) also increases the optimal value of S. When the environment is predictable, the frequency of the superior alternative among models approaches 1, and because of this, social learning is more effective. Thus more costly information and less predictable environments favor less efficient individual learning, whereas, as shown in Fig. 2.2, increasing S also increases the optimal amount of social learning (i.e., d^* increases). Once again, the model suggests that a substantial amount of social learning is advantageous under a wide variety of conditions.

DISCUSSION

The models presented above suggest that the adaptiveness of social learning relative to individual learning depends on two factors:

1. the accuracy of individual learning (or the closely related cost of improving this accuracy), and
2. the chance than an individual's social models experienced the same environment that the individual experiences.

In the context of these models at least, a substantial dependence upon social learning is most adaptive when individual learning is inaccurate (or costly to make accurate), and the chance that an individual's social models experienced the same environment the individual experiences is reasonably high. When environments are not changing too quickly or there is not too much migration among habitats, the occasional use of individually acquired compelling evidence, coupled with faithful copying in the absence of such evidence, is sufficient to keep the locally adaptive behavior common. Increasing the importance of individual learning would entail more errors and would reduce the frequency of the adaptive behavior. In contrast, when environmental change is rapid, or there is extensive migration among habitats, relatively rare instances of individual learning would not be sufficient to maintain a high frequency of the locally adaptive behavior. Under such conditions, individuals must rely on individual learning if they are to have any chance of acquiring locally adaptive behavior.

Similar results derived using different models suggest that the present conclusions are robust. The results presented here are based on very simple models that omit many details that may be important in real cases. It is sensible to wonder if the results follow from the qualitative assumptions, or whether they are peculiar to the particular model analyzed here. Elsewhere (Boyd & Richerson, 1983, 1985, chap. 4) we have analyzed formally quite different models that are based on the same qualitative assumptions about the nature of social learning and individual learning. These models yielded the same qualitative conditions for the evolution of social learning that result from the present model.

As more information on social learning in nonhuman animals accumulates it should be possible to test these results in two different ways: first, by comparing the reliance on social learning for acquiring the same character in different species, and second, by comparing the importance of social learning in the acquisition of different characters in the same species. Consider, for example, the acquisition of food preferences in rodents. According to the models, species of rodents that live in rapidly changing environments should rely more on individual learning for acquiring food preferences than should species living in more constant environments. Similarly, for a particular species, there will be some aspects of diet about which it will be difficult for individuals to learn what is best, but there will be other aspects about which it will be easy for individuals to learn. The models predict that the former will be acquired disproportionately by social learning and the latter disproportionately by individual learning. The several experimental systems of social learning reported in this volume suggest that the qualitative conclusions of the models are testable. We also believe that more detailed models with more precise predictions in specific cases could be derived from the general one developed here.

We have also extended the analysis of these models to an important consideration neglected here. The reader may have wondered if, in very slowly changing environments, genetic transmission is not superior to social learning. Assuming that social learning is inherently a less accurate system of inheritance, or has other costs in excess of genetic transmission such as a need for prolonged juvenile dependency, this suspicion is correct. Nevertheless, results published elsewhere (Boyd & Richerson, 1983, 1985, chap. 4) suggest that there remains a broad range of environments with intermediate heterogeneity or variability under which social learning is favored.

We would like to conclude with some speculations about the more general significance of the study of social learning. The seemingly broad conditions favoring the evolution of social learning, and by implication other forms of the inheritance of acquired variation, are an interesting but troubling result. Modern biology is based on the assumption that the inheritance of acquired variation is absent from biological systems (although such a system of inheritance seemed intuitively plausible to 19th-century observers like Darwin). Similarly, modern comparative psychologists have supposed that complex cognitive processes like social learning are very restricted in importance. On the modern view, humans, through culture, are the only species to make much use of the inheritance of acquired variation. The model presented here seems more consistent with the 19th-century view than the modern one.

There are three hypotheses that can resolve this dilemma:

1. Models of the type discussed here may not account for all the costs of social learning. When these costs are included, social learning may only rarely be advantageous. For example, when socially learned variation becomes important, it can be directly subject to evolutionary processes that produce maladaptations from the genetic point of view (Boyd & Richerson, (1985, chaps. 6–8). Thus, coevolutionary complexities may seriously limit the advantages of social learning (and systems for the inheritance of acquired variation more generally). A version of this hypothesis might be required to account for why only one species (humans) makes extensive use of social learning.

2. Social learning may be a good deal more common than we have supposed. Chapters in this volume suggest that a fair range of animal behaviors, including such important ones as food preferences and predator recognition, are influenced by social learning in a wide range of taxa. It is easy to see how the real empirical difficulty of separating social learning from individual learning and genetic variation, combined with the sense that both biologists and psychologists have that inheritance-of-acquired-variation and social learning explanations bear a special burden of proof, could have led to an underestimate of the importance of social learning.

3. Social learning may be a generally useful system, but one that evolves only with difficulty. Lumsden and Wilson (1981, pp. 325–331) imagine that culture of the human grade of complexity is rare because only the hominid lineage had the "cosmic good fortune" to cross a difficult evolutionary threshold and make extensive use of social learning.

Thus, an understanding of the process of social learning is crucial to our picture of how humans fit into the general framework of evolutionary biology. If the second hypothesis above is even partially correct, the study of social learning has broad implications for our understanding of evolutionary process. The improvements in experimental models of animal social learning reported in this volume, and their suggestion that social learning is indeed widespread, is a most exciting development.

APPENDIX 1

Let $P_{t,k}$ be the probability that a member of cohort t acquires behavior k through ordinary learning. Then, if the frequency of behavior 1 among members of cohort t is q_t, the frequency among members of cohort $t + 1$ is:

$$q_{t+1} = q_t' = q_{t-1}(1 - P_{t,1} - P_{t,2}) + P_{t,1} \qquad (A1)$$

Due to the symmetry of the model, $(1 - p_{t,1} - P_{t,2})$, the fraction of the population that relies on social rather than individual learning is a constant equal to $1 - p_{11} - p_{12} = 1 - p_{21} - p_{22}$ which we label L.

Because the environment is not constant, the fraction of population acquiring behavior 1 will not stabilize at a single equilibrium value. Instead, it will fluctuate randomly, driven by the variations in the environment. Suppose that the fraction of the initial cohort choosing alternative 1 is q_0. Then from Equation (A1), the frequency of alternative 1 in the t th cohort is

$$q_t = q_0 L^t + \sum_{j=0}^{t-1} L^{t-j-1} P_{j,1} \qquad (A2)$$

However, after some time the probability that the frequency of behavior 1 takes on various values during cohorts $t, t - 1, t - 2$ and so on will approach stable equilibrium values. This is called the joint stationary distribution of q_t, $q_{t-1}, q_{t-2}, \ldots$, and it is the probabilistic analog of equilibrium in deterministic systems. To evaluate the effect of social learning on the expected fitness of individuals in the population we first compute the expected fitness in the population given that the environment is in a particular state and the frequency of behavior 1 is some value q_t. Then we average over all combinations of state and frequency using the joint stationary distribution of the q_t and environmental state.

The expected fitness of an individual in cohort t, $E(w)$, is given by

$$E(w) = \int g(q_t|\text{state 1})\text{Prob}(\text{state 1})(W + Dq_t)dq_t \qquad (A3)$$

$$+ \int g(q_t|\text{state 2})\text{Prob}(\text{state 2})(W + D(1 - q_t))dq_t$$

where $g(q_t|\text{state } j)$ is the stationary conditional probability density of q_t given that the environment is in state j. Because of the symmetry of the model this expression can be simplified to become

$$E(w) = W + D E(q_t|\text{state 1}) \qquad (A4)$$

To compute $E(q_t|\text{state 1})$, first reexpress the probability of acquiring alternative 1 by individual learning during cohort t, $P_{1,t}$, as follows

$$P_{1,t} = \theta_t p_1 + (1 - \theta_t)p_2 \qquad (A5)$$

where

$$\theta_t = \begin{cases} 1 \text{ if environment 1} \\ 0 \text{ if environment 2} \end{cases}$$

Next, notice that as t becomes large, the first term on the right-hand side of (A2) becomes small. In the limit of very large t

$$q_t = \sum_{j=0}^{\infty} L^j \left(p_2 + \theta_{t-j-1}(p_1 - p_2) \right) \tag{A6}$$

And thus the expected value of q_t given that cohort t experiences environmental state 1 is

$$E\{q_t|\theta_t = 1\} = \sum_{j=0}^{\infty} L^j (p_2 + (p_1 - p_2)\text{Prob}(\theta_{t-j-1} = 1|\theta_t = 1)) \tag{A7}$$

Where from the assumptions of the model

$$\text{Prob}(\theta_{t-j-1} = 1|\theta_t = 1) = (\tfrac{1}{2} + \tfrac{1}{2}(1 - 2a)^{j+1})\,(1/2) \tag{A8}$$

Combining these expressions and simplifying yields the expression for the expected value of q_t given that cohort t experiences environmental state t, $E(q_t|\theta_t = 1)$, that is identical to Equation (11) except that the parameter a is substituted for m.

APPENDIX 2

Taking the partial derivative of expected individual fitness with respect to S holding q constant yields

$$-\hat{q}_1 \left(\frac{\partial p_1}{\partial S} + \frac{\partial p_2}{\partial S} \right) + \frac{\partial p_1}{\partial S} = \frac{\partial C(S)}{\partial S} \tag{A9}$$

Next notice that changing S is just a change in the scale of measurement of x. Thus

$$p_1(S + \delta S, d, M) = p_1(S, dS/(S + \delta S), MS/(S + \delta S)) \tag{A10}$$

and therefore

$$\frac{\partial p_1}{\partial S} = -\frac{M\partial p_1}{S\,\partial M} - \frac{d\partial p_2}{S\partial d} \tag{A11}$$

Combining these expressions and using the fact that (12) must be an equality if d is at its optimum yields the following expression

$$\frac{M\partial p_1}{S\,\partial M} - q\left(\frac{\partial p_1}{\partial M} + \frac{\partial p_2}{\partial M} \right) = \frac{\partial C}{\partial M} \tag{A12}$$

which using the definitions of p_1 and p_2 becomes

$$\frac{M}{S}\{(1 - q)f(d^* - M) + qf(-d^* - M)\} = -\frac{\partial C}{\partial S} \tag{A13}$$

REFERENCES

Bandura, A. (1986). Social foundations of thought and action: A social cognitive theory. Englewood Cliffs, NJ: Prentice-Hall.

Bonner, J. T. (1980). The evolution of culture in animals. Princeton: Princeton University Press.

Boyd, R., & Richerson, P. J. (1983). The cultural transmission of acquired variation: Effect on genetic fitness. *Journal of Theoretical Biology, 100,* 567–596.

Boyd, R., & Richerson, P. J. (1985). Culture and the evolutionary process. Chicago: University of Chicago Press.

Cavalli-Sforza, L. L., & Feldman, M. W. (1981). Cultural transmission and evolution. Princeton, NJ: Princeton University Press.

Galef, B. G. (1980). Diving for food: Analysis of a possible case of social learning by wild rats *(Rattus norwegicus). J. Comp. Physiol. Psychol., 94,* 416–425.

Lumsden, C., & Wilson, E. O. (1981). Genes, mind, and culture. Cambridge, MA: Harvard University Press.

McGrew, W. C., & Tutin, C. E. G. (1978). Evidence for a social custom in wild chimpanzees? Man. *234,* 234–251.

Pulliam, R., & Dunford, C. (1980). Programmed to learn. New York: Columbia University Press.

Richerson, P. J., & Boyd, R. (1987). Simple models of complex phenomena: The case of cultural evolution. In J. Dupre (Ed.), The latest on the best: Essays on evolution and optimality. Cambridge: MIT Press.

Rosenthal, T. L., & Zimmerman, B. J. (1979). Social learning and cognition. New York: Academic Press.

PART II

Social Influences
on Avoidance Learning

Social Learning and
the Acquisition
of Snake Fear in Monkeys

Susan Mineka
University of Texas at Austin

Michael Cook
University of Wisconsin—Madison

The origins and development of predator avoidance have been of long-standing interest to both primatologists and comparative psychologists. Snake avoidance has been of special interest in part because such a wide range of free-ranging monkeys have been observed to exhibit fearful reactions to the appearance of snakes (e.g., Hall & DeVore, 1965, for chacma baboons [*Papio ursinus*]; Struhsaker, 1967, and Seyfarth, Cheney, & Marler, 1980a, 1980b, for vervet monkeys [*Cercopithecus aethiops*]; J. Robinson, personal communication, February 1985, for the dusky titi [*Callicebus moloch*] and capuchins [*Cebus*]). Behavioral manifestations of this fear of snakes include motor acts such as flight, facial expressions indicative of fear, visual monitoring of the snake, and alarm or distress calls (e.g., Hall & DeVore, 1965; Seyfarth et al., 1980a, 1980b; Struhsaker, 1967).

Some investigators have either suggested or assumed that fear of snakes is *innate* or *spontaneous* (e.g., Bertrand, 1969; Hebb, 1946; Masserman & Pechtel, 1953; Morris & Morris, 1965). These terms have generally been used to imply that snake fear does not result from any *specific* experience, although maturational or general experiential factors may be involved. Other investigators have argued that some form of learning is probably necessary for the development of fear of snakes (e.g., Haselrud, 1938; Schiller, 1952; Wolin, Ordy, & Dillman, 1963; Yerkes & Yerkes, 1936). Yerkes and Yerkes, for example, reached this conclusion based on their finding that adult chimpanzees (*Pan troglodytes*) exhibited greater snake fear than did infant chimps. Similarly, Seyfarth et al.'s (1980b) results indicate that vervet infants make fewer snake alarm calls to snakes than do adults, and make more snake alarm calls to inappropriate, nonsnake objects than do adults. Within a learning model of snake fear, lower levels of fear would be exhibited by infants because they have not yet had the necessary learning experience to show the fear.

Unfortunately, field studies, or studies involving primates living in outdoor environments where snakes may appear (e.g., Yerkes & Yerkes, 1936), cannot be used to examine the role of experience in the development of fear of snakes as such studies fail to control for experiential contributions to the development of snake fear. One methodology that circumvents this problem involves comparing the fear responses of indoor laboratory-reared and wild-reared monkeys to the presence of snakes and snakelike objects. Because only the wild-reared animals could have had experience with snakes, the hypothesis that learning is involved in fear acquisition generates the prediction that wild- but not lab-reared animals will show such fear.

Hebb (1946) and Yerkes and Yerkes (1936) used both laboratory- and wild-reared chimpanzees, but made no systematic comparisons of the two groups. The Yerkes also noted that even their lab-reared chimpanzees may have had experience with snakes in their outdoor enclosures. When Joslin, Fletcher, and Emlen (1964) and Mineka, Keir, and Price (1980) did make systematic comparisons they found that wild-reared rhesus monkeys (*Macaca mulatta*), but not indoor lab-reared rhesus, evinced a fear of both real and toy snakes.[1] Murray and King (1973) replicated these findings with squirrel monkeys (*Saimiri sciureus*), but a recent study by Wiener, Atha, and Levine (1986) raises some questions about the sensitivity of the measures that Murray and King used in their study. Wiener et al. found that lab-reared juvenile and adult squirrel monkeys did show significant behavioral avoidance and cortisol elevations during their first 30-min exposure to a snake. (This response was, however, significantly less than that shown by wild-reared adult squirrel monkeys.) Unfortunately their study, unlike Murray and King's, failed to include multiple test trials or any novel objects other than an empty box for comparison purposes. Thus it is not possible to ascertain the extent to which the reactions they observed in lab-reared squirrel monkeys were specific long-lasting fear reactions to snakes, as opposed to more transient reactions that might occur to a variety of novel objects. Furthermore, Wiener et al. did find additional effects of an observational conditioning experience in the juvenile squirrel monkeys, further indicating that the full-blown fear reaction of wild-reared squirrel monkeys has some significant learned component.

Given that, at least for rhesus monkeys, events experienced by wild-reared but not lab-reared animals appear necessary for the emergence of snake fear, the

[1]Wolin et al. (1963) failed to find evidence of snake fear in *either* wild or lab-reared rhesus monkeys, but this was probably due to the short time the wild-reared animals had spent in the wild: 75% were captured at approximately 6 months of age.

next question arising is, what types of experience are involved? One possibility is direct classical conditioning (cf. Pavlov, 1927; Watson & Rayner, 1920). That is, by virtue of a traumatic experience with a snake, the sight of a snake (a conditioned stimulus—CS) might acquire the capacity to elicit a fear conditioned response (CR). It seems unlikely, however, that every primate that exhibits fear of snakes has had direct traumatic experience with snakes. Further, it would seem maladaptive to rely too heavily on such a method of acquiring predator avoidance, especially if first contact with the predator in question is likely to be injurious or fatal.

It has frequently been suggested that fears in general, and snake fear in particular, may be the consequence of some form of social learning or tradition (Joslin et al., 1964; Marks, 1977; Mineka et al., 1980; Rachman, 1977, 1978). Again, recourse to field observation is unlikely to resolve this issue. Field studies do not provide information about which group members have had prior experience with snakes. Furthermore, field workers usually are unable to isolate a member of the group in order to examine its behavior in the absence of other members. For these reasons, field observations cannot distinguish between instances of *social transmission* and *social enhancement* (cf. Galef, 1976, this volume). Social enhancement implies that although snake fear in Animal B follows its emission by Animal A, the response did not originate as a result of this social interaction but was already in B's repertoire. Social transmission implies that B's fear is a specific consequence of B's social interaction with A, and that B's fear may emerge in later appropriate contexts even if A is not present (i.e., if a snake appears).

A number of studies have provided support for the hypothesis that observational or vicarious learning may be involved in acquisition of fears in primates. Stephenson (1967) showed that fears of arbitrary objects such as kitchen utensils can be acquired by observation in male rhesus monkeys. In Stephenson's study, fear was first directly classically conditioned in male rhesus monkeys, who were later to serve as models, by pairing various objects with an airblast (unconditioned stimulus, US). A male observer was then placed in the same enclosure as the model, affording the observer the opportunity to watch the model behave fearfully in the presence of the object. During subsequent testing in isolation, 3 of the 4 observers exhibited a fear of the object.

There are, unfortunately, a number of interpretetive problems with Stephenson's study. First, because model and observer were placed in the same enclosure, permitting physical contact between them, learning may not have been strictly vicarious; rather, it may have involved direct admonition or a punishment contingency or both. For example, a model would sometimes interfere with an observer's attempts to touch stimuli. Second, when females were used, the opposite result was found. Previously fearful models lost their fear as a result of observing the nonfearful behavior of their observers, a process of vicarious extinction in the models. This sex difference may have been due to higher levels of object manipulation by female observers than by males, but regardless of its cause it raises serious questions about the robustness of the observational conditioning of fear. Further, Stephenson did not conduct any tests for context specificity or persistence of the observationally acquired fear. Yet lack of context specificity and a high level of persistence are important characteristics of fears acquired observationally in natural contexts.

In another unpublished study employing rhesus monkeys (Crooks, 1967, cited in Bandura, 1969), observers heard taped distress vocalizations when models touched particular objects, but not others. When tested alone, the observers showed avoidance of those objects associated with distress, but no avoidance of the remaining objects. Like Stephenson, however, Crooks did not test for context specificity or persistence of the observationally acquired fear.

As discussed above, serious limitations surround both field observations and laboratory studies that have attempted to demonstrate a critical role for social learning in predator recognition by primates. In our work on social transmission of fear in rhesus monkeys, we have attempted to abstract the essence of the opportunities that primates have in the wild to profit from the experiences of their conspecifics with predators, and bring it into the laboratory so that the phenomenon can be studied under controlled conditions. Further, we tried to avoid flaws inherent in field studies or in experiments such as Stephenson's and Crooks', which left unresolved important issues such as the context specificity and persistence of learned fear, or the extent to which the effects were mediated by social enhancement rather than observational conditioning.

Our experimental designs circumvent these problems in a number of ways. First, we tested for context specificity of the observationally acquired fear, that is, whether the fear manifests itself in a place other than where it was first vicariously acquired. That observationally acquired fears generalize in this fashion is important in an evolutionary sense given that, in the wild, predators are almost certain to appear in localities other than that where a monkey first learned about them. Second, we tested for persistence of observationally acquired fear 3 months following acquisition. Persistence of learned fear is important because it would be maladaptive if fear of predators had to be relearned repeatedly. Third, we chose to use as the feared object a snake, rather than an arbitrary object as used by Stephenson and Crooks. The choice of a snake CS was important because it has frequently been noted that characteristics of conditioning vary with use of fear-relevant as opposed to fear-irrelevant stimuli (e.g., Öhman, Dimberg & Öst, 1985; Öhman, Frederikson, Hugdahl, & Rimmo, 1976; Seligman, 1971).

Our goals here are, first, to describe the rationale behind our basic procedures, as well as to describe the results of the initial experiments in this series. Second, we discuss the processes underlying social transmission of snake fear. As Galef has argued (this volume), terms such as social transmission and social enhancement are solely descriptive. In some of our recent work we have attempted to transcend a purely descriptive analysis in order to understand the underlying processes in observational, or vicarious conditioning. Third, we re-view recent evidence concerning how prior experiences with snakes can interfere with or prevent the vicarious acquisition of snake fear. Finally, we discuss our work on the issue of whether there are biological constraints on the acquisition of fears through observational conditioning, that is, whether fear of some stimulus objects is more readily transmitted/acquired than fear of other objects.

BASIC PARADIGM

To understand our experiments on observational conditioning of snake fear, it is important to understand our approach to the measurement of fear in rhesus monkeys. In this regard our work has been heavily influenced by research on human fears and phobias indicating that fear is not a single entity that can be easily measured. Rather, as argued by Lang (e.g., 1968, 1971, 1985), fear should be thought of as occurring in three different, loosely coupled response systems: a cognitive/subjective response system, a behavioral avoidance response system, and a physiological response system. That is, when someone is afraid, they may be experiencing subjective distress ("I feel afraid"), or they may be avoiding some object (behavioral avoidance), or they may be showing intense signs of autonomic arousal. These different components of fear are not always highly correlated (e.g., Hodgson & Rachman, 1974; Mineka, 1979, 1985a, 1985b). Sometimes fear is experienced in only one response system; sometimes it is experienced in all three, but to differing degrees.

Because desynchrony among the fear response systems is common, it is important to indicate which response system is being monitored when acquisition of fear is being studied. There are numerous experiments documenting that observational conditioning of autonomic responses can occur in human observers watching a model being shocked in the presence of a neutral CS (see Green & Osborne, 1985, for a recent review). Such experiments leave open the question of whether fear as indexed by the behavioral or cognitive/subjective response systems can also be acquired observationally. Therefore, in all of our experiments fear is measured in two different response systems: behavioral avoidance and behavioral/subjective distress.

In addition, we measured fear in two different contexts to assure that a fear of snakes acquired in one context was manifest in another context as well. The first context in which we measured fear was the Wisconsin General Test Apparat-us (WGTA, Harlow, 1949), normally used for studying discrimination learning, but adapted for our purposes to measure fear. In this apparatus, monkeys are placed in a cage several feet from the experimenter, who sits behind a one-way screen monitoring the monkey's behavior. The monkeys were initially trained to reach rapidly across an open Plexiglas box containing a wood block (a neutral stimulus) to obtain a desired food treat such as a raisin. Once training had established a baseline of rapid reaching for food, the monkey's reactions to different test stimuli in the Plexiglas box (real and toy snakes, electrical cords, neutral wood blocks, etc.) were tested. Because reaching for food requires the monkey to reach over the stimulus inside the box, if the monkey is afraid of the object, it generally refuses to reach. Thus, long food-reach latencies are indicative of the behavioral-avoidance component of fear. In addition to recording food-reach latency, the experimenter also monitored the occurrence of a dozen different disturbance behaviors that have been shown to occur when monkeys are confined in close proximity to a feared object. These behaviors include withdrawing to the back of the cage, making fear grimaces, ear flapping, clutching the cage, shaking the cage, averting eyes from the stimulus, piloerection, and so forth (cf. Mineka et al., 1980; Mineka, Davidson, Cook, & Keir, 1984). These fear or disturbance behaviors are thought to reflect the behavioral/subjective distress response component of fear.

The second context in which we measured fear was the Sackett Circus (Sackett, 1970), normally used for testing social preferences, but adapted for our purposes to measure behavioral avoidance of feared objects. In the Circus apparatus, there is a central compartment that has doors opening into six outer compartments (in the experiments to be reported only four or five were used). The outer wall of each of these compartments is made of Plexiglas so that stimulus objects (e.g., real and toy snakes, wood blocks, etc.) placed outside and immediately adjacent to the walls can be seen by monkeys inside the compartments. The doors connecting the central compartment with the outer (stimulus) compartments were opened for 5 min, enabling the monkeys to freely move between central and outer compartments. If a monkey was not afraid of any of the objects placed outside the outer compartments, it spent approximately equal amounts of time in each. By contrast, if the monkey was afraid of one or more stimulus objects, it tended to spend little or no time inside those compartments next to feared objects, and spent proportionately more time inside compartments next to non-feared objects (Mineka et al., 1984).

All monkeys were pretested in both situations (WGTA and Sackett Circus) to determine that the wild-reared models exhibited a fear of snakes and that the lab-reared observers did not. Typically, fear in the wild-reared monkeys was manifested by their showing very long, usually maximal 60-second food-reach latencies in the presence of snake stimuli in the WGTA, and by showing very rapid latencies in the presence of neutral stimuli. The wild-reared monkeys also generally showed high levels of disturbance behaviors in the presence of snake stimuli, but no such disturbance in the presence of neutral stimuli. They also tended to spend little or no time in compartments in the Circus adjacent to snake stimuli, and instead showed a marked preference for a compartment adjacent to neutral objects. Lab-reared monkeys, by contrast, manifested their lack of fear by showing rapid food-reach latencies in the presence of all stimuli in the WGTA pretest, and by showing few or no disturbance behaviors in the presence of any stimulus. In the Circus pretests, the lab-reared monkeys tended to spend approximately equal amounts of time with the snake and with neutral stimuli.

Following pretests in the WGTA and Circus, lab-reared observer monkeys were allowed to watch wild-reared model monkeys exhibit their fear of snakes in the WGTA. More specifically, the lab-reared observers were placed in a cage with a Plexiglas front several feet away from the monkey in the WGTA. This allowed the observer to watch the monkey reach (or not reach) for food in the presence of snake and neutral stimuli. The observer could also see any disturbance behaviors emitted by the model. Each session of observational conditioning consisted of 15 forty-sec trials, 6 with snake stimuli and 9 with neutral stimuli. Thus, we conducted a discriminative observational conditioning procedure, with observers seeing models behave fearfully during trials with snake stimuli, and nonfearfully during trials with neutral stimuli. Following two sessions of observational conditioning, observers were tested alone in the Sackett Circus for signs of acquisition of snake fear. This first test in the Circus was followed by four more sessions of observational conditioning in the WGTA, with tests in the Circus following the fourth and sixth sessions. Observers were then tested alone in the WGTA to see whether acquired fear was manifest there as well. Three months later, all observers received follow-up tests for retention of acquired fear in both the Circus and the WGTA.

INITIAL STUDIES

In the first study observers were 6 adolescent/young-adult rhesus monkeys; models were their wild-reared parents, with whom the observers had lived their entire lives (Mineka et al., 1984). Models all showed intense fear of snakes in the pretests, whereas observers did not. The six discriminative observational conditioning sessions proceeded as described above. Five out of the 6 observers acquired an intense fear of snakes, first manifested in the initial Circus test at asymptotic intensity after only 8 min of seeing one of their parents behave fearfully with snakes. The fear was shown on all three measures described above. When tested for retention of the acquired fear 3 months later, there was no diminution in its intensity. Thus, our discriminative observational conditioning procedure was successful in inducing in the lab-reared adolescent/young adult monkeys an intense and long-lasting fear of snakes, observable in two of Lang's (1968, 1971) fear response systems. Related findings have also recently been reported by Wiener et al. (1986). They found evidence of observational learning in juvenile squirrel monkeys (1½ years old) that had been exposed to a snake with their wild-reared mother for a 1-hour period 1 year prior to the test (that is, when the subjects were 6 months old). These previously exposed juveniles showed greater cortisol elevations and more specific "fear" vocalizations than did their naive counterparts.

A question raised by the results of our initial study was the extent to which the parent-child relationship between model and observer contributed to the ease of acquisition of snake fear. Therefore, in a second study using an identical procedure, we used models and observers who were completely unrelated to one another, but were "acquainted" by virtue of having lived together in the same room (not the same cage) in the recent past (Cook, Mineka, Wolkenstein, & Laitsch, 1985). The two models used in this study were again wild-reared monkeys who exhibited an intense fear of snakes. Observers were 10 lab-reared, young adult monkeys who initially did not show fear of snakes.

Results of this experiment were strikingly similar to those described just above. Seven out of 10 observers acquired an intense and persistent fear of snakes. As seen in Figure 3.1, the observers showed a dramatically reduced preference for the snake compartments during posttests relative to the pretest, and a concomitant increase in preference for the neutral compartment. Indeed, observers' pattern of preference during posttest closely resembled that of the models during their pretests. Similarly, in the WGTA, observers demonstrated a pattern of change from pretest to posttest indicating acquisition of a strong fear of snakes. As indicated in Fig. 3.2, observers showed dramatic increases in food-reach latencies in the presence of snakes, but not in the presence of neutral stimuli. Further, as indicated in Fig. 3.3, observers also showed many disturbance behaviors in the presence of snakes during the posttest. Figure 3.2 and 3.3 show also

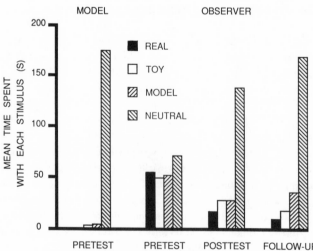

Figure 3.1. Mean amount of time spent with the four different objects in the Sackett Circus for the models in the pretest, and for the observers in the pretest, posttests, and 3-month follow-up. (From Cook et al., 1985.)

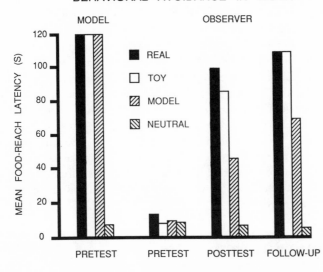

Figure 3.2. Mean food-reach latency in the Wisconsin General Test Apparatus in the presence of the four different objects for the models in the pretest, and for the observers in the pretest, posttest, and 3-month follow-up. (From Cook et al., 1985).

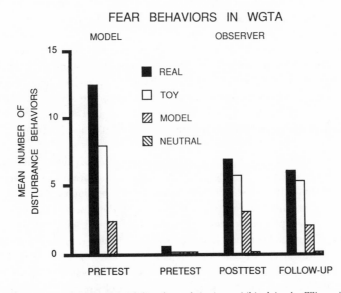

Figure 3.3. Mean number of disturbance behaviors exhibited in the Wisconsin General Test Apparatus in the presence of the four different objects for the models in the pretest, and for the observers in the pretest, posttest, and 3-month follow-up. (From Cook et al., 1985).

that there was no loss of fear at the 3-month follow-up test. Thus, a close social relationship between model and observer is not a major contributing factor in acquisition of snake fear in our observational conditioning paradigm.

To assure that fear acquired by observers in our experiments was similar to that seen in wild-reared monkeys, 2 observers from the previous study then served as models for 8 naive, unrelated lab-reared observers (see Cook et al., 1985, Experiment 2). We wanted to know whether the new models could successfully instill fear in a new set of naive observers. Results indicated that the new observers did acquire a fear of snakes, although it was slightly less intense than that found in the previous study (see Cook et al., 1985, for discussion of possible reasons for this difference in intensity of acquired snake fear). Nonetheless, the fact that monkeys that had acquired snake fear through our paradigm could successfully serve as models was an impressive demonstration of the intensity of their acquired fear.

INDIVIDUAL DIFFERENCES

In the two experiments described above, 1 out of 6 observers from the first experiment (Mineka et al., 1984, Experiment 2) and 3 of 10 observers in the second (Cook et al., 1985, Experiment 1) did not acquire snake fear. These failures of fear acquisition raise intriguing questions as to the source of individual differences in social learning of fear responses. One possibility is that the 4 of 16 observers in the two studies that did not learn may have been bolder or less emotional and would not easily acquire fear under any circumstances. Alternatively, the observational conditioning experiences of the 4 monkeys may have differed from those of the other 12. Model's levels of fear in the presence of snake stimuli vary both from trial to trial and from session to session in ways the experimenter cannot control. These differences in the observational conditioning experiences of observers could contribute to differences in levels of fear acquired by observers.

In a first attempt to understand the source of individual differences in acquired fear, we determined whether there was any relationship between the level of fear shown by a model during observational conditioning and the level of fear its observer exhibited during posttests. During the observational conditioning sessions, the experimenter carefully recorded the disturbance behavior of both model and observer. Therefore, it was possible to correlate a model's level of fear exhibited to the snake stimuli with its observer's level of acquired snake fear exhibited in the posttests. Collapsing both across the fear behaviors shown to the different snake stimuli and across the six sessions of observational conditioning, correlations between the models' level of fear during conditioning and their observers' level of fear during the posttests were .986 in the Mineka et al. (1984) experiment and .95 in the Cook et al. (1985) experiment. These very strong correlations suggest that the major source of individual differences in acquired fear lies in the intensity of the model's fear during observational conditioning.

POSSIBLE MECHANISMS UNDERLYING OBSERVATIONAL CONDITIONING

Observers, as well as models, emit fear behaviors during observational conditioning sessions. This finding is consistent with the literature on human vicarious conditioning showing that observational conditioning is not an unemotional process. Humans who watch models receive an unconditioned stimulus such as shock, and monkeys who watch a model reacting fearfully to snake stimuli, themselves show substantial emotional responses. Indeed, in the second experiment discussed above (Cook et al., 1985, Experiment 1), there was a strong correlation between the models' level of disturbance exhibited to snakes and observers' level of fear exhibited while watching the model ($r = .80$). This suggests the possibility that the observer's response may essentially be an unconditioned response (UR) to a US (the model's fear display). (Or, perhaps, it may be more appropriate to think of it as a CR to a CS if, as may well be the case, observers' responses are based on their prior conditioning history.) Alternatively, something more like a cognitive social inference process may occur in which the observer sees the model reacting fearfully in the presence of snakes and infers that it too should be afraid of snakes. Although these alternative possibilities may be difficult to differentiate experimentally, they do seem theoretically distinct.

The two hypotheses make contrasting predictions about what will happen if an observer can see a model's fear reaction, but not the stimulus to which the model is reacting (e.g., the snake). If an observer's distress in watching the model's fear display is a UR to a US (or a CR to a CS), then it should not matter whether the observer can see the stimulus to which the model is reacting. On the other hand, if the more cognitive social inference process described above occurs, then observers should be less distressed watching a model's fear display if they cannot see the stimulus to which the model is reacting than if they can. To distinguish between these alternatives, we performed an experiment in which 6 lab-reared observers could not see the stimulus to which the model was reacting during observational conditioning; this was accomplished by placing a barrier between the observer and the open Plexiglas box containing test stimuli (Mineka & Cook, submitted for publication). Thus, these Barrier monkeys could witness a model's fear display but could not see the source of the model's distress. Another 6 lab-reared observers (No Barrier group) could see both the model's fear display and the test stimuli, as in our standard observational conditioning paradigm.

The results indicated that during the first session Barrier and No Barrier groups showed equivalent levels of disturbance when watching their models' fear displays. However, by the second session, the level of disturbance in the Barrier group had dropped to almost zero, and stayed at this low level for the remaining four sessions. The level of disturbance in the No Barrier group, by contrast, remained constant across all six sessions. These results suggest that at the outset (Session 1) an observer's distress in watching a model's fear display is like a UR to a US (or a CR to a CS). However, the UR (or CR) appears to be fragile and habituates (or extinguishes) rapidly; by Session 2 observers in the Barrier group stopped showing any significant signs of distress in response to their models' fear displays.

Why then does the disturbance level in the No Barrier monkeys stay constant across the six sessions? It seems likely that by the second session, monkeys in the No Barrier group had already acquired their own fear of snakes, and reacted to the snake stimuli rather than to their models' fear display per se. As mentioned above, in the past we first assessed observers' acquisition of fear after two observational conditioning sessions and generally found their fear to be at asymptotic intensity at that point. In a recent experiment (Mineka & Cook, submitted for publication) we determined whether significant acquisition of snake fear occurs after only one observational conditioning session. Preliminary analysis indicates that significant acquisition of snake fear does occur in one session, although it is not as fully maintained at 3-month follow-up. This finding supports the hypothesis that by Session 2 monkeys in the No Barrier group were showing their own acquired fear of snakes.

To summarize the results discussed thus far, rapid acquisition of snake fear occurs when naive lab-reared monkeys observe wild- or lab-reared monkeys behave fearfully with snakes and nonfearfully with other objects. Once acquired, the fear manifests itself in at least two fear response systems—behavioral avoidance and behavioral distress. It is likely that if we measured autonomic arousal, evidence of fear would be found in the physiological response system as well, given that some of the fear behaviors that occur are probably highly correlated with autonomic arousal (e.g., piloerection, fear withdrawal, cage clutching, etc.).

THE EFFECTS OF PRIOR EXPERIENCES WITH SNAKES ON OBSERVATIONAL CONDITIONING

As discussed by Curio (this volume), in many cases wild animals having observational conditioning experiences will not be as "naive" about the potential predator (e.g., snakes) as observers have been in our experiments. In their natural habitat animals may encounter a potential predator before they see a conspecific reacting fearfully in the presence of that potential predator. For example, an animal unaccompanied by conspecifics may simply encounter the potential predator, and habituate to its presence. Prior experience of this type should produce a phenomenon like that labeled *latent inhibition* in the classical conditioning literature (cf. Lubow, 1973; Lubow & Moore, 1959; Mackintosh, 1974, 1983). With latent inhibition extensive prior exposure to a CS results in retarded subsequent conditioning to that stimulus. Further, an animal may encounter a potential predator in the presence of one or more conspecifics who do *not* react fearfully to its presence. Such prior exposure to a nonfearful model might also be expected to produce interference with subsequent observational conditioning when a fearful model is encountered.

To examine whether one or both of these types of prior exposure to a stimulus object interfere with subsequent observational conditioning, we performed a three-group experiment in which groups differed in the type of prior exposure they experienced before receiving the traditional six-session observational conditioning paradigm (see Mineka & Cook, 1986, for details). Observers in the Immunization group spent six sessions watching *nonfearful* models interact with snake and nonsnake stimuli; these sessions were identical to those described above for observational conditioning except that the models were not afraid of snakes. Observers in the latent inhibition group spent six sessions alone with snake stimuli in the WGTA. Total exposure to snake stimuli in these two

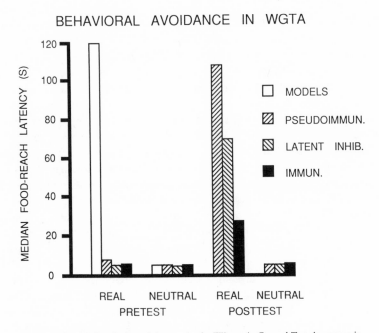

Figure 3.4. Median food-reach latency in the Wisconsin General Test Apparatus in the presence of neutral and real snake stimulus for the models during the pretest, and for the immunization (immuniz), pseudoimmunization (pseudoimmuniz), and latent inhibition (latent inhib) groups in the pretest and posttest. (From Mineka & Cook, 1986.)

conditions was equated. Observers in the pseudoimmunization group spent six sessions watching nonfearful models interact with neutral stimuli. Following these pretreatments, all three groups received six sessions of observational conditioning identical to those described for the experiments previously discussed.

When the three groups were compared for their acquisition of snake fear, significant differences emerged. The immunization group did not show significant acquisition of snake fear, but the other two groups did. Comparing groups, the immunization and pseudoimmunization groups differed significantly on most measures of snake fear, and the latent inhibition group was intermediate and not significantly different from the other two. Figure 3.4 illustrates these results for the WGTA food-reach latency measure. These results suggest that prior observation of nonfearful conspecifics can result in significant interference with the effects of later observational conditioning experiences. Interestingly, inhibition of observational conditioning occurred in only 6 out of 8 observers in the immunization group; the other 2 observers showed levels of acquired fear as high as those of observers from the pseudoimmunization group. The sources of these individual differences remain to be determined.

SELECTIVE ASSOCIATIONS AND OBSERVATIONALLY LEARNED FEAR

Numerous theorists have noted that objects of people's fear and phobias do not constitute a random selection of environmental stimuli. For example, people do not often develop strong fears of hammers, stovetops, or electrical outlets, although these objects may frequently be associated with traumatic experiences or verbal warnings. Instead, people tend to fear heights, snakes, spiders, and so forth. Thus fear of some stimuli is more easily acquired and/or more difficult to extinquish than fear of other stimuli.

One widely cited account of such selective associations is Seligman's preparedness theory (1970, 1971; Seligman & Hager, 1972). According to this theory, as it applies to human fear, humans are evolutionarily "prepared" to associate certain classes of stimuli with aversive consequences because our ancestors who either acquired these fears easily or maintained them over prolonged periods of time possessed a selective advantage. A recent variant of this model has been proposed to Öhman et al. (1985), who distinguished between selective pressures leading to the ready acquisition of fears of animals (e.g., snakes and spiders) as opposed to social fears. Fear of animals is characterized as more reflexive or automatic, and more likely to involve escape/avoidance respones than social fears. Their experimental studies have typically employed nonphobic human subjects, mild shock as a US, and conditioned electrodermal responses (EDRs) as an index of fear. They have typically found that CRs to *fear-relevant* CSs (e.g., slides of snakes and spiders) are very slow to extinguish. In contrast, CRs to *fear-irrelevant* stimuli (e.g., slides of flowers and mushrooms) extinguish readily

(Öhman et al., 1976). Furthermore, evidence of robust conditioning appeared following a single CS-US pairing with fear-relevant CSs, but not with fear-irrelevant CSs (Öhman, Erickson, & Olofsson, 1975). Hygge and Öhman (1978) extended this work on selective associations to a vicarious learning paradigm. They showed that vicariously acquired fear CRs to fear-relevant stimuli also fail to extinguish, whereas vicariously acquired fear CRs to fear-irrelevant stimuli extinguish immediately.

A number of methodological issues complicate interpretation of the foregoing studies. First, it is unclear to what extent, if any, electrodermal responses index fear (see Edelberg & Muller, 1981; Hodes, Cook, & Lang, 1985). Second, as noted by Hygge and Öhman (1978), because humans are used as subjects it is not possible to disentangle experiential from phylogenetic contributions to the selective associations. Indeed other investigators have argued that explanation of such selective associations may well reside in the past experience of individual organisms rather than in the phylogenetic past of the species (e.g., Delprato, 1980; Mackintosh, 1974, 1983). Although evidence on this point is controversial, there are some experiments that implicate biological as opposed to experiential factors in selective associations. For example, Hugdahl and Kärker (1981) found superior conditioning using snakes and spiders as CSs compared with electric outlets. This is in spite of the fact that people are, presumably, as likely to have negative associations to electric outlets as a function of past experience as they are to snakes and spiders.

The observational conditioning paradigm used above allows one to circumvent such problems in interpretation of the causes of differences in conditioning with fear-relevant versus fear-irrelevant CSs. First, the behavioral measures used are probably more valid indices of fear than is electrodermal activity. In addition, by using only laboratory-reared monkeys as observers, the problem of controlling for past experiences with the CSs is averted, because lab-reared monkeys at Wisconsin Primate Laboratory have no experience prior to our experiments with either fear-relevant or fear-irrelevant stimuli (snakes and flowers, respectively).

In an initial attempt to determine whether selective associations occur in the vicarious acquisition of fear in rhesus monkeys, we employed a modified overshadowing paradigm. If two CSs are presented simultaneously in association with a US and the presence of one CS during conditioning causes a failure of the remaining CS to acquire a CR, then overshadowing is said to have occurred (Kamin, 1969; Pavlov, 1927). We hypothesized that if snake and flower stimuli were simultaneously presented in our observational conditioning paradigm, the snake (fear-relevant stimulus) would overshadow conditioning to the simultaneously presented flowers (fear-irrelevant stimulus).

Observers were 10 naive, laboratory-reared monkeys, divided into two groups of 5 subjects each. During the various phases of the experiment, 5 observers witnessed the full range of stimuli (real and toy snakes, brightly colored artificial flowers and neutral objects); the remaining 5 observers were exposed to all the stimuli except the real snake. The procedure during observational conditioning was similar to the one described above except that snake stimuli (real or toy) were always presented simultaneously with brightly colored artificial flower stimuli. Hence, the observers perceived the models reacting fearfully to a compound stimulus consisting of *both* snake and flower components. Following conditioning, flower and snake stimulus components were presented separately to the two observer groups to test for fear acquisition.

During pretests, both models and observers showed little disturbance in the presence of the flower. Following conditioning, both observer groups exhibited an increase in snake fear, but reactivity to neutral objects and flowers did not change significantly from pretest values. Although these results are clearly consistent with predictions of Seligman's and Öhman et al.'s preparedness/selective association theories, they by no means provide conclusive support for either theory. First, the salience of snakes may be greater than that of flowers on a number of stimulus dimensions, and differential salience would be expected to result in superior fear conditioning to snakes. We attempted to control for this possibility by the inclusion of the group that only saw toy snakes thereby removing possible salience differences due to movement, but it is possible that there are other important salience dimensions. An alternative explanation of the overshadowing we observed stems from the possibility that the observer may be able to determine during conditioning that the model is reacting fearfully solely due to the presence of snakes, and not flowers. This might occur, for example, through subtle behavioral/postural cues emitted by the model and detected by the observer, but not by the experimenter.

A final methodological problem is that demonstration of overshadowing requires the inclusion of a control group for which only the overshadowed stimulus (in the present case the fear-irrelevant CS) is present during conditioning. This group controls for the possibility that the overshadowed CS may be incapable of supporting conditioning under any circumstances. Such a control group would require models that react fearfully in the presence of flowers alone. Although it is possible that such a fear could be instilled via direct classical conditioning (i.e., pairing flowers with a noxious US), there is no guarantee that fear of flowers would be either quantitatively or qualtatively equal to the fear shown by models to snakes. Comparisons between the effects of watching these different types of models would be problematic because, as discussed above, the level of fear exhibited by the model largely determines the level of fear acquired by its observer.

Our solution to this methodological problem involved the use of videotapes.[2] An initial experiment assessed whether observers would acquire the

---

[2]We would like to acknowledge and thank C. T. Snowdon for originally suggesting this idea. We would also like to thank J. Schultz for his technical expertise and assistance in preparing the edited videotapes.

same level of snake fear following exposure to *videotaped* models as they acquired following exposure to live models. Two models were videotaped in color (see Mineka, Cook, & Ekman, 1987, for details). One tape was made of each model, showing the same sequence of trials employed in the typical, live-model observational conditioning sessions. Six naive lab-reared monkeys then received six conditioning sessions as in the basic paradigm. To maximize the probability of observer fear acquisition, *both* tapes were shown during each of the six sessions; consequently, observers received twice as much exposure to fearful model behavior in the presence of snakes as in earlier studies (e.g., Cook et al., 1985; Mineka et al., 1984). Furthermore, the number of fear/disturbance behaviors shown by the videotaped models in this study was substantially higher than the mean number of such behaviors shown in past studies using live models. Again, this was purposefully done in order to increase the chance of obtaining vicarious conditioning of snake fear. The procedures for observer pretests, postests, and follow-up were similar to the basic paradigm described for previous studies.

The results substantially conformed to those obtained from studies in which observers watched live models react to snakes. Specifically, whereas observers displayed little or no fear of snake and nonsnake stimuli at pretest, following the taped discriminative observational conditioning sessions, observers showed greatly elevated levels of fear to snake, but not to nonsnake stimuli. This acquired fear was maintained at 3-month follow-up.

Given this initial success with the response of observers to videotaped model performances, a second experiment was performed to pursue the question of selective associations (Cook, Mineka, & Ekman, 1987). In this experiment, videotapes were altered so as to affect observer perception of stimuli to which the taped model was reacting. The original, unedited videotapes had fearful models from past experiments reacting fearfully on some trials to a live boa constrictor and nonfearfully on other trials in the presence of brightly colored artificial flowers. These original videotapes were then edited in two different ways for two different groups of observers. For one group of observers, images of the live boa constrictor were edited out and replaced by images of brightly colored flowers. Thus, observers watching this tape would perceive a model reacting fearfully to flowers (CS+ trials). Also, for this videotape images of flowers were replaced by images of toy snakes so that observers would perceive a model reacting nonfearfully to toy snakes (CS− trials). This group was designated FL+/SN− inasmuch as flowers were a CS+ for fearful model behavior, and snakes were a CS− for nonfearful model behavior.

The videotape shown to the second group of observers was edited in the opposite fashion so observers perceived models reacting fearfully to toy snakes on some trials and nonfearfully to flowers on other trials. This group was designated SN+/FL−. Note that the two groups were exactly equated for the model's fear performances that they saw; they differed only in which stimulus they saw the model reacting to with fear. Videotapes for both groups also showed the model reacting nonfearfully to the neutral wood blocks on trials interspersed between the CS+ and CS− trials.

Naive observers were initially pretested in the Circus and the WGTA with flowers and toy snakes. They then observed the videotapes (either SN+/FL− or FL+/SN) for 12 sessions, with Circus tests after every 4 training sessions. The live snake was used only on the final trials of the WGTA posttest. The pretests had indicated little or no fear of any of the stimuli prior to conditioning. Following conditioning, the SN+/FL− observers showed that they had acquired a fear of both real and toy snakes, but had failed to acquire a fear of flowers. In contrast the FL+/SN− observers failed to acquire a fear of either flowers or snakes. These results are illustrated for the WGTA food-reach latency measure in Figure 3.5.

The results of this study strongly suggest that there are constraints on the kinds of stimuli to which monkeys will acquire fear. Fear of even toy snakes is easily acquired, but a fear of flowers is not. A similar conclusion was reached by Curio, Ernst, and Vieth (1978; see also Curio, this volume). They found observer blackbirds acquired a significantly higher level of fear when the stimulus paired with alarm cries was a predator-like stuffed noisy friarbird than when the stimulus was a plastic bottle. Different from our results, however, Curio et al. did find significant conditioning to the plastic bottle (the fear-irrelevant stimulus) in their blackbirds.

One possible explanation of why we found no acquisition of flower fear is

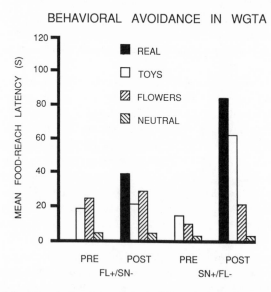

Figure 3.5.   Mean food-reach latency in the Wisconsin General Test Apparatus in the presence of the four different objects during the pretest and posttest for the observers in the SN+/FL− group and the FL+/SN− group. (From Cook et al., 1987.)

that the discriminative conditioning paradigm we used may have required too difficult a discrimination in the FL+/SN— condition. By this view, aversive conditioning might be possible using a flower CS if a simpler paradigm were employed in which a FL+ group viewed only fearful model performances in the presence of flowers, i.e., without any interspersed SN— trials. Such a group would be more like the single SN+ group in the first videotape study described above (Mineka, Cook, & Ekman, 1987). We are currently conducting this study, showing observers a modified version of the videotape shown the FL+/SN— observers on which all snake trials have been deleted. Preliminary results are consistent with those in the previous study: FL+ monkeys do not appear to acquire a fear of flowers.

Another possible objection to our conclusion that the snake/flower videotape study demonstrates selective associability stems from the possibility that the flowers we used may be incapable of supporting excitatory conditioning under any circumstances. To test for this possibility, we are conducting a study in which a videotaped flower stimulus is paired with delivery of a food treat for one group, i.e., flowers are serving as a CS+ in an appetitive classical conditioning paradigm. A second group has a videotaped toy snake as a CS+ for food. If the FL+ group shows acquisition of an excitatory CR (e.g., conditioned activity, cf. Holland & Rescorla, 1975), then it will be clear that our flowers are not simply inadequate CS+s in general but rather do not easily become associated with fear CRs.

CONCLUSIONS

The significance of the studies reviewed above can be viewed from both practical and theoretical perspectives. On a practical level, ethologists and comparative psychologists interested in reintroducing endangered primate species into the wild have devoted considerable effort to training their animals to forage for food, climb trees, and so on. However, little attention has been given to the problem of training predator avoidance. The present review not only suggests that such training may be essential for some species, but also provides a general framework through which it can be accomplished. On a theoretical level, the present studies contribute substantially to an understanding of how predator recognition/ avoidance may develop in free-ranging primates. The results may also contribute to an understanding of the origins of human fears and phobias (see Mineka, in press, for further discussion).

That our paradigm adequately models predator avoidance learning in the wild is supported by congruence between aspects of the laboratory phenomenon and what we should reasonably expect to see concerning predator avoidance in nature. As discussed above, acquired snake fear is rapid, strong, persistent and not context specific. Further, our research on selective associability in vicarious acquisition of snake fear suggests ways in which the learning process is constrained. Our data are a first step in demonstration of phylogenetic history affecting parameters of learning.

ACKNOWLEDGMENTS

Preparation of this chapter was supported by BNS-8507340 from the National Science Foundation to S. Mineka. The research described in this chapter has been generously supported by grants from the University of Wisconsin Graduate School and by Grants BNS-8216141 and BNS-8507340 from the National Science Foundation.

REFERENCES

Bandura, A. (1969). *Principles of behavior modification.* New York: Holt, Rinehart & Winston.

Bertrand, M. (1969). The behavioral repertoire of the stumptail macaque: A descriptive and comparative study. In H. Hofer, A. Schulz, & D. Starck (Eds.), *Bibliotheca Primatologica* (No. 11). New York: S. Karger AG.

Cook, M., Mineka, S., & Ekman, J. (1987). Observational conditioning of fear to fear-relevant versus fear-irrelevant stimuli in rhesus monkeys. Manuscript in preparation.

Cook, M., Mineka, S., Wolkenstein, B., & Laitsch, K. (1985). Observational conditioning of snake fear in unrelated rhesus monkeys. *Journal of Abnormal Psychology, 93,* 355–372.

Crooks, J. (1967). *Observational learning of fear in monkeys.* Unpublished manuscript, University of Pennsylvania.

Curio, E., Ernst, U., & Vieth, W. (1978). The adaptive significance of avian mobbing: II. Cultural transmission of enemy recognition in blackbirds: Effectiveness and some constraints. *Zeitschrift Tierpsychologie, 48,* 184–202.

Delprato, D. (1980). Hereditary determinants of fears and phobias. *Behavior Therapy, 11,* 79–103.

Edelberg, R., & Muller, M. (1981). Prior activity as a determinant of electrodermal recovery rate. *Psychophysiology, 18,* 17–25.

Galef, B. (1976). Social transmission of acquired behavior: A discussion of tradition and social learning in vertebrates. In J. Rosenblatt, R. Hinde, E. Shaw, & C. Beer (Eds.), *Advances in the study of behavior* (Vol. 6, pp. 77–100). New York: Academic Press.

Green, G., & Osborne, J. (1985). Does vicarious instigation provide support for observational learning theories? A critical review. *Psychological Bulletin, 97,* 3–17.

Hall, K., & DeVore, I. (1965). Baboon social behavior. In I. DeVore (Ed), *Primate behavior: Field studies of monkeys and apes* (pp. 53–110). New York: Holt, Rinehart and Winston.

Harlow, H. (1949). The formation of learning sets. *Psychological Review, 56,* 51–65.

Haselrud, G. (1938). The effect of movement of stimulus objects upon avoidance reactions in chimpanzees. *Journal of Comparative Psychology, 25,* 507–528.

Hebb, D. (1946). On the nature of fear. *Psychological Review, 53,* 259–276.

Hodes, R., Cook, E., & Lang, P. (1985). Individual differences in autonomic response: Conditioned association or conditioned fear? *Psychophysiology, 22,* 545–560.

Hodgson, R., & Rachman, S. (1974). II. Desynchrony in measures of fear. *Behaviour Research and Therapy, 12,* 319–326.

Holland, P., & Rescorla, R. (1975). Second-order conditioning with food unconditioned stimulus. *Journal of Comparative and Physiological Psychology, 88,* 459–467.

Hugdahl, K., & Kärker, A.-C. (1981). Biological vs. experiential factors in phobic conditioning. *Behaviour Research and Therapy, 19,* 109–115.

Hygge, S., & Öhman, A. (1978). Modeling processes in the acquisition of fears: Vicarious electrodermal conditioning to fear-relevant stimuli. *Journal of Personality and Social Psychology, 36,* 271–279.

Joslin, J., Fletcher, H., & Emlen, J. (1964). A comparison of the responses to snakes of lab- and wild-reared rhesus monkeys. *Animal Behavior, 12,* 348–352.

Kamin, L. (1969). Predictability, surprise, attention and conditioning. In B. Campbell & R. Church (Eds.), *Punishment and aversive behavior* (pp. 279–296). New York: Appleton Century Crofts.

Lang, P. (1968). Fear reduction and fear behavior: Problems in treating a construct. In J. Shlein (Ed.), *Research in psychotherapy* (Vol. 3, pp. 90–102). Washington, DC: American Psychological Association.

Lang, P. (1971). The application of psychophysiological methods to the study of psychotherapy and behavior modification. In A. Bergin & S. Garfield (Eds.), *Handbook of psychotherapy and behavior change: An empirical analysis* (pp. 75–125). New York: Wiley.

Lang, P. (1985). The cognitive psychophysiology of emotion: Fear and anxiety. In A. Tuma & J. Maser (Eds.), *Anxiety and the anxiety disorders* (pp. 131–170). Hillsdale, NJ: Lawrence Erlbaum Associates.

Lubow, R. (1973). Latent inhibition. *Psychological Bulletin, 79,* 398–407.

Lubow, R., & Moore, A. (1959). Latent inhibition: The effect of nonreinforced preexposure to the conditioned stimulus. *Journal of Comparative and Physiological Psychology, 52,* 415–419.

Mackintosh, N. (1974). *The psychology of animal learning.* London: Academic Press.

Mackintosh, N. (1983). *Conditioning and associative learning.* New York: Oxford University Press.

Marks, I. (1977). Phobias and obsessions: Clinical phenomena in search of a laboratory model. In J. Maser & M. Seligman (Eds.), *Psychopathology: Experimental models* (pp. 174–213). San Francisco: Freeman.

Masserman, J., & Pechtel, C. (1953). Conflict-engendered neurotic and psychotic behavior in monkeys. *Journal of Nervous and Mental Disorders, 118,* 408–411.

Mineka, S. (1979). The role of fear in theories of avoidance learning, flooding and extinction. *Psychological Bulletin, 86,* 985–1010.

Mineka, S. (1985a). Animal models of anxiety-based disorders: Their usefulness and limitations. In A. Tuma & J. Maser (Eds.), *Anxiety and the anxiety disorders* (pp. 199–244). Hillsdale, NJ: Lawrence Erlbaum Associates.

Mineka, S. (1985b). The frightful complexity of the origins of fears. In F. Brush & J. B. Overmier (Eds.), *Affect, conditioning, and cognition: Essays on the determinants of behavior* (pp. 55–73). Hillsdale, NJ: Lawrence Erlbaum Associates.

Mineka, S. (in press). A primate model of phobic fears. In H. Eysenck & I. Martin (Eds.), *Theoretical foundations of behavior therapy*. Plenum.

Mineka, S., & Cook, M. (1986). Immunization against the observational conditioning of snake fear in rhesus monkeys. *Journal of Abnormal Psychology, 95*, 307–318.

Mineka, S., Cook, M., & Ekman, J. (1987). Observational conditioning of snake fear in rhesus monkeys using videotaped models. Manuscript in preparation.

Mineka, S., & Cook, M. (Submitted for publication). Possible mechanisms underlying observational conditioning of fear in monkeys.

Mineka, S., Davidson, M., Cook, M., & Keir, R. (1984). Observational conditioning of snake fear in rhesus monkeys. *Journal of Abnormal Psychology, 93*, 355–372.

Mineka, S., Keir, R., & Price, V. (1980). Fear of snakes in wild- and lab-reared rhesus monkeys. *Animal Learning and Behavior, 8*, 653–663.

Morris, R., & Morris, D. (1965). *Men and snakes*. London: Hutchinson.

Murray, S., & King, J. (1973). Snake avoidance in feral and laboratory-reared squirrel monkeys. *Behavior, 47*, 281–289.

Öhman, A., Dimberg, U., & Öst, L.-G. (1985). Biological constraints on the learned fear response. In S. Reiss, & R. Bootzin (Eds.), *Theoretical issues in behavior therapy* (pp. 123–175). New York: Academic Press.

Öhman, A., Ericksson, A., & Olofsson, C. (1975). One-trial learning and superior resistance to extinction of autonomic responses conditioned to potentially phobic stimuli. *Journal of Comparative and Physiological Psychology, 88*, 619–627.

Öhman, A., Fredrikson, M., Hugdahl, K., & Rimmo, P.-A. (1976). The premise of equipotentiality in human classical conditioning: Conditioned electrodermal responses to potentially phobic stimuli. *Journal of Experimental Psychology: General, 105*, 313–337.

Pavlov, I. (1927). *Conditioned reflexes*. London: Oxford University Press.

Rachman, S. (1977). The conditioning theory of fear acquisition: A critical examination. *Behaviour Research and Therapy, 15*, 375–388.

Rachman, S. (1978). *Fear and courage*. San Francisco: Freeman.

Sackett, G. (1970). Unlearned responses, differential rearing experiences, and the development of social attachments by rhesus monkeys. In L. Rosenblum (Ed.), *Primate behavior: Development in field and laboratory research* (Vol. 1, pp. 112–140). New York: Academic Press.

Schiller, P. (1952). Innate constituents of complex responses in primates. *Psychological Review, 59*, 177–191.

Seligman, M. (1970). On the generality of the laws of learning. *Psychological Review, 77*, 406–418.

Seligman, M. (1971). Phobias and preparedness. *Behavior Therapy, 2*, 307–320.

Seligman, M., & Hager, J. (1972). *Biological boundaries of learning*. New York: Meredith.

Seyfarth, R., Cheney, D., & Marler, P. (1980a). Monkey responses to three different alarm calls: Evidence of predator classification and semantic communication. *Science, 210*, 801–803.

Seyfarth, R., Cheney, D., & Marler, P. (1980b). Vervet monkey alarm calls: Semantic communication in a free-ranging primate. *Animal Behavior, 28*, 1070–1094.

Stephenson, G. (1967). Cultural acquisition of a specific learned response among rhesus monkeys. In D. Starck, R. Schneider, & H. Kuhn (Eds.), *Progress in primatology.* Stuttgart: Gustav Fisher Verlag.

Struhsaker, T. (1967). Auditory communication among vervet monkeys. In S. Altmann (Ed.), *Social communication among primates (Cercopitheous aethips)* (pp. 281–324). Chicago: University of Chicago Press.

Watson, J., & Rayner, R. (1920). Conditioned emotional reactions. *Journal of Experimental Psychology, 3,* 1–14.

Wiener, S., Atha, K., & Levine, S. (1986). Influence of early experience on the development of fear in the squirrel monkey. *Primate Report Abstracts,* 11th Congress of the International Primatological Society, *14,* 29.

Wolin, L., Ordy, J., & Dillman, A. (1963). Monkeys' fear of snakes: A study of its basic and generality. *Journal of Genetic Psychology, 103,* 207–226.

Yerkes, R., & Yerkes, A. (1936). Nature and conditions of avoidance (fear) in chimpanzees. *Journal of Comparative Psychology, 21,* 53–66.

Cultural Transmission of Enemy Recognition by Birds

E. Curio
Arbeitsgruppe für Verhaltensforschung
Fakultät für Biologie, Ruhr-Universität
Bochum, GFR.

INTRODUCTION

Birds, like other animals, are endowed with diverse structural and behavioral devices to escape from or fend off their predators. As a result of coevolution of prey and predator, behavioral devices for predator avoidance may become part of the prey species' behavioral repertoire. Predator avoidance, for instance, is often finely tuned to sympatric predators and is preprogrammed so that individual learning is unnecessary (Curio, 1969, 1975; Giles, 1984; Seghers, 1970, 1973). Individual learning of predator avoidance may even be unfeasible because of its deadly cost (Smith, 1975, 1977). When the threat from predators is relatively unpredictable, for example, as the result of invasion by a previously absent predator species (see Robertson & Norman, 1977, for a brood parasite; Diamond, 1985) or of a change in hunting behavior of a sympatric, hitherto innocuous species (Steiniger, 1950), phenotypic plasticity can come to safeguard prey. One way to achieve learning to avoid a particular predator is by cultural transmission of avoidance of predator-associated stimuli, one of many forms of tradition in animals (see Mainardi, 1980). Formation of single species or multispecies flocks, an ingredient of predator harassment, would appear particularly conducive to this sort of learning.

The practical difficulty with experimental work on cultural transmission lies in the fact that any transmission procedure relies on the existence of at least one knowledgeable teacher. For experimental purposes an experimentally naive bird can be exposed to a neutral object and to a teacher that has been tricked into harassment of that object (the latter is shielded from view of the teacher). This method was adopted in our studies of cultural transmission in the European blackbird (*Turdus merula*) and in the Australian zebra finch (*Taeniopygia guttata*). The research capitalized on the preexisting mobbing of owls displayed by both species.

The selective review that follows relies exclusively on our work (Curio, Ernst, & Vieth, 1978; Vieth, Curio, & Ernst, 1980), for although there is valuable work on cultural transmission of enemy recognition in chimpanzees (*Pan troglodytes*) (see Menzel, Davenport, & Rodgers, 1972) and in rhesus monkeys (*Macaca mulatta*) reviewed by Mineka in this volume, the present research is the only firm evidence for cultural transmission of enemy recognition in birds.

The present report addresses four interrelated questions with particular attention given to the natural environment.

1. What are the properties of the learning mechanism underlying cultural transmission?

2. What constraints on such learning exist and can they be related to the life-style of individual species?

3. Does cross-species tutoring of enemy recognition occur?

4. Which animal in the teacher/learner dyad is the beneficiary?

GENERAL EXPERIMENTAL PROCEDURE
OF BLACKBIRD EXPERIMENTS

Objects to be conditioned were exposed to the learner in a presentation box. Learner blackbirds (Lr) were exposed to the presentation box prior to the start of training to control for a response elicited by the stimulus background itself (Trial 1). Thereafter, one of two objects chosen to be conditioned via a conspecific's mobbing behavior (either an Australian honeyeater (*Philemon corniculatus*) dummy or a multicolored plastic bottle) was offered in the presentation box (Trial 2). The criteria for selecting a conditioning object were as follows: (1) It had to be novel. (2) It had to be unlike any predator that is recognized innately, i.e., without prior experience with it. (3) It had to be similar in size to a dangerous predator.

The second criterion, the one most difficult to attain, was examined with a *novelty test* (Trial 2). This test yielded a *novel stimulus value*. The CS was then paired with a conspecific teacher's (Tr) mobbing (Trial 3). Mobbing, which served as a UCS, sympathetically induced mobbing in the Lr. A (final) test of learning (Trial 4) served to determine whether the behavior of Lr had been altered as a consequence of Trial 3, as predicted by the cultural transmission hypothesis.

We used only a few Tr blackbirds, thus minimizing variation of the UCS. Both Trs and Lrs were trapped in the wild. Response strength (RS) was scored as mobbing elements (calls plus tail and wing flicks)/min.

The aviary of the Lr was separated from that of the Tr (Figure 1) by a hallway 1 m wide. Each of the two birds could look into one of four compartments of the presentation box, which was located in the middle of the hallway. Before a trial the compartment exposed to either bird was empty. By rotating the box around its vertical axis the Lr was shown the potential CS while the Tr was simultaneously shown the opposite compartment containing a little owl (*Athene*

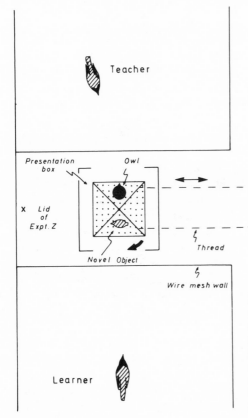

Figure 4.1. Experimental apparatus with presentation box between the aviaries of Teacher (Tr) and Learner (Lr) blackbird. Experimenter (E) is hidden from both behind white canvas. Little owl and novel object are shown in position for training the Lr. Lid in Experiment Z covered Ho between presentations to both Tr and Lr. (modified from Vieth et al., 1980).

noctua). The presence of the owl elicited vigorous mobbing by the Tr. Juxtaposition of the stimuli ensured that the Lr associated the Tr's mobbing with the CS alone. At the end of the 5-min presentation, the box was rotated back to its original position, i.e., the stimulus objects were removed from the view of both birds. (For further procedural details see Curio et al., 1978, and Vieth et al., 1980).

CULTURAL TRANSMISSION OF ENEMY RECOGNITION

Baseline Experiments with a Honeyeater

One-Trial Learning as the Basic Process. Before looking at the conditioning of blackbird mobbing by the pairing of a mobbing conspecific Tr to a novel object, the object's novel stimulus value needed to be determined. Birds are known to fear a novel object prior to any adverse experience with it (Berlyne, 1967; Curio, 1969, 1975; Hogan, 1965). This investigation started with Trial 2 of an experiment that controlled for change in response to the honeyeater (Ho) as a consequence of repeatedly seeing it (Experiment II, in Figure 4.2a).

Comparison of the response to the empty presentation box in Trial 1 with the response to the box containing Ho in Trial 2, and comparison of the latter with the response to the empty box presented for the second time (Experiment III, in Figure 4.2a) demonstrates that Ho elicits a stronger response than does the empty box. The unreinforced responses to Ho continued to exceed responses to the empty box on all subsequent trials, in spite of some habituation to the Ho. Hence, Ho seems to engender some initial fear, independent of reinforcement (i.e., pairing with a mobbing Tr).

On Trial 3, in response to the vigorous mobbing response of the Tr in the aviary behind the presentation box, the Lr joined the Tr in mobbing (Figure 4.2a, Experiment I). Lr's response strength was 2.9 times greater, on the average, than the original response to Ho when it was first seen in Trial 2. In the learning test (Trial 4), 2 hr later, evidence for conditioning was found. Responding to Ho exceeded the response of control subjects (Experiment II). Response strength (RS) had increased by a factor of 2.2 as compared to the novel stimulus value as a consequence of events during Trial 3. One must conclude from the results of Experiments I and II that the significant rise in stimulus value of Ho on Trial 4 was a *consequence of social elicitation on Trial 3* and not of sensitization by repeatedly seeing Ho.

During all trials the Lr could freely perceive the behavior of the Tr. Positive feedback may have occurred between Lr and Tr that, especially on Trial 4, might have confounded the increase in RS in the learning test (Trial 4). Lr's initially weak response could have been enhanced by sympathetically inducing mobbing by the Tr that, in turn, could have potentiated the Lr's response and so on. To

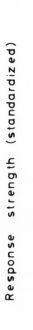

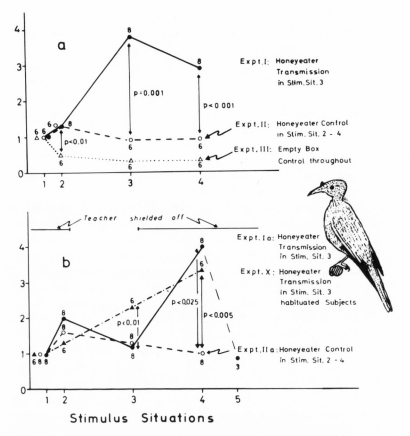

Figure 4.2. Training of Learner blackbird (Lr) to respond to honeyeater (Ho) in experiments with the Teacher (Tr) being visible to Lr (a) on all trials (see text), or (b) only before and after training trial (Trial 3). Trials were spaced in time as indicated, with 30-min interval between Trials 1 and 2. Response strength after Trial 1 standardized with reference to initial empty box response. Number of Lrs at each data point as indicated. For details see text (modified from Curio et al., 1978).

control for this possibility, a white canvas cloth that shielded Tr from Lr was removed from shortly after Trial 2 till shortly after Trial 3. Thus transmission of Tr's response to Ho was permitted only during Trial 3 (Figure 4.2b). The Tr was not induced to call when it heard the Lr's vocal response during Trial 4. As before, the Ho again appeared to be an initially effective, though comparatively weak, stimulus in all three new experiments (Ia, IIa, X); the novelty response of 21 birds fell short of being significantly different from the response to the empty box control on Trial 1, perhaps because the box itself had been seen for the second time and habituation may have reduced RS.

The most striking result is seen in Experiment Ia, the counterpart to

Experiment I in Figure 4.2a. This result demonstrates cultural transmission of Ho recognition in the absence of any feedback effect of Tr during Trial 4. Also important, however, is the fact that despite an unusually low RS during training (Trial 3) the Lr exhibited the same RS on Trial 4 as did Lrs In Experiment I. From this one must conclude that behavior of the Lr during training is not a predictor of the efficacy of transmission evidenced in Trial 4. The reason for the comparatively strong decrement in Trial 3 of Experiment Ia was likely of external origin (Curio et al., 1978).

Does Habituation to an Innocuous Object Prevent Conditioning to It?   In the wild, a bird may encounter a dangerous animal unwarned and theoretically the bird might even become habituated to it. The bird might thus lose the fear of novelty inherent in the first encounter. Can a tradition of enemy recognition even then protect a novice from a fatal encounter? An affirmative answer to this question would considerably enhance the realism of cultural transmission as an antipredator device in the wild. Blackbirds that had been habituated to Ho during five presentations 16–25 days earlier were subjected to the same conditioning procedure as those Lrs in Experiment Ia (Fig. 4.2b, Experiment X). As can be seen, the Lrs learned to mob Ho after only one trial, to an extent that compares favorably with Lrs trained after seeing Ho for the first time (Experiment Ia). Thus a bird habituated to a potentially dangerous creature would not become blind to a later lesson from a knowledgeable Tr if the occasion arose. It remains less clear why during transmission Lrs were induced to respond more strongly in the present experiment than in Experiment Ia. In any case, the discrepancy indicates again that the behavior during transmission is unsuitable as a predictor of the outcome of the learning process.

To further support the conclusions of the habituation/conditioning experiment a stimulus object was chosen as CS that can be assumed to elicit no avoidance response whatsoever in the wild. Starlings (*Sturnus vulgaris*) coexist with blackbirds, are innocuous to them, and are familiar to them. Accordingly, any initial fear of starlings should have been eliminated through life-long habituation. When 7 experimentally naive blackbirds were presented a mounted starling it did not elicit significantly more responding than an empty box (1.4/min, $p = .12$, binomial test, two-tailed). In fact, Lrs seemed to respond less to the starling than to the novel Ho. When Lrs were conditioned with Tr visible (see Fig. 4.2b), the starling CS yielded a test-trial response which, though weak, significantly exceeded the novel stimulus value (1.7/min, $p < .01$, Wilcoxon test, two-tailed). Furthermore, the RS did not differ significantly from the learned value to Ho after experimental habituation (Experiment X, stimulus situation 4: 3.2, $p = .14$, Mann Whitney U-test, two tailed). The possibly diminished efficacy of experimentally transmitting information about the starling might be due to the naturally occurring long period of fear via habituation that blackbirds have experienced to starlings. Hence, habituation may set a limit to what can become conditioned later on, though other interpretations are possible. Habituation of a bird to an initially effective predator stimulus may be site-specific (e.g., Shalter, 1975, 1978). Predators in the wild tend to appear under ever-changing circumstances of space and time. The hypothesis of cultural transmission of enemy recognition would be more realistic if it could be shown that RS increases with a change in site of encountering Ho. To test this idea a sample of experimentally naive blackbirds was trained in the way indicated in Figure 4.2b, but tested with Ho shifted to the opposite side of the Lr's aviary; the Ho was presented in front of a piece of grey cardboard (30 x 25 cm), 30 cm in front of and outside the aviary, and 100 cm above ground level. The manner of presentation thus resembled previous experiments except in site of presentation of the CS and absence of the box. The test response to the CS at the novel site was the highest obtained (12.4/min, Experiment IV in Table 4.1) and it differed significantly from the RS observed under normal conditions (Experiment Ia). Hence, the outcome of conditioning can be potentiated by changing the site of the CS between training and testing. This result supports the hypothesis that cultural transmission is a process of considerable benefit to the Lr.

Table 4.1

Upper Half: Strength of Learned Response to Honeyeater (Ho) With the Tr Visible only during Training (Trial 3, see Fig. 4.2b) as a Function of Encountering Ho at the Original Site or at a Novel Site (Exps. Ia and IV). Lower Half: Control for Sensitization to Ho: Repeated Presentation of Ho, on Trials 2 and 3, Resulted in Habituation to "Ho + Site of Presentation" (Exp. IIa) or in Dishabituation (Exp. V). Responses Standardized With Reference to Empty Box Control (Trial 1)

Experiment	Experimental Paradigm	n	Response Strength (standardized) 1/min	Third Exposure to Ho on Trial 4 as a	Level of Significance one-tailed
Ia	Ho presented at site of reinforcement	8	4.2	Test of Learning	$p < .025$
IV	Ho presented at *novel* site	6	12.4	Test of Learning	$p < .001$
IIa	Ho presented at *original* site after habituation to "Ho + Site of Presentation" on Trials 2 and 3	8	1.2	Test of Sensitization	$p < .001$
V	Ho presented at *novel* site on Trial 4 after habituation to "Ho + Site of Presentation" on Trials 2 and 3	6	4.0	Test of Sensitization	

The above result is consistent with the idea that habituation occurs during all trials prior to the test trial and hence reduces response during testing. In order to separate the role of habituation per se, the response-eliciting power of Ho on Trial 4 at the original site (box) was compared with that with the site of presentation changed, as described above (Experiment IIa vs. Experiment V in Table 4.1), after habituating the subject to Ho in Trials 2 and 3. Results indicated that there was a significant increase in RS after the change of site such that the response obtained was about the same as it was after conditioning *without* change of site (Experiment Ia). Therefore, *both* social reinforcement and change of site combined to yield the maximum response referred to above (Experiment IV).

The increase in RS induced by the change of site in Experiment V leaves one finding unexplained. Why does RS on Trial 4 exceed the *novel* stimulus value of Ho on Trial 2 by a factor of almost 3? If habituation alone diminished the response observed on Trial 4 of the sensitization experiments (IIa, also II), dishabituation through change of site should have yielded a response comparable only to the initial stimulus value of Ho. Because a much stronger response was obtained, one must assume that repeated exposure of blackbirds to Ho in some way sensitizes their responsivity without any social elicitation (perhaps due to the movement associated wih each presentation). This would mean that the "sensitization" control curves reflect the net effect of habituation and sensitization, that is, of decremental and incremental effects that occur simultaneously (see also Hinde, 1960). How the interplay of both processes translates into the response as it occurs in nature, following repeated encounters with an apparently innocuous creature, remains an open question.

A Control for Conditioning to the Experimental Context.   Transmission of recognition of Ho occurred against the visual background of the presentation box rotated in exactly the same way on each trial. To what extent was learning specific to the Ho? Three Lrs trained in Experiment I were tested on a fifth trial (1 hr after Trial 4) with the empty box rotated. The birds failed to respond more strongly than on Trial 1 (Figure 4.2b). This finding suggests that the Lr separates the Ho from its environment when learning to mob it. Cultural transmission can hence be said to be object-specific. The question remains whether this perceptual separation is simply due to the box being visible before and between stimulus presentations and thereby losing any conditioned stimulus value in excess of that of the empty box on Trial 1.

Conditioning an Unnatural Object:
Examining Constraints of Learning

The successful transmission of response to Ho raises the question of whether blackbirds are capable of becoming conditioned to objects that would pose no threat in the real world. The experiment to be reported addresses the question of constraints on sensitivity to the CS, that is, whether there is "preparedness for learning" *sensu* Seligman and Hager (1972; see also Shettleworth, 1984).

In Experiment VI, a multicolored plastic bottle of similar overall length and the same novelty as Ho was presented to new Lrs as was the Ho in Experiment I (in Figure 2a). The initial response to the bottle proved to be only about as strong as that to the empty box (Experiment VI, Figure 4.3). However, both objects were clearly discriminated as evidenced by RS on Trial 2 in Experiments III, VI and VII. As can be further seen, response to the bottle, similar to that to Ho, was reinforced by Tr mobbing.

To portray the extent to which responses to Ho differed from those to the bottle, thus implying different perceptual mechanisms, RS values have been juxtaposed in Figure 4.4. The Ho elicited an initially stronger response than the bottle. Hence, body size alone cannot account for the releasing values of both novel objects. The Ho must possess additional specific features absent from the bottle. Also, responses during both training and test revealed a difference in the same direction, despite nearly constant mobbing by the Tr each time. From this finding it follows that there are constraints on learning: Transmission of information about different CS objects was not equally effective.

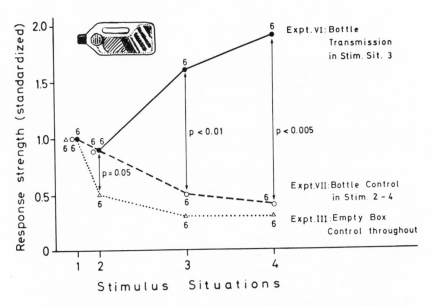

Figure 4.3. Strength of response in four stimulus situations analogous to Trials 1 through 4 in Fig. 4.2, involving social reinforcement of a multicolored bottle (modified from Curio et al., 1978).

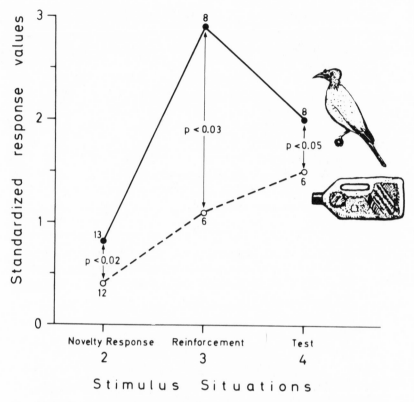

Figure 4.4. Comparison of cultural transmission as evidenced by recognition of Ho (upper curve, Experiment I) and recognition of a multicolored bottle (Experiment VI). RS standardized by subtracting the empty box RS value from the respective experiment from each mean RS value (see Figs. 4.2 and 4.3, respectively). For details see Figure 4.2.

The Adaptedness of the Culturally Transmitted Response

The socially acquired antipredator response should benefit Lr if it improved its protection in future encounters with the predator. The hypothesis was approached in two ways. First, the level of the conditioned mobbing of Ho was compared with the response to a stuffed little owl (the one used to trigger harassment in the Tr). When presented with the owl, 6 Lrs that had been tutored from one to several days before (Experiment X, Figure 4.2b) responded to the owl indistinguishably from their response to Ho (Table 1 in Curio et al., 1978). This result supports the hypothesis that the socially transmitted response quantitatively matches a true antipredator response. (This conclusion holds irrespective of whether blackbirds recognize owls innately, as do various other songbirds [refs. in Curio, 1975]. There are no available data concerning blackbirds.)

Second, the pattern of avoidance behavior of tutored Lrs was examined in some detail to assess more directly the benefit gained from the acquired response. Since proximity to a harassed predator can result in death or injury (Curio & Regelmann, 1985), knowledgeable prey animals should stay farther away from the predator than others (other things being equal). To study avoidance in inexperienced and tutored birds, the distance from the Ho at which birds landed while flying about in the aviary was scored. Three branches at a distance from Ho of 1 m, 2 m, and 3 m and at a height of 3 m, 2 m, and 1 m, respectively, above ground served as perches. These perches were oriented perpendicular to a line connecting Ho and the opposite wall. On each exposure in Trial 4 the Ho was presented at a novel site after social tutoring (Experiment IV), or after habituating birds to Ho in the old place (Experiment V, cf. Table 4.1). As can be seen in Figure 4.5, birds tutored by a Tr tended to avoid Ho significantly more often than habituated birds. On average, they stayed 2.5 m away from Ho as compared to 1.9 m for controls ($p < .008$, $n_{IV,V} = 6, 8$, Mann-Whitney U-test, two-tailed). Because the control birds flew about more often in the presence of Ho than tutored birds (Figure 4.5), the increase in RS by the tutored birds (Table 4.1) must have been due to their increased vocalizing and wing/tail flicking behavior. The increased RS may indicate that there was greater fear, and fear may have produced flight inhibition (unpublished data). The comparison is a conservative one because the change of site of Ho in the control for sensitization (Experiment V) led to an unforeseen increase of RS, thereby diminishing the difference in RS between groups. From this comparison it follows that tutored birds not only mob the dangerous object more strongly than naive birds, but also

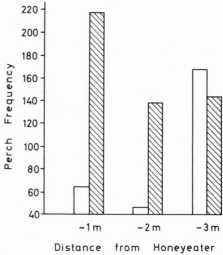

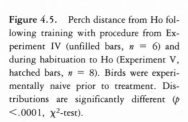

Figure 4.5. Perch distance from Ho following training with procedure from Experiment IV (unfilled bars, $n = 6$) and during habituation to Ho (Experiment V, hatched bars, $n = 8$). Birds were experimentally naive prior to treatment. Distributions are significantly different ($p < .0001$, χ^2-test).

stay farther away from the dangerous object when they encounter it in a new place.

Do Learners Pass on the Information Received?

During training (in the presence of Tr) and following training (in the absence of Tr), Lr emits a conditioned response to the stimulus that is indistinguishable from that given to a natural predator (Experiments I, Ia; previous section). Thus, it was expected that trained Lrs would be able to serve as Trs for experimentally naive Lrs. To what extent can information be passed on successively from a trained Lr to a new Lr (Experiment Z)?

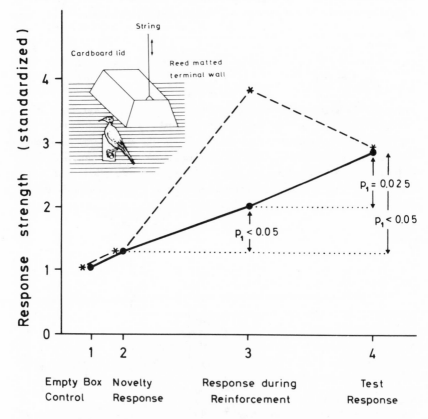

Figure 4.6. Response strength (RS) of 6 birds that passed on information from conspecific to conspecific (heavy line, "chaining experiment," Z). First Tr was trained in Experiment I with the usual procedure (Fig. 4.1); for all subsequent birds both Tr and Lr were simultaneously exposed to the uncovered Ho as shown in inset figure (for site of Ho see x in Fig. 4.1). Baseline RS in Experiment I is shown for comparison (dashed line). (Data appear in Curio et al., 1978.)

The sequence of presentations was the same as in Experiment Ia (Figure 4.2b). After Trial 4, the Lr replaced the original Tr in its aviary to become the new Tr and so on. Once the original Lr was tutored, the presentation method of Trial 3 was changed such that the trainee and the new Tr saw Ho simultaneously. Ho was presented at the terminal wall between aviaries (x in Figure 4.1) by uncovering it (Figure 4.6). For Trial 4 Ho was again presented to the Lr in the old position (with the Tr visually isolated from the Lr). Each bird served first as a Lr and then as a Tr for the next bird.

As can be seen (Figure 4.6), responses of 6 birds during conditioning *and* testing exceeded those during the initial control presentation of Ho, as in Experiment I. The test response was, on average, virtually of the same strength as that of birds that received first-hand information as in Experiment I. Even the last individual tested emitted a response equaling the average. Hence, information about Ho can be passed on along a chain of 6 birds without any detectable decrement.

RS during conditioning was significantly lower in Experiment Z than it was in Experiment I ($p < .05$, Mann Whitney U-test, two-tailed). This is probably due to the persistently lower RS of the 6 Trs (see Fig. 9 in Curio et al., 1978) that, in Trial 3, responded for the second time without reinforcement and, also to presentation of Ho in the same place where Trs had seen it during their own training. As in Experiment Ia (see Figure 4.2b), the response during conditioning is not a reliable predictor of RS in the test, but the reason may be different. In the present case, the increase of RS after Trial 3 may well be due to Ho appearing at a place different from where it was presented during training. The incremental effect of a change of site on RS subsequent to conditioning (Experiment IV in Table 4.1) is a sufficient explanation for the observed rise in RS.

Do the Teacher's Vocalizations Suffice to Impart Cultural Transmission?

During conditioning, the Tr provided the Lr with a compound visuo-acoustic stimulus. But mobbing calls alone suffice to attract many birds and make them mob (Curio, 1971; Regelmann & Curio, 1983). In order to know if these calls alone can bring about transmission, Ho was presented in conjunction with a taped train of blackbird high-threshold mobbing "tix" calls (88/min) of natural loudness. The Ho appeared in a grey plastic box inserted into a wall of the Lr's aviary, with the loudspeaker immediately beneath it (Fig. 1 in Vieth et al., 1980). The experimental protocol was as above with the exception that the test trial (No. 4) was repeated 1 day later and again 8 days later. This extension of the experiment served to determine how long the transmitted response to Ho was observable.

In Experiment VIII, 6 Lrs responded both during conditioning and testing

(Trials 3 and 4) significantly more vigorously than birds in a sensitization control test (Experiment XI, Figure 4.7a). The test responses of the Lrs were not significantly lower than those obtained with the complete Tr involving sight as well as vocalization ($p = .41$, $n_{1,2} = 6,17$, Mann-Whitney U-test, two-tailed, see Figure 4.7a). As can also be seen in Figure 4.7, the response persisted for at least 8 days, ruling out any aftereffects of the motor coordination system as an explanation, and strongly reinforcing the notion of the adaptedness of transmission (see also the last section).

As had been found earlier, transmission of Ho was successful even after habituation to Ho (Figure 4.2b, Experiment X). The acoustic reinforcer alone is incapable, however, of imparting the response to a Lr previously habituated to Ho. Rather RS declines continually over the course of Ho presentations (Figure 4.7a, Experiment IX). This means that the sight of a harassing Tr contains reinforcing properties that cannot be replaced by taped calls alone.

Will other species' mobbing calls also produce mobbing in response to Ho? In Experiment XII (a pilot experiment) a taped multispecies mobbing chorus containing the calls of great tit (*Parus major*), blue tit (*P. caeruleus*), chaffinch (*Fringilla coelebs*), and nuthatch (*Sitta europaea*), the mobbing calls of a total of seven birds, was employed with the procedure used in Experiments VIII and IX. We found that the response was about as effectively transmitted as in Experiment VIII involving conspecific mobbing calls (Figure 4.7b, Experiment XII). Again, the difference between the test response and that obtained with the complete mobbing blackbird fell short of significance ($p = .08$, $N_{1,2} = 7, 17$, Mann-Whitney U-test, two-tailed). The response-eliciting value that these alien species' calls have remains to be explored. Because they were composed of the calls of seven harassers of four species, every single call may be less effective than a blackbird call. Significantly, chaffinch mobbing calls are more effective in attracting chaffinches than mobbing calls of 20 sympatric songbird species (Fleuster, 1973).

PREDATOR HARASSMENT DEPENDENT ON PERSONAL AFFILIATION

Blackbird Trs engage in predator harassment irrespective of whether a conspecific is nearby. Cultural transmission of enemy recognition is therefore not dependent on any affiliation between the Tr and the Lr. However, in the domesticated zebra finch (*Taeniopygia guttata*) sympathetic induction of predator mobbing, a precondition of transmission, is contingent on presence of the pair-mate. A finch allowed to see both an owl (*Glaucidium brasilianum*) and its pair-mate in an adjacent cage shielded from the owl displayed a response about as strong as when it experienced its mate in its own cage harassing the owl (Figure 4.8). By contrast, a model bird (a potential Tr) adjacent to a randomly selected flock member shielded from view of the owl, responded as weakly as it did on a control trial with no owl or when isolated from any conspecific. Hence, there must be

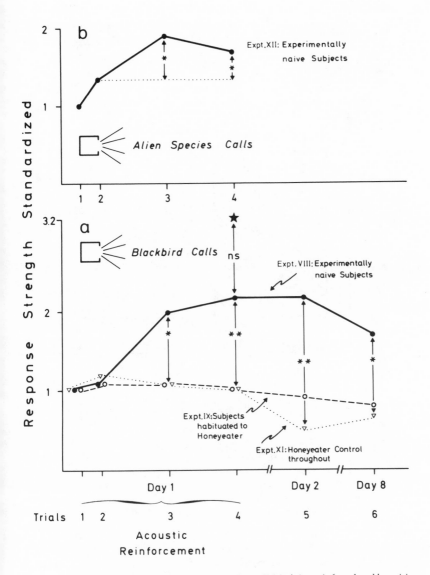

Figure 4.7. Mobbing to honeyeater (Ho) on Trials 4 through 6 produced by pairing Ho on Trial 3 with audiotape recording of (a) conspecific mobbing calls, or (b) alien multispecies mobbing chorus. Trials 1 through 4 were as in Fig. 4.2. Trials 5 and 6 were repetitions of Trial 4. Birds in Experiment IX had been habituated to Ho 7–34 days earlier. *$p < .05$, **$p = .025$. $N = 6$ birds in (a) and $n = 7$ birds in (b). "Star" represents RS after reinforcement with a live conspecific teacher for comparison (see Fig. 4.2). (Modified from Vieth et al., 1980).

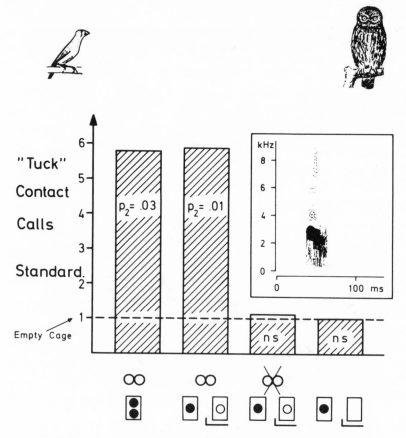

Figure 4.8. Mobbing an owl by zebra finches as a function of pair bond. RS measured by "tuck" contact calls/min (4-min presentations) standardized with reference to RS elicited by empty cage (dotted line). Filled circles are for model birds (one for each combination of birds) in presence of owl. Unfilled circles are for observer birds in presence of model in an adjacent cage (owl not visible). Inset figure: Sonogram of "tuck" contact call. (Data from Hoffmann, 1979, and Stevens, 1979).

positive feedback between the harasser and its mate for the response to occur. This feedback is probably the harassment induced in the observer bird, that, incidentally, is also aimed in the direction of the unseen owl (see also Frankenberg, 1981). When all components of harassment are examined, it turns out that the correlation in RS between mates, as measured by an increase or a decrease of any component of the response, is 100% as compared to 42% among unpaired birds (Stevens, 1979). Sympathetic induction remains unimpaired when an observer female can only hear its model male (Lombardi & Curio, 1985).

Despite species differences in social behavior, the sympathetic induction of predator harassment by zebra finches might well form the basis of cultural transmission analogous to that in blackbirds.

CONCLUSIONS

The Learning Paradigm

The Nature of the Learning Process. Captive, learner (Lr) blackbirds (*Turdus merula*) were successfully tutored to recognize an innocuous, nonraptorial novel bird (Ho) as potentially dangerous, as a consequence of perceiving a conspecific teacher (Tr) exhibit mobbing behavior directed to Ho. The behavioral changes induced in the Lr consisted of a considerable increase in mobbing of the Ho (Figure 4.2), an increase in avoidance of Ho, and a suppression of flight behavior (Figure 4.5). Tutoring makes the components of the harassment behavior covary in a direction enhancing protection of the Lr (see Curio, 1969; Curio & Regelmann, 1985). Thus it appears to be unnecessary to consider various aspects of the behavior separately as is sometimes the case in socially transmitted fear of predators (Mineka & Keir, 1983).

The learning process appears to involve classical conditioning to the novel object, with two qualifications:

1. The CS elicits a weak yet measurable response (Figures 4.2, 4.3), a priori, in the experimentally naive Lr. Thus conditioning would appear to enhance a preexistent, though slight, fear of novelty. Fear of novelty in the blackbird is not entirely stimulus-nonspecific as some stimuli (e.g., the Ho) initially elicit somewhat more fear than others (e.g., the bottle or the presentation box; see also Curio, 1969, 1975). That the response is a novelty response is demonstrated by the fact that it rapidly extinguishes when the stimulus is repeatedly presented (Figures 4.2, 4.3, 4.7a). A parallel phenomenon has recently been reported. In two bird species the innate stimulus-specific rejection of noxious insects required the constant reinforcement of unpleasant experience to maintain rejection behavior (Schuler, 1982; Schuler & Hesse, 1985).

2. There is a dearth of information on the ontogenetic processes that bring about responsiveness to both visual and acoustic components of mobbing (see Figure 4.7). Harassment by conspecifics and by alien species (Figure 4.7b) is not necessarily a UCS, but may develop through learning processes. There are indications that the acoustic components are responded to as a result of learning (Refs. in Curio et al., 1978; Seyfarth & Cheney, 1980), yet in fledgling great tits (*Parus major*) mobbing calls of two vocally unfamiliar and three potentially familiar sympatric species have both been responded to alike by "freezing"; calls of one other vocally unfamiliar species induced definitely less fear than those of the most potent species, a potentially familiar one (Kretzschmar, personal communication).

Another question concerns the information encoded in the Tr's behavior during conditioning. Despite the Tr's rather weak mobbing in Experiment Z, probably due to a change of aviary, the Lrs' responses in the test were invariably strong. Thus, the learning process under scrutiny here differs from others in that the behavior serving as an UCS that is paired with the CS is simultaneously induced in Lr. The strength of Lr's response triggered by Tr's behavior at a gross level, appears not to determine the efficacy of transmission. Regardless of whether RS during conditioning had been strong (Experiments I, VI, VIII) or weak (Experiments Ia, Z) test responses were, on average, strong. Variation of RS during conditioning could not be ascribed to the Tr's RS that triggered the response because the TR's RS was virtually constant. Though the factors that suppressed strong mobbing by Lr during learning could not be unequivocally identified, it seemed certain they were of external origin (Curio et al., 1978). If inhibitory factors arose from within the animal (e.g., by habituation to Ho), lack of performance during training had been a reliable predictor of a weak response during test (Experiment IX, Figure 4.7). Similarly, when looking at intra-individual variation, RS of the test response appeared to be contingent on RS of the conditioning response (Vieth et al., 1980).

Although the strength of the learned response could have been due to a change in presentation site (see Table 4.1), the possibility cannot be ruled out that not all received information was contained in scored elements of Tr's mobbing behavior. This idea is supported by the unprecedented precision of information transfer in the chaining experiment (Figure 4.6). As Frankenberg (1981) has shown, predator harassment must contain subtler information than has been recorded. Even before onset of overt predator mobbing by a Tr blackbird, an observer blackbird is already alerted, as shown by its reduced escape latency. Furthermore, the location of the predator is also conveyed to the observer bird via harassment, though it is not clear how this is accomplished (Frankenberg, 1981; see also the previous section).

To the experienced human observer the Tr's harassment does not appear to vary as a function of having a Lr close by. That is, the Tr does not modify its behavior specifically to facilitate transmission and would, therefore, be called a "demonstrator" by some (e.g., Mainardi, 1980). Instead the nature of the CS to be transmitted is of greater importance in determining the strength of conditioning than is the Tr's performance: In spite of Tr's virtually identical response level, Ho was more effectively conditioned than either the unnatural bottle (Figure 4.4) or the presentation box (Experiment Ia, Figure 4.2).

Constraints on learning can be attributed in part to the nature of the CS. Although the socially learned response to Ho was comparable to the response to an owl (a natural predator), the learned response to an equally novel plastic bottle was significantly inferior, despite the same level of training (Figure 4.4). With regard to Lr's responses preceding the final test response, either the greater "novelty response" to Ho or the greater RS during training with Ho could be responsible for this intriguing difference. RS during training might play the pivotal role. If one examines Lr's responses on all trials during each minute of the 5 min of stimulation, one finds that Ho and the bottle differed markedly in effectiveness *only* during the *training* trial. Whereas response to the Ho peaked in the second minute, response to the bottle did so in the fifth minute. Since responses generally do not vary in peak time as a function of RS, the different time courses must be caused by differences in *CS quality*, independent of the associated RS level (Vieth et al., 1980). From this finding it follows that the CS interacts with the reinforcer during conditioning in a way that determines the differential outcome of learning observed during test. Another even more remarkable constraint lies in the species-specific social relationship between Lr and Tr (see below).

The Compensatory Relationship Between the Readiness to Learn and the Strength of the Social Reinforcer. Habituation to Ho does not impair social transmission by complete Tr mobbing (Experiments Ia and X in Figure 4.2b). Similarly, using the same procedure, a starling dummy can assume a releasing value not statistically different from Ho when conditioned. By contrast, if birds habituated to Ho are tutored by an incomplete reinforcer, represented by taped stationary mobbing calls, enemy recognition of Ho fails to come about, whereas nonhabituated individuals so treated learn as usual (Experiments IX and VIII, Figure 4.7). Thus impaired learning through habituation of the CS can be compensated for by presentation of the complete compound reinforcer. This is the first demonstration in a *learning* paradigm of a compensatory relationship between the animal's internal state, as reflected by its perceptual pathways, and the external stimulus that serves as reinforcement (see Baerends, Brouwer & Waterbolk, 1955, for a nonlearning paradigm).

The Adaptiveness of Cultural Transmission and Who is the Beneficiary?

Because cultural transmission has been demonstrated only with captive birds, it seems appropriate to examine whether it would occur in the wild as well. The most direct answer (i.e., to rigorously demonstrate cultural transmission of enemy recognition in the wild), however, may remain an empty hope. An affirmative answer to this question might be suggested by an assessment of the benefits that would accrue to Lrs in the wild. Furthermore, for a functional explanation of cultural transmission to be complete one would also have to answer the question, Who is the beneficiary, the Tr or the Lr joining it?

The following facts strongly support the notion that *Lr* benefits:

1. Subsequent to transmission, RS elicited by a novel bird (i.e., a potentially dangerous creature) matches the existing response to an owl.

2. Transmission induces, apart from increased RS, an enhanced avoidance of the reinforced Ho (Figure 4.5).

3. Following tutoring a novel bird comes to elicit a stronger response than an unnatural, potentially innocuous object (Figure 4.4).

4. After transmission, the memory for the Ho lasts for at least 8 days, in spite of intervening unreinforced extinction trials (Figure 4.7).

5. Habituation to the CS prior to transmission does not impair learning (Figure 4.2b); having encountered a potential danger in the absence of a knowledgeable Tr in the wild should not blind a Lr to later beneficial lessons. (Strangely, captive rhesus monkeys become less fearful of snakes when tutored after preexposure to snakes, Mineka, this volume.)

6. After transmission, a change of site of Ho enhances the acquired response dramatically (Table 4.1; see also Shalter, 1975, 1978). Predators in the wild often appear to their prey under ever-changing circumstances.

7. There is circumstantial evidence that wild blackbirds can educate others in enemy recognition (Curio et al., 1978).

The foregoing list suggests that cultural transmission benefits the Lr, yet it does not permit one to assess the magnitude of the benefit, nor does it shed light on the costs involved. To clarify these issues observations need to be carried out in the wild.

The benefit to the Tr is less clear. Because predator harassment involves a cost of possible death or injury (Curio & Regelmann, 1985), a compensatory benefit has to be invoked. Evidence is accumulating that the benefit of harassment derives from driving off a predator, thus forestalling later surprise attack (Curio & Regelmann, 1985). Hence, the Tr, or any initiator of a mobbing party in the wild, acts in its own self-interest. This view is compatible with the fact that with blackbirds, the Tr does not demonstrably modify its harassment when tutoring, and also that the Lr mobs while being tutored. While acquiring knowledge about enemies, the Lr simply exploits harassment, even that of other species (Figure 4.7b), to its own advantage. Incidentally, this seems to be the first demonstration of cross-species tutoring of enemy recognition in birds. Observational evidence of the transmission of raptor recognition from dwarf mongooses (*Helogale undulata*) being tutored by hornbills (*Tockus* spec.) to recognize raptors (Rasa, 1981) has not yet been experimentally confirmed.

In species like the zebra finch, with less conspicuous mobbing and with long-lasting social ties, a different functional explanation is needed. Here a bird with a free view of a predator (corresponding to Trial 3 of the blackbird experiments), mobs only if its pair mate is close (Figure 4.8); the behavioral pattern of the zebra finch is similar to that of the rhesus monkey (Mineka, this volume): neither does the informed model bird emit the full mobbing response, nor does the observer bird respond fully, when the relationship is solely one of flock companions. (Similarly, in food luring, domestic cockerels have been shown to tailor their vocal signals both to the nature of the food referent *and* to that of the conspecific receiver (Marler, Dufty, & Pickert, 1986a, 1986b). In this case egoistic benefits cannot suffice to bring about the full response. Thus the door is open to cheating, e.g., withholding vital information, if no benefit is expected from passing it on. A qualitative species difference, such as this one, seems to transcend mere species differences in the *"salience of stimuli"* and the *"motivation"* of the subjects involved (Shettleworth, 1984) and, thus, appears to mirror a genuine constraint of the learning mechanism, i.e., on the behavior of both the potential tutor and the potential learner.

ACKNOWLEDGMENTS

My sincere thanks go to all who were involved in the experimental work: H.-W. Böcking, U. Ernst, E. Frankenberg, W. Hoffmann, E. Kretzschmar, C. Lombardi, B. Stevens, and W. Vieth. W. Windt critically read the manuscript. I also gratefully acknowledge the stimulating discussions in the Tuesday colloquium of the Arbeitsgruppe. Dr. W. Scherzinger generously donated the Brazilian pygmy owl. The Deutsche Forschungsgemeinschaft supported the work over many years by various grants.

REFERENCES

Baerends, G. P., Brouwer, R., & Waterbolk, H. T. (1955). Ethological studies on *Lebistes reticulatus* (Peters): I. An analysis of the male courtship pattern. *Behaviour, 8,* 249–334.

Berlyne, D. E. (1967). Arousal and reinforcement. *Nebraska Symposium on motivation* (pp. 1–110). Lincoln, NE: University of Nebraska Press.

Curio, E. (1969). Funktionsweise und Stammesgeschichte des Flugfeinderkennens einiger Darwinfinken (Geospizinae). *Zeitschrift für Tierpsychologie, 26,* 394–487.

Curio E. (1971). Die akustische Wirkung von Feindalarmen auf einige Singvögel. *Journal für Ornithologie, 112,* 365–372.

Curio E. (1975). The functional organization of anti-predator behaviour in the pied flycatcher: A study of avian visual perception. *Animal Behaviour, 23,* 1–115.

Curio, E., Ernst, U., & Vieth, W. (1978). The adaptive significance of avian mobbing. II. Cultural transmission of enemy recognition in blackbirds: Effectiveness and some constraints. *Zeitschrift für Tierpsychologie, 48,* 184–202.

Curio, E., & Regelmann, K. (1985). The behavioural dynamics of great tits (*Parus major*) approaching a predator. *Zeitschrift für Tierpsychologie, 69,* 3–18.

Diamond, J. M. (1985). Rats as agents of extermination. *Nature, 318,* 602–603.

Fleuster, W. (1973). Versuche zur Reaktion freilebender Vögel auf Klangattrappen verschiedener Buchfinkenalarme. *Journal für Ornithologie, 114,* 417–428.

Frankenberg, E. (1981). The adaptive significance of avian mobbing. IV. "Alerting others" and "Perception advertisement" in blackbirds facing an owl. *Zeitschrift für Tierpsychologie, 55,* 97–118.

Giles, N. (1984). Development of the overhead fright response in wild and predator-naive three-spined sticklebacks, *Gasterosteus aculeatus* L.. *Animal Behaviour, 32,* 276–279.

Hinde, R. A. (1960). Factors governing the changes in strength of a partially inborn response, as shown by the mobbing behaviour of the chaffinch (*Fringilla coelebs*): III. The interaction of short-term and long-term incremental and decremental effects. *Proceedings of the Royal Society of London, Series B, 153,* 398–420.

Hoffmann, W. (1979). *Antworten von Zebrafinken auf bekannte und fremde Vogelarten. II. Der Einfluss von Vorerfahrung und Paarpartner.* Thesis, Ruhr-Universität, Bochum.

Hogan, J. A. (1965). An experimental study of conflict and fear: An analysis of behavior of young chicks toward a mealworm. I. The behavior of chicks which do not eat the mealworm. *Behaviour, 25,* 45–97.

Lombardi, C. M., & Curio, E. (1985). Social facilitation of mobbing in the zebra finch *Taeniopygia guttata. Bird Behaviour, 6,* 34–40.

Mainardi, D. (1980). Tradition and the social transmission of behavior in animals. In G. W. Barlow & J. Silverberg (Eds.), *Sociobiology: Beyond nature/nurture?* (pp. 227–255), AAAS Selected Sympos. *35.* Boulder, CO: Westview Press.

Marler, P., Dufty, A., & Pickert, R. (1986a). Vocal communication in the domestic chicken: I. Does sender communicate information about the quality of a food referent to a receiver? *Animal Behaviour, 34,* 188–193.

Marler, P., Dufty, A., & Pickert, R. (1986b). Vocal communication in the domestic chicken: II. Is a sender sensitive to the presence and nature of a receiver? *Animal Behaviour, 34,* 194–198.

Menzel, E. W., Jr., Davenport, R. K., & Rodgers, C. M. (1972). Protocultural aspects of chimpanzees' responsiveness to novel objects. *Folia Primatologica, 17,* 161–170.

Mineka, S., & Keir, R. (1983). The effects of flooding on reducing snake fear in rhesus monkeys: 6-month follow-up and further flooding. *Behaviour Research and Therapy, 21,* 527–535.

Rasa, O. A. E. (1981). Raptor recognition: An interspecific tradition? *Naturwissenschaften, 68,* 151–152.

Regelmann, K., & Curio, E. (1983). Determinants of brood defence in the great tit *Parus major* L.. *Behavioral Ecology and Sociobiology, 13,* 131–145.

Robertson, R. J., & Norman, R. F. (1977). The function and evolution of aggressive host behavior towards the brown-headed cowbird (*Molothrus ater*). *Canadian Journal of Zoology, 55,* 508–518.

Schuler, W. (1982). Zur Funktion von Warnfarben: Die Reaktion junger Stare auf wespenähnlich schwarz-gelbe Attrappen. *Zeitschrift für Tierpsychologie, 58,* 66–78.

Schuler, W., & Hesse, E. (1985). On the function of warning coloration: A black and yellow pattern inhibits prey-attack by naive domestic chicks. *Behavioral Ecology and Sociobiology, 16,* 249–255.

Seghers, B. H. (1970). Behavioral adaptations of natural populations of the guppy, *Poecilia reticulata,* to predation. *American Zoologist, 10,* 489.

Seghers, B. H. (1973). *An analysis of geographic variation in the antipredator adaptations of the guppy, Poecilia reticulata.* Ph.D. thesis, University of British Columbia.

Seligman, M. E. P., & Hager, J. L. (1972). *Biological boundaries of learning*. New York: Appleton-Century-Crofts.

Seyfarth, R. M., & Cheney, D. L. (1980). The ontogeny of vervet monkey alarm calling behavior: A preliminary report. *Zeitschrift für Tierpsychologie, 54,* 37–56.

Shalter, M. D. (1975). Lack of spatial generalization in habituation tests of fowl. *Journal of Comparative and Physiological Psychology, 89,* 258–262.

Shalter, M. D. (1978). Effect of spatial context on the mobbing reaction of pied flycatchers to a predator model. *Animal Behaviour, 26,* 1219–1221.

Shettleworth, S. J. (1984). Learning and behavioural biology. In J. R. Krebs & N. B. Davies (Eds.) *Behavioural ecology* (2nd ed., pp. 170–200). Boston: Blackwell Scientific Publications.

Smith, S. M. (1975). Innate recognition of coral snake pattern by a possible avian predator. *Science, 187,* 759–760.

Smith, S. M. (1977). Coral-snake pattern recognition and stimulus generalisation by naive great kiskadees (Aves: Tyrannidae). *Nature, 265,* 535–536.

Steiniger, F. (1950). Beiträge zur Soziologie und sonstigen Biologie der Wanderratte. *Zeitschrift für Tierpsychologie, 7,* 356–379.

Stevens, B. (1979). *Die Antworten von Zebrafinken auf bekannte und fremde Vogelarten. I. Die Analyse von Antwortmass und Reizeinfluss*. Thesis, Ruhr-Universität, Bochum.

Vieth, W., Curio, E., & Ernst, U. (1980). The adaptive significance of avian mobbing. III. Cultural transmission of enemy recognition in blackbirds: Cross-species tutoring and properties of learning. *Animal Behav., 28,* 1217–1229.

5

Direct and Observational Learning by Redwinged Blackbirds (Agelaius Phoeniceus): The Importance of Complex Visual Stimuli

J. Russell Mason
U.S. Department of Agriculture,
Animal and Plant Health Inspection Service,

Denver Wildlife Research Center
c/o Monell Chemical Senses Center,
Philadelphia, Pennsylvania

INTRODUCTION

Redwing blackbirds (*Agelaius phoeniceus*, Mason & Reidinger, 1983a), European starlings (*Sturnus vulgaris*, Schuler, 1980), house sparrows (*Passer domesticus;* Greig-Smith & Rowney, 1987), and a variety of other avian species (e.g., Japanese quail, *Corturnix japonica;* Czaplicki, Borrebach, & Wilcoxin, 1976) learn to avoid visual cues associated with sickness. For redwings, visual stimuli appear relatively more important than taste in avoidance acquisition (Mason & Reidinger, 1983a), and certain colors seem to be more effective conditioned stimuli than others. For example, avoidance generalization is broad for hues of red, but relatively narrow for hues of green (Mason & Reidinger, 1983b). Ecologically, the differential effectiveness of color is predictable, since red is used frequently by animals to advertise unpalatability (*aposematic coloration;* Terhune, 1977). Green serves this function rarely, if ever, and is more often associated with the *cryptic* coloration used by palatable prey for concealment from predators (Brower, Cook, & Croze, 1967; Wickler, 1968).

Besides direct acquisition of avoidance, red-wings will learn by observing conspecifics or other birds such as common grackles (*Quiscalus quiscula;* Mason, Arzt, & Reidinger, 1984a). Such vicariously acquired avoidance closely resembles avoidance acquired as a function of direct experience. For example, vicarious learning occurs in a single trial, and resistance to extinction is usually similar to

99

that exhibited when birds learn directly. These findings have clear implications for theories of mimicry that make the assumption that avian predators learn to avoid unpalatable prey (Alcock, 1969a, 1969b; Avery, 1985; Mason & Reidinger, 1983b). One implication is that not all predators need to experience the unpleasant and potentially lethal consequences of attacking unpalatable aposematic prey in order to learn to avoid them (Mason et al., 1984a).

Given the ease with which avoidance responses are vicariously acquired, it is not surprising that preferences can be acquired through observation as well. For example, in the laboratory, redwings will prefer color-food combinations that they have seen presented to demonstrator birds (Mason & Reidinger, 1981). In a similar vein, chaffinches (*Fringilla coelebs*), white wagtails (*Motacilla alba*) and Tennessee warblers (*Vermivora peregrina*) are more likely to sample new foods when exposed to conspecifics doing so (Davies, 1976; Rubenstein, Barnett, Ridgely, & Klopfer, 1977; Tramer & Kemp, 1979).

One potentially important difference between vicariously acquired preference and avoidance responding is that, for the former, aposematic colors (e.g., orange) do not appear to be more effective stimuli than cryptic colors (e.g., green), at least in terms of resistance to extinction (Mason & Reidinger, 1981). Another difference is that several training trials are often necessary to elicit vicarious color preference responding, whereas avoidance is usually elicited in a single trial. These findings suggest that preferences may be acquired more slowly or with greater difficulty than aversions. Nevertheless, the existence of reliable observational acquisition of color preferences raises the issue of whether observationally acquired preferences or aversions exert greater control over behavior. The answer to this question is important with regard to mimicry, since predators are likely to observe attacks by conspecifics on both models and their mimics, and, in some cases, observed attacks on the latter may exceed observed attacks on the former, since mimics are more numerous (Brower, 1960). In the case of observed attacks on models, observers should learn avoidance, but in the case of attacks on mimics, preference should accrue. If avoidance and preference were to exert equal control over behavior, and mimics were more numerous than models, then observers should develop preferences for both models and mimics.

At least one experiment has addressed this issue (Mason et al., 1984a). As conspecifics watched, individual redwings were trained to prefer or avoid food paired with yellow. During subsequent tests, the demonstrators and half of the observers were assessed in visual isolation. The remaining observers were tested in visual contact with another observer that had watched a demonstrator exhibit behavior opposite to that exhibited by its own demonstrator. For demonstrators and observers tested in isolation, color aversions were more resistant to extinction than color preferences. For the observers tested together, avoidance was again more resistant to extinction than preference. Moreover, once preferences had extinguished, they were replaced by avoidance. Such findings suggest that observationally acquired avoidance may exert relatively greater control over behavior than observationally acquired preference.

An unanswered question is the importance of stimulus complexity as a variable influencing direct and observational acquisition of responding. In Batesian mimicry, the importance of this variable is suggested by the fact that unpalatable or toxic models (e.g., Monarch butterflies, *Danaus plexippus*) and their palatable mimics (e.g., Viceroy butterflies, *Limenitis archippus*) employ both aposematic coloration (e.g., orange) and patterns (e.g., stripes) as warnings to potential predators. Aposematic coloration and striping may have even greater importance in Mullerian mimicry, in which both models and "mimics" are unpalatable (Wickler, 1968), and in Mertesian mimicry, in which direct encounters between a predator and a model or mimic are usually fatal for the predator (Wickler, 1968).

The present experiments were designed to assess the relative importance of color and pattern cues in food aversions and food preferences exhibited by birds. Both direct and vicarious acquisition of responding were examined, and for avoidance learning, an attempt was made to manipulate the intensity (malaise, mere unpalatability) of the unconditioned stimulus. One assumption was that, together, pattern and color cues would produce avoidance that was more resistant to extinction than that produced by either of these cues alone. Another assumption was that "complex" stimuli (colors and stripes) might not facilitate preference learning, insofar as aposematic cues are rarely used by palatable prey (outside the context of mimicry).

EXPERIMENT 1

Experiment 1 was performed to test the proposition that, together, color and pattern cues would enhance the resistance to extinction of a directly acquired avoidance response, relative to either color or pattern cues alone.

Method

Thirty decoy-trapped experimentally naive adult male red-wing blackbirds (mean weight: 70.2 ± 2.3 g) were individually housed (cage dimensions: 61 cm × 36 cm × 41 cm), and a 6:18 hr light/dark cycle was used to maximize feeding, without reducing the total quantity of food consumed (Mason et al., 1983a, 1983b; Rogers, 1974, 1978). Water was always available. Before the experiment began, the birds were permitted free access to food (Purina Flight Bird Conditioner [PFBC]) presented in hoppers attached to the center of the fronts of the cages.

On each of the 4 days prior to conditioning, food hoppers were removed from the cages for the first 2 hr following light onset. This induced mild food deprivation, because redwings consume the greatest portion of their daily ration during this period (Mason, Dolbeer, Arzt, Reidinger, & Woronecki, 1984c). During the third hour of light, each bird was presented with a food cup (7.5 cm diameter) containing 20 g of PFBC. After 60 min, the cups were removed from the cages, and the amount of PFBC remaining was recorded. Food hoppers were then returned to the cages, and the birds were left undisturbed until light onset of the following day.

Birds were assigned to six matched groups ($n = 5$/group) on the basis of mean pretreatment consumption. The bird with the highest consumption was assigned to the first group, that with the next highest to the second group, and so on. On the day of conditioning, all groups were food deprived for 2 hr, and then presented with cups containing 20 g of PFBC. White rectangles (17.5 cm × 12.5 cm) on which four evenly spaced vertical black stripes (1 cm width) had been drawn were attached to the backs of the cups presented to Groups S-E (stripe-experimental) and S-C (stripe-control). These training stimuli are depicted in Fig. 5.1A. Orange rectangles (17.5 cm × 12.5 cm) were attached to the backs of cups presented to Groups O-E (orange-experimental) and O-C (orange-control). Orange rectangles (17.5 cm × 12.5 cm) with four evenly spaced vertical black stripes (1 cm width) were attached to the backs of cups presented to Groups SO-E (striped orange-experimental) and SO-C (striped orange-control).

After each bird had consumed 1 g of food, or after 30 min had passed, the food cups were removed, and Groups O-E, S-E and SO-E were gavaged (i.e., orally intubated) with methiocarb solution (2 mg/kg). As a control, Groups O-C, S-C and SO-C were gavaged with propylene glycol, the carrier for the methiocarb

Figure 5.1. Diagram showing stimuli and food cups presented to birds in Groups S-E and S-C on the day of conditioning (A) and during testing (B). All other groups were treated similarly, except that stimulus cards differed.

(Mason & Reidinger, 1982a; Mason & Reidinger, 1983a, 1983b). Methiocarb (3,5-dimethyl-4-[methylthio] phenol methylcarbamate) is a bird repellent that reliably elicits one-trial avoidance learning similar to that elicited in redwings by 0.15 M lithium chloride (Mason & Reidinger, 1983b). Intubation was completed in all cases within 15 min of the end of the feeding trial. Thirty minutes later, food hoppers were replaced on the cages, and the birds were left undisturbed until light onset of the following day.

On each of the 4 days immediately following conditioning, the birds were food deprived for 2 hr, and then given two-choice tests. Testing involved the presentation of two food cups, each containing 20 g of PFBC, spaced 5 cm apart at the center of the front of each cage. For Groups S-E and S-C, white S+ rectangles with vertical stripes were attached to the back of one of the cups in each pair. Attached to the back of the other cup was a white So rectangle with horizontal stripes. These test stimuli are depicted in Fig. 5.1B. For Groups O-E and O-C, orange (S+) rectangles were attached to the back of one of the cups in each pair. Attached to the back of the other cup was a red (So) rectangle. For Groups SO-E and SO-C, vertically striped orange S+ rectangles were attached to the back of one of the cups in each cage; horizontally striped red So rectangles were attached to the back of the other cup.

After 1 hr, the cups were removed from the cages, and the amount of PFBC remaining was recorded. Food hoppers were then replaced on the cages, and the birds were left undisturbed until light onset of the following day.

Results and Discussion

All experimental groups (O-E, S-E, SO-E) avoided food paired with S+ stimuli during testing ($ps < .05$). However, there were significant differences among groups in resistance to extinction ($ps < .05$). Groups S-E and O-E extinguished after 2 or 3 days of testing, respectively, whereas Group SO-E exhibited conditioned avoidance on all 4 test days ($p < .05$; Figure 5.2). None of the control groups (O-C, S-C, SO-C) exhibited differential consumption ($ps > .25$).

The results of Experiment 1 are consistent with prior findings (Mason & Reidinger, 1983a, 1983b). As in these other investigations, birds learned avoidance after a single pairing of visual cues and malaise. Also, as previously reported for scrub jays (*Aphelocoma coerulescens;* Terhune, 1977), color alone appeared to elicit relatively more durable avoidance than stripes. The present findings extend these observations by suggesting that complex stimuli appeared to enhance resistance to extinction (Group SO-E), relative to that elicited by color (Group O-E) or pattern (Group S-E) alone. Such differential effectiveness suggests that increasing discriminability (e.g., by use of multiple cues) offers an advantage to aposematic prey by increasing their discriminability to potential predators (Guilford, 1986).

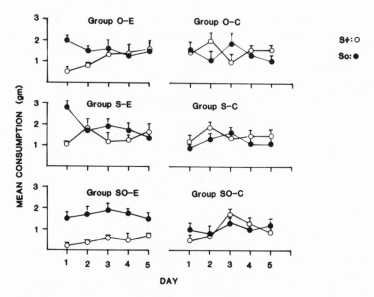

Figure 5.2. Experiment 1 two-choice test results. All experimental groups showed conditioned avoidance. However, Groups O-E and S-E extinguished by test day 3, and Group SO-E exhibited avoidance on all test days. Control groups (O-C, S-C, SO-C) failed to exhibit differential behavior. Capped vertical bars represent standard errors of the means.

EXPERIMENT 2

Experiment 1 demonstrated that color and pattern cues together produce greater resistance to extinction than either cue alone. Experiment 2 was designed to investigate whether similar findings would obtain when avoidance responding was acquired vicariously. Since observational learning by redwing mirrors direct acquisition of color avoidance responding in terms of resistance to extinction (e.g., Mason et al., 1984a) and generalization of responding (personal observation), a reasonable prediction was that a complex stimulus might be more effective than a simple stimulus (e.g., color only) for vicariously acquired avoidance.

Method

Forty decoy-trapped adult male redwings (mean weight 68.5 ± 3.0 g) were adapted to the food deprivation regime and assigned to eight groups (n = 5/group) on the basis of consumption, as previously described.

Groups were paired, and the cages of birds in Groups O-E (orange-experimental) and O-EW (orange-experimental watching); O-C (orange-control) and O-CW (orange-control watching); SO-E (striped orange-experimental) and SO-EW (striped orange-experimental watching); and SO-C (striped orange-control) and SO-CW (striped orange-control watching) were placed adjacent to and in view of one another (Mason & Reidinger 1982a; Mason et al., 1984a). Stripes per se were not used as stimuli because they were the least effective stimuli in Experiment 1.

On the day of conditioning, all birds were food deprived for 2 hr, and then Groups O-E and O-C were given orange S+ rectangles paired with PFBC. Groups SO-E and SO-C were given vertically striped orange S+ rectangles paired with PFBC. The birds in the other two groups (O-C, SO-C) were given food in plain metal cups without colored rectangles attached. When birds in Groups O-E, O-C, SO-E and SO-C had consumed at least 1 g of PFBC, or after 30 min had passed, food was removed from the cages and the birds were intubated. Groups O-E and SO-E were gavaged with methiocarb (2 mg/kg), and Groups O-C and SO-C were gavaged with propylene glycol. Birds in Groups O-EW, O-CW, SO-EW and SO-CW were left undisturbed. One hour following gavage, food hoppers were replaced on the cages. The birds were then visually isolated from one another with pieces of cardboard, and left undisturbed until light onset of the following day.

On each of the next 5 days, all birds were food deprived for 2 hrs, and then given two-choice tests. Groups O-E, O-C, O-EW and O-CW were given tests in which orange S+ and red So rectangles were attached to the backs of food cups. Groups SO-E, SO-C, SO-EW and SO-CW were given tests with vertically striped orange S+ and horizontally striped red So rectangles. After completion of each test period, all birds were left undisturbed with free access to PFBC until light onset of the following morning.

Results and Discussion

Groups O-E and O-EW avoided food paired with orange S+ rectangles for three or two test sessions, respectively ($ps < .01$; Figure 5.3). Groups SO-E and SO-EW also avoided food paired with S+ stimuli ($ps < .01$), but differential behavior was exhibited by these groups for 5 days. No significant differential consumption was exhibited by birds in the control groups (i.e., Groups O-C, O-CW, SO-C, SO-CW).

The results of Experiment 2 confirm prior observations (e.g., Mason & Reidinger, 1982a). Color avoidance was acquired vicariously after a single conditioning trial. Moreover, resistance to extinction of the observationally acquired response was similar to that of avoidance acquired as a function of direct experience. Finally, regardless of how avoidance was acquired, complex stimuli appeared to enhance resistance to extinction, relative to color alone.

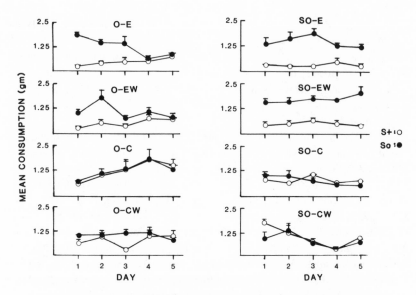

Figure 5.3. Responses exhibited by Groups O-E, O-EW, O-C, O-CW, SO-E, SO-EW, SO-C and SO-CW in two-choice tests in Experiment 2. Groups O-E and O-EW expressed avoidance on test days 1–3 and 1–2, respectively, whereas Groups SO-E and SO-EW expressed avoidance on all test days. Groups O-C, O-CW, SO-C and SO-CW did not exhibit differential consumption. Capped vertical bars represent standard errors of the means.

EXPERIMENT 3

An unanswered question is whether complex stimuli are generally more effective than simple stimuli, or whether they enhance avoidance responding alone. Just as aposematic colors (e.g., orange) are no more effective than cryptic colors (e.g., green) in preference learning, it may be that complex stimuli are no more effective than simple stimuli outside aversive contexts. Experiment 3 was designed to assess this possibility.

Method

Twenty decoy-trapped adult male redwings (mean weight: 70.2 ± 2.0 g) were adapted to the food deprivation regime, and assigned to four groups ($n =$ 5/group) on the basis of consumption.

Birds in Group O-EW (orange-experimental watching) were placed in cages adjacent to birds in Group O-E (orange-experimental). Birds in Group SO-EW (striped orange-experimental watching) were placed in cages adjacent to birds in Group SO-E (striped orange-experimental). At the beginning of the third hour of light on each of the next 4 days, Groups O-E and SO-E were given

PFBC in cups with orange or vertically striped orange rectangles attached. Birds in Groups O-EW and SO-EW were given PFBC in plain metal cups. After 60 min, the amount of PFBC remaining was recorded. After each trial, the birds were left undisturbed with free access to PFBC until the following morning.

Immediately following training, all birds were visually isolated from one another, and given two-choice tests during the third hour of light for 4 days. Birds in Groups O-E and O-EW were given food in two cups with orange S+ or red So rectangles attached. Birds in Groups SO-E and SO-EW were given food in cups with vertically striped orange S+ or horizontally striped red So rectangles attached. After 60 min, the cups were removed from the cages and consumption was measured. After each test, the birds were left undisturbed with free access to PFBC until light onset of the next day.

Results and Discussion

During testing, all groups preferred PFBC paired with their respective S+ (ps < .05; Figure 5.4). However, differential consumption extinguished rapidly. By the third test session, only Group O-EW continued to exhibit color preference responding. No group exhibited differential consumption during the fourth or fifth test session.

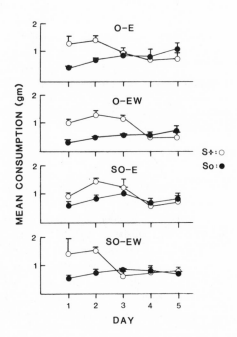

Figure 5.4. Preferences expressed by Groups O-E, O-EW, SO-E, and SO-EW in two-choice tests in Experiment 3. All groups showed preference acquisition, but only Group O-EW exhibited differential consumption for more than 2 days. Capped vertical bars represent standard errors of the means.

The results of Experiment 3 are consistent with other observations. Red-wings (Mason & Reidinger, 1981), wood pigeons (*Columba palumbus;* Murton, 1971) and European starlings (Williamson & Grey, 1975) are capable of developing food preferences, either as a result of direct experience or observation. However, unlike the results of Experiments 1 and 2, no evidence was obtained to suggest that color and pattern cues together facilitated preference, relative to color alone. Although it is arguable that complex stimuli might have been more effective than simple stimuli if an "appropriate" color such as green had been used, previous work (e.g., Mason & Reidinger, 1981) has suggested that aposematic colors are no more effective than cryptic colors for resistance to extinction of a color preference response.

When Experiments 2 and 3 are compared, visually mediated avoidance appears more resistant to extinction than visually mediated preference. This impression is consistent with previous work (Mason et al., 1984a). Not only are direct and vicariously acquired avoidance responses more resistant to extinction, but in addition, avoidance responses are more likely to affect the behavior of conspecifics.

EXPERIMENT 4

In the preceding experiments, avoidance responding was mediated by the experience or observation of malaise in association with visual cues. Experiment 4 was designed to assess whether a merely unpalatable flavor (one not associated with sickness) would elicit color avoidance learning as a function of direct experience. On the basis of other evidence (e.g., Alcock, 1970), avoidance acquisition was predicted, although it also was expected that differential responding would be less durable than that elicited by sickness (Barker, 1976). As in Experiment 1, different groups of birds were trained and tested with color cues only, or with color and pattern cues together.

Method

Twenty decoy-trapped adult male redwings (mean weight 69.2 ± 2.0 g) were adapted to the food deprivation regime, and assigned to two groups ($n =$ 10/group) on the basis of consumption. Both groups were then given five training trials (one trial/day). On each day of training, birds were food deprived for 2 hr, and then given stimulus rectangles paired with dimethyl anthranilate (DMA) adulterated food (0.8% w/w). DMA is widely used as a grape flavoring in human foods, but is unpalatable to birds in the laboratory (Mason, Arzt, & Reidinger, 1984b) and in the field (Mason, Glahn, & Reidinger, 1985).

For Group O-E (orange-experimental), food adulterated with DMA was presented in a cup with an orange S+ rectangle attached. Group SO-E (striped-orange experimental) was treated similarly, except that vertically striped orange S+ rectangles were attached to food cups. On each of the 5 days following training, both groups were food deprived for 2 hr, and then given two-choice tests. Group O-E was given food cups with orange S+ and red So rectangles attached, and Group SO-E was given cups with vertically striped orange S+ and horizontally striped So rectangles attached. All food cups contained plain (un-adulterated) PFBC. After 2 hr, consumption was measured. PFBC was returned to the cages in plain metal cups, and the birds were left undisturbed until light onset of the following day.

Results and Discussion

Both groups exhibited avoidance of PFBC paired with their respective S+ (ps < .05; Figure 5.5). However, as in Experiments 1 and 2, color and pattern together (Group SO-E) elicited avoidance that appeared more resistant to extinction than avoidance exhibited toward color alone (Group O-E).

That DMA was as effective as methiocarb was not expected, and this result is inconsistent with previous reports. Alcock (1970) found that chickadees (*Parus atricapillis*) showed stronger avoidance of mealworms when ingestion was paired with malaise, than when ingestion merely was associated with an unpleasant taste (i.e., an unspecified concentration of NaCl). Possibly, the discrepancy between avoidance elicited by NaCl and that elicited by DMA reflects the sensory modalities stimulated by the latter compound. Dimethyl anthranilate is an olfactory and trigeminal stimulant for birds, and it also may have gustatory properties

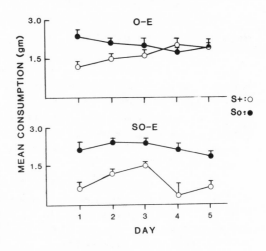

Figure 5.5. Avoidance expressed by Groups O-E and SO-E in two-choice tests in Experiment 4. Group SO-E showed greater resistance to extinction than Group O-E. Capped vertical bars represent standard errors of the means.

(Mason, Adams, & Clark, 1987). Sodium chloride is primarily a taste stimulus. In our laboratory, DMA has been found to be 200%, 150%, and 125% more effective than 0.1 M NaCl, 0.0001 M quinine HCl, and 0.001 M sucrose octaacetate in reducing or eliminating consumption of foods by redwing blackbirds (Mason, unpublished observation).

EXPERIMENT 5

Because DMA elicited color avoidance responses that were as resistant to extinction as those elicited by methiocarb, Experiment 5 was designed to test whether observers of birds given DMA paired with a visual stimulus would also exhibit visually mediated avoidance. As in previous experiments, different groups of birds were trained and tested with color cues only, or with color and pattern cues together.

Method

Twenty decoy-trapped redwings (mean weight: 69.2 ± 2.0 g) were adapted to the food deprivation regime, and assigned to four groups ($n = 5$/group) on the basis of consumption. Groups O-E (orange-experimental) and SO-E (striped orange-experimental) were given training (4 days) identical to that described in Experiment 4. Birds in Groups O-EW (orange-experimental watching) were placed in cages adjacent to those of group O-E, and birds in Group SO-EW (striped orange-experimental watching) were placed in cages adjacent to those of Group SO-E. After conditioning, all birds were visually isolated, and given two-choice tests identical to those described in Experiment 4 for 5 days.

Results and Discussion

Groups O-E and SO-E (i.e., demonstrators presented with DMA adulterated food) showed less consumption during training than did Groups O-EW and SO-EW (i.e., observers presented with unadulterated food) ($ps < .05$). During testing, all groups avoided food paired with their respective S+ stimuli ($ps < .05$; Figure 5.6), and as in the previous experiments, complex stimuli appeared to elicit avoidance that was more resistant to extinction than that elicited by color alone.

The present results confirm those of Experiment 4. DMA served as an effective unconditioned stimulus, and complex stimuli produced learning that was more resistant to extinction than learning elicited by color cues alone. In addition, observers of birds given DMA paired with visual stimuli exhibited avoidance, although the cues used by observers remain unclear. Demonstrators

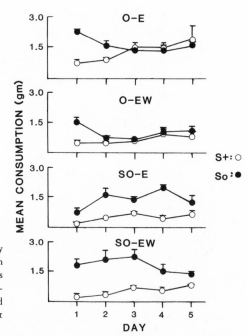

Figure 5.6. Avoidance expressed by Groups O-E, O-EW, SO-E and SO-EW in two-choice tests in Experiment 5. Groups SO-E and SO-EW expressed greater resistance to extinction than Groups O-E and O-EW. Capped vertical bars represent standard errors of the means.

exhibited few signs of discomfort (only bill wiping was observed occasionally). Possibly, the demonstrator's decreasing consumption of DMA adulterated food during training provided sufficient information to observers. Alternatively, it may be that "vicarious" learning in the present experiment was actually learning through direct experience. Observers may have detected DMA volatiles from the demonstrators' food and associated the volatiles with the S+ cue.

GENERAL DISCUSSION

Various passerine species learn to avoid visual cues associated with sickness. Moreover, prior investigations have demonstrated that the breadth of response generalization depends, in part, on the intensity (Czaplicki et al., 1976; Duncan & Shepherd, 1965) and color (Mason & Reidinger 1983b) of the conditioned stimulus. The present experiments extend these observations by suggesting that stimulus complexity influences the resistance to extinction of an avoidance response. Experiments 4 and 5 further suggest that this facilitative effect may not depend on malaise.

That complexity should facilitate learned avoidance is predictable on an ecological basis, because black stripes against an aposematic background (e.g., red, orange) are used by animals to advertise unpalatability (Cott, 1940). In this regard, the observation that malaise may not be a precondition for learned avoidance is interesting, because, in mimicry, some model prey (e.g., Monarch butterflies) sequester toxicants from plants that differ considerably in the amount of toxicant contained (Fink & Brower, 1981). One outcome of this variation is that models range from being palatable to being lethal. Differential toxicity may result in greater predation on toxic individuals, but the present results suggest that this may not necessarily be the case. Strong learned avoidance of merely unpalatable individuals may occur.

There are no ready explanations for the lack of effect of complex stimuli on food preference extinction, although one plausible speculation is that the extent to which some passerines attend to visual stimuli depends on the context (aversive or appetitive) in which the cues are presented. This speculation is at least consistent with laboratory demonstrations that redwings learn more about what to avoid than what to approach in some feeding situations (Mason & Reidinger, 1982b). Regardless, the finding that aposematic colors selectively facilitate avoidance responding highlights the possible role of "unlearned" factors in the development and maintenance of a conditioned response.

Beyond learning as a function of direct experience, the present results confirm and extend previous observations of vicariously acquired avoidance. As in other work, one training trial was sufficient for avoidance acquisition. Once established, conditioned responses were as resistant to extinction as those acquired directly, and complex cues appeared to be more effective conditioned stimuli than color alone. One implication of such durable vicariously acquired avoidance is that social interactions among predators (even predators of different species; Mason et al., 1984a) may influence the frequency of attacks on aposematic prey. A second implication is that the use of redundant aposematic cues (i.e., pattern, color) by prey could provide extra protection from predators by enhancing resistance to extinction of the avoidance response. In the simplest case, fewer observed attacks on unpalatable prey would be needed to maintain avoidance of both model and mimic organisms.

From the perspective of an avian predator, socially acquired avoidance, albeit imperfect (e.g., the occasional rejection of a palatable mimic of an unpalatable model) could lead to more efficient foraging than learning by direct experience. In the case of Batesian mimicry (unpalatable model, palatable mimic), observationally acquired avoidance would allow the predator to reject models without wasting limited foraging time. Of course, mimics would also be avoided at the cost of rejecting harmless prey. Presumably, the disadvantages of mistakenly rejecting mimics is outweighed by the advantages of avoiding models. In the case of Mullerian mimicry, the advantage of observational learning to the predator is more clear, since both models and mimics are unpalatable. However, vicariously acquired avoidance would be of the greatest advantage to predators in Mertesian mimicry (deadly models and mimics), because any direct encounter between a predator and a model or mimic is lethal to the predator. Indeed, in the absence of observational learning, it is difficult to conceive how Mertesian mimicry might evolve.

Broadly, the present experiments suggest that a knowledge of stimulus effectiveness in laboratory studies of direct and vicarious avoidance learning will further understanding of aposematic signals used in model-mimic systems. Provided that laboratory experiments of visually mediated avoidance learning fit within a broader ecological context, one might predict that the stronger the avoidance response (e.g., the greater the resistance to extinction) in the laboratory, the more effective (and, perhaps, the more common) the stimulus complex in nature. This prediction is consistent with the observation that aposematic animals use both color and pattern cues to deter potential predators (Cott, 1940). Strong avoidance acquisition after experience with a model prey (or after observation of prey sampling by a conspecific) could deter even brief sampling excursions by birds, thus decreasing the likelihood of encountering a mimic (and weakening the learned association). Strong acquisition might also permit the number of mimics to exceed the number of models without damage to the mimetic complex (Brower, 1960).

SUMMARY

Learned avoidance and preference by birds for some foods is mediated by visual cues. Learning can occur either through direct experience or observation. For avoidance, *aposematic* colors such as red are more effective conditioned stimuli than *cryptic* colors such as green. For preference, both red and green appear to be equally effective. Ecologically, the differential effectiveness of color is predictable, because the aposematic colors are used frequently by animals to advertise unpalatability, whereas the cryptic colors serve this function rarely. An unanswered question is the importance of pattern cues as a variable influencing direct and observationally acquired preference and avoidance. The potential significance of striping is suggested by the observation that aposematic animals often are striped as well as brightly colored. The present experiments were designed to address this issue using redwinged blackbirds as subjects. Experiments 1 and 2 assessed whether complex stimuli (pattern and color cues) elicited greater resistance to extinction than simple stimuli (pattern or color cues) in avoidance learning. Experiment 3 investigated whether complex stimuli might facilitate resistance to extinction of color preference responding. Experiments 4 and 5 assessed whether complex stimuli would enhance learned avoidance of visual stimuli associated with merely unpalatable food. Both direct and vicariously acquired avoidance were more resistant to extinction when complex stimuli were employed. Resistance was enhanced regardless of whether the unconditioned stimulus was malaise or unpalatability. Conversely, resistance to extinction of color preferences was not affected by the use of complex stimuli. These results suggest that the strength of visually mediated food avoidance learning may depend on the number of available discriminative cues. Ecologically, such findings are consistent with the observation that the use of multiple aposematic cues may confer greater protection from predators than the use of simple cues, such as color, alone.

REFERENCES

Alcock, J. (1969a). Observational learning by fork-tailed flycatchers (*Muscivora tyrannus*). *Animal Behavior, 17,* 652–657.

Alcock, J. (1969b). Observational learning in three species of birds. *Ibis, 111,* 308–321.

Alcock, J. (1970). Punishment levels and the response of black capped chickadees (*Parus atricapillus*) to three kinds of artificial seeds. *Animal Behavior, 18,* 592–599.

Avery, M. L. (1985). Application of mimicry theory to bird damage control. *Journal Wildlife Management, 49,* 1116–1121.

Barker, L. M. (1976). CS duration, amount and concentration effects in conditioning taste aversions. *Learning Motivation, 7,* 265–273.

Brower, L. P. (1960). Experimental studies of mimicry. Part IV. The reactions of starlings to different proportions of models and mimics. *American Naturalist, 44,* 271–281.

Brower, L. P., Cook, L. M., & Croze, H. J. (1967). Predator responses to artificial Batesian mimics released in a neotropical environment. *Evolution, 21,* 11–23.

Cott, H. B. (1940). *Adaptive coloration in animals.* London: Methuen.

Czaplicki, J. A., Borrebach, D. E., & Wilcoxin, H. C. (1976). Stimulus generalization of an illness-induced aversion to different intensities of colored water in Japanese Quail. *Animal Learning Behavior, 4,* 45–48.

Davies, N. B. (1976). Food, flocking and territorial behavior of the Pied Wagtail (*Motacilla alba yarelli*). *Journal of Animal Ecology, 45,* 235–253.

Duncan, C. L., & Shepherd, P. M. (1965). Sensory discrimination and its role in the evolution of Batesian mimicry. *Behaviour, 24,* 270–282.

Fink, L. S., & Brower, L. P. (1981). Birds can overcome the cardenolide defense of monarch butterflies in Mexico. *Nature, 291,* 67–70.

Greig-Smith, P. W., & Rowney, C. M. (in press). Effects of colour on the aversions of starlings and house sparrows to five chemical repellents. *Crop Protection.*

Guilford, T. (1986). How do warning colors work? Conspicuousness may reduce recognition errors in experienced predators. *Animal Behavior, 34,* 286–287.

Mason, J. R., Adams, M. A., & Clark, L. (1987). The repellency of anthranilate derivatives to starlings (*Sturnus vulgaris*): Chemical correlates and sensory mediation. Manuscript submitted for publication.

Mason, J. R., Arzt, A. H., & Reidinger, R. F. (1984a). Comparative assessment of food preferences and aversions acquired by observational learning. *Auk, 101,* 796–803.

Mason, J. R., Arzt, A. H., & Reidinger, R. F. (1984b). Evaluation of dimethyl anthranilate as a non-toxic bird repellent for feedlot settings. In J. Caslick (Ed.), *Proceedings of the First Eastern Animal Damage Control Conference* (pp. 259–263). Ithica, NY: Cornell University Press.

Mason, J. R., Dolbeer, R. A., Arzt, A. H., Reidinger, R. F., & Woronecki, P. P. (1984c). Taste preferences of male red-winged blackbirds among dried samples of ten corn hybrids. *Journal of Wildlife Management, 48,* 611–616.

Mason, J. R., Glahn, J. F., & Reidinger, R. F. (1985). Field trial of dimethyl anthranilate as a non-toxic bird repellent in cattle and swine feedlots. *Journal of Wildlife Management, 49,* 636–642.

Mason, J. R., & Reidinger, R. F. (1981). Effects of social facilitation and observational learning on feeding behavior of the red-winged blackbird (Agelaius phoeniceus). *Auk, 98,* 778–784.

Mason, J. R., & Reidinger, R. F. (1982a). Observational learning of food aversions in red-winged blackbirds (Agelaius phoeniceus). *Auk, 99,* 548–554.

Mason, J. R., & Reidinger, R. F. (1982b). The relative importance of reinforced versus nonreinforced stimuli in visual discrimination learning by redwinged blackbirds (Agelaius phoeniceus). *Journal of General Psychology, 107,* 219–226.

Mason, J. R., & Reidinger, R. F. (1983a). Color and taste influence methicarb-induced aversion learning in blackbirds, *Journal of Wildlife Management, 47,* 383–393.

Mason, J. R., & Reidinger, R. F. (1983b). Generalization of and effects of pre-exposure on color-avoidance learning by red-winged blackbirds (Agelaius phoeniceus). *Auk, 100,* 461–468.

Murton, R. K. (1971). The significance of a specific search image in the feeding behavior of the wood-pigeon. *Behaviour, 40,* 10–42.

Rogers, J. G. (1974). Responses of caged red-winged blackbirds to two types of repellents. *Journal of Wildlife Management, 38,* 418–423.

Rogers, J. G. (1978). Some characteristics of conditioned taste aversions in red-winged blackbirds. *Auk, 95,* 362–369.

Rubenstein, D. I., Barnett, R. J., Ridgely, R. S., & Klopfer, P. H. (1977). Adaptive advantages in mixed species feeding flocks among seed eating finches in Costa Rica. *Ibis, 119,* 10–21.

Schuler, W. (1980). Factors influencing learning to avoid un palatable prey in birds relearning new alternative prey and similarity of appearance of alternative prey. *Zeitschrift für Tierpsychologie, 54,* 105–143.

Terhune, E. C. (1977). Components of a visual stimulus used by Scrub jays to discriminate a Batesian model. *American Naturalist, 111,* 435–451.

Tramer, E. J., & Kemp, T. R. (1979). Diet-correlated variations in the social behavior of wintering Tennessee Warblers. *Auk, 96,* 186–187.

Wickler, W. (1968). *Mimicry in plants and animals.* New York: McGraw-Hill.

Williamson, P., & Grey, L. (1975). Foraging behavior of the starling (Sturnus vulgaris) in Maryland. *Condor, 77,* 84–89.

PART III

Social Influences on Foraging and Feeding

Communication of Information Concerning Distant Diets in a Social, Central-Place Foraging Species: Rattus norvegicus[1]

Bennett G. Galef, Jr.
McMaster University
Hamilton, Ontario

In environments characterized by an unpredictable and patchy distribution of foods, social birds or mammals that forage from a central site (e.g., a burrow, roost, or nesting site) can benefit from exchange of information with conspecifics about the availability and distribution of foods (Bertram, 1978; DeGroot, 1980; Erwin, 1977; Waltz, 1982; Ward & Zahavi, 1973). Relatively unsuccessful foragers able to extract relevant information from their more successful fellows could learn both the identity of foods successful foragers are exploiting and the locations of those foods. Such socially-acquired information could enhance the foraging efficiency of relatively unsuccessful individuals.

Wild Norway rats are social, central-place foragers; in natural circumstances, each rat lives as a member of a colony inhabiting a fixed system of burrows; when foraging, colony members disperse from their burrow, feed, and then return to it (Calhoun, 1962; Telle, 1966). Thus, Norway rats are an ecologically appropriate choice for laboratory experiments examining ways in which social interaction might facilitate food acquisition in a social, central-place foraging species.

---

[1]An article similar to the present one has been published, under the title "Olfactory communication among rats: Information concerning distant diets," in D. Duvall (Ed.), *Chemical signals in vertebrates IV: Ecological, evolutionary and comparative aspects of vertebrate chemical signalling.* (1986). New York: Plenum.

THE LABORATORY PARADIGM

The procedures used in the studies described below simulated a natural situation in which a foraging rat ingests a food at some distance from its burrow, returns to its burrow, and then interacts with a burrow-mate. Our initial purpose was to discover whether, as a result of such interaction (1) the burrow-mate could acquire information concerning the food the forager had eaten and (2) whether the burrow-mate would use the information acquired from its fellow when selecting foods for ingestion.

The Basic Experiment

During the experiments described below, subjects were housed in same-sex pairs in cages divided in half by screen partitions. To simplify exposition, I refer to the "successful forager" in each pair as a *demonstrator* and the other member of that pair as an *observer*.

The basic experiment, schematized in Figure 6.1, was carried out in five steps:

Step 1. Demonstrator and observer were maintained together with ad lib access to Purina Laboratory Rodent chow and water for a 2-day period of familiarization with both apparatus and cage-mate.

Step 2. The demonstrator was moved to the opposite side of the screen partition from its observer and food-deprived for 24 hr to ensure that the demonstrator ate when given the opportunity to do so.

Step 3. Chow was removed from the observer's side of the cage (in preparation for testing) and the demonstrator was moved to a cage in a

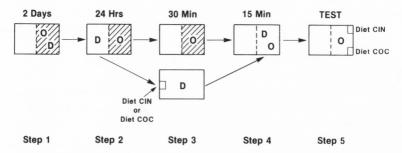

Figure 6.1. Schematic diagram of the procedure of the basic experiment. O = observer; D = demonstrator; hatching indicates maintenance diet present in cage. (Galef & Wigmore, 1983. Copyright 1983 by Bailliere Tindall. Reprinted by permission of the publisher and authors.)

separate room and allowed to feed for 30 min on either cinnamon-flavored diet (Diet Cin) or cocoa-flavored diet (Diet Coc).

Step 4. The demonstrator was returned to the observer's side of the cage and demonstrator and observer were allowed to interact for 15 min.

Step 5. The demonstrator was removed from the experiment and the observer was offered a choice between two weighed food cups, one containing cinnamon-flavored diet (Diet Cin) and one containing cocoa-flavored diet (Diet Coc).

Figure 6.2 shows the mean amount of Diet Coc, as a percentage of total amount eaten, ingested during testing (Step 5) by observers whose demonstrators had eaten either Diet Coc or Diet Cin during Step 3 of the experiment. As can be seen in Figure 6.2, (1) those observers whose demonstrators ate Diet Coc ate a far greater percentage of Diet Coc than did those observers whose demonstrators ate Diet Cin, and (2) effects of demonstrators' diet on observers' diet preference were still observable 48–60 hr after interaction of demonstrator and observer. The results of this first experiment clearly show both that an observer rat can extract from a demonstrator information identifying the diet that demonstrator had eaten at a time and place distant from the locus of demonstrator-observer interaction and that this extracted information is sufficient to bias its recipient's subsequent selection of diet.

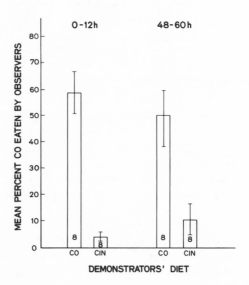

Figure 6.2.   Mean amount of cocoa-flavored diet ingested, as a percentage of total amount eaten, by observers whose demonstrators ate either cocoa- or cinnamon-flavored diet. CO = cocoa-flavored diet; Cin = Cinnamon-flavored diet. (Galef & Wigmore, 1983. Copyright 1983 by Bailliere Tindall. Reprinted by permission of the publisher and authors.)

Variations on a Theme

We have repeated the basic experiment described above many times: with a variety of different diets (Galef & Wigmore, 1983), with hungry and replete observers, with male demonstrator-observer pairs and female ones, with wild and domesticated rats, with demonstrator-observer pairs familiar with one another and with pairs that had never met prior to their interaction during Step 4 of the experiment, with both old demonstrators and observers and young ones, and with observers selecting distinctively flavored fluids rather than solids for ingestion (Galef, Kennett, & Wigmore, 1984). In every case, we have seen robust enhancement of observers' preferences for their respective demonstrators' diets. Similarly, Posadas-Andrews and Roper (1983) and Strupp and Levitsky (1984), using rather different paradigms, have repeatedly observed demonstrator influence on subsequent diet selection by observers. The phenomenon of demonstrator influence on observer diet preference seems a general one in Norway rats, not dependent on some restricted set of experimental parameters for its expression.

Effects of the Passage of Time

In the basic experiment illustrated in Figure 6.1, observers and demonstrators interacted immediately after demonstrators had eaten diets and observers had the opportunity to choose between diets immediately following extraction of information from their respective demonstrators. Free-living rats must expend time in returning from a feeding site to their burrows. In the field, foragers departing from their burrows must expend further time in reaching a feeding site. If the capacity of rats to transmit information concerning a food eaten at a distance from their burrow functions in information exchange in natural settings, communication must occur even if there are delays both between a successful forager's ingestion of a food and its return to its burrow and between the interaction of a successful forager with other rats and the latter's arrival at a potential feeding site. In terms of the laboratory analogue illustrated in Figure 6.1, rats must be able to tolerate delays between Steps 3 and 4 and between Steps 4 and 5 and still successfully exchange information.

Figures 6.3a and 6.3b show the results of experiments in which independent groups of subjects experienced varying delays (1) between a demonstrator feeding and its interaction with an observer and (2) between an observer interacting with a demonstrator and its choosing between diets.

As can be seen in Figure 6.3a, for at least 4 hr after feeding on a diet, demonstrators continued to emit cues sufficient to permit observers to identify their respective demonstrators' diets (Galef & Kennett, 1985). Data presented in Figure 6.3b indicate that observers can use diet-identifying information obtained from demonstrators for 12 to 24 hr after receiving it (Galef, 1983). Both the time

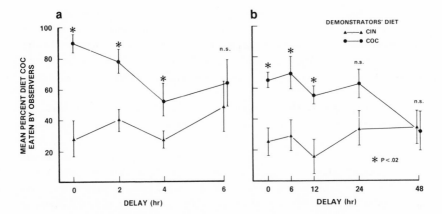

Figure 6.3. Mean amount of cocoa-flavored diet ingested, as a percentage of total amount eaten, by observers whose demonstrators ate Diet Cin or Diet Coc: (3a) as a function of time between ingestion by demonstrator and interaction with observer, (3b) as a function of time between interaction of demonstrator and observer and initiation of testing. (Galef & Wigmore, 1983. Copyright 1983 by Bailliere Tindall. Reprinted by permission of the publisher and authors.)

course of emission of diet-identifying cues by demonstrators and observer retention of diet-identifying information obtained from demonstrators seem appropriate to permit use of the information transmission system under investigation in natural environments.

Handling of Multiple Messages

Although there is relatively little information available concerning social life in free-living wild rat colonies, it seems reasonable to suppose that each colony member, prior to departing from its colony's burrow system on a foraging expedition, might have the opportunity to acquire information from several conspecifics about foods they had recently ingested. It is, thus, possible that an individual rat, remaining in its burrow and interacting with a succession of colony-mates returning from successful foraging trips, could collect information concerning the entire range of foods returning foragers had exploited.

If rats in their burrows are to make use of information received from a succession of returning colony-mates, they must be able to distinctively encode and store information extracted from each informant. The results of several studies indicate that rats have such a capacity (Galef, 1983). Our method was similar to that outlined in Figure 6.1. However, in the present experiment, each observer, instead of interacting during Step 4 with a single observer that had eaten either Diet Cin or Coc, interacted (in counterbalanced order) for 15 min with each of a series of four demonstrators, one of which had eaten vinegar-flavored diet (Diet Vin), one a coffee-flavored diet (Diet Cof), one a casein and cornstarch-based died (Diet NPT), and one *either* Diet Coc *or* Diet Cin. During testing of observers (Step 5 of Figure 6.1), each observer was offered a choice between Diets Cin and Coc. As can be seen in the left-hand panel of Figure 6.4, those observers one of whose four demonstrators had eaten Diet Coc preferred Diet Coc, whereas those observers one of whose four demonstrators had eaten Diet Cin preferred that diet. Of course, it might have been that the two diets selected for testing (Diets Cin and Coc) were simply the most salient of those offered to demonstrators. To control for this possibility, the entire experiment was repeated using Diets Cin, Coc, and NPT as irrelevant diets and Diets Cof and Vin as critical test items. As can be seen in the right-hand panel of Figure 6.4, those observers one of whose four demonstrators ingested Diet Cof preferred Diet Cof, whereas those observers one of whose four demonstrators ingested Diet Vin preferred Diet Vin. These findings are consistent with the hypothesis that a rat remaining in its burrow and interacting with a succession of returning successful foragers is able to construct an inventory of foods currently available in the larger environment and exploited by its fellows.

Transmission of Aversions to Distant Diets

Naive rats could benefit not only from information acquired from conspecifics concerning diets those conspecifics have eaten, but also from information about toxic diets more knowledgeable individuals have learned to avoid. We therefore undertook experiments simulating situations in which a rat departs from its burrow, ingests a novel, toxic food, returns to its burrow, and while suffering toxicosis interacts with a burrow-mate. We then presented the burrow-mate with a choice between the novel food its demonstrator had been trained to avoid and a second novel food (Galef, Wigmore, & Kennett, 1983).

Our experimental method was similar to that employed in the basic experiment (see Figure 6.1) except that each demonstrator, after eating either Diet Cin or Diet Coc for 30 min (Step 3 of Figure 6.1), was injected intraperitoneally with 1% of body weight of either 2% (w/vol) LiCl or saline solution. Demonstrators then interacted with observers for either 30 min or 2 hr (Step 4 of Figure 6.1). As can be seen in Figure 6.5, observers exhibited a marked preference for their respective demonstrators' diets even if demonstrators were suffering toxicosis during the period that observers interacted with them.

Analysis of the causes of failure of transfer of aversion indicated that although (1) the diet-identifying cues emitted by a demonstrator are adequate conditional stimuli for taste aversion learning (observers, themselves poisoned after interacting with demonstrators fed either Diet Cin or Diet Coc, developed aversions to their respective demonstrators' diets, Galef et al., 1983) and (2)

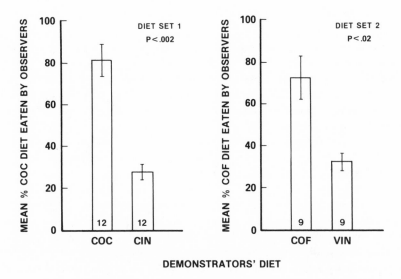

Figure 6.4.   Mean percent Diet Coc (left-hand panel) or Diet Cof (right-hand panel) eaten by observers one of whose demonstrators ingested, respectively, either Diet Cin or Coc, or either Diet Cof or Vin. (Galef, 1983. Copyright 1983 by the American Psychological Association. Reprinted by permission of the author and publisher.)

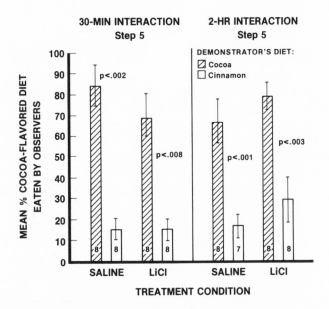

Figure 6.5.   Mean amount of cocoa-flavored diet, as a percentage of total amount eaten, ingested by observers whose demonstrators ate either cocoa-flavored or cinnamon-flavored diet and were then injected with LiCl solution or saline. (Galef, Wigmore, & Kennett, 1984. Copyright 1984 by the American Psychological Association. Reprinted by permission of the authors and publisher.)

demonstrators emit cues adequate to serve as unconditional ˈimuli in a taste-aversion learning paradigm (Bond, 1982; Lavin, Freise, & Coombes, 1980), observers do not, at least under the conditions we employed, associate CS and UCS. Rats seem to transmit information about what foods to eat more readily than information about what foods to avoid (Galef, 1985; for an interesting exception see Gemberling, 1984).

USE OF EXTRACTED INFORMATION IN ORIENTATION OF FORAGING

Although the experiments described above indicate that a successful forager can provide information about diets it has ingested far from the locus of information transfer, these studies do not provide evidence that such information can be used by its recipients to facilitate their later foraging. To investigate the usefulness of socially transmitted information in increasing foraging efficiency, we introduced our subjects into the environment depicted in overhead schematic in Figure 6.6. The rule here was that each of three discriminable foods was available at a different, fixed location: cheese-flavored diet (CH Diet) in the central arm of the maze, cocoa-flavored diet (CO Diet) in the right arm, and cinnamon-flavored diet

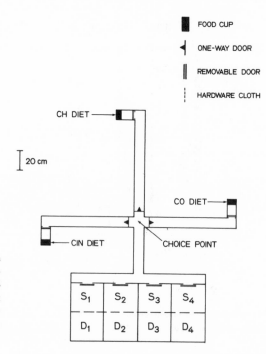

Figure 6.6.   Plan view of apparatus. Ch = cheese-flavored diet; Cin = Cinnamon-flavored diet; Co = cocoa-flavored diet; S = subject; D = demonstrator. (Galef & Wigmore, 1983. Copyright 1983 by Bailliere Tindall. Reprinted by permission of the publisher and authors.)

(CIN Diet) in the left. Only one of the three diets was accessible to a subject on any given day, and the particular diet available to a subject on any day was randomly selected.

Each subject (S_n in Figure 6.6) was given four trials/day using a correction procedure. On the first trial of each day, each subject had no information as to which food was available, and therefore had only one chance in three of selecting the correct arm of the maze. If it chose the correct arm, it could eat for a few minutes. If it didn't, it was locked in the arm it had chosen for a few minutes and the first trial was repeated until the subject found the food. Trials 2, 3, and 4 of each day were run in the same fashion.

Each subject could, in effect, tell the experimenter when it understood this little world by exhibiting more or less perfect performance in its first choices on Trials 2, 3, and 4 of each day. Once a given subject had reached the necessary criterion of performance on Trials 2, 3, and 4, testing was instituted.

On each test day, for 15 min prior to Trial 1 of that day, each subject was allowed to interact with a demonstrator rat (D_n in Figure 6.6) that had eaten the diet that was going to be available to that subject on that day. That is, if cheese-flavored diet was going to be available to S_3 on a given day, S_3's demonstrator, D_3, was fed cheese-flavored diet for 30 min and then allowed to interact with S_3 for 15 min prior to initiating Trial 1 of testing of S_3.

To determine whether subjects were capable of using information acquired from demonstrators to enhance foraging efficiency, we compared the probability of a correct response on the first choice of the first trial of each day of testing (when information from a demonstrator was available to subjects) with the probability of a correct response on the first choice of the first trial of each of the last days of training (when no information from a demonstrator was available to subjects). As can be seen in the left-hand panel of Figure 6.7, 4 of our 7 subjects were able to use the information provided by their respective demonstrators to facilitate location of unpredictable foods (Galef & Wigmore, 1983).

As indicated in a preceding section, rats can distinctively encode diet-identifying information extracted from a series of conspecifics. We have also found that they can use such diet-identifying information, embedded in a series of like messages, to orient foraging trips. In another experiment (Galef, 1983), during testing, instead of allowing each subject to interact with a single demonstrator predicting the food to be available on a given day, we had each subject interact with 4 demonstrators; 3 had eaten irrelevant foods (Diets NPT, Vin, and Cof) and one had eaten the food to be available to the subject on that day. As can be seen in the right-hand panel of Figure 6.7, subjects were still able to extract and use the relevant information in selecting an arm of the maze for initial exploration on test days.

In more recent experiments we have found (Galef, Mischinger, & Malenfant, 1987) that rats trained to follow conspecifics to food in a multi-armed maze will follow a leader that has recently eaten a desirable food with higher proba-

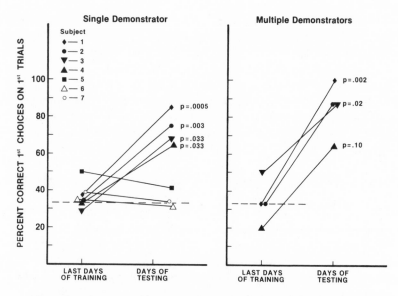

Figure 6.7.   Percentage of correct first choices on first trials by subjects at the end of training and during testing in the apparatus illustrated in Figure 6.5. (Galef, 1983; Galef & Wigmore, 1983. Copyright 1983 by Bailliere Tindall and the American Psychological Association. Reprinted by permission of the authors and publishers.)

bility than they will follow a leader that has recently eaten an undesirable food. Nine of 10 followers that had been trained to avoid ingesting a novel, highly palatable diet (by feeding them the novel diet and then poisoning them) were less likely to follow leaders that had eaten the averted diet than to follow leaders that had eaten the followers' normal maintenance diet.

These data suggest that a rat in its burrow, interacting with a number of successful foragers, could choose among them and follow those exploiting the most desirable food. The ability to identify the diet eaten by a conspecific, together with a spontaneous tendency to follow others on foraging expeditions (Galef, Mischinger, & Malenfant, 1987) could result, in natural circumstances, in communication of information as to the locations where valuable foods are to be found.

THE NATURE OF MESSAGES PASSING
FROM DEMONSTRATORS TO OBSERVERS

Implication of Olfactory Signals

An obvious question arising from the experiments described above concerns the means by which an observer rat acquires information from a demonstrator as to the diet that demonstrator has been eating. We have developed several converging lines of evidence, each consistent with the hypothesis that olfactory cues passing from demonstrator to observer are sufficient to allow observer identification of demonstrators' diets.

In order to examine the mode of communication of diet-identifying information from demonstrator to observer, it was necessary to gain some control over their interaction. We employed a procedure similar to that depicted in Figure 6.1, but with one important modification. During the period of demonstrator-observer interaction (Step 4 of Figure 6.1), the members of each demonstrator-observer pair were on opposite sides of the screen partition dividing their cage.

As can be seen in Figure 6.8, observers had no trouble in developing a preference for their respective demonstrators' diets when separated from their demonstrators by a screen during interaction. However, as can also be seen in Figure 6.8, if the screen partition was replaced by a clear Plexiglas partition, demonstrator influence on observer diet preference was completely abolished (Galef & Wigmore, 1983).

Further, we have conducted an experiment in which each demonstrator,

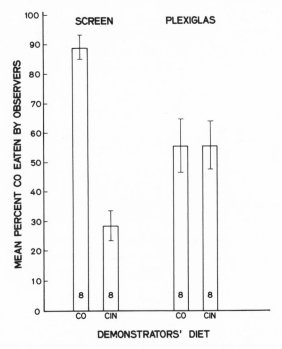

Figure 6.8. Mean amount of cocoa-flavored diet ingested, as a percentage of total amount eaten, by observers whose demonstrators ate cinnamon- or cocoa-flavored diet. Left-hand bars, observer and demonstrator separated by a screen partition during interaction. Right-hand bars, observer and demonstrator separated by a Plexiglas partition during interaction. (Galef & Wigmore, 1983. Copyright 1983 by Bailliere Tindall. Reprinted by permission of the publisher and authors.)

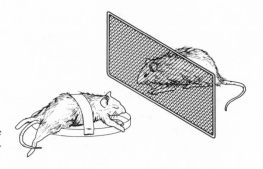

Figure 6.9. Illustration of procedure during interaction of anesthetized demonstrator and observer.

after eating either Diet Cin or Diet Coc, was anesthetized and placed 2 in. from and facing a screen partition, with its observer on the other side of the screen (see Figure 6.9). During subsequent preference testing, observers still exhibited (Figure 6.10) a robust preference for their respective demonstrators' diets (Galef & Wigmore, 1983). Also, as one would expect if olfactory cues play an important role in information transfer between demonstrator and observer, observers rendered anosmic by passing zinc-sulfate solution through their nares (Alberts & Galef, 1971) failed to exhibit a preference for their respective demonstrators' diets. Control rats whose nasal passages had been rinsed with saline solution continued to exhibit a preference for their respective demonstrators' diets (See Figure 6.11).

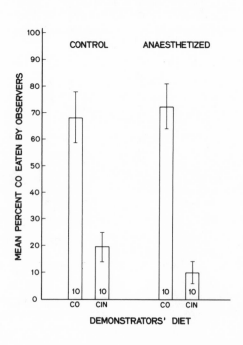

Figure 6.10. Mean amount of Diet Coc eaten by observers, as a percentage of total amount ingested. Left-hand bars, observers interacting with intact demonstrators. Right-hand bars, observers interacting with anesthetized demonstrators, as depicted in Figure 6.9. (Galef & Wigmore, 1983. Copyright 1983 by Baillière Tindall. Reprinted by permission of the publisher and authors.)

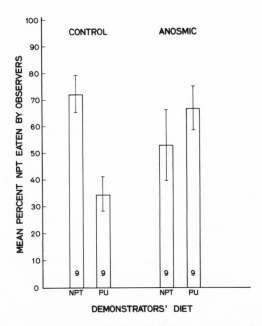

Figure 6.11. Mean amount of Diet NPT ingested, as a percentage of total amount eaten, by observers whose demonstrators ate either Diet NPT or Pu. Left-hand bars, observers' nasal cavities rinsed with saline. Right-hand bars, observers' nasal cavities rinsed with $ZnSO_4$, i.e. anosmic. (Galef & Wigmore, 1983. Copyright 1983 by Bailliere Tindall. Reprinted by permission of the publisher and authors.)

Last, but not least, humans, as well as rats, can use olfactory cues emitted by a previously fed rat to tell what diet that rat has been eating. A human observer presented with a dozen rats in random sequence, half having eaten Diet Coc and half Diet Cin, could, by sniffing their breaths, tell with better than 85% accuracy which rat had eaten which diet (Galef & Wigmore, 1983).

CAUSES OF DEMONSTRATOR INFLUENCE ON OBSERVER DIET PREFERENCE

The simplest behavioral explanation of the observed influence of demonstrators on observers' subsequent diet selection would be something like the following. Rats are always somewhat hesitant to ingest unfamiliar foods (Barnett, 1958; Galef, 1970). As the result of interacting with a demonstrator that has eaten a Diet X and therefore smells of Diet X, an observer rat has been exposed to cues associated with Diet X and should be somewhat familiar with that diet. Therefore, an observer rat that has interacted with a Diet-X-fed demonstrator should

131

eat Diet X in preference to other roughly equipalatable, but totally unfamiliar, diets.

We have conducted a number of experiments designed to test the adequacy of explanations of demonstrator influence on observer diet preference in terms of demonstrator-induced diet familiarity of the sort described above (Galef, Kennett, & Stein, 1985). In every case, the results of our studies have been contrary to the most straightforward predictions from the familiarity hypothesis.

For example, if reduced diet novelty, resulting from observer exposure to diet-identifying cues during interaction with a demonstrator, were responsible for subsequent demonstrator influence on observer diet preference, one would expect observers choosing between two familiar diets to be relatively immune to demonstrator influence on their diet selection. Any additional familiarity with one test diet, resulting from a brief period of interaction with a demonstrator fed that diet, should be overwhelmed by observers' extensive previous experience with both test diets.

We conducted an experiment much like that outlined in Figure 6.1 except that during the 2-day period of familiarization (Step 1 of Figure 6.1), observers in a Cin/Coc pre-exposure group were left alone in their cages and allowed ad lib access to two food bowls, one containing Diet Cin and one containing Diet Coc. Following 2 days of feeding on both Diets Cin and Coc, each observer was exposed for 15 min to an unfamiliar demonstrator that had eaten either Diet Coc or Diet Cin (Step 4 of Figure 6.1). Each observer was then tested for its preference between Diets Coc and Cin (Step 5 of Figure 6.1). Observers in the control group were treated identically to those in the Cin/Coc pre-exposure group except that during familiarization (Step 1 of Figure 6.1), observers in the control group had access to two food bowls containing a powdered form of their standard maintenance diet.

The main results of the experiment are presented in Figure 6.12, which shows the mean amount of Diet Coc, as a percentage of total amount eaten, ingested by observers in Cin/Coc pre-exposure and control groups. As can be seen in the figure, the diet eaten by demonstrators profoundly affected the food choice of observers in both groups. This finding renders unlikely interpretation of the effects of demonstrator influence on observer diet preference as resulting solely from familiarity with the taste or smell of a diet experienced during 15 min of interaction with a demonstrator. Further, simply feeding a rat either Diet Cin or Coc for 15 min (or, for that matter, for 24 hr) prior to offering it a choice between Diets Cin and Coc had no effect on subjects' subsequent choice of diet (Galef et al., 1985).

In the face of such data, it is difficult to maintain the hypothesis that demonstrator influence on observer diet preference is the result of a simple increase in observers' familiarity with their respective demonstrators' diets. An obvious alternative is that the presence of a demonstrator is necessary if experience of diet-identifying cues is to alter observers' subsequent diet preference. It is this hypothesis that has been the guiding principle in our recent research.

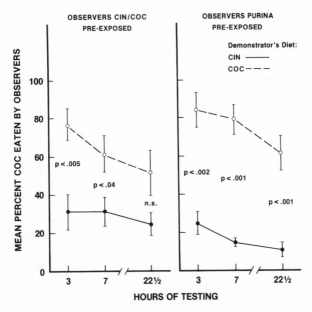

Figure 6.12. Mean amount of Diet Coc ingested by observers either pre-exposed or not pre-exposed to Diets Cin and Coc and whose demonstrators ate either Diets Cin or Coc. (Galef, Kennett & Stein, 1985. Copyright 1985 by the Psychonomic Society, Inc. Reprinted by permission of the authors and publishers.)

Analysis of Olfactory Cues

Assume, for the sake of argument, that I am correct in asserting that demonstrators do not alter their observers' subsequent diet preference by simply making diet-identifying cues available to observers, rather that demonstrators provide important contextual cues, as well as diet-identifying cues, necessary for demonstrator influence on observer diet preference. If so, then analysis of the message passing from demonstrator to observer presents two separable problems: (1) determination of the source of the diet-identifying cues emitted by demonstrators and (2) determination of the source and nature of the contextual cues, also emitted by demonstrators, that act in concert with the diet-identifying cues to alter observers' subsequent diet preference.

Diet Identifying Cues. In order to look more closely at the cues involved in demonstrator influence on observer diet preference, we again changed our experimental procedures slightly. The new procedure was similar to that described in Figure 6.1, but differed both in the way in which demonstrators were made to emit diet-identifying cues (Step 3) and in the treatment of demonstrators and observers during the period of their interaction (Step 4). Rather than feed all demonstrators during Step 3 of the procedure, we employed a variety of techniques for attaching diet-identifying cues to demonstrators. Some demonstrators were allowed to eat Diet Cin or Diet Coc for 30 min, as was done in the basic experiment. Other demonstrators were anesthetized and their faces dusted with either Diet Cin or Diet Coc. Yet other demonstrators were anesthetized and tube-fed one of two distinctively flavored fluids. Some observers, instead of interacting with a demonstrator during Step 4 of the procedure, spent 30 min interacting with a surrogate rat (constructed of cotton-batting and surgical gauze) one end of which had been dusted with either Diet Cin or Coc. Further, instead of permitting demonstrator and observer to interact freely during Step 4, each anesthetized demonstrator was placed in the screen tube of the apparatus illustrated in Figure 6.13. Observers were introduced into the bucket-shaped area of the enclosure, left there for 30 min, then moved back to their respective home-cages for testing (Step 5 of Figure 6.1).

As can be seen in Figure 6.14, 30-min observer interaction with a surrogate demonstrator, dusted with either Diet Coc or Diet Cin, failed to affect observer diet preference during testing (Step 5), providing further evidence of the inadequacy of simple exposure to a diet to produce alterations in observer diet preference. In contrast, exposure to a fed demonstrator, an anesthetized demonstrator powdered with diet, or an anesthetized demonstrator tube-fed a flavored solution each had the capacity to alter observers' diet selection during testing.

The finding that diet applied to the faces of demonstrators enhanced diet preference in their observers indicates that ingestion of a diet by a demonstrator is not critical in demonstrator production of diet-identifying cues. The finding that demonstrators stomach-loaded with a flavored solution also induced observers to increase their preference for the solution placed in the stomach of demonstrators indicates that particles of food clinging to the fur and vibrissae of demonstrators are not necessary for transmission of diet-identifying information to observers. Taken together the results of the present study (Galef et al., 1985; Galef & Stein, 1985) show that both particles of food on the exterior of rats and portions of diet

Figure 6.13.   Illustration of apparatus used to analyze diet-identifying and contextual cues. (Galef & Stein, 1985. Copyright 1985 by the Psychonomic Society, Inc. Reprinted by permission of the authors and publisher.)

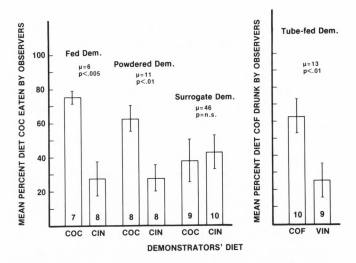

Figure 6.14. Left-hand panel: Mean amount of cocoa-flavored diet eaten, as a percentage of total amount ingested, by observers interacting with demonstrators or surrogates. Right-hand panel: Mean amount of coffee-flavored solution, as a percentage of total amount drunk, ingested by observers whose demonstrators were tube-fed with either coffee- or vinegar-flavored solution.

in the stomach of rats provide cues sufficient to permit observers to identify their respective demonstrators' diets.

Contextual Cues.　The results of the studies presented in Figure 6.14 also suggest that a demonstrator rat provides a context within which exposure to diet-identifying cues alters observers' subsequent diet preference. Observer preference was not affected by exposure to a diet presented on a surrogate, but was affected by exposure to the same diet presented on the face of a rat. Further, the procedure employed in these studies provides an opportunity to define more precisely the nature of the contextual cues which, in combination with diet-identifying cues, produce demonstrator influence on observer diet preference.

We allowed observers to interact for 30 min in the apparatus illustrated in Figure 6.13 with demonstrators treated in one of four ways: (1) Observers in the powdered-face group interacted with anesthetized demonstrators whose faces had been rolled in either Diet Cin or Diet Coc. (2) Observers in the dead-powdered-face group interacted with demonstrators that had been sacrificed by anesthetic overdose and had their faces rolled in either Diet Cin or Diet Coc prior to the demonstrators' introduction into the apparatus. (3) Observers in the powdered-rear group interacted with anesthetized demonstrators whose rear ends were rolled in Diet Cin or Diet Coc. These demonstrators were introduced into the screen tube of the apparatus illustrated in Figure 6.13 with their rear ends inside the bucket and their heads outside of it. Last, (4) observers in the surrogate group were allowed to interact in the apparatus with a rat-size cotton-batting stuffed length of tubular gauze one end of which had been rolled in either Diet Cin or Diet Coc.

Figure 6.15 presents a measure of the degree of influence of the various sorts of demonstrators on their respective observers' subsequent diet preferences during testing (Step 5 of Figure 6.1). The summary descriptive statistic, cocoa-demonstrator/cinnamon-demonstrator ratio, was calculated by dividing the mean percentage of Diet Coc eaten during testing by observers whose demonstrators had been coated with Diet Coc by the mean percentage Diet Coc eaten during testing by observers whose demonstrators had been coated with Diet Cin. Each histogram in the figure summarizes data from 16–20 observers, half of which interacted with demonstrators coated with Diet Coc and half with demonstrators coated with Diet Cin. The greater the Cocoa-demonstrator/Cinnamon-demonstrator ratio the greater the influence of demonstrators' diets on observers' subsequent diet preference.

To summarize the results of a series of statistical analyses discussed in detail elsewhere (Galef & Stein, 1985): (1) Observers in powdered-face groups consistently exhibited a significant tendency to choose for ingestion the diets applied

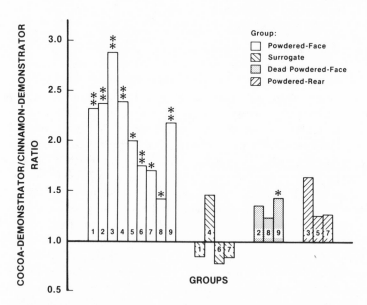

Figure 6.15.   Cocoa-demonstrator/Cinnamon-demonstrator ratios of groups of observers interacting with demonstrators and surrogates in the apparatus illustrated in Figure 6.13. Observers were randomly assigned across groups labeled with the same integer. * = p < .05, ** = p < .01. (Galef & Stein, 1985. Copyright 1985 by the Psychonomic Society, Inc. Reprinted by permission of the authors and publisher.)

to their respective demonstrators. (2) Observers in surrogate groups exhibited no tendency to select the same diet for ingestion that their respective demonstrators had been fed. (3) Observers in dead-powdered-face and powdered-rear groups were both significantly less affected in their diet selection by demonstrators than were observers in powdered-face groups, and significantly more affected by demonstrators than were observers in surrogate groups. Taken together these findings suggest (1) that simple exposure of an observer rat to the smell of a diet is not sufficient to enhance observer preference for that diet, and (2) that the contextual cues emitted by demonstrator rats, producing preference for a diet in their observers, are both widely distributed and most concentrated at the anterior end of live rats. These findings do not, of course, satisfactorily resolve the issue of the nature or origins of the effective contextual cues emitted by demonstrator rats. Determination of the active chemicals involved in potentiating observer preference for demonstrators' diets must await biochemical analyses. We will attempt such analyses in the future, but I suspect that identification of the critical agent or agents will prove as difficult in the present case as it has in other attempts to chemically define mammalian pheromones.

SUMMARY AND CONCLUSIONS

The series of studies described above provide compelling evidence that naive rats have the capacity to extract information from recently fed conspecifics, permitting identification of the food conspecific individuals have eaten. Recipients of such information are biased in their subsequent food selection by diet-related cues they experience during interaction with a fed individual. Recipients of diet-identifying information, acquired during social interaction, can use that information to orient their subsequent foraging activities.

Information concerning distant diets is contained in olfactory signals passing from recently fed rats to naive ones. These olfactory cues both permit recipient identification of the diet eaten by a conspecific and provide an as yet undefined social context that results in subsequent enhanced preference for diets eaten by informants.

Norway rats, like honeybees, the only other species of social, central-place foragers whose sharing of information concerning distant diets has been examined in detail (Gould, 1976; von Frisch, 1967; Wenner, 1971), possess a number of behavioral mechanisms for the social enhancement of foraging efficiency (See Galef, 1977, 1983, 1984a, for reviews). The convergent evolution of social learning mechanisms in species as phyletically diverse as bees and rats suggests that laboratory study of social effects on feeding in other social, central-place foragers should prove fruitful.

Social learning provides a relatively little understood alternative to individual learning for the development of adaptive feeding repertoires. Social, central-place foraging species, both vertebrate and invertebrate, offer as yet unexplored opportunities for increased understanding of the mechanisms of social learning and the development of diet choice.

ACKNOWLEDGMENTS

The research described here was supported by grants from the Natural Sciences and Engineering Research Council of Canada and the McMaster University Research Board.

I thank my collaborators, Stephen Wigmore, Moni Stein, Deborah Kennett, Anna Mischinger, Sandra Vegeris, Cathy Maskell, Toni Hammond and Cecelia Malinski for their enthusiasm for and dedication to this research program. I also thank Mertice Clark, Harvey Weingarten, and Tom Zentall whose thoughtful critiques of earlier drafts have made this manuscript far more "user friendly" than it would otherwise have been.

REFERENCES

Alberts, J. R., & Galef, B. G., Jr. (1971). Acute anosmia in the rat: A behavioral test of a peripherally-induced olfactory deficit. *Physiology and Behavior, 6,* 619–621.

Barnett, S. A. (1958). Experiments on "neophobia" in wild and laboratory rats. *British Journal of Psychology, 49,* 195–201.

Bertram, B. C. R. (1978). Living in groups: Predators and prey. In J. R. Krebs & N. B. Davies (Eds.). *Behavioral ecology* (pp. 64–96) Sunderland, MA: Sinauer.

Bond, N. W. (1982). Transferred odor aversions in adult rats. *Behavioral and Neural Biology, 35,* 417–412.

Calhoun, J. B. (1962). *The ecology and sociology of the Norway rat.* Bethesda, MD: U.S. Department of Health, Education, and Welfare.

DeGroot, P. (1980). Information transfer in a socially roosting weaver bird (*Quelea quelea: Ploceinae*): An experimental study. *Animal Behaviour, 28,* 1249–1254.

Erwin, R. M. (1977). Foraging and breeding adaptations to different food regimes in three seabirds: The common tern, *Sterna hirundo,* Royal tern, *Sterna maxima,* and black skimmer, *Rynchops niger, Ecology, 58,* 389–397.

Galef, B. G., Jr. (1970). Aggression and timidity: Responses to novelty in feral Norway rats. *Journal of Comparative and Physiological Psychology, 70,* 370–381.

Galef, B. G., Jr. (1977). Mechanisms for the social transmission of food preferences from adult to weanling rats. In L. M. Barker, M. Best, & M. Domjan (Eds.), *Learning mechanisms in food selection* (pp. 123–150). Waco, TX: Baylor University Press.

Galef, B. G., Jr. (1983). Utilization by Norway rats (R. norvegicus) of multiple messages concerning distant foods. *Journal of Comparative Psychology, 97* 364–371.

Galef, B. G., Jr. (1984a). Social learning in wild Norway rats. In T. D. Johnston & A. T. Pietrewicz (Eds.), *Issues in the ecological study of learning* (pp. 143–166). Hillsdale, NJ: Lawrence Erlbaum Associates.

Galef, B. G., Jr. (1984b). Reciprocal heuristics: A discussion of the relationships of the study of learned behavior in laboratory and field, *Learning and Motivation, 15,* 479–493.

Galef, B. G., Jr. (1985). Direct and indirect behavioral pathways to the social transmission of food avoidance. In P. Bronstein & N. S. Braveman (Eds.), *Experimental assessments and clinical applications of conditioned food aversions* (pp. 203–215). (Annals of the New York Academy of Science, Vol. 443.)

Galef, B. G., Jr., & Kennett, D. J. (1985). Delays after eating: Effects on transmission of diet preferences and aversions. *Animal Learning and Behavior, 13,* 39–43.

Galef, B. G., Jr., Kennett, D. J., & Wigmore, S. W. (1984). Transfer of information concerning distant food in rats: A robust phenomenon. *Animal Learning and Behavior, 12,* 292–296.

Galef, B. G., Jr., Kennett, D. J., & Stein, M. (1985). Demonstrator influence on observer diet preference: Effects of familiarity and exposure context in *R. norvegicus. Animal Learning and Behavior, 13,* 25–30.

Galef, B. G., Jr., Mischinger, A., & Malenfant, S. A. (1987). Hungry rats' following of conspecifics to food depends on the diets eaten by potential leaders. *Animal Behaviour, 35,* 1234–1239.

Galef, B. G., Jr., & Stein, M. (1985). Demonstrator influence on observer diet preference: Analyses of critical social interactions and olfactory signals. *Animal Learning and Behavior, 13,* 131–138.

Galef, B. G., Jr. & Wigmore, S. W. (1983). Transfer of information concerning distant foods: A laboratory investigation of the 'information-centre' hypothesis. *Animal Behaviour, 31,* 748–758.

Galef, B. G., Jr., Wigmore, S. W., & Kennett, D. J. (1983). A failure to find socially mediated taste aversion learning in Norway rats (*R. norvegicus*). *Journal of Comparative Psychology, 97,* 458–463.

Gemberling, G. A. (1984). Ingestion of a novel flavor before exposure to pups injected with lithium chloride produces a taste aversion in mother rats (*Rattus norvegicus*). *Journal of Comparative Psychology, 98,* 285–301.

Gould, J. L. (1976). The dance-language controversy. *Quarterly Review of Biology, 51,* 211–244.

Lavin, M. J., Freise, B., & Coombes, S. (1980). Transferred flavor aversions in adult rats. *Behavioural and Neural Biology, 28,* 25–33.

Posadas-Andrews, A., & Roper, T. J. (1983). Social transmission of food-preferences in adult rats. *Animal Behaviour, 31,* 265–271.

Strupp, B. J., & Levitsky, D. A. (1984). Social transmission of food preferences in adult hooded rats (*Rattus norvegicus*). *Journal of Comparative Psychology, 98,* 257–266.

Telle, H. J. (1966). Beitrag zur Kenntnis der Verhaltensweise von Ratten, vergleichend dargestellt bei *Rattus norvegicus* und *Rattus rattus. Zeitschrift für Angewandte Zoologie, 53,* 129–196.

Von Frisch, K. (1967). *The dance language and orientation of bees.* Cambridge: Belknap Press.

Waltz, E. C. (1982). Resource characteristics and the evolution of information centers. *American Naturalist, 119,* 73–90.

Ward, P., & Zahavi, A. (1973). The importance of certain assemblages of birds as 'information-centres' for food finding. *Ibis, 115,* 517–534.

Wenner, A. M. (1971). *The bee language controversy.* Boulder, CO: Educational Programs Improvement Corp.

7

Mechanisms, Ecology, and Population Diffusion of Socially Learned, Food-Finding Behavior in Feral Pigeons

Louis Lefebvre
McGill University

Boris Palameta
University of Cambridge,
McGill University

INTRODUCTION

The study of socially learned feeding behavior has traditionally focused on two distinct approaches: field descriptions of behavioral innovations thought to have been socially transmitted and controlled laboratory experiments on the mechanisms underlying social learning. Although social learning is often said to be rare in animals (e.g., Boyd & Richerson, 1983), field observations of possible social influences on a variety of learned food searching and handling behavior have been reported in the literature. A list (not intended to be exhaustive) of these field reports, along with some observations made in captivity, is presented in Table 7.1. Although such reports are intriguing in their diversity and often spectacular nature, many of them are frustratingly speculative and anecdotal. Skeptics can thus easily claim that social learning in animals has not been rigorously documented.

When attempts have been made in the laboratory to investigate the nature of the mechanisms involved in social learning phenomena, most of the experimental designs and tasks used have been unrelated to the types of behavior reported to be learned in the field, e.g., pigeons pecking at a disk (Bullock & Neuringer, 1977; Skinner, 1962) or at a Ping-Pong ball (Epstein, 1984), rats (Corson, 1967; Gardner & Engel, 1971; Jacoby & Dawson, 1969) and cats (Chesler, 1969; John, Chesler, Bartlett, & Victor, 1968) pressing on a lever,

Table 7.1
Reports of Possible Socially Transmitted Foraging Behavior

Reference	Species	Description of Behavior
Carpenter, 1887	Crab-Eating Macaque	Cracking oysters with stones
Manders, 1911	Crow	Pulling gristle from bones
Schorger, 1921	Magpie	Preying on livestock
Stephens, 1921		
Berry, 1922		
Bent, 1937	Black Vulture	Locating clumped food patches
Bent, 1940	Belted Kingfisher	Fish-catching by fledglings
Stager, 1941	Peregrine Falcon	Preying on bats
Bent, 1942	Ash-Throated Flycatcher & Black Phoebe	Insect-catching by fledglings
Morley, 1942	Marsh Tit	Taking bait from traps
*†Swynnerton, 1942	One species of Swallow (*Hirundo puella*) learning from another (*H. rustica*)	Avoiding noxious insects
Cushing, 1944	Various Birds of Prey	Nestlings and fledglings learning to recognize live prey items
Gibson-Hill, 1947	Great Frigatebird	"Play-fishing" for inanimate objects by juveniles
Buxton, 1948	Great Tit	Eating peanuts
Fisher & Hinde, 1949	Eleven species of British birds, especially Great & Blue Tits	Removing or tearing milk bottle tops to drink milk
von Steiniger, 1950	Norway Rat	Preying on sparrows and avoiding noxious foods
Liers, 1951	Canadian Otter	Young learning to recognize live prey items
Patterson, 1956	Greenfinch	Feeding on seeds of a shrub-fruit by cracking the stones
L. Tinbergen, 1960	Great Tit	Acquiring a "searching image" for a previously ignored prey item (*Panolis* caterpillars)
Hall, 1962	Chacma Baboon	An inexperienced individual increasing its diet range by eating the same foods as more experienced conspecifics
Stenhouse, 1962	Redpoll	Feeding on peach and apricot blossoms
*Ewer, 1963	Meerkat	Young learning to recognize live prey items
Stonehouse & Stonehouse, 1963	Ascension Island Frigatebird	Juveniles catching inanaimate objects from each other in mid-air: "play-kleptoparasitism"

(Continued)

TABLE 7.1 (*Continued*)

Reference	Species	Description of Behavior
*Hall & Goswell, 1964	Patas Monkey	Juveniles eating previously avoided novel foods (eggs, parsnips, black currant juice)
Hall & Schaller, 1964	California Sea Otter	Juveniles collecting and opening mussels, urchins, abalone, etc.
*†Turner, 1964	Sparrows & Chaffinches learning from each other, as well as from conspecifics	Eating previously avoided novel foods (colored bits of dough)
Bowman & Billeb, 1965	Galapagos Finch (*Geospiza difficilis*)	Puncturing the skin of seabirds and feeding on the blood
Kawai, 1965	Japanese Macaque	Washing sand from potatoes and wheat by dipping them in water
Kruuk & Turner, 1967	Cheetah	Prey-capture and killing by juveniles
*†Millikan & Bowman, 1967	One species of Galapagos Finch (*Geospiza conirostris*) learning from another (*Cactospiza pallida*)	Manipulating sticks to pry food items out of narrow cracks
Newton, 1967	Goldfinch & Linnet	Differences between populations in preferred seed diet
Norton-Griffiths, 1967	Oystercatcher	Fledglings opening mussels
Schaller, 1967	Tiger	Prey-capture and killing by juveniles
Ashmole & Tovar, 1968	Inca Tern	"Play-fishing" for inanimate objects by juveniles
Horn, 1968	Brewer's Blackbird	Locating clumped food patches
Morse, 1968	Nuthatch	Manipulating fallen pine bark scales to pry off attached scales, thus exposing insects
*†Rothschild & Ford, 1968	Starling learning from Mistle Thrust	Avoiding noxious novel food (grasshopper)
van Lawick-Goodall, 1968	Chimpanzee	Juveniles "fishing" for termites
*Alcock, 1969	Fork-Tailed Flycather	Eating previously avoided novel food (mimics of noxious butterflies)
†Cook, Brower, & Alcock, 1969	Mixed-species Flycatcher and Kiskadee flocks	Avoiding noxious foods
Marais, 1969	Chacma Baboon	Cracking fruit of the baobab tree by pounding it with stones
†Maclean, 1970	American Robin learning from Cedar Waxwing	Feeding on juniper berries by hovering

(*Continued*)

TABLE 7.1 *(Continued)*

Reference	Species	Description of Behavior
Murton, 1970	Wood Pigeon	Locating clumped food patches
Ewer, 1971	Black Rat	Feeding on nuts suspended from a wire
Hoese, 1971	Atlantic Bottlenose Dolphin	Capturing fish by herding them onto a sand bank
Stokes, 1971	Red Jungle Fowl	Chicks learning to recognize food items
Lecroy, 1972	Common Tern & Roseate Tern	Fish-catching by juveniles
*Menzel, 1972	Chimpanzee	Using large branches as ladders to avoid electric wiring at the base of trees and gain access to upper branches and leaves
Ransom & Rowell, 1972	Anubis Baboon	Infants learning to recognize food items
Schaller, 1972	Lion	Prey-capture and killing by juveniles
†Taylor, 1972	House Finch possibly learning from Hummingbird	Feeding on nectar from artificial feeders by hovering
Gandolfi & Parisi, 1973	Norway Rat	Diving and fishing for molluscs
*Jones & Kamil, 1973	Blue Jay	Manipulating sticks to reach otherwise inaccessible food
*Radakov, 1973	Pollock fish	Locating clumped food patches
*Rasa, 1973	Dwarf Mongoose	Infants learning to recognize live prey items
*Tayler & Saayman, 1973	Indian Ocean Bottlenose Dolphin	Manipulating a scraper to dislodge algae from sides and bottom of tank
van Lawick-Goodall, 1973	Chimpanzee	One population feeding on novel foods (papaya and grapefruit) which are avoided by another population
Krebs, 1974	Great Blue Heron	Locating clumped food patches
Barash, Donovan & Myrick, 1975	Glaucous-Winged Gull	Dropping clams on hard surfaces to crack them
Strum, 1975	Olive Baboon	Systematic predation on small birds and mammals
*Beck, 1976	Pigtailed Macaque	Manipulating a rake to reach an otherwise inaccessible food tray
Edwards, 1976	Moose	Young learning to recognize food items
*†Greenberg, 1976	Blue Spiny Lizard learn-	Eating previously avoided novel

(Continued)

TABLE 7.1 (*Continued*)

Reference	Species	Description of Behavior
	ing from Desert Iguana	food (lettuce)
*Jouventin, Pasteur, & Cambefort, 1976	Forest Baboon	Avoiding noxious food
*Welker, 1976	Galago	Capturing fish from water bowls
†Kushlan, 1977	Mixed-species Egret flocks	Locating clumped food patches
†MacDonald & Henderson, 1977	Mixed-species flocks of insectivorous tropical birds	Locating clumped food patches
†Rubenstein, Barnett, Ridgely, & Klopfer, 1977	Mixed-species Finch flocks	Locating clumped food patches
Sussmann, 1977	Ring-Tailed Lemur	Infants learning to recognize food items
†Greig-Smith, 1978	Mixed-species Sunbird and White-Eye flocks	Locating clumped food patches
*Wyrwicka, 1978	Cat	Kittens preferring the same diet as their mothers
McGrew, Tutin, & Baldwin, 1979	Chimpanzee	Differences between populations in "termite-fishing" techniques
Sugiyama & Koman, 1979	Chimpanzee	Cracking nuts with stones, and using various methods, including stick tools, to reach the lower branches and swing up into a fig tree with an unclimbable trunk
Springer, 1980	Coyote	Catching fish
*Weigl & Hanson, 1980	Red Squirrel	Cracking hickory nuts
Barnard & Sibly, 1981	Sparrow	Locating clumped food patches
†Caldwell, 1981	Mixed-species Heron flocks	Locating clumped food patches
Cambefort, 1981	Chacma Baboon and Vervet Monkey	Using artificial "clues" to find hidden bait
Waite, 1981	Rook	Locating clumped food patches
Barclay, 1982	Little Brown bat	Locating clumped food patches
Beck, 1982	Herring Gull	Dropping shellfish on hard surfaces to shatter them
Gayou, 1982	Green Jay	Manipulating twigs to probe under bark for insects
Nishida & Hiraiwa, 1982	Chimpanzee	Differences between populations in preferred ant species eaten

(*Continued*)

TABLE 7.1   (*Continued*)

Reference	Species	Description of Behavior
*Pitcher, Magurran, & Winfield, 1982	Minnow and Goldfish	Locating clumped food patches
Knight & Knight, 1983	Bald Eagle	Locating clumped food patches
McGrew, 1983	Chimpanzee	Differences between populations in preferred animal diet
Strum, 1983	Anubis Baboon	Scavenging gazelle carcasses
Takasaki, 1983	Chimpanzee	Eating novel food (mango)
Aisner & Terkel, 1985	Black Rat	Stripping and eating pine cones
*Anderson, 1985	Tonkean Macaques	Manipulating metal rods to reach otherwise inaccessible food
Erwin, Hafner, & Dugan, 1985	Little Egret	Locating clumped food patches
*Gaudet & Fenton, 1985	Three species of Vespertilionid Bats	Removing mealworms from alligator clips
Hamilton & Tilson, 1985	Chacma Baboon	Catching fish
Lopez & Lopez, 1985	Killer Whale	Hunting seals on shore, by "intentional stranding"
*Sumita, Kitahara-Frisch, & Norikoshi, 1985	Chimpanzee	Cracking walnuts with stones
Watts, 1985	Gorilla	Infants learning to recognize food items
*King, 1986	Orangutan	Manipulating ladles to extract food from cylindrical containers
*Lefebvre & Hewitt, 1986	Chimpanzee	Willingness to engage in profitable food exchange with a human experimenter
Whitehead, in press	Mantled Howling Monkey	Infants learning to recognize food items

*Observations made of captive animals
†Interspecific social learning

dogs pulling a food cart (Adler & Adler, 1977). (Exceptions to this trend include studies of food searching in great tits [Krebs, MacRoberts, & Cullen, 1972] and mixed-species pairs of chickadees [Krebs, 1973], acquisition of food preferences and diving behavior in rats [reviewed in Galef, 1985], cream-tub opening by chickadees [Sherry & Galef, 1984] and the ontogeny of food recognition in chicks [Suboski & Bartashunas, 1984].) Many laboratory studies have been unsuccessful in convincingly identifying the processes by which information is acquired during social learning because of inadequate controls or use of tasks that are too easy to allow discrimination between alternative explanations. Thus, the complexity of the information passed from one animal to another has yet to be precisely determined (see critical reviews by Davey, 1981; Davis, 1973; Galef, 1976; Mackintosh, 1974).

A third, more recent, tradition in social learning research has attempted to provide general theoretical models applicable to both human and nonhuman cases. This approach deals with mathematical models of cultural transmission at the population level (Boyd & Richerson, 1985; Cavalli-Sforza & Feldman, 1981; Fagen, 1981; Lumsden & Wilson, 1981; Mundinger, 1980; Pulliam, 1983). The goal of these models is to describe the rate of cultural diffusion under various conditions and to predict the kinds of environments where a capacity for culture is likely to be favored. Despite the complexity and mathematical rigor of the models, their assumptions and predictions are by and large empirically untested.

We believe that a thorough investigation of social learning in animals must simultaneously answer questions stemming from all three traditions. In fact, the processes that each of these traditions specifically deals with, i.e., mechanisms, ecology and population dynamics, may often interact at the causal level. For example, an arbitrarily chosen behavior that can be socially learned by an individually tested observer in the laboratory may not spread in a population studied in its natural environment. In the field, an innovation will only spread if it provides some advantage with respect to behavioral alternatives already present in the population. In the laboratory, these alternatives are unavailable to the animal during the experiment. Thus, we could theoretically see social learning in a wide variety of arbitrary laboratory situations, but rarely in the field. Second, population factors may affect social learning in a way that makes learning in the field very different from learning in a cage. The simultaneous presence of several observers and several demonstrators in the field may accelerate or inhibit learning. Third, the rate at which a behavioral innovation spreads in a population may depend on the amount of information transmitted during a demonstration, a variable that can only be determined in the controlled conditions of a laboratory experiment. Finally, differences in ecological variables may result in different social learning capacities in different species.

In this chapter, we present a case study indicating how the three traditions can be combined through an investigation of social learning of food-finding techniques in the feral pigeon (*Columba livia*). Specifically we address three questions: (1) what is the nature of the information transmitted from a demonstrator to an observer? (2) how does an innovation spread in a natural population? and (3) what ecological variables favor social learning? The feral pigeon is a good subject species for a study of this type because it is both easy to work with in the laboratory and easy to observe in the field, especially in urban environments. Feral pigeons eat an extremely wide range of foods and colonize many habitats. Thus occasions for learning occur frequently. Pigeons also feed in flocks and are thus exposed to the foraging techniques of conspecifics on a regular basis. Finally, pigeons are known to be able to learn from conspecifics in the laboratory (Epstein, 1984; Skinner, 1962; Zentall & Hogan, 1976).

THE NATURE OF THE INFORMATION TRANSMITTED

Social learning of foraging behavior has been attributed to a variety of mechanisms. The most complex of these mechanisms, observational learning, occurs when an animal copies a specific technique used by a conspecific searching for food by interacting with a specific set of features in the environment. As several authors have pointed out (e.g., Davis, 1973), the observer might be influenced by various aspects of the demonstrator's behavior: (1) the mere act of foraging (social facilitation), (2) the features in the environment with which the demonstrator is interacting (local enhancement), or (3) the precise food-finding technique (observational learning).

In order to show rigorously that observational learning underlies the diffusion of a feeding innovation, five conditions must be met: (1) inexperienced animals that are not given demonstrations by a conspecific model should not be able to learn the innovation by themselves; (2) animals given only information about where to find food (local enhancement) should not learn, or should learn more slowly, than animals given full demonstrations of both how and where to find food; (3) animals given partial experience at feeding by themselves in conditions similar to social test conditions should also not learn or should learn more slowly than animals given full demonstrations; (4) animals having observed a demonstration should be able to perform the innovation in the absence of the model, i.e., should not need social facilitation by the feeding model; (5) animals should use specific features of the model's technique when they perform the innovative feeding behavior. No study has yet examined all of these conditions in a single test case.

In a recent series of experiments, we have found that all five of the above conditions apply to pigeons learning to find seed hidden under a paper cover. Pigeons and several other Columbids routinely search for hidden seed by using their beaks to remove obstacles such as soil, sand, leaves, (Goodwin, 1983). Paper piercing is thus sufficiently similar to natural food-searching behavior to be ecologically valid as a laboratory task. On the other hand, it is sufficiently different from normal food searching for its introduction into feral pigeon flocks to be considered novel. Palameta and Lefebvre (1985) have tested conditions 1, 2, and 4. When experimentally naive pigeons could search for food during the model's demonstration, birds given full demonstrations learned very quickly, whereas birds shown only where to look learned at a slower rate (Figs. 7.1D and 7.1C, respectively). Furthermore, birds that had a model showing them only how to pierce the paper cover but not why (the model had no food under its cover)

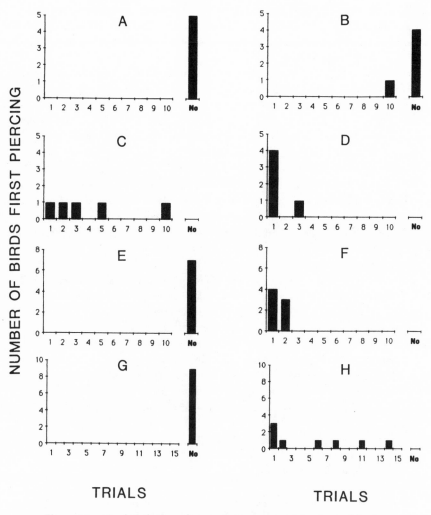

Figure 7.1. Number of pigeons first piercing on a given trial under the following experimental conditions: (A) no model; (B) model pierces but does not eat; (C) model does not pierce, but eats through pre-cut hole; (D) model pierces and eats; (E) same as C, except model removed before observer test; (F) same as D, except model removed before observer test; (G) same as A, except prior observer experience at feeding from uncovered box; (H) same as D, except prior observer experience at feeding from uncovered box. (A) to (F) modified from Palameta and Lefebvre (1985).

failed to learn, with one exception (Figure 7.1B). Thus, it appears that a reward must be associated with the motor act for it to be copied. Birds given no model whatsoever never learned (Figure 7.1A). When the experimentally naive pigeons could only search for food after the demonstration, birds that got a full demonstration learned, but those that were only shown where to look did not (Figures 1F and 7.1E, respectively).

Condition 3 was tested by allowing birds to have 4 days of experience at feeding from an uncovered food box prior to being tested with the paper cover (Lefebvre, 1985a). None of the birds tested without a model pierced within the 15 trials of the experiment, whereas all the birds given a model learned to pierce (Figures 7.1G and 7.1H). Palameta (1985) offers evidence that condition 5 also applies to pigeons. He presented experimentally naive birds with either correct or incorrect information from a model. Pigeons could find hidden seed either by piercing the center of a lid covering the seed or by pushing aside an unpierceable variant of this cover. Lids that required piercing and lids that required pushing were visually indistinguishable. For observers that were given the wrong information, either their model would pierce but observers were required to push or the model would push but observers were required to pierce. Birds given correct information, i.e., with lid types that matched those of their model, took significantly fewer pecks to find food than those given the wrong information. It appears that observers relied on specific information provided by the model, to the extent of being "fooled" by incorrect demonstrations.

Taken together, the experiments described here strongly suggest that observational learning is responsible for the social transmission of paper-piercing behavior in feral pigeons. Further experiments on the precision of technique imitation may have important consequences for cognitive ethology. An animal may rarely be able to tell the experimenter what it knows about its own behavior, but it may more easily show by imitation what it knows about the behavior of a conspecific.

DIFFUSION IN A POPULATION

Having isolated the mechanisms involved in the social learning of paper piercing by pigeons, we can now ask how population characteristics affect the spread of this behavior in a group setting. A novel food-finding behavior that is readily learned by individually caged observers often does not spread to more than a few pigeons in an aviary flock (Giraldeau & Lefebvre, 1986, 1987). Instead of performing the novel food-finding behavior, many birds in a flock will exploit discoveries of individuals that find food, a behavior that Barnard and Sibly (1981) have called *scrounging*. Kawai (1965) has also reported scrounging in the Japanese macaque troop that learned to separate sand from wheat by throwing it into the water. Of 6 individuals that were frequently seen to snatch wheat from other monkeys, 2 animals never learned the cleaning technique. In fact, Giraldeau and Lefebvre (1987) have shown experimentally that scrounging blocks observational learning; pigeons that passively obtain food from their demonstrator's performance of a novel food-finding behavior (removal of a stopper to allow grain to fall into a tray) are very poor at learning this behavior relative to birds that get no food during the demonstration. Scrounging opportunities were manipulated in these experiments by tilting a tray separating the cages of observer and model. As seed fell into the tray when the model removed the stopper on its seed container, the observer either obtained seed (i.e., scrounged) if the tray was tilted towards it, or did not obtain seed if the tray was kept horizontal. When birds in the scrounger group could no longer scrounge (the tray was horizontal), they learned to remove the stopper at the same rate as experimentally naive pigeons. Thus scrounging during a demonstration was equivalent to getting no demonstration at all. After repeated associations between the demonstrator's behavior and free food, observers may have learned to depend on the demonstrator for scrounging opportunities. In a captive flock, scroungers selectively followed birds that performed the food-finding behavior (Giraldeau & Lefebvre, 1987).

In theory, whether an animal will learn to perform a novel behavior or to scrounge from others' discoveries depends on the relative frequencies of performers and scroungers within the group. Through such frequency-dependent learning, the proportion of scroungers and performers in a group should eventually reach an equilibrium (Giraldeau, 1984). If the equilibrium point is reached when scroungers and performers obtain equal feeding payoffs, this is the learned equivalent of an evolutionarily stable strategy (Harley, 1981). If payoffs are unequal, one type or the other may be "making the best of a bad job" (Dawkins, 1980).

The potential effects of frequency-dependent learning were assessed by monitoring the diffusion of paper piercing in an aviary flock after the introduction of a pretrained demonstrator. In the aviary, only 4 out of 10 birds acquired the innovation, whereas 6 birds scrounged exclusively. In contrast, diffusion of the novel behavior was much more rapid in a feral pigeon population tested in the field (Figure 7.2A). When the urban flock was presented with the paper-piercing task at one of its main foraging sites, 24 previously naive birds learned, whereas only 4 birds specialized on scrounging (Lefebvre, 1986). Demonstrators in this case were 4 pretrained pigeons, randomly chosen from the flock when it was captured, individually tagged, and released back to the capture site. Natural shaping (Galef, 1980) and spontaneous individual learning are unlikely explanations for the rapid diffusion of paper piercing in the urban flock because (1) prior experience at feeding from a pierced box or even widening a partially pierced hole in a paper cover were not prerequisites for subsequent performance of the task, (2) a second urban flock with no pretrained demonstrators learned much more slowly than the flock with demonstrators and then only because of accidental tearing due

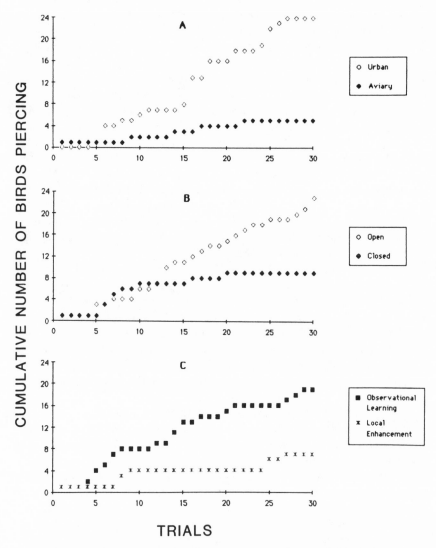

Figure 7.2. Cumulative number of pigeons piercing as a function of trials (A) in an urban flock and an aviary flock presented with paper-covered food boxes; (B) in computer simulations comparing an open and a closed population, under equivalent conditions of frequency-dependent learning and learning rate distributions; (C) in computer simulations comparing two equally open populations with frequency distributions of learning rates typical of observational learning and local enhancement, respectively, under equivalent conditions of frequency-dependence. (A) modified from Lefebvre (1986).

to birds walking on rain-soaked paper covers, (3) birds in the aviary flock showed no tendency to approach or pierce the paper-covered box prior to the introduction of a demonstrator.

Why is diffusion more rapid in an urban flock than in a laboratory flock? Foraging flocks of urban pigeons are open populations, with infrequent attendance by some individuals and a fairly high turnover rate of residence by more regular birds (Lefebvre, 1985b). This means that experienced piercers are often absent and that naive newcomers arrive frequently. These effects presumably combine to destabilize a frequency-dependent equilibrium between piercers and scroungers. Stochastic simulations show that given the existence of frequency-dependent learning, the effect of an open population is sufficient to produce diffusion curves (Figure 7.2B) similar to those obtained empirically. In these simulations, the frequency-dependent effect starts as soon as one animal has learned. It reaches an equilibrium point (no further learning) when the proportion of piercers reaches .18, (i.e., 2 of 11), the proportion of birds that accounted for 98% of piercings in the aviary. The value used to estimate openness of the population, (i.e., 8% of birds replaced per trial) is based on a combination of the three effects known to occur in the field: (1) occasional visits by transients, (2) sporadic attendance by regulars and (3) turnover rate of residents (Lefebvre, 1985b).

Using the same parameters, we can also see that the amount of information transmitted from demonstrator to observer will affect the slope of the diffusion curves (Figure 7.2C). As Palameta and Lefebvre (1985) have shown, different amounts of information lead to different frequency distributions of learning rates (See Figure 7.1). The contrasting learning rate distributions used in the simulations were based on those depicted in Figs. 7.1C and 7.1E (local enhancement) and Figures 7.1D, 7.1F and 7.1H (observational learning) respectively. The simulations show that differences in mechanisms of transmission not only lead to different learning rates for caged observers faced with a single model, but also to different diffusion rates of a novel behavior in a population. Thus, as we suggested in the introduction, mechanisms and population factors are not simply different levels of explanation, but also interacting levels of causation.

All of the diffusion curves presented in Figure 7.2 share one characteristic; all differ from the basic sigmoid function, derived from the logistic equation, that is a typical feature of previous mathematical models of cultural transmission (Cavalli-Sforza & Feldman, 1981; Fagen, 1981; Lumsden & Wilson, 1981). Caution should be exercised in selecting assumptions for these mathematical models: If the assumptions are unrealistic and do not reflect processes known to affect diffusion curves, the general validity of the models will suffer. More specifically, failure to consider, for instance, the potential inhibitory effects of frequency-depedent learning might lead one to predict wrongly the rapid cultural diffusion of behavioral traits in cases where diffusion would, in fact, stop at very low values (Giraldeau & Lefebvre, 1987).

SPECIES DIFFERENCES IN SOCIAL LEARNING

Observational learning, like many other forms of complex learning, is often perceived to be a kind of taxonomic status symbol (Beck, 1982) with the result that considerations of species differences are often biased from the start. Secondary sources, although commonly assuming that examples of social learning in "higher" mammals, particularly primates, are indicative of complex mental processing, are more skeptical when considering the intricacy or even existence of socially learned behavior in other species (e.g., Barnett, 1981; Clementson-Mohr, 1982; Lumsden & Wilson, 1981). Yet our data indicate that social learning in the pigeon may be a complex process at the cognitive level, in that it can involve the acquisition of precise, detailed information. Furthermore, we have seen that pigeons learn new food-finding techniques very quickly, whereas some primates seem very slow at social learning. For instance, novel food-handling techniques spread to 20–30 Japanese macaques over a period of 10 years (Kawai, 1965), as opposed to 55 days in pigeons (Lefebvre, 1986). Cambefort (1981) has shown that observational learning of a simple food-finding task is also very slow in vervet monkeys.

Lefebvre, Maine, and Horrocks (unpublished data) have found similar results in vervets using a paper-piercing task analogous to the one described earlier. Peanuts or banana slices were hidden inside hollow pieces of bamboo with paper covers taped over holes that allowed access to the food. The baited pieces of bamboo were presented to a small feral troop of vervet monkeys at one of its regular foraging sites in Barbados. One juvenile male spontaneously learned to find the food, but the behavior failed to spread to any other animal in the troop despite the fact that (1) the juvenile demonstrated the paper-tearing technique a total of 76 times, (2) an average of 9.6 troop members per demonstration were within observational distance (10 m), (3) naive monkeys intently watched demonstrations from very close quarters (within 1 m) on 14 occasions, (4) no scrounging by the others or overt defense of the unopened bamboos by the juvenile ever occurred, (5) monkeys were hungry throughout the tests, because they immediately accepted unconcealed food offered at the end of a few randomly selected trials, and (6) animals were familiar with the experimenters, with bamboo, and with the foods offered.

We believe that ecological variables, not subjective assessments of intelligence, are most likely to explain species differences in social learning of foraging behavior. Feral pigeons are both gregarious and highly opportunistic foragers (Goodwin, 1960; Murton, Coombs, & Thearle, 1971; Murton & Westwood, 1966). An opportunistic life-style, favored by an unpredictable food supply and frequent exposure to novel potential foods, requires the rapid processing of new environmental information. Situations where an opportunistic animal could most efficiently acquire such information from an experienced conspecific are, even if rare, likely to be critical. Gregarious living ensures that conspecifics are always there to be copied.

In fact, group living may provide not only opportunities for social learning, but also the selective pressure for its evolution. One frequent consequence of gregariousness is competition for limited resources among group members. Those members that can obtain the most information by watching others may be at a competitive advantage, particularly in species with frequent exposure to novel foraging opportunities, in which learning is important. Thus, group living may provide the fuel for a cognitive arms race in which increasingly complex social learning mechanisms, which allow for the rapid copying of others' innovative behavior, are positively selected. If individual differences in food preference (Giraldeau & Lefebvre, 1985), habitat use (Lefebvre & Giraldeau, 1984) and foraging skills (Giraldeau, 1984) are overlaid on these effects, novel behavior may be introduced and diffused at a high rate in pigeon populations.

Comparative studies of social learning abilities in related species are one way of testing hypotheses about the importance of ecological factors. Klopfer (1959) first proposed that propensity to imitate was associated with opportunistic feeding habits. More specifically, he predicted that the more opportunistic a species is, the more it needs to attend to the effects of potentially unpalatable novel foods on conspecifics. This prediction is supported by his (1961) study in which learning of a food avoidance response by pairs of birds was retarded in the greenfinch relative to the great tit, a more opportunistic species. Gandolfi (1975) has also pointed out the potential importance of opportunism. More recently, Sasvári (1979, 1985) has reported apparent differences in social learning abilities in several tit and thrush species. Sasvári concluded that these differences correlate with species differences in opportunism: Great tits and blackbirds are claimed to be both the best social learners in their respective groups and the most opportunistic in terms of habitat use.

The problem with comparative studies is that differences in performance on a given task can always be attributed to factors other than the one specifically being tested. For instance, opportunism in habitat use often means colonization of humanized environments. This implies a tolerance for humans that could in itself explain the results of a comparative learning experiment. Clearly, adequate controls are needed for such nonspecific effects.

Social learning studies have a unique position in comparative learning research because they often feature a built-in control group: animals that are tested without a demonstrator. If the task is easy enough for learning to occur without a demonstrator then the *relative* rate of learning in animals given demonstrations and animals not given demonstrations is an appropriate comparative measure. Variables that are nonspecific to the social learning process per se, e.g., tolerance of the human experimenter, response to caging and to the testing apparatus, motor or cognitive difficulty of the task to be learned, should influence both groups in the same way. The relationship between the observer and the model, e.g., mate, stranger, dominant, and so forth, should also be controlled, because differences in social structure (i.e., the network of relationships between group members) are thought to lead to species differences in social learning in primates (Cambefort, 1981).

Columbids are a convenient group for such comparative studies. Learning abilities of *Columba livia* and *Streptopelia risoria* have been well studied in the lab. Some of the most well known avian opportunistic colonizers are Columbids: *C. livia* in temperate regions, *S. decaocto* in Europe (Coombs, Isaacson, Murton, Thearle, & Westwood, 1981) *S. senegalensis* in Africa (Goodwin, 1983), *S. chinensis* introduced in Australia (Frith, 1982). All of these species are gregarious in addition to being opportunistic. If we wish to study these two variables separately, we need a species that is gregarious but conservative and specialized or a species that is opportunistic but solitary. One suitable species is the Zenaida dove of Barbados (*Zenaida aurita*), which is reported to be both highly opportunistic in urban areas of the island (Haverschmidt, 1969; Pinchon, 1963) and non-gregarious (Devas, 1970). A recent study of this species provides quantitative confirmation of these reports (Lefebvre, unpublished data). Typical foraging group size for coastal populations is around 1.5 individuals. Pairs of birds defend exclusive year-found territories. This is in marked contrast to the typical foraging group size of *C. livia* in Barbados and in central Montréal, which is around 40–50 birds (Lefebvre, unpublished data). If gregariousness is not an important factor and opportunism is by itself a sufficient condition for social learning to evolve, then *Z. aurita* and *C. livia* should not differ in a comparative test. If on the contrary gregariousness is a necessary condition, then *C. livia* should outperform *Z. aurita*. These predictions are currently being tested using a task similar to the ones described in this chapter.

CONCLUSION

The study of cultural learning has too often been conducted in disciplines that are relatively isolated from each other, e.g., psychology, population biology, ethology. This has led to the development of three discrete research traditions that emphasize learning mechanisms, mathematical models of cultural diffusion and evolution, and field descriptions, respectively. By combining the three approaches, i.e., by doing field experiments based on controlled laboratory work and by taking into account variation in ecological parameters of the species tested, we can achieve a more thorough understanding of both how and why social learning is important to animals.

ACKNOWLEDGMENTS

Funding for this work was provided by an NSERC operating grant to L.L. and NSERC and FCAR scholarships to B.P. We are grateful to Alastair Inman for writing the simulation program and to Luc-Alain Giraldeau and Patrick Bateson for their stimulating comments and criticism.

REFERENCES

Adler, L. L., & Adler, H. E. (1977). Ontogeny of observational learning in the dog (*Canis familiaris*). *Developmental Psychobiology, 10,* 267–271.

Aisner, R., & Terkel, J. (1985). *Habitat exploitation through cultural transmission: Pine cone feeding behavior in black rats.* Paper presented at the 19th International Ethological Conference, Toulouse, France.

Alcock, J. (1969). Observational learning by fork-tailed flycatchers (*Muscivora tyrannus*). *Animal Behaviour, 17,* 652–657.

Anderson, J. R. (1985). Development of tool use to obtain food in a captive group of *Macaca tonkeana. Journal of Human Evolution, 14,* 637–646.

Ashmole, N. P., & Tovar, H. (1968). Prolonged parental care in royal terns and other birds. *Auk, 85,* 90–100.

Barash, D. P., Donovan, P., & Myrick, R. (1975). Clam dropping behavior of the glaucous-winged gull (*Larus glaucescens*). *Wilson Bulletin, 87,* 60–64.

Barclay, R. M. R. (1982). Interindividual use of echolocation calls: eavesdropping by bats. *Behavioral Ecology and Sociobiology, 10,* 271–275.

Barnard, C. J., & Sibly, R. M. (1981). Producers and scroungers: A general model and its application to feeding flocks of house sparrows. *Animal Behaviour, 29,* 543–550.

Barnett, S. A. (1981). *Modern ethology.* New York: Oxford University Press.

Beck, B. B. (1976). Tool use by captive pigtailed macaques. *Primates, 17,* 301–310.

Beck, B. B. (1982). Chimpocentrism: Bias in cognitive ethology. *Journal of Human Evolution, 11,* 3–17.

Bent, A. C. (1937). *Life histories of North American birds of prey. Part 1.* United States National Museum Bulletin 167.

Bent, A. C. (1940). *Life histories of North American cuckoos, goatsuckers, hummingbirds and their allies.* United States National Museum Bulletin 176.

Bent, A. C. (1942). *Life histories of North American flycatchers, larks, swallows and their allies.* United States National Museum Bulletin 179.

Berry, S. S. (1922). Magpies versus livestock: An unfortunate new chapter in avian depredations. *Condor, 24,* 13–17.

Bowman, R. I., & Billeb, S. L. (1965). Blood-eating in a Galapagos finch. *Living Bird, 4,* 29–44.

Boyd, R., & Richerson, P. J. (1983). The cultural transmission of acquired variation: Effects on genetic fitness. *Journal of Theoretical Biology, 100,* 567–596.

Boyd, R., & Richerson, P. J. (1985). *Culture and the evolutionary process*. Chicago: University of Chicago Press.

Bullock, D., & Neuringer, A. (1977). Social learning by following: an analysis. *Journal of the Experimental Analysis of Behavior, 27*, 127–135.

Buxton, E. J. M. (1948). Tits and peanuts. *British Birds, 41*, 229–232.

Caldwell, G. S. (1981). Attraction to tropical mixed-species heron flocks: proximate mechanism and consequences. *Behavioral Ecology and Sociobiology, 8*, 99–103.

Cambefort, J. P. (1981). A comparative study of culturally transmitted patterns of feeding habits in the chacma baboon *Papio ursinus* and the vervet monkey *Cercopithecus aethiops*. *Folia Primatologica, 36*, 243–263.

Carpenter, A. (1887). Monkeys opening oysters. *Nature, 36*, 53.

Cavalli-Sforza, L. L., & Feldman, M. W. (1981). *Cultural transmission and evolution: A quantitative approach*. Princeton: Princeton University Press.

Chesler, P. (1969). Maternal influence in learning by observation in kittens. *Science, 166*, 901–903.

Clementson-Mohr, D. (1982). Towards a social-cognitive explanation of imitation development: In G. Butterworth & P. Light (Eds.), *Social cognition: Studies of the development of understanding* (pp. 53–74). Chicago: University of Chicago Press.

Cook, L. M., Brower, L. P., & Alcock, J. (1969). An attempt to verify mimetic advantage in a neotropical environment. *Evolution, 23*, 339–345.

Coombs, C. F. B., Isaacson, A. J., Murton, R. K., Thearle, R. J. P., & Westwood, N. J. (1981). Collared doves (*Streptopelia decaocto*) in urban habitats. *Journal of Applied Ecology, 18*, 41–62.

Corson, J. A. (1967). Observational learning of a lever-pressing response. *Psychonomic Science, 7*, 197–198.

Cushing, J. E. (1944). The relation of nonheritable food habits to evolution. *Condor, 46*, 265–271.

Davey, G. C. L. (1981). *Animal learning and conditioning*. London: Macmillan.

Davis, J. M. (1973). Imitation: a review and critique. In P. P. G. Bateson & P. H. Klopfer (Eds.), *Perspectives in ethology* (Vol. 1, pp. 43–72). New York: Plenum.

Dawkins, R. (1980). Good strategy or evolutionarily stable strategy? In G. W. Barlow & J. Silverberg (Eds.), *Sociobiology: Beyond nature/nurture?* (pp. 331–367). Boulder, CO: Westview Press.

Devas, R. P. (1970). *Birds of Grenada, St. Vincent and the Grenadines*. St. George's, Grenada: Careenage Press.

Edwards, J. (1976). Learning to eat by following the mother in moose calves. *American Midland Naturalist, 96*, 229–232.

Epstein, R. (1984). Spontaneous and deferred imitation in the pigeon. *Behavioural Processes, 9*, 347–354.

Erwin, R. M., Hafner, H., & Dugan, P. (1985). Differences in the feeding behavior of little egrets (*Egretta garzetta*) in two habitats in the Camargue, France. *Wilson Bulletin, 97*, 534–538.

Ewer, R. F. (1963). The behavior of the meerkat, *Suricata suricatta* (Schreber). *Zeitschrift für Tierpsychologie, 20*, 570–607.

Ewer, R. F. (1971). The biology and behavior of a free-living population of black rats (*Rattus rattus*). *Animal Behaviour Monographs, 4*, 127–174.

Fagen, R. M. (1981). *Animal play behavior.* New York: Oxford University Press.

Fisher, J., & Hinde, R. A. (1949). The opening of milk bottles by birds. *British Birds, 42,* 347–357.

Frith, H. J. (1982). *Pigeons and doves of Australia.* Adelaide: Rigby.

Galef, B. G., Jr. (1976). Social transmission of acquired behavior: A discussion of tradition and social learning in vertebrates. In J. S. Rosenblatt, R. A. Hinde, E. Shaw, & C. Beer (Eds.), *Advances in the study of behavior* (Vol. 6, pp. 77–100). New York: Academic Press.

Galef, B. G., Jr. (1980). Diving for food: Analysis of a possible case of social learning in wild rats *(Rattus norvegicus). Journal of Comparative and Physiological Psychology, 94,*416–425.

Galef, B. G., Jr. (1985). Social learning in wild Norway rats. In T. D. Johnston & A. T. Pietrewicz (Eds.), *Issues in the ecological study of learning* (pp. 143–166). Hillsdale, NJ: Lawrence Erlbaum Associates.

Gandolfi, G. (1975). Social learning in non-primate animals. *Bollettino di Zoologia, 42,* 311–329.

Gandolfi, G., & Parisi, V. (1973). Ethological aspects of predation by rats, *Rattus norvegicus* (Berkenhout), on bivalves *Unio pictorum,* L. and *Cerastoderma lamarcki* (Reeve). *Bollettino di Zoologia, 40,* 69–74.

Gardner, E. L., & Engel, D. R. (1971). Imitational and social facilitatory aspects of observational learning in the laboratory rat. *Psychonomic Science, 25,* 5–6.

Gaudet, C. L., & Fenton, M. B. (1984). Observational learning in three species of insectivorous bats (Chiroptera). *Animal Behaviour, 32,* 385–388.

Gayou, D. C. (1982). Tool use by green jays. *Wilson Bulletin, 94,* 593–594.

Gibson-Hill, C. A. (1947). Notes on the birds of Christmas Island. *Raffles Museum and Library, Singapore, Bulletin, 18,* 87–165.

Giraldeau, L.-A. (1984). Group foraging: The skill pool effect and frequency-dependent learning. *American Naturalist, 124,* 72–79.

Giraldeau, L.-A., & Lefebvre, L. (1985). Individual feeding preferences in feral rock dove flocks. *Canadian Journal of Zoology, 63,* 189–191.

Giraldeau, L.-A., & Lefebvre, L. (1986). Exchangeable producer and scrounger roles in a captive flock of feral pigeons: A case for the skill pool effect. *Animal Behaviour, 34,* 797–803.

Giraldeau, L.-A., & Lefebvre, L. (1987). Scrounging prevents cultural transmission of food-finding behaviour in pigeons. *Animal Behaviour, 35,* 387–394.

Goodwin, D. (1960). Comparative ecology of pigeons in inner London. *British Birds, 53,* 201–212.

Goodwin, D. (1983). *Pigeons and doves of the world* (3rd ed.). Ithaca, NY: Cornell University Press.

Greenberg, N. (1976). Observations of social feeding in lizards. *Herpetologica, 32,* 348–352.

Greig-Smith, P. W. (1978). Imitative foraging in mixed-species flocks of Seychelles birds. *Ibis, 120,* 233–235.

Hall, K. R. L. (1962). Numerical data, maintenance activities and locomotion of the wild chacma baboon, *Papio ursinus. Proceedings of the Zoological Society of London, 139,* 181–220.

Hall, K. R. L., & Goswell, M. J. (1964). Aspects of social learning in captive patas monkeys. *Primates, 5,* 59–70.

Hall, K. R. L., & Schaller, G. B. (1964). Tool-using behavior of the California sea otter. *Journal of Mammalogy, 45,* 287–298.

Hamilton, W. J., III, & Tilson, R. L. (1985). Fishing baboons at desert waterholes. *American Journal of Primatology, 8,* 255–257.

Harley, C. B. (1981). Learning the evolutionarily stable strategy. *Journal of Theoretical Biology, 89,* 611–633.

Haverschmidt, F. (1969). The *Zenaida* dove on Barbados. *Ibis, 111,* 613.

Hoese, H. D. (1971). Dolphin feeding out of water in a salt marsh. *Journal of Mammalogy, 52,* 222–223.

Horn, H. S. (1968). The adaptive significance of colonial nesting in the Brewer's blackbird (*Euphagus cyanocephalus*). *Ecology, 49,* 682–694.

Jacoby, K. E., & Dawson, M. E. (1969). Observation and shaping learning: a comparison using Long Evans rats. *Psychonomic Science, 16,* 257–258.

John, E. R., Chesler, P., Bartlett, F., & Victor, I. (1968). Observation learning in cats. *Science, 159,* 1489–1491.

Jones, T., & Kamil, A. (1973). Tool-making and tool-using in the northern blue jay. *Science, 180,* 1076–1078.

Jouventin, P., Pasteur, G., & Cambefort, J. P. (1976). Observational learning of baboons and avoidance of mimics. Exploratory tests. *Evolution, 31,* 214–218.

Kawai, M. (1965). Newly acquired pre-cultural behavior of the natural troop of Japanese monkeys on Koshima Inlet. *Primates, 6,* 1–30.

King, B. J. (1986). Individual differences in tool-using by two captive orangutans (*Pongo pygmaeus*). In D. M. Taub & F. A. King (Eds.), *Current perspectives in primate social dynamics* (pp. 469–475). New York: Van Nostrand Reinhold.

Klopfer, P. H. (1959). Social interactions in discrimination learning with special reference to feeding behavior in birds. *Behaviour, 14,* 282–299.

Klopfer, P. H. (1961). Observational learning in birds: the establishment of behavioural modes. *Behaviour, 17,* 71–80.

Knight, S. K., & Knight, R. L. (1983). Aspects of food finding by wintering bald eagles. *Auk, 100,* 477–484.

Krebs, J. R. (1973). Social learning and the significance of mixed-species flocks of chickadees (*Parus* spp.). *Canadian Journal of Zoology, 51,* 1275–1288.

Krebs, J. R. (1974). Colonial nesting and social feeding as strategies for exploiting food resources in the great blue heron (*Ardea herodias*). *Behaviour, 51,* 99–134.

Krebs, J. R., MacRoberts, M. H., & Cullen, J. M. (1972). Flocking and feeding in the great tit *Parus major*—an experimental study. *Ibis, 114,* 507–530.

Kruuk, H., & Turner, M. (1967). Comparative notes on predation by lion, leopard, cheetah and wild dog in the Serengeti Area, East Africa. *Mammalia, 31,* 1–26.

Kushlan, J. A. (1977). The significance of plumage colour in the formation of feeding aggregations of Ciconiiforms. *Ibis, 119,* 361–364.

Lecroy, M. (1972). Young common and roseate terns learning to fish. *Wilson Bulletin, 84,* 201–202.

Lefebvre, L. (1985a). *Cultural transmission of a novel food-finding behavior in pigeons.* Paper presented at the 19th International Ethological Conference, Toulouse, France.

Lefebvre, L. (1985b). Stability of flock composition in urban pigeons. *Auk, 102,* 886–888.

Lefebvre, L. (1986). Cultural diffusion of a novel food-finding behaviour in urban pigeons: An experimental field test. *Ethology, 71,* 295–304.

Lefebvre, L., & Giraldeau, L.-A. (1984). Daily feeding site use of urban pigeons. *Canadian Journal of Zoology, 62,* 1425–1428.

Lefebvre, L., & Hewitt, T. A. (1986). Food exchange in captive chimpanzees. In D. M. Taub & F. A. King (Eds.), *Current perspectives in primate social dynamics* (pp. 476–486). New York: Van Nostrand Reinhold.

Liers, E. E. (1951). Notes on the river otter (*Lutra canadensis*). *Journal of Mammalogy, 32,* 1–9.

Lopez, J. C., & Lopez, D. (1985). Killer whales (*Orcinus orca*) of Patagonia, and their behavior of intentional stranding while hunting nearshore. *Journal of Mammalogy, 66,* 181–183.

Lumsden, C. J., & Wilson, E. O. (1981). *Genes, mind and culture: the coevolutionary process.* Cambridge, MA; Harvard University Press.

MacDonald, D. W., & Henderson, D. G. (1977). Aspects of the behaviour and ecology of mixed-species bird flocks in Kashmir. *Ibis, 119,* 481–491.

Mackintosh, N. J. (1974). *The psychology of animal learning.* New York: Academic Press.

Maclean, S. F. (1970). Social stimulation modifies the feeding behavior of the American robin. *Condor, 72,* 499–500.

Manders, N. (1911). An investigation into the validity of Müllerian and other forms of mimicry, with special reference to the islands of Bourbon, Mauritius, and Ceylon. *Proceedings of the Zoological Society of London, 2,* 696–749.

Marais, E. (1969). *The soul of the ape.* New York: Atheneum.

McGrew, W. C. (1983). Animal foods in the diets of wild chimpanzees (*Pan troglodytes*): Why cross-cultural variation? *Journal of Ethology, 1,* 46–61.

McGrew, W. C., Tutin, C. E. G., & Baldwin, P. J. (1979). Chimpanzees, tools, and termites: cross-cultural comparisons of Senegal, Tanzania and Rio Muni. *Man, 14,* 185–214.

Menzel, E. W. (1972). Spontaneous invention of ladders in a group of young chimpanzees. *Folia Primatologica, 17,* 87–106.

Millikan, G. C., & Bowman, R. I. (1967). Observations on Galapagos tool-using finches in captivity. *Living Bird, 6,* 23–41.

Morley, A. (1942). Effects of baiting on the marsh-tit. *British Birds, 35,* 261–266.

Morse, D. H. (1968). The use of tools by brown-headed nuthatches. *Wilson Bulletin, 80,* 220–224.

Mundinger, P. C. (1980). Animal cultures and a general theory of cultural evolution. *Ethology and Sociobiology, 1,* 183–223.

Murton, R. K. (1970). Why do some bird species feed in flocks? *Ibis, 113,* 534–536.

Murton, R. K., Coombs, C. F. B., & Thearle, M. J. P. (1972). Ecological studies of the feral pigeon *Columba livia* var. II: Flock behavior and social organization. *Journal of Applied Ecology, 9,* 875–899.

Murton, R. K., & Westwood, N. J. (1966). The foods of the rock dove and feral pigeon. *Bird Study, 13,* 130–146.

Newton, I. (1967). Evolution and ecology of some British finches. *Ibis, 109,* 33–99.

Nishida, T., & Hiraiwa, M. (1982). Natural history of a tool-using behavior by wild chimpanzees in feeding upon wood-boring ants. *Journal of Human Evolution, 11,* 73–99.

Norton-Griffiths, M. (1967). Some ecological aspects of the feeding behavior of the oystercatcher (*Haematopus ostralegus*) on the edible mussel *Mytilus edulis*. *Ibis, 109,* 412–424.

Palameta, B. (1985). *Cognitive mechanisms of observational learning in canaries and pigeons.* Paper presented at the 19th International Ethological Conference, Toulouse, France.

Palameta, B., & Lefebvre, L. (1985). The social transmission of a food-finding technique in pigeons: What is learned? *Animal Behaviour, 33,* 892–896.

Pettersson, M. (1956). Diffusion of a new habit among greenfinches. *Nature, 177,* 709–710.

Pinchon, R. (1963). *Faune des Antilles françaises: les oiseaux.* Fort-de-France: Muséum National d'Histoire Naturelle.

Pitcher, T. J., Magurran, A. E., & Winfield, I. J. (1982). Fish in larger shoals find food faster. *Behavioral Ecology and Sociobiology, 10,* 149–151.

Pulliam, H. R. (1983). On the theory of gene-culture co-evolution in a variable environment. In R. L. Mellgren (Ed.), *Animal cognition and behavior* (pp. 427–443). Amsterdam: North-Holland.

Radakov, D. V. (1973). *Schooling in the ecology of fish.* New York: Wiley.

Ransom, T. W., & Rowell, T. E. (1972). Early social development of feral baboons. In F. E. Poirier (Ed.), *Primate socialization* (pp. 104–144). New York: Random House.

Rasa, O. A. E. (1973). Prey-capture, feeding techniques and their ontogeny in the African dwarf mongoose, *Helogale undulata rufula*. *Zeitschrift für Tierpsychologie, 32,* 449–488.

Rubenstein, D. I., Barnett, R. J., Ridgely, R. S., & Klopfer, P. H. (1977). Adaptive advantages of mixed-species feeding flocks among seed-eating finches in Costa Rica. *Ibis, 119,* 10–21.

Rothschild, M., & Ford, B. (1968). Warning signals from a starling *Sturnus vulgaris* observing a bird rejecting unpalatable prey. *Ibis, 110,* 104–105.

Sasvári, L. (1979). Observational learning in great, blue and marsh tits. *Animal Behaviour, 27,* 767–771.

Sasvári, L. (1985). Different observational learning capacity in juvenile and adult individuals of congeneric bird species. *Zeitschrift für Tierpsychologie, 69,* 293–304.

Schaller, G. B. (1967). *The deer and the tiger.* Chicago: University of Chicago Press.

Schaller, G. B. (1972). *The Serengeti lion.* Chicago: University of Chicago Press.

Schorger, A. W. (1921). An attack on live stock by magpies (*Pica pica hudsonia*). *Auk, 38,* 276–277.

Sherry, D. F., & Galef, B. G., Jr. (1984). Cultural transmission without imitation: Milk bottle opening by birds. *Animal Behaviour, 32,* 937–938.

Skinner, B. F. (1962). Two "synthetic social relations". *Journal of the Experimental Analysis of Behavior, 5,* 531–533.

Springer, J. T. (1980). Fishing behavior of coyotes on the Columbia River, Southcentral Washington. *Journal of Mammalogy, 61,* 373–374.

Stager, K. E. (1941). A group of bat-eating duck hawks. *Condor, 43,* 137–139.

Stenhouse, D. (1962). A new habit of the redpoll *Carduelis flammea* in New Zealand. *Ibis, 104,* 250–252.

Stephens, T. C. (1921). Magpies and live stock. *Auk, 38,* 458–459.

Stokes, A. W. (1971). Parental and courtship feeding in red jungle fowl. *Auk, 88,* 21–29.

Stonehouse, B., & Stonehouse, S. (1963). The frigate bird *Fregata aquila* of Ascension Island. *Ibis, 103b,* 409–422.

Strum, S. C. (1975). Primate predation: Interim report on the development of a tradition in a troop of olive baboons. *Science, 187,* 755–757.

Strum, S. C. (1983). Baboon cues for eating meat. *Journal of Human Evolution, 12,* 327–336.

Suboski, M. D., & Bartashunas, C. (1984). Mechanisms for social transmission of pecking preferences to neonatal chicks. *Journal of Experimental Psychology: Animal Behavior Processes, 10,* 182–194.

Sugiyama, Y., & Koman, J. (1979). Tool-using and -making behavior in wild chimpanzees at Bossou, Guinea. *Primates, 20,* 513–524.

Sumita, K., Kitahara-Frisch, J., & Norikoshi, K. (1985). The acquisition of stone-tool use in captive chimpanzees. *Primates, 26,* 168–181.

Sussmann, R. W. (1977). Socialization, social structure, and ecology of two sympatric species of *Lemur*. In S. Chevalier-Skolnikoff & F. E. Poirier (Eds.), *Primate biosocial development* (pp. 515–528). New York: Garland.

Swynnerton, C. F. M. (1942). Observations and experiments in Africa by the late C. F. M. Swynnerton on wild birds eating butterflies and the preference shown. *Proceedings of the Linnean Society of London, 154,* 10–46.

Takasaki, H. (1983). Mahale chimpanzees taste mangoes-toward acquisition of a new food item. *Primates, 24,* 273–275.

Tayler, C. K., & Saayman, G. S. (1973). Imitative behaviour by Indian Ocean bottlenose dolphins (*Tursiops aduneus*) in captivity. *Behaviour, 44,* 286–298.

Taylor, P. M. (1972). Hovering behavior by house finches. *Condor, 74,* 219–221.

Tinbergen, L. (1960). The natural control of insects in pinewoods. I. Factors influencing the intensity of predation by songbirds. *Archives Néerlandaises de Zoologie, 13,* 265–343.

Turner, E. R. A. (1964). Social feeding in birds. *Behaviour, 24,* 1–46.

van Lawick-Goodall, J. (1968). The behaviour of free-living chimpanzees in the Gombe Stream reserve. *Animal Behaviour Monographs, 1,* 161–311.

van Lawick-Goodall, J. (1973). Cultural elements in a chimpanzee community. In E. Menzel (Ed.), *Precultural primate behavior* (pp. 144–184). Basel: Karger.

von Steiniger, F. (1950). Beiträge zur soziologie und sonstigen Biologie der Wanderratte. *Zeitschrift für Tierpsychologie, 7,* 356–379.

Waite, R. K. (1981). Local enhancement for food-finding by rooks (*Corvus frugilegus*) foraging on grassland. *Zeitschrift für Tierpsychologie, 57,* 15–36.

Watts, D. P. (1985). Observations on the ontogeny of feeding behavior in mountain gorillas (*Gorilla gorilla beringei*). *American Journal of Primatology, 8,* 1–10.

Weigl, P. D., & Hanson, E. V. (1980). Observational learning and the feeding behavior of the red squirrel (*Tamiasciurus hudsonicus*): The ontogeny of optimization. *Ecology, 61,* 213–218.

Welker, C. (1976). Fishing behaviour in *Galago crassicaudatus* E. Geoffroy, 1812 (Prosimiae; Lorisiformes; Galagidae). *Folia Primatologica, 26,* 284–291.

Whitehead, J. M. (in press). Development of feeding selectivity in mantled howling monkeys (*Alouatta palliata*). In *Proceedings of the Xth Congress of the International Primatological Society.* Cambridge: Cambridge University Press.

Wyrwicka, W. (1978). Imitation of mother's inappropriate food preference in weanling kittens. *Pavlovian Journal of Biological Science, 13,* 55–72.

Zentall, T. R., & Hogan, D. E. (1976). Imitation and social facilitation in the pigeon. *Animal Learning & Behavior, 4,* 427–430.

Social Learning
About Food by Humans

Paul Rozin
University of Pennsylvania

INTRODUCTION

There is a strong tendency for psychologists to think of food as essentially a source of energy. Among research psychologists, this tendency derives from the fact that the study of food has been firmly rooted in the tradition of homeostasis and energy balance. The emphasis has been on eating as a response to a need for energy. This view of eating, especially for humans, is reinforced by the great concern about food intake and weight in American society (the home of most research psychologists) and the fact that food plays a relatively muted social role in American society. The study of food in psychology has been, in large part, the study of amount eaten. A typical introductory psychology text deals with food only in terms of energy regulation, and considers disorders of eating (obesity, anorexia) as problems in impulse control, set points, and the like. The social environment is seen as a nuisance variable, which may modulate a basically biological, nutrition-driven system.

How wrong and how odd this is. First, a fundamental psychological and biological aspect of the human omnivore's interaction with foods is the attainment of adequate nutrients, as well as sufficient energy. Indeed, food selection is a major force in the evolution of animals, and food habits are a major predictor of the appearance and physiology of particular animal species. Second, for humans, food is one of the major sources of pleasure. Third, the use of food is quintessentially social for humans. Consider these examples: (a) In India, rules about who can eat food prepared by whom make food a major vehicle through which the structure of society (e.g., the caste system) and the family (Appadurai, 1981; Marriott, 1968; see discussion below) is maintained; (b) Males entering puberty among the Hua in Papua New Guinea are prohibited from eating any food touched, raised, or prepared by a fertile female (Meigs, 1984); (c) in most cultures, special occasions are marked by special foods; (d) the positive expression made by the newborn infant in response to sweet, and the negative expression made in response to bitter, develop into a means of communication between the infant and its caretaker (Chiva, 1985); (e) in common with all other mammals, food serves as a center for human parent-infant interaction, as a result of the obligatory nursing phase in development; (f) many problems in feeding, such as the refusal of all but a few types of foods by many 2- to 4-year-olds, anorexia nervosa, and obesity, have strong social determinants.

It is primarily through the process of enculturation that the human om-nivore learns what is food and what is not. Other omnivores must rely much more on individual experience, a daunting prospect. Omnivores such as rats and roaches do manage adaptive selection of diets. The role of social factors in roaches is unexplored. Research on rats continues to reveal more and more forms of social transmission (Galef, 1986; see chapter by Galef in this volume), though there is still a qualitative gap between the role of social factors in food selection in humans and any other species.

The human omnivore brings few biological biases to the task of food selection: innate tendencies to avoid bitter and perhaps irritation, and to consume items that produce sweet sensations; a suspicion of new foods, coupled with a curiosity about them, and some special abilities to link the flavors of foods with their consequences (Rozin, 1976). Over the first year or so of life, the human infant tends to put anything it reaches into its mouth (Davis, 1939; Rozin, Hammer, Oster, Horowitz, & Marmara, 1986). Preserving the infant's safety is largely the task of a vigilant parent. During the first decade of life, the child acquires its culture's basic culinary attitudes, including those concerning what is edible and what is not. Given the young child's tendency to mouth all sorts of things, much early learning is about what not to eat (Davis, 1939; Rozin et al., 1986). Learning about the edibility of specific objects can occur quite rapidly, and need not involve social mediation (Davis, 1928, 1939).

The flexibility of the feeding system is illustrated by the variety of its end points. Consider the massive differences between the almost purely carnivorous diet of Eskimos and the plant-dominated diets of many tropical cultures, or between the elaborate cuisines of India or France and the relatively limited amounts of food processing carried out by some hunter-gatherers.

The fate of surviving feral children (Zingg, 1940) provides another per-spective on this flexibility. Some feral children (appropriately, those believed to have been reared by wolves or other wild animals) ate raw meat almost exclusively, even after some time in captivity. Others ate roots and berries or mixed diets.

Children learn more than culinary rules. They learn about the social meaning of food. Consider the case of India, home to almost one fifth of the world's people. For Hindu Indians, food is a moral substance. It is not an impersonal nutrient package, bought in a supermarket, but the bearer of the mark of its particular maker. The food one eats has something like an essence of its preparer. One can harm one's status or persona by consuming food prepared by a person of inferior rank. Indeed, one can reconstruct the elaborate caste structure of India just from examining who can eat whose food (Marriott, 1968). In India, food is a material form of nurture: when shared, or passed from preparer to eater, it can cement or enhance relations. When avoided, it can preserve social distance (Appadurai, 1981). Needless to say, all of these attitudes are learned.

There should be no doubt that food has many social functions. It does not follow from this that the learning of these social functions is itself a social process, though it seems very likely that it is.

THE TARGET OF EXPLANATION.

There are three aspects of food selection (Rozin, 1979). One is *use;* the amounts of different foods that are consumed, which is determined largely by availability and cost. A second aspect is *preference,* which refers to a choice of one item rather than another. Preference presumes availability; cost is one of many factors that influence it. A third aspect of food selection is *liking,* an affective response to foods. Liking is usually indexed by self-report, but can also be measured using facial expressions (e.g., Ekman & Friesen, 1975). Liking can be used comparatively, in the sense, "I like X better than Y." This statement is not equivalent to the statement, "I prefer X to Y." The latter statement describes a choice; the "like" statement describes a motivation or mental state. It is possible to like X better than Y but prefer Y, if for example, Y is cheaper or X may be harmful to one's health.

Because liking is a powerful determinant of preference, likes and preferences are often congruent. The liking-preference distinction is easy to measure in humans, but more difficult in animals, because of the absence of self-report. It is, however, possible to draw a distinction between liking and preference even in animals, based in large part on their expressive behavior to foods (Grill & Norgren, 1978; Pelchat, Grill, Rozin, & Jacobs, 1983).

In spite of the important distinction between liking and preference, the two terms are often used interchangeably. I will sometimes intentionally commit this same error, by using the term *food preferences* to include food likes.

SOURCES OF VARIATION
IN FOOD PREFERENCES AND ATTITUDES

What accounts for both universals and individual differences in food preferences? The factors that account for both universals and individual differences can be described as biological (genetically determined), cultural, or individual (unique). We have already indicated that because of the open-endedness of omnivore food selection systems, there are few biological universals in food selection. There is some genetic basis for individual differences in selection and preference, based on sensory differences (e.g., bitter sensitivity; Fischer, Griffin, England, & Garn, 1961), and on differences in the ability to process certain nutrients (e.g., lactose intolerance; Simoons, 1978). However, most individual differences cannot be attributed to genetic differences; in some studies the food preferences of identical twins are not more similar than those of fraternal twins (Rozin & Millman, 1987) or even unrelated persons (Greene, Desor, & Maller, 1975).

It is surely the case that the best predictor of human food preferences is culture or ethnic group. The range and cost of most foods available to humans throughout the world are essentially determined by cultural variables. Availability and price are powerful determinants of food choice. The preparation of foods (flavorings, cooking techniques) is determined by culture, as is the pattern of introduction of foods to children.

Individual differences in preferences that cannot be accounted for in terms of biological or cultural differences must be attributed to differences in individual experience. This is not to say that such experiences are independent of culture, but rather that they are not uniform within the culture. Such experiences may or may not be "social" (in the sense that an acquired taste aversion is probably not social). To what extent can we account for within-culture variation? Surprisingly, although within-culture variation is substantial, there is no single factor that accounts for much of it. Neither gender nor age (outside of extremes) is an important predictor. The obvious within-culture variable is the family (a very social vehicle).

Because the family is surely the primary means through which culture-wide culinary values are transmitted, it is also likely to be a means for propagating within-culture (that is, between-family) differences in food preferences and likes. In order to study the role of the family in within-culture variation, parent-child resemblance that results from culture-wide preferences must be factored out. This can be done in two ways. First, measures of resemblance (e.g., correlation in pattern of food preferences across a number of foods, for a parent-child pair) can be computed for parent-child and pseudoparent-child pairs. A pseudoparent is a parent from the same general community who is not the parent of the child in question. Pseudoparent-child correlations represent resemblance resulting from culture-wide influences, and the difference between pseudoparent-child and parent-child resemblances is attributable to within-family effects. Two studies have made the appropriate measurements.

Birch (1980b) compared the preferences of preschoolers, who ranked eight actually tasted foods (e.g., eight vegetables) in terms of preference, with the rankings made by their parents or by the (pseudo) parents of other children in her study. She reports that parent-child resemblance (tau; approximately .13) is not significantly higher than pseudoparent-child resemblance (approximately .09). Pliner (1983) compared the pattern of preferences for 47 foods (rated on a questionnaire) of college students and their parents. She reports modest correlations (r = .20), which are significantly higher than student-pseudoparent correlations (r = .10). Using this same technique, correlations for siblings are notably higher (phi = .50 compared to .18 for child and pseudosibling [Pliner & Pelchat, 1986].

A second approach is to compute separate correlations for individual foods, in which each parent and child contribute one pair of points for each food. Even though the set of parents and children share a common culture, any positive correlation represents within-family resemblance. Ritchey and Olson (1983) report no significant correlation between parents' attitudes to sweets and the sweet preferences of their young children. In a different study, the mean correlation across 22 different foods for college students and their parents is .15 (Rozin, Fallon, & Mandell, 1984).

The surprisingly low parent-child correlations are not a result either of limitations in the sample or of unreliability. The same sample that generated low preference correlations yielded substantial parent-child correlations for a different food-related attitude: sensitivity to contamination and disgust (Rozin et al., 1984). Here, parent-child correlations were about .50.

One must remember that parent-child resemblances, modest as they are, include both common genetic and experiential components. Estimates of the role of genetic factors in food preference vary widely (Greene et al., 1975; Krondl, Coleman, Wade, & Miller, 1983; Rozin & Millman, 1987). It is likely that most of the modest parent-child resemblance is attributable to common environment. In this regard, it is noteworthy that for both food preferences and disgust and contamination sensitivity, mother-father resemblance may be higher than the resemblance of either parent to the offspring (Rozin et al., 1984). Mother-father resemblance comes from two sources: assortative mating and common experience. There is reason to believe that assortative mating plays a strong role in spouse resemblance; however, food preferences were one of only a few domains in which *some* spouse similarity could be attributed to common experience (Price & Vandenberg, 1980).

We are left with the mystery of a lot of within-culture variance, and little to explain it. Later in the chapter, this topic is discussed in terms of processes that might be involved in the acquisition of preferences.

WAYS IN WHICH SOCIAL FACTORS
INFLUENCE FOOD PREFERENCES

Our focus is on explaining attitudes (preferences). However, attitudes are often dependent on beliefs (e.g., "I avoid sugar because I believe it is toxic"). Most beliefs have sociocultural origins. Furthermore, there is an enormous amount of social learning that goes on in the acquisition of beliefs. By preschool years, children have learned that certain foods are appropriate only at breakfast (Birch, Billman, & Richards, 1984), whereas these same children have yet to learn that certain combinations of favored foods (e.g., chocolate and meat) are unacceptable in their culture. That is, if a preschooler likes A and B, then he will like A + B (Fallon, Rozin, & Pliner, 1984; Rozin, Fallon, & Augustoni-Ziskind, 1986).

Taken in the broadest sense, beliefs also include self-knowledge. Thus, the developing awareness that certain internal states indicate a need for food (hunger) or water (thirst) is almost surely, in part, social. Learning to label one's "internal" states may be fundamental in coming to understand and respond to them. Bruch (1961), with good reason, suggests that learning to label internal states has a strong social component; hunger awareness depends on parental responses to child-initiated cues indicating energy deficit.

Social factors influence food preferences both directly and indirectly. A classification of such effects has been presented by Galef (1976; 1985) and Birch (1986, 1987). What follows is a slight modification of their schemes.

Indirect Social Action. Social agents are not present in indirect cases; rather, they have determined what is to be learned and/or the conditions of learning. Food traditions and attitudes are represented in "culture," and hence are established by social forces. These traditions are acquired in the process of enculturation, but this learning does not necessarily involve social mediation. The most potent indirect effect of social factors on preferences comes through control of availability (discussed in the next section).

Direct social effects, or social learning of values, can be divided into two categories. In *inadvertent social agency,* a social presence is essential to learning. However, the social agent is not explicitly oriented to the learning task. In other words, social learning, but no teaching, occurs. In *active social agency,* or teaching, the social agent participates in the learning task, for the purpose of producing a change. The agent is a teacher.

FOOD PREFERENCES: A TAXONOMY

The analysis of learning processes is facilitated if there is clarity about what is being learned. Every adult in every culture has a set of attitudes toward objects in the world, as to their appropriateness and desirability as food. The acquisition of this categorization, and the assignment of objects to appropriate categories, is a major feature of food enculturation. Fallon and I (Fallon & Rozin, 1983; Rozin & Fallon, 1980, 1981) have explored these attitudes in American adults, using a combination of questionnaires and interviews. We believe that there are three basic reasons for accepting or rejecting potential foods. Each of these (Table 8.1) in one form motivates acceptance, and in the opposite form motivates rejection. The three reasons are reviewed here.

Sensory-Affective Factors. Some items are accepted or rejected because of liking or disliking for their sensory aspects: taste, smell, and to a lesser extent, appearance. Items accepted primarily on such grounds are "good tastes," whereas those rejected on such grounds are "distastes." Most commonly, when we say we like or dislike a food, we are referring to sensory-affective factors. Individual differences in hedonic responses to particular sensory-affective factors probably account for most within-culture variance in food preferences (e.g., liking for hot pepper, lima beans, beer, yogurt).

Anticipated Consequences. Some items are accepted or rejected primarily because of beliefs about the consequences of ingesting them. These may refer to rapid effects, such as satiation, nausea, or increased social status, or more delayed effects, such as increased risk of contracting cancer or gaining weight. Items rejected because of negative anticipated consequences are called dangerous, whereas those accepted because of positive anticipated consequences are called beneficial.

Ideational Factors. Some substances are rejected or accepted primarily because of our knowledge of what they are, their origins, or their symbolic meanings. Ideational factors play a modest role in food acceptance, and a major role in food rejection. There are two distinct categories of ideational rejection.

1. *Inappropriate.* Inappropriate items are considered inedible, and hence are refused. They account for most items in the world: sand, paper, bark, grass, and so forth. These items may or may not be viewed as bad tasting or dangerous. They are inoffensive. The primary reason for rejection is that they are not considered to be food. Most culture-wide rejections fall into this category.

2. *Disgusting.* Disgusting items are also rejected on ideational grounds, but they are considered offensive. They have a strong negative sensory-affective loading and are likely to elicit nausea. They are so offensive that they are contaminants: if they touch an edible food, they tend to render it inedible. Disgusting items (Table 8.1), unlike other categories of items, are heavily loaded on two dimensions in our taxonomy. Almost all disgusts are animals

Table 8.1

Psychological Categories of Acceptance and Rejection*

Dimensions	Rejections				Acceptances			
	Distaste	Danger	Inappropriate	Disgust	Good Taste	Beneficial	Appropriate	Transvalued
Sensory-affective	−			−	+			+
Anticipated consequences		−				+		
Ideational		?	−	−		?	+	+
Examples	Beer, chili, spinach	Allergy foods, carcinogens	Grass, sand	Feces, insects	Saccharine	Medicines	Ritual food	Leavings of heroes or deities

*Source: Fallon & Rozin, 1983

172

or animal products, with feces as the apparently universal disgust substance (Angyal, 1941; Rozin & Fallon, 1987).

Our taxonomy is a simplification. Most rejections and acceptances are motivated by reasons that fall into more than one category. Indeed, a number of studies have identified multiple bases for food acceptance, including a number of social factors, such as prestige (e.g., Krondl & Lau, 1982; Schutz, Rucker, & Russell, 1975; Worsley, 1982). Thus, milk is good tasting and beneficial; cockroaches are disgusting, but also may be dangerous. Nonetheless, many items fall pretty well within a single category; that is, there is a primary reason for accepting or rejecting them.

The taxonomy discussed above provides a framework for discussing acquisition of preference. We focus on the acquisition of good tastes because this involves a hedonic/value change, in contrast to beneficial, which represents assimilation of information about the consequences of food without a necessary change in liking. We then briefly consider the changes in liking that occur in the acquisition of distaste (as opposed to danger) and disgust (as opposed to inappropriate).

SOCIAL FACTORS IN THE ACQUISITION OF LIKES

Our interest is in the acquisition of likes (good tastes); the acquisition of intrinsic value (liking a food for its sensory properties) as opposed to extrinsic value (preferring a food because of its effects).

Exposure

In many contexts, preference and liking increase with exposure (Zajonc, 1968). This effect has been demonstrated for food (Birch & Marlin, 1982; Pliner, 1982). Zajonc attributes this effect to *mere* exposure. Zajonc's mere exposure hypothesis stands as a valid empirical generalization, but it is very difficult to prove that mere exposure is a mechanism for the acquisition of liking, because exposure is also a necessary condition for other mechanisms of acquired likes to operate. The term *mere* may simply refer to the fact that no contingencies can be identified in the situation in which acquisition takes place. One account for the "mere" exposure (contingency-free) effect is opponent process theory (Solomon, 1980). According to this view, the organism strives for hedonic equilibrium by internally generating affective processes that oppose the affective processes generated by external stimuli. With continued exposure, the opponent process becomes more effective; both larger in amplitude and longer in duration. For the case of food, this would mean that on experiencing an unpleasant-tasting food, a pleasure opponent process would be generated. With repeated samplings, the opponent would grow in strength. If the opponent process overcompensated for the

negative affect induced by the food, the net effect could be an acquired preference. This process has been suggested as a mechanism for the acquisition of liking
for initially aversive mouth "burn" of chili peppers (Rozin, Ebert, & Schull,
1982).

Exposure (whether mere or as a condition for operation of other forces) is a
prime example of indirect social effects. Sociocultural forces, in the form of
culinary traditions, have a major influence in determining availability, and hence
exposure, to foods. Cultural factors also influence exposure in other ways. Feeding of sugar water in the first months of life is an option that is socially (paren-
tally) determined for infants. This practice influences sugar preferences at 6
months of age (Beauchamp & Moran, 1984). Preferences for a variety of initially
unpalatable substances (e.g., alcohol, chili pepper, tobacco) depend on socially
mediated exposure and social pressures that encourage people to partake of these
substances during the period in which they are not yet liked (Rozin, 1982).

Associative Processes
(Non-Social or Indirect Social Effects)

We review a number of established mechanisms for the acquisition of likes,
moving from those with least to those with most social involvement. The least
"social" mechanism is conditioning based on satiating effects of foods. Flavors (in
foods) paired with high satiety (high caloric loads) become more liked, by hungry
subjects, than flavors paired with lower caloric loads (Booth, Mather, & Fuller,
1982). Social effects in this instance are most indirect, and operate only by
controlling food availability.

A second type of conditioning involves pairing of already liked tastes with
neutral, less liked, or disliked foods. This procedure is employed at least occasionally by 36% of a sample of American parents (Casey & Rozin, 1987). Flavor
conditioning has been demonstrated in the laboratory by pairing of flavors with
sugar (Zellner, Rozin, Aron, & Kulish, 1983). Pairing of flavors may account for
the development of liking for black coffee. Coffee is usually drunk with much
sugar. Some people gradually cut out the sugar and come to enjoy the un-
sweetened flavor of coffee. This sequence is, to a large extent, programmed
socially, because parents have much control over the beverages consumed by their
children and the amount of sugar that goes into their food. Culinary constraints,
an indirect social effect, also operate, in specifying, for example, the appropriate
contexts for sugar.

Direct Social Effects

The most powerful force in the acquisition of culture, both in food and other
domains, is direct social effects. The most general effect seems to be that the
perception by a child that an object or attitude is valued by respected others
(parents, other adults, older siblings, certain peers) causes the child to come to

value that object or attitude more. This process has some of the mystery of "mere exposure." One immediately wants to know *why* it occurs. There is evidence in favor of operation of the "perception of value by others" in the acquisition of food preferences. (In many studies of children, preference is confounded with liking; most studies measure preference changes rather than liking changes. However, when no obvious extrinsic factors are involved, we may assume that liking and preference are congruent.)

Duncker (1938) showed that preschool children's food preferences could be influenced by observation of choices made by other people. The "other" figure in this study selected a food less preferred by the subject from a choice of foods offered to the model. The same choice was subsequently offered to the subject. Subjects' preference moved significantly in the direction of the food chosen by the model. This effect depended on the relation between the child and the "model." The effect was clearest when the model was a friend or another child perceived as powerful. Adult strangers did not produce a significant effect. Duncker also presented stories to children in which a fictional hero preferred a particular food. These stories also influenced subsequent food preference. These effects were most substantial in the younger children (as young as 2.5 years), perhaps because the mode of presentation had more ecological validity for younger children. The effects measured in Duncker's (1938) study disappeared on retest 8 to 10 days after training.

Marinho (1942) confirmed and extended Duncker's work on fictional heroes. She demonstrated that the effects of social influence on food choice was greater and more persistent in children who did not have a strong initial preference for the food in question, and that, under ideal conditions, the induced preference change could last for months.

Birch and her collaborators have conducted the most systematic investigation of social influence in acquisition of preferences by children (see reviews of this work, and this field by Birch, 1986, 1987). In a well-controlled study in a nursery school setting, Birch (1980a) examined the influence of peers on preschoolers' preferences. She used a preference technique that produced reliable rankings on nine foods. The training part of the study involved a comparison of two vegetables that had previously been part of the ranking tests for all children. Birch seated children so that the target child was at a lunch table occupied by three to four children each of whom had a vegetable preference opposite to that of the target child. The target child always chose last from both vegetables offered by the teacher. By the third day (trial), the target child's preference had shifted significantly toward the vegetable preferred by his/her peers. A substantial preference change (mean shift upwards of 2.5 ranks in the nine foods) appeared in tests made in the absence of peers. This preference shift did not occur in children who were not exposed to peers with opposite preferences. Birch's study clearly demonstrates, under controlled conditions, that peers are capable of exerting significant social influence on preference among familiar foods. The influence in this case is probably inadvertent.

The influence of approval by a significant adult (teacher) was investigated in the same nursery-school setting (Birch, Zimmerman, & Hind, 1980). After a pretest in which the child's rank order preference for nine snacks was determined, a relatively neutral snack was selected for each child. Each child in the study received this snack twice a day, for 21 days, under a set of conditions that were different for 4 different groups. In this critical group (reward), children were offered the snack by the teacher as a reward for performing some desirable behavior. This manipulation was intended to establish a positive social-affective context and indicate value of the snack to a respected elder. Children in the reward group showed a substantially higher ranking of the critical snack in a post-manipulation preference test (a mean improvement of about 3 rank units out of 9). This effect, slightly attenuated, was still present in a test 6 weeks later (see Fig. 8.1). Three control groups allowed for an interpretation of the mechanism of enhancement in the reward group. In one (familiarity), the critical snack plus six others were simply offered at snack time, at the same frequency (twice/day) as in the reward condition. In another, entirely Nonsocial condition, the critical snack was left in the child's locker. In a third condition, Noncontingent attention, the teacher offered the child the critical snack twice each day, but not as a reward for specific behaviors.

As indicated in Fig. 8.1, the nonsocial (also a mere exposure) condition produced a minimal, transitory effect, and the familiarity condition produced no effect at all. The noncontingent attention manipulation produced a substantial effect that was, in the final test at 6 weeks post manipulation, about the same as

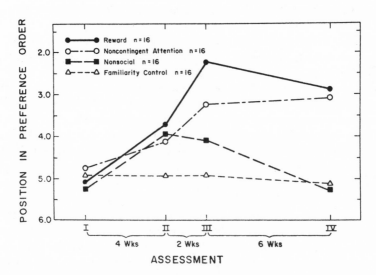

Figure 8.1.   Effect of presentation context on snack food preferences of preschoolers across successive assessments (from Birch, Zimmerman, & Hind, 1980).

the reward effect. These results indicate that experience of a food in a positive social context can enhance preference for the food. The data do not indicate whether perception of valuation by an adult other is critical; this was clearly the case in the reward condition, but not explicit in the noncontingent attention condition, and the latter was only marginally less effective than the former. Of course, it is possible that by presenting a snack to a child in a positive context, a teacher is indicating that she values the snack. In the classification of social effects that we have adopted, the reward condition clearly represents a teaching situation, whereas noncontingent attention could involve either teacher or inadvertent social agency. There is an alternate, Pavlovian interpretation of the reward effects that does not invoke the child's evaluation of the attitudes of others. On this view, the food (CS) is associated with a positive social-affective context (US) (Birch 1986, 1987; Rozin & Zellner, 1985; and see discussion in next section).

Birch's work represents the clearest laboratory demonstration of the operation of social-affective factors. It is consistent with observations of acquisition of likes for foods in natural settings. Rozin and Schiller (1980) studied the acquisition of liking for the initially unpleasant hot burn of chili pepper in its traditional home, a Mexican rural community. They showed, by preference measurements, that an initial dislike for the burn becomes a like at 5 to 8 years of age. Both interviews with parents and observations at mealtime indicate that parents offer young children piquant foods, but do not force or even pressure the children to consume these foods. Offering is typically accomplished by placing some hot sauce on a tortilla and offering it to the child. Refusal by the child is readily accepted, and the same item is offered without piquant sauce. In the social context of a family readily eating and obviously enjoying the piquant food, the child comes to gradually accept more and more hot sauce (salsa) on his food, and to consume more and more of foods that are piquant at the time of serving (e.g., in which the chili peppers are part of the cooking). By 5 to 7 years of age, the child, without any overt pressure, is adding hot sauce to his or her food. This sequence, which seems typical of many food socialization situations, is best interpreted as something between Birch's reward and noncontingent attention situations. On the one hand, adults do not use chili pepper as a reward; on the other hand, they clearly indicate their enjoyment of it.

To what extent do American parents realize and utilize the principles of acquisition of liking that we have discussed? In keeping with these principles, American parents, with generally negative attitudes to consumption of sweets, typically do not think it is acceptable to offer children sweets in a positive context (Ritchey & Olson, 1983). A survey of beliefs and practices of 76 American parents concerning development of food likes to their young children reveals that the two most popular techniques, participation in preparation of the relevant food, and displays indicating that adults like the food, both involve direct social mediation (Casey & Rozin, 1987). The "adults like" technique is in line with the laboratory results of Birch and her predecessors. However, although using the target food as a reward was very effective in Birch's hands, it was never spontaneously suggested by the parents in this study. When queried, a majority of parents thought it would be ineffective.

Mode of Operation of Social-Affective Influence

Unfortunately, in our attempts to understand food socialization, we cannot turn to a very informative literature on the socialization process in general. Given its central importance, socialization has received surprisingly little attention by psychologists (see Damon, 1983, for a review). There are evaluative theories that essentially hold that children value the attitudes of respected others, and want to be like them. This provides, in some way, the motivation for development or change in values. Processes such as imitation, modeling, and identification are invoked in this regard. All could be relevant to food socialization.

A more tractable (but not necessarily more correct) view emphasizes associative processes (e.g., Aronfreed, 1968; see also Martin & Levey, 1978). To some extent, the associationist view is different from the evaluative positions described above, and to some extent it offers an explanation for these processes, such as modeling. The associative position has some appeal, particularly because Pavlovian processes seem to be involved in a number of ways in the acquisition of food preferences (Rozin & Zellner, 1985). With respect to food socialization, the Pavlovian approach holds that social factors somehow induce an emotionally positive or pleasant state in a person in the presence of a relevant food object. The co-occurrence of food (CS) and pleasant affect (US) causes the food to become more liked. The social stimulus is presumably responsible for inducing a positive US in the child (this is Birch's [1986, 1987] account for the social influence effects she reports). The social stimulus could be something as vague as the child's perception of the pleasure of a respected elder, but more specific alternatives are available.

Tomkins (1963) suggests two sequences of events that could "transfer" an emotional response from adult to child. Both sequences focus on the face as a critical element in social transmission, but the conception might hold as well for other verbal or nonverbal cues. Tomkins's formulation depends on the assumption that when a person executes a facial display, these actions themselves induce the relevant emotion. Therefore, if an appropriate (e.g., smiling-pleasant) expression is induced on the face of a child, this would produce the corresponding emotion (the necessary US for a Pavlovian model of socialization). In one route to this end point, Tomkins suggests that there is a strong tendency for the child to assume, involuntarily, the same facial expression that it sees in respected others. In the second route, the child explicitly models such expressions. In either case, a respected other eating and enjoying a particular food would induce the corresponding emotion in the child, in association with the food. Tomkins's position, or variants of it, constitue a reasonable, but unproven, model of food socialization. It offers an explicit pathway from the social world to acquired and stable hedonic change in the individual.

The Agents of Socialization

The family (especially parents or guardians) is the most likely source of social cues that foster food (and other) socialization. As indicated in the discussion on accounting for variance in food selection, the family must play a critical role in transmission of culture-wide food values. What is surprising is how little within-culture variation is accounted for by the family. There is a further puzzlement in this literature.

Any reasonable model of the transmission of food preference (values, attitudes) via the family would emphasize the role of the mother. Traditionally, the mother is more involved in the selection and preparation of food, and, most critically for children, the mother is more often present and involved in feeding situations. However, relevant studies do not reveal reliably greater mother-child than father-child resemblance in preferences. Burt and Hertzler (1978), Pliner (1983), and Pliner and Pelchat (1986) all report no difference in these correlations. Both Birch (1980b) and Rozin et al. (1984) report small effects favoring the mother, though the difference is reversed for disgust sensitivity (Rozin et al., 1984). There is no simple way to explain why the mother's greater involvement with actual feeding of the child is not expressed in the child's preferences. However, there is an explanation of why the mother's critical role in selection of foods (via control of shopping) does not produce an exposure bias toward her preferences by her children. It seems that mothers are more influenced by the father's food preferences than by their own in making food purchases (Burt & Hertzler, 1978; Weidner, Archer, Healy, & Matarazzo, 1985). Hence, in terms of exposure effects, there may be a father bias that might compensate for the bias in favor of the mother as a result of her greater contact with the child in feeding situations.

Views of modeling that depend on identification would predict higher resemblance among same-sex child parent pairs. In the only study that examined this issue, significantly higher correlations of patterns of food preferences between college students and their same-sex parent as opposed to opposite-sex parent were found (Pliner, 1983). One can be thankful for this meaningful result, but it should not obscure the fact that many of the findings from the literature on parent influences on children's food preferences are in conflict with both accepted views of socialization and common sense.

Overjustification: The Negative Effect
of Instrumental Contingencies

There are conditions under which forces intended to promote socialization inadvertently operate to reduce the liking for socially valued items. This phenomenon, described as the overjustification effect (Lepper, 1980), can be derived from self-perception theory (Bem, 1967), which in turn has relations to the idea of cognitive dissonance. The basic position is that people infer their attitudes from their own behavior (Bem, 1967). Subjects seek to explain their actions (e.g., selection and consumption of a food). If such an action can be explained by extrinsic forces, no further "account" need be given. However, in the absence of extrinsic causal explanations, an internal account is encouraged, and one such account is that the action was intrinsically desirable. In the absence of external justification, the operation of cognitive consistency causes an increase in liking for a selected and/or consumed food. The overjustification position (Lepper, 1980) carries this logic one step further. If a clear extrinsic account for behavior is available, there will be a reduction in existing intrinsic motivation (i.e., a reduction in liking). There is considerable evidence for overjustification in the developmental literature (see Lepper, 1980; 1983, for reviews). An extension of this view (Pliner, Rozin, Cooper, & Woody, 1985) holds that in the absence of any intrinsic motivation (liking), the presence of clear extrinsic factors will block the acquisition of liking.

We consider the evidence for this general position in the food domain, working from the most fundamental background assumptions (cognitive consistency and self-perception), through overjustification as a way of decreasing intrinsic value, to extrinsic reward as a way of blocking the acquisition of liking.

There is one classic study on cognitive dissonance in food selection. Smith (1961) examined the effectiveness of various techniques in inducing liking for grasshoppers by adults. Adults were induced to sample grasshoppers under conditions of low or high financial inducement and under the urging of a warm or cold "communicator." The dissonance (and self-perception) views predict that when consumption is accomplished without any obvious external motivator (cold communicator, low financial reward), there is most likely to be a positive shift in intrinsic value, to reduce dissonance and/or satisfactorily account for one's own behavior. This is the result reported by Smith.

Overjustification was demonstrated in a study in which children, in a mealtime setting, were told stories in which food A was used as a reward, and eating of food B was rewarded. Subsequent ratings indicated that children liked food A more (Lepper, Sagotsky, Dafoe, & Greene, 1982). Birch and her colleagues have brought the overjustification effect into actual eating situations and have successfully produced overjustification with preschoolers. Following determination of children's preference-rankings of nine foods, a mid-ranked food was subjected to an instrumental reward contingency. Children were told that if they ate this food, they would be allowed to play. Consumption of the food increased. However, when the instrumental contingency was discontinued, preference for the rewarded food dropped below initial levels in 9 of 12 subjects (Birch, Birch, Marlin, & Kramer, 1982).

A second study (Birch, Marlin, & Rotter, 1984) both extended these findings and related them to the claim that salient tangible rewards, as opposed to feedback about performance, was the critical external factor that promoted an overjustification effect (Lepper 1980, 1983). Contrary to Lepper's prediction, both types of contingencies produced a negative shift in preference.

I know of no direct experimental tests of the claim that extrinsic factors block the acquisition of likes, but there are suggestive data. A questionnaire study on acquisition of liking for medicines and foods indicated that oral medicines (clearly consumed for extrinsic reasons) rarely come to be strongly liked, even though they are paired with positive events (Pliner et al., 1985). Furthermore, opiate-addicted patients who are in methadone programs, and receive thousands of "trials" in which they consume their methadone "medicine" in an orange-flavored beverage, do not show any enhancement for liking of this beverage (Pliner et al., 1985). On the basis of studies on acceptance of a new food, soya, Woodward (1945) suggests that emphasis on the nutritive value of foods implies that the foods do not taste good. In spite of the fact that there is, in nature at least, a relation between goodness of taste and goodness of nutrition, there seems to be a commonly held view among adults in the United States that if something tastes very good it probably isn't good for one's health. This view is surely acquired; it is probably not present in traditional cultures and is absent in young children, who believe, for example, that if something is bad for you, it will taste bad (Fallon et al., 1984; Rozin et al., 1986).

American parents often reward ingestion of a food as a way of increasing its preference, and much less often use the food as a reward (Casey & Rozin, 1987). Hence, their behavior is not in line with the suggestions of the research literature.

There can be no question of the importance of social factors in the acquisition of likes. The overjustification effect can be recast (outside of self-perception theory) to bring it in line with the positive results on social enhancement of preference. If Birch's children like foods more because they are perceived as valued by others, they may like rewarded foods less because they infer that such foods are not liked by adults; indeed, it is necessary that the adults bribe them to eat such foods.

One serious problem for the overjustification position is the acquisition of likes for a family of innately unpalatable foods (e.g., tobacco, alcohol, chili peppers, strong-tasting foods). Children or adolescents usually begin consumption of these items under social pressure; in spite of a disliked taste, consumption of these items confers the benefits of appearing adult and "in" (Rozin, 1982). This extrinsic motivation regularly shifts to an intrinsic motivation; people usually come to like the same properties of these substances that were initially aversive. The social valuation forces that potently support the acquisition of liking are present in the typical use of innately unpalatable substances, and apparently overwhelm the opposing force of extrinsic motivation.

ACQUISITION OF DISLIKES AND DISGUST

There is no literature on the acquisition of dislikes in a social context. The only documented mechanism of acquired distastes is the taste-aversion phenomenon: if ingestion of a food is followed by nausea, the food tends to become disliked (Pelchat & Rozin, 1982). Other food-negative event pairings tend to produce an avoided (dangerous) but not distasteful food. Taste aversions can account for only a small percentage of acquired dislikes. We know of no other mechanism to account for the remainder. It is highly likely that social factors (e.g., the perception that respected others dislike an item) produce distastes, but there is no evidence on this point.

The case of disgust is different, because disgust is an inherently social category. The set of objects that give rise to disgust is culturally determined. The objects are almost always of animal origin (Angyal, 1941; Rozin & Fallon, 1981, 1987), and always include feces. Disgust appears to be an entirely acquired category; infants will mouth just about anything (Rozin et al., 1985). The weight of evidence is against a present-at-birth rejection of decay odors (Petó, 1936), and a critical feature of disgust, contamination, does not appear until 7 or 8 years of age (Fallon et al., 1984).

At a minimum, disgust is heavily influenced by indirect social factors, because the category of disgust objects is culturally transmitted. Direct social effects are almost certainly involved. It is likely that the toilet training experience provides the foundation for disgust (Rozin & Fallon, 1987). Parental verbal and nonverbal expressions in the presence of the child's feces are the most likely forces that convert a desired substance into a disgusting substance. Although feces do not assume full disgust properties until age 7 or 8, when contamination appears, feces are clearly rejected after the time of toilet training (perhaps as some combination of dangerous and distasteful). Because the earliest disgust substance, feces, is surely learned in a social context, to the extent that further disgusts are acquired with feces as a base (e.g., mud, on the grounds of similarity to feces, or objects that are associated with or have contact with feces), these acquisitions ultimately have a social base.

CONCLUSION

Although our current knowledge of mechanisms of social learning in the acquisition of food preferences is modest, we can be quite confident that social factors and social learning are of overwhelming importance in the development of attitudes to foods. The critical point is that it is very difficult to extract even a simple learning situation in humans from the social context. Consider the following episode. A solitary person, Milton, opens a carton of chocolate milk and is greeted by the odor of decay. Milton now finds that he can no longer drink chocolate milk, and that it induces nausea (and perhaps, disgust; see Rozin, 1986, for actual examples of this type). This apparently asocial encounter cannot be understood outside of a social context. First of all, the chocolate milk is itself a product of culture, and its presence as an available food is determined by many social factors, some culture-wide, others local (e.g., it was purchased by a friend or family member). More centrally, the odor of decay is not inherently offensive. Decayed milk is acceptable in certain contexts, for example, cheese or yogurt. Milton has learned, probably directly from others, the tradition that chocolate milk shouldn't smell like cheese; decay outside of a particular context is disgusting. Milton's disgust response to decay probably dates back to his toilet training, and the association of decay odor with negative displays and attitudes of his caretakers, an inherently social encounter. He is and has been surrounded by social indications of the undesirability of decay, outside of its narrow acceptable context. Therefore, Milton's solitary Pavlovian experience is imbued with social influence. Indeed, there are very few examples of truly nonsocial learning about food; a chapter on social learning about foods in humans is almost equivalent to a chapter on learning about foods.

ACKNOWLEDGMENTS

The preparation of this paper was supported by funds from the John D. & Catherine T. MacArthur Network on the Determinants and Consequences of Health-promoting and health-damaging behavior.

REFERENCES

Angyal, A. (1941). Disgust and related aversions. *Journal of Abnormal and Social Psychology, 36,* 393–412.

Appadurai, A. (1981). Gastropolitics in Hindu South Asia. *American Ethnologist, 8,* 494–511.

Aronfreed, J. A. (1968). *Conduct & conscience The Socialization of internalized control over behavior.* New York: Academic Press.

Beauchamp, G., & Moran, M. (1984). Acceptance of sweet and salty tastes in 2-year-old children. *Appetite, 5,* 291–305.

Bem, D. (1967). Self-perception: An alternative interpretation of cognitive dissonance phenomena. *Psychological Review, 74,* 183–200.

Birch, L. L. (1980a). Effects of peer models' food choices and eating behaviors on preschooler's food preferences. *Child Development, 51,* 489–96.

Birch, L. L. (1980b). The relationship between children's food preferences and those of their parents. *Journal of Nutritional Education, 12,* 14–18.

Birch, L. L. (1987). The acquisition of food acceptance patterns in children. In R. Boakes, D. Popplewell, & M. Burton (Eds.), *Eating habits.* (pp. 107–130) Chichester, England: Wiley.

Birch, L. L. (1986). Children's food preferences: Developmental patterns and environmental influences. In C. Whitehurst & R. Vasta (Eds.), *Annals of child development* Vol. 4. Greenwich, CT: JAI.

Birch, L. L., Billman, J., & Richards, S. (1984). Time of day influences food acceptability. *Appetite, 5,* 109–12.

Birch, L. L., Birch, D., Marlin, D. W., & Kramer, L. (1982). Effects of instrumental consumption on children's food preference. *Appetite, 3,* 125–34.

Birch, L. L., & Marlin, D. W. (1982). I don't like it; I never tried it: Effects of exposure to food on two-year-old children's food preferences. *Appetite, 4,* 353–60.

Birch, L. L., Marlin, D. W., & Rotter, J. (1984). Eating as the "means" activity in a contingency: Effects on young children's food preferences. *Child Development, 55,* 432–39.

Birch, L. L., Zimmerman, S. I., & Hind, H. (1980). The influence of social-affective context on the formation of children's food preferences. *Child Development, 51,* 856–61.

Booth, D. A., Mather, P., & Fuller, J. (1982). Starch content of ordinary foods associatively conditions human appetite and satiation, indexed by intake and eating pleasantness of starch-paired flavors. *Appetite, 3,* 163–84.

Bruch, H. (1961). Transformation of oral impulses in eating disorders: A conceptual approach. *Psychiatric Quarterly, 35,* 458–480.

Burt, J. V., & Hertzler, A. A. (1978). Parental influence on the child's food preference. *Journal of Nutrition Education, 10,* 127–28.

Casey, R. D., & Rozin, P. (1987). Changing children's food likes and dislikes: A survey of parent's beliefs and practices. Unpublished data.

Chiva, M. (1985). *Le doux et l'amer.* Paris: Presses Universitaires de France.

Damon, W. (1983). *Social and personality development.* New York: W. W. Norton.

Davis, C. (1928). Self-selection of diets by newly-weaned infants. *American Journal of Diseases of Children, 36,* 651–79.

Davis, C. (1939). Results of the self-selection of diets by young children. *Canadian Medical Association Journal, 41,* 257–61.

Duncker, K. (1938). Experimental modification of children's food preferences through social suggestion. *Journal of Abnormal and Social Psychology, 33,* 489–507.

Ekman, P., Friesen, W. V. (1975). *Unmasking the Face.* Englewood Cliffs, NJ: Prentice-Hall.

Fallon, A. E., Rozin, P. (1983). The psychological bases of food rejections by humans. *Ecology of Food and Nutrition, 13,* 15–26.

Fallon, A. E., Rozin, P., Pliner, P. (1984). The child's conception of food: The development of food rejections with special reference to disgust and contamination sensitivity. *Child Development, 55,* 566–75.

Fischer, R., Griffin, F., England, S., Garn, S. M. (1961). Taste thresholds and food dislikes. *Nature, 191,* 1328.

Galef, B. G. Jr. (1976). Mechanisms for the social transmission pf acquired food preferences from adult to weanling rats. In L. M. Barker, M. Best, & M. Domjan (Eds.), *Learning mechanisms in food selection* (pp. 123–148). Waco, TX: Baylor University Press.

Galef, B. G. Jr. (1985). Direct and indirect behavioral pathways to the social transmission of food avoidance. *Annals of the New York Academy of Sciences, 443,* 203–215.

Galef, B. G. Jr. (1986). Social interaction modifies learned aversions, sodium appetite, and both palatability and handling-time induced dietary preferences in rats. *Journal of Comparative Psychology, 100,* 432–439.

Greene, L. G., Desor, J. A., Maller, O. (1975). Heredity and experience: their relative importance in the development of taste preference in man. *Journal of Comparative and Physiological Psychology, 89,* 279–284.

Grill, H. J., & Norgren, R. (1978). The taste-reactivity test. I. Mimetic responses to gustatory stimuli in neurologically normal rats. *Brain Research, 143,* 263–269.

Krondl, M., Coleman, P., Wade, J., Miller, J. (1983). A twin study examining the genetic influence on food selection. *Hum. Nutrit: Appl. Nutrit, 37,* 189–98.

Krondl, M., Lau, D. (1982). Social determinants in human food selection. In L. M. Barker (Ed.), *Psychobiology of human food selection* (pp. 139–51). Westport, CT: AVI.

Lepper, M. R. (1980). Intrinsic and extrinsic motivation in children: Detrimental effects of superfluous social controls. In W. A. Collins (Ed.), *Minnesota Symposium on Child Psychology* (Vol. 14, pp. 155–214). Hillsdale, NJ: Lawrence Erlbaum Associates.

Lepper, M. R. (1983). Social-control processes and the internalization of social values: An attributional perspective. In E. T. Higgins, D. N. Ruble, & W. W. Hartup (Eds.), *Social cognition and social development* (pp. 294–330). New York: Cambridge University Press.

Lepper, M. R., Sagotsky, G., Dafoe, J. L., & Greene, D. (1982). Consequences of superfluous social constraints: Effects on young children's social inferences and subsequent intrinsic interest. *Journal of Personality and Social Psychology, 42,* 51–65.

Marinho, H. (1942). Social influence in the formation of enduring preferences. *Journal of Abnormal and Social Psychology, 37,* 448–68.

Marriott, M. (1968). Caste ranking and food transactions: A matrix analysis. In M. Singer & B. S. Cohn (Eds.), *Structure and change in Indian society* (pp. 133–171). Chicago: Aldine.

Martin, I., & Levey, A. B. (1978). Evaluation conditioning. *Advances in Behavior Research & Therapy, 1,* 57–102.

Meigs, A. (1984). *Food, sex and pollution. A New Guinea religion.* New Brunswick, NJ: Rutgers University Press.

Pelchat, M. L., Grill, H. J., Rozin, P., & Jacobs, J. (1983). Quality of acquired responses to tastes by Rattus norvegicus depends on type of associated discomfort. *Journal of Comparative Psychology, 97,* 140–153.

Pelchat, M. L., & Rozin, P. (1982). The special role of nausea in the acquisition of food dislikes by humans. *Appetite, 3,* 341–51.

Petó, E. (1936). Contribution to the development of smell feeling. *British Journal of Medical Psychology, 15,* 314–20.

Pliner, P. (1982). The effects of mere exposure on liking for edible substances. *Appetite, 3,* 283–90.

Pliner, P. (1983). Family resemblance in food preferences. *Journal of Nutritional Education, 15,* 137–40.

Pliner, P., & Pelchat, M. L. (1986). Similarities in food preferences between children and their siblings and parents. *Appetite, 7,* 333–342.

Pliner, P., Rozin, P., Cooper, M., & Woody, G. (1985). Role of specific postingestional effects and medicinal context in the acquisition of liking for tastes. *Appetite, 6,* 243–252.

Price, R. A., & Vandenberg, S. G. (1980). Spouse similarity in American and Swedish couples. *Behavior Genetics, 10,* 59–71.

Ritchey, N., & Olson, C. (1983). Relationship between family variables and children's preference for consumption of sweet foods. *Ecology of Food and Nutrition, 13,* 257–266.

Rozin, P. (1976). The selection of food by rats, humans and other animals. In J. Rosenblatt, R. A. Hinde, C. Beer, & E. Shaw (Eds.), *Advances in the study of behavior,* (Vol. 6, pp. 21–76). New York: Academic Press.

Rozin, P. (1979). Preference and affect in food selection. In J. H. A. Kroeze (Ed.), *Preference behavior and chemoreception* (pp. 289–302). London: Information Retrieval.

Rozin, P. (1982). Human food selection: The interaction of biology, culture and individual experience. In L. M. Barker (Ed.), *The psychobiology of human food selection* (pp. 225–54). Bridgeport, CT: AVI.

Rozin, P. (1986). A survey of one-trial acquired likes and dislikes in humans: Disgust as a US, food predominance, and negative learning predominance. *Learning & Motivation, 17,* 180–189.

Rozin, P., Ebert, L., & Schull, J. (1982). Some like it hot: A temporal analysis of hedonic responses to chili pepper. *Appetite, 3,* 13–22.

Rozin, P., & Fallon, A. E. (1980). The psychological categorization of foods and nonfoods: A preliminary taxonomy of food rejections. *Appetite, 1,* 193–201.

Rozin, P., & Fallon, A. E. (1981). The acquisition of likes and dislikes for foods. In J. Solms & R. L. Hall (Eds.), *Criteria of food acceptance: How man chooses what he eats. A Symposium* (pp. 35–48). Zurich: Forster.

Rozin, P., & Fallon, A. E. (1987). A perspective on disgust. *Psychological Review, 94,* 23–41.

Rozin, P., Fallon, A. E., & Augustoni-Ziskind, M. (1986). The child's conception of food: The development of categories of acceptable and rejected substances. *Journal of Nutritional Education, 18,* 75–81.

Rozin, P., Fallon, A. E., & Mandell, R. (1984). Family resemblance in attitude to food. *Developmental Psychology, 20,* 309–14.

Rozin, P., Hammer, L., Oster, H., Horowitz, T., & Marmora, V. (1986). The child's conception of food: Differentiation of categories of rejected substances in the 1.4 to 5 year range. *Appetite, 7,* 141–151.

Rozin, P., & Millman, L. (1987). Family environment, not heredity, accounts for family resemblances in food preferences and attitudes. *Appetite, 8,* 125–134.

Rozin, P., & Schiller, D. (1980). The nature and acquisition of a preference for chili pepper by humans. *Motivation and Emotion, 4,* 77–101.

Rozin, P., & Zellner, D. A. (1985). The role of Pavlovian conditioning in the acquisition of food likes and dislikes. *Annals of the New York Academy of Science, 443,* 189–202.

Schutz, H., Rucker, M. H., & Russell, G. F. (1975). Food and food-use classification systems. *Food Technology, 29,* 50–64.

Simoons, F. J. (1978). The geographic hypothesis and lactose malabsorption: A weighing of the evidence. *Digestive Disorders, 23,* 963–80.

Smith, E. E. (1961). The power of dissonance techniques to change attitudes. *Public Opinion Quarterly, 25,* 625–39.

Solomon, R. L. (1980). The opponent-process theory of acquired motivation. *American Psychologist, 35,* 691–712.

Tomkins, S. S. (1963). *Affect, imagery, consciousness. Vol. II. The negative affects.* New York: Springer.

Weidner, G., Archer, S., Healy, B., & Matarazzo, J. D. (1985). Family consumption of low fat foods: Stated preference versus actual consumption. *Journal of Applied Social Psychology, 15,* 773–779.

Woodward, P. (1945). The relative effectiveness of various combinations of appeal in presenting a new food: soya. *American Journal of Psychology, 58,* 301–323.

Worsley, A. (1980). Thought for food: Investigations of cognitive aspects of food. *Ecology of Food and Nutrition, 9,* 65–80.

Zajonc, R. B. (1968). Attitudinal effects of mere exposure. *Journal of Personality and Social Psychology, 9 (Part 2),* 1–27.

Zellner, D. A., Rozin, P., Aron, M., & Kulish, C. (1983). Conditioned enhancement of human's liking for flavors by pairing with sweetness. *Learning and Motivation, 14,* 338–50.

Zingg, R. M. (1940). Feral man and extreme cases of isolation. *American Journal of Psychology, 53,* 487–517.

PART IV

Social Learning of Arbitrary Responses

9

Experimentally Manipulated Imitative Behavior in Rats and Pigeons

Thomas R. Zentall
University of Kentucky

INTRODUCTION

Historically, researchers investigating the capacity of animals to learn by imitation have considered two types of phenomena, the acquisition of "natural" behaviors such as bird song and food preferences, and the acquisition of arbitrary behaviors such as bar pressing. The acquisition of arbitrary behaviors has been viewed by some as a means of circumventing problems associated with distinguishing social elicitation of species-typical behavior from social learning (Thorpe, 1963).

The techniques of operant conditioning provide a set of procedures that, at least in principle, should be readily applicable to the study of imitative acquisition of arbitrary behaviors by animals. However, application of operant procedures to the study of imitation has proven less straightforward than one might anticipate. Problems in controlling for nonimitative effects of social interaction on behavior acquisition have proven particularly troublesome. In the present chapter, I am concerned with the assessment of imitative learning effects and the isolation of such effects from other social and nonsocial learning effects.

A WORKING DEFINITION OF IMITATION

In common parlance, imitation is the performance of a novel behavior by an observing organism resulting from the observation of that behavior performed by a demonstrator. For example, a young child sees his father reading a newspaper and then picks up a newspaper and pretends to read. The low probability of the child's behavior prior to the parent's behavior and the close temporal proximity of the two behaviors, together with the knowledge that such response matching is not atypical in the human species, allows one to conclude that imitation has occurred. What if the evidence is not so clear? What if the likelihood of performance of a target behavior by an observer does not shift from almost zero to very probable following observation of the model's performance?

In nonprimate species, imitative effects reported in the literature have often been small. When one does see evidence of imitation in a single animal it is generally because the animal is strongly predisposed to engage in the target behavior (e.g., feeding behavior or bird song). However, many definitions of imitation specifically exclude such species-typical behaviors. Thorpe (1963), for example, defines imitation as "the copying of a novel or otherwise improbable act or utterance, or some act for which there is clearly no instinctive tendency" (p. 135). An increase in species-typical behavior seen when an animal is exposed to a conspecific engaged in that behavior has been called contagious behavior (Thorpe, 1963). For example, satiated chicks began to eat again when a hungry chick was introduced into their enclosure and began eating (Tolman, 1964). Because eating is a well-established response, the presence of an eating conspecific may produce an increase in motivation or may reflexively elicit pecking in the satiated observer. Although such behavioral change is socially produced, it is not at all clear that the behavioral change is the result of learning.

One strategy to ensure that learning is involved in socially induced alterations in behavior is to insist that the copied behavior be improbable or *arbritrary*. When imitation of arbitrary behaviors has been examined, large imitation effects have not been found. Thus, imitation of behavior is probably not a very important determinant of behavior generally. However, for theoretical reasons, the very existence of any imitative behavior is of considerable importance. When the expected magnitude of an imitation effect is small, one typically compares the performance of animals exposed to a performing demonstrator with the performance of a group of control animals. The measure of imitation is the statistical reliability of increased rate of behavior acquisition by the observation group as compared with the control group. Of course, the control group must be exposed to conditions that allow one to separate nonimitational factors (both social and nonsocial) from imitative behavior.

Many studies of this type have suffered from theoretical and methodological problems. For example, studies in which an observer has been reinforced for following a demonstrator in a T-maze (Bayroff & Lard, 1944; Church, 1957a, 1957b) should not be interpreted as demonstrations of imitation because the demonstrator merely served as a discriminative stimulus (i.e., one could substitute a moving block of wood for the demonstrator or one could indicate the correct path with a stripe on the floor leading to the goal box).

A further problem with much experimental research on imitation is that imitation manipulations often have been compared with inappropriate control conditions. For example, it is difficult to interpret studies that compared the barpress acquisition of rats exposed to a barpressing conspecific with the barpress acquisition of rats that have been shaped to barpress by an experimenter (Corson, 1967; Jacoby & Dawson, 1969; Powell, 1968; Powell & Burns, 1970; Powell, Saunders, & Thompson. 1968). This design can be thought of as an applied approach to research, because there is no concern for the vast differences in the procedures to which subjects in the two groups were exposed. The only question asked was whether one treatment would lead to faster learning than another. Furthermore, the results of such studies have been inconclusive. Although observational learning has sometimes led to faster learning than shaping (Corson, 1967; Jacoby & Dawson, 1969), faster learning by shaping than by observational learning has also been reported (Powell, 1968; Powell & Burns, 1970; Powell, Saunders, & Thompson, 1968).

In yet other experiments, researchers have failed to control for social factors unrelated to imitation. Comparison of an imitation group with a group that acquired the barpress response on its own (by trial and error) fails to consider the potential effect on barpress acquisition of the mere presence of another animal. Zajonc (1965) referred to the effects of mere presence of a conspecific on target behavior as social facilitation. He showed that mere presence can have an important effect on the behavior of species as diverse as cockroaches (Zajonc, Heingartner, & Herman, 1969) and humans (Zajonc & Sales, 1966). Zajonc (1965) proposed that the effect of social facilitation is to increase drive or general arousal in the observing animal. He then argued that according to Hull's (1943) theory of learning, an increase in drive should increase the probability of occurrence of dominant (i.e., highly probable) behaviors and decrease the probability of nondominant (i.e., less probable) behaviors. Interestingly, Zajonc's theory of social facilitation predicts that the mere presence of a conspecific should retard the acquisition of a new response (i.e., one that is by definition a nondominant response). Thus social facilitation theory cannot be used to explain instances of imitative learning. Although there is considerable support for social facilitation theory, the effect of mere presence is an empirical question and its effects must be assessed or controlled for in any measure of imitative learning.

Gardner and Engel (1971) recognized the need to control for social facilitation effects, but the observers they included for this purpose were exposed to demonstrators that were performing an important part of the task the observers were to learn. In Gardner and Engel's study, experimentally naive rats observed a conspecific either barpressing and eating food pellets from a pellet dispenser or just eating food pellets from the dispenser. However, training rats to approach and eat from the dispenser when a pellet is delivered is an important part of task acquisition. Thus, in fact, Gardner and Engel did not include a social facilitation control group (i.e., rats exposed to the mere presence of a conspecific).

Another factor that needs to be controlled for in imitation experiments is the degree to which the demonstrator makes some aspect of the environment more salient. Lorenz (1935) observed that penned ducks may not notice an opening in their enclosure through which they might escape, unless they happened to be near another duck at the time of its escape. The opening is made more salient by observing a duck pass through it. Thus, if a duck sees a conspecific pass through a hole in a fence, it may increase the likelihood that the observer will follow, but this may not be imitation. Thorpe (1963) has referred to this phenomenon as local enhancement (i.e., the increase in salience of important stimuli produced by observing a demonstrator make contact with those stimuli). Facilitated learning, found when observers are permitted access to the demonstrator's manipulandum (e.g., Herbert & Harsh, 1944; Jacoby & Dawson, 1969; Oldfield-Box, 1970), can also be attributed to local enhancement (see also Denny, Clos, & Bell's chapter in this volume).

Behavior acquired through imitation should be arbitrary (i.e., should not be already learned or a predisposed species-typical behavior), should not be capable of being produced by social facilitation (i.e., the mere presence of a conspecific), and should not be due to local enhancement (i.e., merely drawing the observer's attention to task-relevant stimuli).

Our research in the area of animal imitation began in an attempt to assess the existence of imitation under conditions that adequately controlled for such nonimitative social learning. Our conclusion (quite different from that of Galef, chapter 1) is that imitative behavior is a reliable phenomenon that can be found under a variety of conditions in both rats and pigeons.

IMITATION OF BARPRESSING BY RATS

The purpose of our initial study (Zentall & Levine, 1972) was to assess imitative learning under conditions that controlled for social facilitation, as well as to assess the role of observation of one component of the response to be learned (i.e., observation of a magazine trained rat) in acquisition of the barpress response by rats.

The design involved the duplicate-cage method (Warden & Jackson, 1935) consisting of two operant chambers placed side by side with clear Plexiglas walls between them. Each operant chamber had its own bar and water delivery system. The physical separation of the observer's bar from that of the demonstrator was introduced in order to eliminate any facilitation due to local enhancement of barpress acquisition by observers. Any tendency for an observer to attend to a demonstrator's bar because the demonstrator's bar was being manipulated should have distracted the observer from its own bar, and thus should have retarded barpress acquisition.

Four groups of experimentally naive observer rats acquired the barpress response for water reinforcement. Group OB (the imitation group) observed a demonstrator rat barpressing for water reinforcement. Group OD observed a magazine-trained demonstrator rat consuming water (each OD demonstrator's magazine was yoked to an OB demonstrator's magazine). The purpose of Group OD was to assess facilitation of barpress acquisition by the observation of a portion of the response to be learned. Observers must learn where and under what conditions water will be delivered (e.g., the sound of the solenoid-operated water dipper can serve as a cue for approaching the dipper). Group ON observed an experimentally naive demonstrator (neither barpressing nor drinking) and thus served as a social facilitation (mere presence) control. Group OE observed an empty box and allowed for the assessment of social facilitation effects by providing a nonsocial, trial and error baseline for barpress acquisition.

The observers' barpress acquisition curves are presented in Figure 9.1. The results were (a) the imitation group (Group OB) learned significantly faster than the partial imitation group (Group OD). Observation of the entire response to be learned was more beneficial than observation of part of that response. (b) Group OD learned significantly faster than the group that observed an experimentally naive rat (Group ON). Observation of part of the response to be learned was beneficial as compared with observation of no part of that response. (c) Group ON learned significantly *slower* than the group exposed to an empty box (Group OE). Thus, the mere presence of another rat retarded barpress acquisition. (d) Group OD did not learn significantly faster than Group OE. It appears that the facilitative effects of imitation on learning for Group OD were washed out by the retarding effects of a conspecific's presence on learning.

The social facilitation effect, although in the opposite direction from that

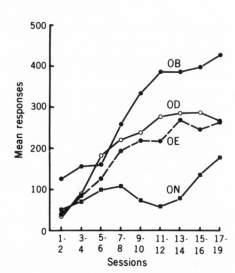

Figure 9.1. Acquisition of barpress response for rats observing a barpressing rat (OB), a yoked drinking rat (OD), a rat neither drinking nor barpressing (ON), or an empty box (OE).

predicted by Gardner and Engel (1971), supports Zajonc's theory of social facilitation. According to Zajonc, the presence of a conspecific will facilitate performance only if the behavior is a dominant behavior or, in the case of barpressing, is well learned. If the behavior has not yet been learned, as was the case in the present study, the presence of a conspecific should inhibit or retard performance.

But two other explanations can be proposed for retarded acquisition of the barpress when a rat is in the presence of a nonbarpressing demonstrator. Slower learning in the presence of a conspecific may occur if the conspecific is viewed by the observer as a salient, meaningful stimulus that distracts the observer from the task to be learned. This explanation will be called the distraction hypothesis. Alternatively, it is possible that Group ON's experimentally naive demonstrator (engaged in nonbarpressing behavior) serves as a model for irrelevant behavior, and thus slows acquisition of the reinforced response by inducing imitation of inappropriate behaviors. This third explanation will be called the imitation hypothesis.

To distinguish among the three hypotheses proposed to explain retarded acquisition by Group ON, relative to Group OE, a second experiment was conducted (Levine & Zentall, 1974). Well-trained barpressing rats were exposed either to an empty box or to an experimentally naive conspecific (under high or low water deprivation).

According to Zajonc's theory of social facilitation, the presence of a conspecific should increase the probability of dominant responses. For well-trained barpressing rats, barpressing should be a dominant response, and thus one that should be facilitated by the presence of a conspecific.

According to the distraction hypothesis, the introduction of a conspecific should disrupt barpressing, regardless of the target rat's behavior. Similarly, according to the imitation hypothesis, the presence of a nonbarpressing conspecific should facilitate nonbarpressing through imitation, thus barpressing should be disrupted.

Two levels of water deprivation were used to examine the effects of a manipulation known to affect drive level in rats. Also, if conspecific-produced drive affected barpressing by rats, the design would allow assessment of the interaction between a social drive and a water-deprivation drive.

Under both levels of water deprivation barpressing occurred at a higher rate in the presence of a conspecific than in the absence of a conspecific. This finding supports Zajonc's theory of social facilitation, and argues against both a distraction or an imitation explanation of the difference in barpressing between Groups OE and ON. The results are presented in Figure 9.2. Not only does the mere presence of a conspecific increase drive in an observer but this socially-produced drive appears to add algebraically to the existing water-deprivation-produced drive.

The first two experiments demonstrated that social facilitation effects can be separated from those of imitation. Not only is social facilitation an inappropri-

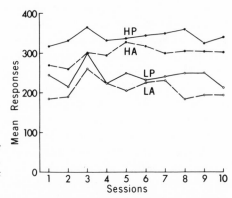

Figure 9.2. Mean barpress responses for trained rats under high (H, 23h) or low (L, 4h) water deprivation with a conspecific present (P) or absent (A).

ate explanation for the facilitation of bar press acquisition by rats under the present conditions, but social facilitatory effects appear to reliably retard bar press acquisition.

Imitative effects can also be found during the extinction of bar press performance by rats. Using a procedure similar to that used by Zentall and Levine (1972), rats exposed to bar press demonstrators during bar press acquisition and then extinguished in the presence of those demonstrators showed significantly greater resistance to extinction than a number of control groups (Henning & Zentall, 1981).

IMITATION OF PASSIVE AVOIDANCE BY RATS

Most imitation research with rats has used tasks that have involved appetitive consequences of behavior. It seems likely, however, that any predisposition to imitate the behavior of another animal, or learn the consequences of some behavior through observation, ought to be at least as strong when the consequences of the behavior produce fear or pain in the animal being observed (i.e., learning through observation ought to have more immediate and potentially important consequences for the survival of an observing animal in nature, if the observed behavior has aversive consequences).

Lore, Blanc, and Suedfeld (1971) conducted an experiment in which observer rats in an experimental group were permitted to see another rat learning to passively avoid making nose contacts with a candle flame. Observer rats in a control group viewed a candle and another rat, but no candle contacts could be made by the demonstrator (the candle was isolated in a third compartment between the observer and the demonstrator). When permitted access to the candle flame, observers in the experimental group made fewer nose contacts with the flame than observers in the control group.

Some aspect of demonstrator contact with the flame appeared to play a role in observer learning, but it was not clear that observation of the consequences of nose-flame contact was involved. It is possible that some general arousal-producing cue provided by the demonstrator was responsible for facilitated learning. For example, an olfactory cue such as the smell of singed whiskers or the release of a pheromone may have provided a general alerting cue or resulted in an unconditioned fear response. Similarly, an auditory fear- or pain-produced response by the demonstrator may have altered or frightened the observer. Finally, it is possible that a general visual cue, such as the sight of the demonstrator in rapid retreat (after having made contact with the candle) may have sensitized the observing animal. To the extent that general, arousal-producing cues made the observer more sensitive to pain, increased the observers motivational level, or just resulted in less observer activity, one need not invoke an imitational process to account for facilitated acquisition.

The purpose of our experiment (Bunch & Zentall, 1980) was to replicate the results of Lore et al. and to assess the nonimitational components of facilitated learning. We included three groups of observers with 12 rats in each group. The observe-candle-contact group (E) and no-contact group (NC) were identical to Lore et al.'s two groups of observers. A third group of observers, nonvisual-contact control (NVC), was treated exactly as was Group E, with the exception that a sheet-metal strip placed between the observer and the demonstrator's candle prevented the observer from seeing demonstrator-candle contacts. (To control for the observation of a candle by Group E, a second candle, accessible to neither rat, was placed between the demonstrator's and the observer's compartments.) When the three groups of observers were later exposed to the candle flame, the two control groups (Groups NVC and NC) made a comparable number of flame contacts, whereas significantly more rats in Group E made five or fewer candle contacts than in the two control groups combined (see Figure 9.3). Thus, general arousal-producing cues contributed little to facilitated learning by the candle-contact observers, and the major facilitative effect can be attributed to visual imitation of the passive avoidance response.

Interestingly, a social facilitation effect emerged from the present candle-contact study as well. Although the demonstrators learned the candle avoidance response in the presence of the observers, the observers learned in the absence of a conspecific. Thus comparison of demonstrator learning with observer learning allows for the assessment of social facilitation. Significantly more rats in the combined observer control groups (Groups NVC and NC) made five or fewer candle contacts than in the two demonstrator groups (Groups DE and DNV) combined. Thus, the presence of another rat increased the probability of contacting the candle. This finding is in agreement with Zajonc's social facilitation theory because, prior to learning, contacting the candle would have to be considered a dominant behavior.

The present experiment demonstrated both imitation and social facilitation

Figure 9.3. Number of rats making 0 or 1 candle-flame contact during the first 6 min (hatched bars), and number of rats making 5 or fewer candle-flame contacts to a criterion of 20 min without a contact (combined hatched plus open bars). Group E observed demonstrators (Group DE) learning not to make contact with the candle flame. For Group NVC observation of candle-flame contact by demonstrators (Group DNV) was visually obscured. Group NC observed a candle flame and another rat but no candle-flame contacts were made.

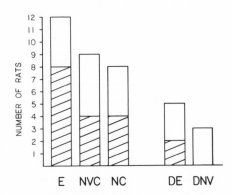

in the context of passive avoidance learning. Thus earlier findings of imitation and social facilitation were confirmed and extended.

The problem in interpreting the results of experiments in which animals observe conspecifics performing aversively motivated tasks is the possibility that general fear conditioning may be responsible for the observed facilitation. For example, in the candle contact experiments the candle, a novel stimulus (CS), may have become associated with an aversive stimulus (US), another rat in pain, through the process of Pavlovian conditioning. In fact, the mere presence of another animal in distress may be sufficient to sensitize an observer (i.e., make it more fearful). We included a control for another animal in distress (Group NVC) and we also tried to control for novel stimulus conditioning by exposing Group NVC to a candle, but the candle (CS) and the distressed demonstrator (US) may not have been sufficiently "paired" to promote conditioning.

Another way to reduce the likelihood of Pavlovian conditioning is to use demonstrators that have been well trained to make an avoidance response. Del Russo (1975) found that observation of a demonstrator performing a discriminated (active) shock-avoidance task facilitated acquisition of that task (but see Sanavio & Savardi, 1979). The use of a well-trained demonstrator that is successfully avoiding shocks should reduce the likelihood that the demonstrator would serve as an aversive US.

Other studies have controlled for fear induced in the observer by the demonstrator's response to pain by exposing observers to a demonstrator performing either a relevant discrimination (the same as the observer's task) or an irrelevant discrimination (one different from the observer's) (Kohn, 1976; Kohn & Dennis, 1972). In these studies facilitated learning occurred only when the stimulus associated with a correct response for the observer was the same as that for the demonstrator.

Thus, there is evidence that observation of performance of a discriminated avoidance task can facilitate acquisition of that task. Such data provide additional evidence for the existence of imitative behavior in rats.

IMITATION OF KEYPECKING BY PIGEONS

Although we and others have demonstrated reliable imitation effects with rats, the ability to imitate motor behavior clearly requires substantial visual-stimulus processing; rats are not known for their superior visual acuity. Unfortunately, imitation research that has used animals with better visual discriminative ability than the rat has been quite spotty. Warren, Bryant, Petty, and Byrne (1975) have reported social facilitation but no imitation in active avoidance learning by goldfish, and Klopfer (1957) has reported some evidence for passive avoidance imitation in ducks under nonlaboratory conditions. More recently, evidence for visually mediated imitative behavior has been reported in blackbirds (see Mason's chapter in this volume), and in monkeys (see Mineka's chapter in this volume).

The purpose of our experiment (Zentall & Hogan, 1976) was to study imitative learning of an "arbitrary" appetitively reinforced response in another visually dominant species, the pigeon. Keypecking in magazine-trained pigeons was assessed following various conditions of observation. Keypeck observers were exposed to a demonstrator pecking a lighted key for grain reinforcement. Consummatory observers were exposed to a demonstrator eating (the eating demonstrator's grain feeder was yoked to that of the keypeck demonstrator). Consummatory observers served as a control for the motivational effects of being in the presence of a conspecific that is eating. Naive observers were exposed to an experimentally naive demonstrator (a social facilitation control). Empty compartment observers were exposed to an empty compartment (a baseline condition against which to assess other learning). Information observers were exposed to keylight-grain pairings in an empty adjacent compartment (a control for non-social events that occurred in the demonstrator's compartment).

When the observers' keys were lit, keypeck observers were significantly more likely to peck (79% of birds pecked) than either consummatory observers or naive observers (30% and 36% of birds pecked, respectively). Thus the results indicate the presence of imitation. The results appear in Table 9.1. Additionally,

Table 9.1

Performance of Pigeons Exposed to a Keypecking
Demonstrator (KPO), an Eating Demonstrator (CO),
a Merely Present Demonstrator (NO), an Empty
Compartment (EO), or an Empty Compartment with
Key-light/grain Pairings (IO)

	Condition				
	KPO	CO	NO	EO	IO
Number of birds in each condition	14	10	14	14	10
Number of birds pecking	11	3	5	1	1

consummatory observers and naive observers were significantly more likely to peck (30% and 36% of the birds pecked, respectively) than empty compartment observers and information observers (7% and 10% of the birds pecked, respectively). Thus the results also indicate the presence of social facilitation, though the social facilitation effect was not in the same direction as it was in the previously described rat experiments (Levine & Zentall, 1974; Zentall & Levine, 1972). It may be that the mere presence of a conspecific affects different species differently. Nonetheless, the results are inconsistent with Zajonc's social facilitation theory.

IMITATION OF DISCRIMINATED KEYPECKING BY PIGEONS

The research presented in this chapter has assessed the extent to which imitative learning can contribute to the acquisition of simple responses (e.g., barpressing and keypecking). Although care has been taken to control for nonimitation factors, including socially produced changes in motivation level due to the mere presence of a conspecific, it is possible that additional increments in motivation can accrue from being in the presence of an active conspecific or a conspecific that is performing *any* reinforced response. Being in the presence of an active conspecific may induce activity in an observer through contagion, and increased activity may lead indirectly to facilitated acquisition of a target response such as barpressing. One approach to this problem would be to find a control task that (a) if it were imitated would not facilitate the acquisition of the target response, but (b) would result in the same level of reinforced activity as the target task. One way to accomplish this would be to have observer pigeons learn a successive discrimination task after having observed a conspecific perform the same task (imitation group) or the reverse of the observer's task (control group). The advantage of this procedure is (a) it controls for general activity (overall amount of pecking and feeding) and (b) it separates the period of observation from the period of performance. The separation of observation opportunity from performance assessment, as well as the use of a mere complex learning task (discrimination learning), should eliminate contagion effects on performance.

Groesbeck and Duerfeldt (1971) have examined the imitation of a visual discrimination by rats. Observation of a demonstrator knocking down the correct cue card for water reinforcement, on an elevated Y maze, facilitated later learning of the same discrimination, relative to a number of control conditions. However, Groesbeck and Duerfeldt (1971) made no assessment of the relevance of the cue cards observed to the cue cards later to be discriminated by the observers (i.e., the cue card that was correct for the demonstrator was always correct for the observer).

On the other hand, Kohn (1976) found that rat observers learned a visually discriminated avoidance task faster after having observed a demonstrator rat perform that discrimination than after having observed a demonstrator perform the reverse of the discrimination to be learned. Unfortunately, a third group of observer rats that observed demonstrators performing a totally different discrimination actually learned their discrimination slightly faster than rats that observed performance of the discrimination to be learned. Performance of the third group should have been at a level midway between the other two groups; thus Kohn's data are difficult to interpret.

There have also been reports of facilitated acquisition of discrimination learning through observation by birds. Cronhelm (1970) trained 7-day-old chicks on a multiple schedule of reinforcement. When the response key was illuminated with one color, responses were reinforced according to a fixed-interval schedule of reinforcement (i.e., the first response after 30 sec was reinforced). When the response key was illuminated with another color, responses were reinforced according to a variable-interval schedule of reinforcement (i.e., the first response after a variable duration with a mean of 30 sec was reinforced). Variable-interval schedules generally result in much higher rates of responding than the fixed-interval schedule. Observer chicks that were present during discrimination acquisition performed the discrimination themselves (in the presence of the demonstrator) at a level significantly above the initial level of performance shown by the demonstrator chicks. Unfortunately, the observer chicks had four more sessions of adaptation to the novel experimental chamber and the presence of another chick than did the demonstrators with which they were compared. The additional period of adaptation could have reduced fear of the experimental apparatus and reduced the possible distractive influence of the other chick. Although it is more efficient use of animals to compare observer performance with that of demonstrators, it is generally more appropriate to compare the performance of observers with that of an independent control group.

Klopfer (1957) also reported a demonstration of facilitated discrimination learning through observation by birds. Ducks that observed other ducks learn to approach one food dish and avoid another, distinctive food dish wired for shock never made contact with the wired food dish when admitted to the pen. Furthermore, new observers that observed only the avoidance behavior of the old observers showed perfect avoidance behavior, though they had never observed the consequences of making contact with the wired food dish. Interpretation of the results is made difficult, however, by the fact that the demonstrators were present not only during the period of observation but also during the test. Thus the results could have been influenced by social flocking. On the other hand, it should be noted that avoidance of the wired food dish by the first observers persisted after removal of the original demonstrators. Thus, some direct avoidance learning must have occurred, and one cannot argue that the observers were simply "following" the demonstrators.

The purpose of our experiments (Edwards, Hogan, & Zentall, 1980) was to assess the ability of pigeons to benefit from the observation of an appetitively motivated visual discrimination. Daily observation by observers of demonstrator pigeons trained to perform a color discrimination (red +, green −, or green +, red −) to a stringent criterion was followed by training with the same or the reverse discrimination. In the first experiment, both demonstrators and observers were exposed to 30-sec trials with 10-sec intertrial intervals, and reinforcement was provided for responding on a variable-interval 60-sec schedule. In the second experiment, both demonstrators and observers were exposed to 10-sec trials with 30-sec intertrial intervals and response independent reinforcement was provided at the end of each trial (automaintenance). The change in procedure from the first experiment to the second experiment was made in order to emphasize the temporal relations among the discriminative stimulus, the demonstrator's pecking response, and reinforcement provided the demonstrator. The results of the two experiments were quite similar. In both cases, birds for which the observed discrimination was consistent with the discrimination to be learned, learned significantly faster than birds for which the observed discrimination was the reverse of the discrimination to be learned. Thus, it is clear from the results of the present experiment and other experiments cited above that observation of a conspecific performing a discrimination can facilitate acquisition of that discrimination.

CONCLUSIONS

Imitation can be defined as a savings either in time or trials to learn a task that accrues to an observer from being exposed to a demonstrator (usually a conspecific) performing that task. Imitative behavior, like many other psychological concepts, is best defined by what it is not. Imitative behavior must be distinguished from the following: social facilitation (effects on performance of the mere presence of a conspecific), contagion (the elicitation of species-typical behavior by a conspecific engaged in that behavior, e.g., eating), local enhancement (the increase in saliency of task-relevant environmental stimuli through their contact with the demonstrator). One can control for social facilitation through the use of a social facilitation control group (see Zentall & Hogan, 1972). One can preclude contagion effects by examining the acquisition of new, arbitrary behavior. And one can avoid local enhancement effects by separating (spatially and temporally) the demonstrator's task stimuli (e.g., the manipulandum) from that of the observer. With regard to local enhancement, however, it has been argued that it is not just the locale that can be enhanced but also the stimuli at that locale (see Galef, chapter 1 of this volume; Spence, 1937). If an observer attends better to the location of the demonstrator's manipulandum (e.g., operant bar) because it is being pressed by the demonstrator it should, by default, attend less to its own bar. But if the observer attends better to the demonstrator's bar, it might also show generalized attention to its own bar due to the similarity between the two bars. One approach to resolving this problem would be to reduce the similarity between the demonstrator's manipulandum and that of the observer. But altering the similarity between the two manipulandi would also reduce the similarity between the two tasks, and would thus make the procedure inappropriate for the assessment of imitation.

The problem is that stimulus enhancement can be proposed as an explanation for facilitated acquisition by observers whenever external stimuli are involved in the task to be imitated. There are three approaches to this problem. First, one can select behavior to be imitated that does not involve external stimuli such as bars or keys. Behavior such as rearing on hind legs or turning in a circle would satisfy this criterion. Findings of faster acquisition following observation would provide strong evidence for the existence of imitative behavior in animals. Second, one could train demonstrators to respond to the manipulandum in different ways (e.g., bar pressing and bar biting). If observers acquired the specific behavior to which they were exposed, a very strong case would be made for imitative learning (see Dawson & Foss, 1965, for some suggestive positive evidence and see Meltzoff's chapter for the general application of such a procedure in support of imitative behavior by newborn human infants). Third, if stimulus enhancement increases the probability of task-stimulus contact, one would expect it to *retard* the acquisition of a passive avoidance response. There is evidence, however, that observation of passive avoidance learning can facilitate acquisition of that response (Bunch & Zentall, 1980; Lore et al., 1971).

The potential problem with the kind of analytic approach to the assessment of imitative learning that has been developed in the present chapter is that by so narrowing the region of evidence that will be accepted as convincing, we may have created for the animal an environment that is so "unnatural" that imitative behavior will not occur, not because it does not exist, but because the behavior and context does not elicit imitation as a learning "strategy." One would hope that the dilemma raised by such narrowing of behavior and context does not present us with a situation analogous to that of the drunk looking for his car keys under the street lamp, not because he lost them there, but because that is the only place where there is light enough to see.

I think it is too early to abandon hope for the laboratory study of imitation with operant procedures. Even if one cannot find evidence for imitative behavior under the stringent conditions described above, because the context does not encourage the appearance of imitative behavior, perhaps one can prime the animal to process social cues by exposing it to a task in which social cues are relevant (e.g., a task that requires cooperative behavior) prior to the assessment of imitative behavior (see Hogan's chapter in this volume).

In the final analysis it may be that imitative behavior cannot best be studied under artificial laboratory conditions and the appropriate assessment of such social behavior will have to await the proper combination of more natural settings with rigorously controlled environmental manipulation. Ultimately, it is the cleverness of the experimenter that allows us to discover how clever the animal is.

ACKNOWLEDGMENTS

This research was supported by NIMH Grants MH 19757, MH 24092, and MH 35378. Preparation of this chapter was supported by NSF Grant BNS-8418275. I thank David E. Hogan, Charles A. Edwards, John M. Levine, and Gail B. Bunch for their participation in the research reported here, and Bennett G. Galef, Jr., for his helpful comments on this manuscript.

REFERENCES

Bayroff, A. G., & Lard, K. E. (1944). Experimental social behavior of animals. III. Imitational learning of white rats. *Journal of Comparative Physiological Psychology, 37,* 165–171.

Bunch, G. B., & Zentall, T. R. (1980). Imitation of a passive avoidance response in the rat. *Bulletin of the Psychonomic Society, 15,* 73–75.

Church, R. M. (1957a). Transmission of learned behavior between rats. *Journal of Abnormal Social Psychology, 54,* 163–165.

Church R. M. (1957b). Two procedures for the establishment of "imitative behavior." *Journal of Comparative and Physiological Psychology, 50,* 315–318.

Corson, J. A. (1967). Observational learning of a lever pressing response. *Psychonomic Science, 7,* 197–198.

Cronhelm, E. (1970). Perceptual factors and observational learning in the behavioural development of young chicks. In J. H. Crook (Ed.), *Social behavior in birds and mammals: Essays on the social ethology of animals and man* (pp. 393–439). New York: Academic Press.

Dawson, B. V., & Foss, B. M. (1965). Observational learning in budgerigars. *Animal Behaviour, 13,* 470–474.

Del Russo, J. E. (1975). Observational learning of discriminative avoidance in hooded rats. *Animal Learning and Behavior, 3,* 76–80.

Edwards, C. A., Hogan, D. E., & Zentall, T. R. (1980). Imitation of an appetitive discriminatory task by pigeons. *Bird Behaviour, 2,* 87–91.

Gardner, E. L., & Engel, D. R. (1971). Imitational and social facilitatory aspects of observational learning in the laboratory rat. *Psychonomic Science, 25,* 5–6.

Groesbeck, R. W., & Duerfeldt, P. H. (1971). Some relevant variables in observational learning of the rat. *Psychonomic Science, 22,* 41–43.

Henning, J. M., & Zentall, T. R. (1981). Imitation, social facilitation, and the effects of ACTH 4-10 on rats' bar-pressing behavior. *American Journal of Psychology, 94,* 125–134.

Herbert, M. J., & Harsh, C. M. (1944). Observational learning by cats. *Journal of Comparative Psychology, 37,* 81–95.

Hull, C. L. (1943). *Principles of Behavior.* New York: Appleton.

Jacoby, K. E., & Dawson, M. E. (1969). Observation and shaping learning: A comparison using Long Evans rats. *Psychonomic Science, 16,* 257–258.

Klopfer, P. H. (1957). An experiment on empathic learning in ducks. *American Naturalist, 91,* 61–63.

Kohn B. (1976). Observation and discrimination learning in the rat: Effects of stimulus substitution. *Learning and Motivation, 7,* 303–312.

Kohn, B., & Dennis, M. (1972). Observation and discrimination learning in the rat: Specific and nonspecific effects. *Journal of Comparative and Physiological Psychology, 78,* 292–296.

Levine, J. M., & Zentall, T. R. (1974). Effect of a conspecific's presence on deprived rats' performance: Social facilitation vs. distraction/imitation. *Animal Learning and Behavior, 2,* 119–122.

Lore, R., Blanc, A., & Suedfeld, P. (1971). Empathic learning of a passive-avoidance response in domesticated *Rattus norvegicus. Animal Behaviour, 19,* 112–114.

Lorenz, K. (1935). Der kumpan in der umwelt des vogels; die artgenosse als ausloesendes moment socialer verhaltensweisen. *Journal fur Ornithologie, 83,* 137–213, 289–413.

Oldfield-Box, H. (1970). Comments on two preliminary studies of "observation" learning in the rat. *Journal of Genetic Psychology, 116,* 45–51.

Powell, R. W. (1968). Observational learning vs shaping: A replication. *Psychonomic Science, 10,* 263–264.

Powell, R. W., & Burns, R. (1970). Visual factors in observational learning with rats. *Psychonomic Science, 21,* 47–48.

Powell, R. W., Saunders, D., & Thompson, W. (1968). Shaping, autoshaping, and observational learning with rats. *Psychonomic Science, 13,* 167–168.

Sanavio, E., & Savardi, U. (1979). Observational learning of a discriminative shuttlebox avoidance by rats. *Psychological Reports, 44,* 1151–1154.

Spence, K. W. (1937). Experimental studies of learning and the higher mental processes in infra-human primates. *Psychological Bulletin, 34,* 806–850.

Thorpe, W. H. (1963). *Learning and instinct in animals* (2nd ed.). Cambridge, MA: Harvard University Press.

Tolman, C. W. (1964). Social facilitation of feeding behaviour in the domestic chick. *Animal Behaviour, 12,* 245–251.

Warden, C. J., & Jackson, T. A. (1935). Imitative behavior in the rhesus monkey. *Journal of Genetic Psychology, 46,* 103–125.

Warren, J. L., Bryant, R. C., Petty, F., & Byrne, W. L. (1975). Group training in goldfish (*carasius auratus*): Effects on acquisition and retention. *Journal of Comparative and Physiological Psychology, 89,* 933–938.

Zajonc, R. B. (1965). Social facilitation. *Science, 149,* 269–274.

Zajonc, R. B., Heingartner, A., & Herman, E. M. (1969). Social enhancement and impairment of performance in the cockroach. *Journal of Personality and Social Psychology, 13,* 83–92.

Zajonc, R. B., & Sales, S. M. (1966). Social facilitation of dominant and subordinate responses. *Journal of Experimental Social Psychology, 2,* 160–168.

Zentall, T. R., & Hogan, D. E. (1976). Imitation and social facilitation in the pigeon. *Animal Learning and Behavior, 4,* 427–430.

Zentall, T. R., & Levine, J. M. (1972). Observational learning and social facilitation in the rat. *Science, 178,* 1220–1221.

Learning in the Rat
of a Choice Response by
Observation of S-S Contingencies

M. Ray Denny
Carla F. Clos
R. Charles Bell
Michigan State University

INTRODUCTION

This chapter describes a program of research that contributes to the analysis of the mechanisms mediating observational learning. [1] The basic design is one in which a hungry rat observes two distinctive environmental events, one having a positive consequence (food pellet) and the other a negative consequence (no pellet). These events, downward movement of two radically different levers (bars), are ones that the rat, if so permitted, could bring about by itself. Initially, though, the bars are inaccessible and operated solely by a hidden experimenter. When the rat clearly indicates it has learned the unique correlation between the movement of the positive, or S+, bar and the availability of food, both bars are made accessible to the rat to determine whether it will make the S+ event happen. Unlike many other observational learning experiments this procedure ensures that the rat has observed the relevant environmental events because it must use these events to

---

[1] For us, observational learning refers to a mode of response acquisition via stimulus-stimulus contingencies that is purposeful and directive in nature. It may involve multiple observational trials but occurs without overt responding (like Bandura's, 1965, no-trial learning). Imitation, commonly used interchangeably with observational learning, is distinguished here by the addition of a model. Information can clearly be gained with or without a model, although certain responses (conditioned taste aversion) require a model.

perform correctly on a go/no-go discrimination by approaching a distal food tray after the S+ bar has been activated and inhibit approach after the S− bar has been activated. Failure to make this critical check of the observing response may help explain the many failures to demonstrate imitative behavior from Thorndike (1898) on.

Although our paradigm resembles blocked discriminative autoshaping (Browne, 1976), there is an important difference. The exact nature of the to-be-learned response (mechanical barpress) is not demonstrated to the subject in an autoshaping procedure. On autoshaping trials, the bar is simply inserted and the insertion correlated with food.

Other experiments have eliminated the model in observational learning and found that observers come to make the target response when given the opportunity to do so. For example, this was demonstrated by Groesbeck and Duerfeldt (1971) with rats when the experimenter knocked down the correct stimulus panel, by Jacobson and Sisemore (1976) with humans in a lever-pressing task, and by Suboski and Bartashunas (1984) with chicks in a situation in which a moving arrow simulated pecking.

Our experimental paradigm can be conceptualized as a type of subordinate S-S ("what leads to what") latent learning à la Tolman. The significate in the sign-significate relation at hand is movement of the S+ bar (itself a sign for the food pellet) and the sign is the chamber containing the two bars. But unlike the largely unsuccessful Spence-Lippitt (1946) tests of latent learning of the late 1940s (e.g., Grice, 1948; Kendler, 1947) the animal's current motivational state is now relevant to the goal object used. According to Tolman (1932), the docile rat should have the necessary means-end readiness[2] in its repertoire and should eventually manifest the appropriate behavior route to the significate (downward movement of the S+ bar as a stimulus) by pressing the S+ bar when the opportunity arises, simply because it has learned the subordinate S-S relation. And since the terminal food pellet significate is motivationally relevant here, latent learning (observational learning) should occur.

Another way to describe our research program is in terms of the hypothesis that originally triggered it. Associate R. Charles Bell constructed the original hypothesis from naturalistic observations and from a general perusal of the Russian literature. His cognitive hypothesis can be stated formally as follows: A reward is an unconditioned stimulus to scan cognitively back in time in search of some precondition (cue stimulus) that consistently precedes this reward. With repeated scannings, the animal then executes, whenever possible, actions that

---

[2]To Tolman a means-end readiness is "equivalent to what in ordinary parlance we call a 'belief' (a readiness or disposition) to the effect that an instance of this *sort* of stimulus situation, if reacted to by an instance of this *sort* of response, will lead to that *sort* of further stimulus situation" (Tolman, 1959, p. 113).

lead to the precondition for this reward. On reflection, any differences between Bell's hypothesis[3] and our interpretation of Tolman appear minor.

INITIAL RESEARCH

Our standard procedure used experimentally naive rats. First, individual rats engaged in brief preliminary exploration of the observation apparatus with the well-differentiated bars inoperable (see Figure 10.1). At least 10 97-mg Noyes pellets were available in the food tray during exploration. Next, 5 additional reward pellets were individually delivered while the rat was confined to the tunnel; a pellet was delivered only after the rat had left the food tray and faced the closed tunnel door before returning to the food tray. Both hooded and albino rats, 110–200 days old, at 90%–95% of ad lib weight were used (more highly deprived rats bit the tunnel door and visited the food tray excessively).

Observational training began on the following day and only occurred when the rat was looking toward the test chamber. This was no problem, because, with very few exceptions, the rats promptly turned toward the tunnel door after visiting the food tray. In the go/no-go discrimination, half the observing animals were trained with the activation of the left bar as S+ and the activation of the right bar as S−. The tip of the activated left bar had a total excursion of 8.5 cm and made a sharp click when it struck the chamber floor. The right bar when activated had a downward excursion of 2.2 cm, turned on a dim light above the bar, and produced a faint click from the microswitch.

A food pellet was not dropped through the tube on S+ trials until after the rat had turned around in the tunnel to face the food tray. Thus the moving bars and attendant stimuli, rather than the slight noise that the pellet made when it hit the tray, maintained exclusive stimulus control of go/no-go behavior. Activation of the S− bar was followed by nonreinforcement. The intertrial interval (ITI) was a Poisson distribution of time intervals with a mean of 10 sec and a range of 1 to 60 sec. This meant that wait time could not become a reliable cue for leaving the door and approaching the food tray. The ITI started after the rat returned to the door from the food tray or after the rat had waited 10 sec at the door on S− trials. If the rat was not present at the door at the end of the scheduled time, the ITI was prolonged.

---

[3]According to Bell his principle helps explain operant learning. The internal stimuli produced by the operant serve as a precondition for reward; thus, the response is repeated so as to produce those stimuli that consistently precede reward. Operant conditioning is essentially a special case of this reinforcement principle because the preconditional stimulus is confounded with the operant response. In this chapter, learning is demonstrated in the more general case in which the precondition for reward is separated from the response.

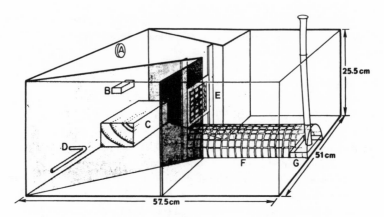

Figure 10.1. The two-choice observation apparatus. The funnel-shaped compartment is called the test chamber. (A)Light. (B)Right bar. (C)Wooden block present only in Experiments 1 and 2. (D)Left bar. (E)Hardware cloth tunnel door in up position. Door is down during observational training. (F)Hardware cloth tunnel. (G)Food tray. Pellet is dropped through tube. The experimenter activates the bars from behind the stimulus panel and can observe the subject through the near wall opposite to the tunnel. The subject cannot see the experimenter until after it turns toward the food tray.

Trials were administered in blocks of twenty, 10 S+ and 10 S− trials randomly distributed; and generally one or two blocks were presented daily until the discrimination criterion was reached. The criterion was (a) inhibiting on 9 out of 10 S− trials by continuing to face the test chamber for at least 10 sec after the S− bar moved, and (b) leaving the tunnel door for the food tray in less than 10 sec on all 10 S+ trials of a block (well-trained subjects left in 1 or 2 sec).

Once the criterion was met, the tunnel door was raised and the subject was allowed to enter the test chamber. The tunnel door closed behind the rat. On this trial a rat typically explored for a while before pressing a bar. Contact of the left bar was recorded as a barpress if the lever was displaced from the "up" position (.45 rad from horizontal) to the horizontal position. Contact of the right bar was recorded as a barpress if the light turned on. After the subject pressed a bar it was returned to its home cage. Thus, with respect to the food tray the subject was neither reinforced nor nonreinforced for barpressing on this or any test trial, though conditioned reinforcement could possibly occur from the light on the right or the sharp click of the left bar. For this reason, the initial test trial was viewed as a critical test of the learning (Adler, 1955). On each of the three succeeding days (test days 2, 3, and 4) the rat was placed in the tunnel and given one block of 20 go/no-go booster trials followed immediately by a test as described above. On test days 5, 6, and 7 the rat was tested both prior to and following the block of 20 booster trials. This gave a total of 10 test trials over a 7-day period. Following the 7 test days, subjects received additional observational training with the cues reversed (movement of the S+ bar became S− and vice versa). Upon reaching the same criterion as used for the original discrimination the subjects were given 10 test trials in the same fashion for 7 days.

Male Rats Trained First to Barpress (Experiment 1)

When this research began (Denny, Bell, & Clos, 1983), some of us doubted that a naive rat that had learned to discriminate between the two bars just by watching from the tunnel would actually press either bar when bars were made accessible. Consequently, the initial phase of Experiment 1 involved the conventional training of each rat to press both bars about equally well before they received observational training in the tunnel. We were simply concerned with whether the rats would press the bar whose operation was uniquely correlated with food. Seven male rats were employed as subjects. Training the rats to press either bar to receive reinforcement at the end of the tunnel was a laborious task. In nearly every case, the bars had to be baited with wet mash and the wet mash gradually faded. Shaping was also employed. Presumably the delayed reinforcement involved in entering the tunnel and traversing its length to the food tray as well as learning two responses more or less simultaneously made the learning difficult. All rats were trained until barpress latency was 10 sec. Subjects were reinforced equally often on each bar. In the observational training that followed, the S+ bar was always the nonpreferred bar.

The 7 rats learned the go/no-go discrimination in a mean of 232 trials, including the criterial block. Six of them pressed the S+ bar on the initial test trial, and those 6 pressed the S+ bar on an average of 83% of the 10 test trials. The other rat (trained to right bar as S+) pressed the S− bar 80% of the time. Despite criterial learning in the tunnel, the 6 reversed rats persisted in pressing the old S+ bar on an average of 85% of the test trials.

These generally positive results encouraged us to eliminate the barpress pretraining in Experiment 2 to see whether observational training alone would produce appropriate responding during test[4] and to investigate further the failure on test of the S-S reversal learning.

---

[4]Others (Corson, 1967; Jacoby & Dawson, 1969) have found that observational training alone is an easier method for getting an operant started than conventional methods.

S-S Observational Reversal Learning in Experimentally Naive Rats (Experiment 2)

By this time an explanation of the rats' failure to reverse on test in Experiment 1 became apparent. According to elicitation theory, rats learn a particular barpress during test trials through consistent responding in the test chamber situation (Denny & Adelman, 1955). This S-R learning is protected from extinction because reversal training in the tunnel is in a different stimulus context than the context in which barpress learning occurred. For extinction to take place, the original and the competing response must occur in similar stimulus contexts (Denny, 1971). The test of this interpretation was to reverse a group on the go/no-go discrimination before it had received any test trials. Without test trials to mediate the S-R learning, the original S-S learning should be extinguished by learning the S-S reversal. Thus, the hypothesis under test is that the new S+ bar is consistently pressed only if reversal training precedes all test trials.

Twelve male rats were divided into two groups of 6 rats each. One group received the standard training outlined earlier, that is, tested before reversal, TBR (see Table 10.1). The other group was reversed before testing (RBT in Table 10.1), with the reversal training beginning on the day after the criterion was met. Group RBT was given a second reversal followed by a second testing session of 10 trials.

Table 10.1
Outline of the Experimental Phases for the Observational Learning Groups

	Phase				
Group	1	2	3	4	5
TBR	Observational learning		Test (BT)	Observational learning (reversal)	Test (BT)
RBT	Observational learning	Observational learning (reversal)	Test (BT)	Observational learning (reversal)	Test (BT)
C-TBR	Observational learning		Test	Observational learning (reversal)	Test (BT)
ETC	Observational learning + 120 BT	Observational learning (reversal)	Test (BT)	Observational learning (reversal)	Test (BT)

Note. TBR = Tested Before Reversed; RBT = Reversed Before Tested; C-TBR = Control-Tested Before Reversed; ETC = Extra Trials Control; BT = Booster Trials.

212

The original go/no-go discrimination was learned in a mean of 219.2 trials (N = 12). The first reversal had a mean of 210.4 trials, and there was no significant difference between TBR and RBT on this measure (p > .4). The second reversal (RBT only) was learned in a mean of 196.6 trials (n = 5).

All TBR subjects pressed the S+ bar on initial test and on an average of 87% of the test trials during the first test session. As in Experiment 1, though, TBR subjects failed to reverse. They pressed the new S+ on only 18% of the test trials. Five of the 6 rats in RBT, however, did reverse. All 5 pressed the new S+ bar on the initial test and on an average of 92% of the first 10 test trials (one rat never pressed either bar). The difference between groups on the 10 test trials following the first reversal (TBR Phase 5 and RBT Phase 3) was highly significant. Furthermore, after a second observational reversal, the 5 RBT rats that had learned to barpress failed to reverse on test. They pressed the new S+ bar on an average of 4% of the tests in Phase 5. Again, the intervening barpressing during test trials prevented reversal, supporting our hypothesis.

Absence of an Overtraining Effect on S-S Reversal (Experiment 3)

Because TBR had 120 more trials (booster trials) on the original go/no-go discrimination than RBT before reversal training, overtraining could have produced the failure of TBR to reverse in Experiment 2. This would seem unlikely because overtraining, if anything, typically facilitates rather than hinders reversal learning. But a direct test was in order.

Eighteen males were evenly divided into three groups. An extra trials control (ETC) group received 120 overtraining trials, 20 per day, after reaching the original criterion and prior to reversal. After reversal training and after reaching reversal criterion, ETC received its initial set of 10 test trials, and then was reversed and tested again (see Table 10.1). There were two groups tested before reversal, one without the booster trials during the initial testing phase (C-TBR) and one with the 120 extra training trials as in Experiment 2 (TBR). All groups received booster trials during test days following a reversal.

All three groups showed similar observational learning, with means to criterion of 196.7, 196.7, and 213.3 on the original go/no-go discrimination and means of 250, 216.7, and 220 on first reversal for ETC, C-TBR, and TBR, respectively.

All 6 ETC rats pressed the new S+ bar on the initial test trial, and on the average pressed it 93.3% of the 10 test trials, clearly showing reversal of the directed response and that 120 overlearning trials do not prevent reversal. When ETC was reversed for the second time, this time after 10 test trials, it failed to reverse, as was true of all groups tested before reversal. The new S+ bar was pressed on only 10% of the 10 test trials.

Five of 6 TBR subjects pressed the S+ bar on the first test trial. The 4 rats in TBR that showed good learning on initial test continued to press the original S+ on an average of 97.5% of the 10 test trials after reversal training. Likewise, all 6 rats in C-TBR pressed the S+ bar on the initial test trial and on 86.7% of the first set of 10 test trials, and then pressed the old S+ an average of 95% of the 10 test trials following reversal training.

In short, C-TBR and TBR, groups that differed only on whether 120 extra trials were received during testing, did not differ significantly on reversal of bar preference ($p > .53$); whereas TBR and ETC, which differed only on whether they received test trials prior to reversal training, did differ significantly on reversal performance ($p < .02$). Overtraining has no effect on S-S reversal. What is relevant for S-S reversal is whether or not the subject has received test trials, S-R learning, prior to reversal.

ASSESSMENT OF THE GENERALITY OF OBSERVATIONAL LEARNING: IS SEX A FACTOR?

With few exceptions (e.g., Oldfield-Box, 1970) studies on the observational learning of barpressing in rats have not tested for sexual dimorphism (Corson, 1967; Del Russo, 1971; Gardner & Engel, 1971; Huang, Koski, & DeQuardo, 1983; Jacoby & Dawson, 1969; Powell, 1968; Strobel, 1972; Zentall & Levine, 1972). The results obtained when we first ran females to test for gender differences (Clos & Denny, 1983) were not as clear-cut as those obtained with male subjects. On test, TBR females contacted the S+ bar on an average of only 42% of the first 10 test trials, with performance marked by variability (range from 0 to 80%). Only 2 out of the 5 subjects pressed the S+ bar on the initial trial. In contrast, RBT females responded more similarly though not as well as male subjects, with 4 out of 5 pressing the S+ bar on the initial test and an 82% average response to the most recent S+ bar in Phase 3. Like males, RBT females failed to reverse in Phase 5, pressing the most recent S+ bar on only 18% of the test trials. The effect of sex appeared to depend on whether testing occurred before or after reversal.

A possible explanation for the observed sex difference is suggested by the fact that the females required a longer period of pretraining—more food associations and extended training of the observing response. If during this extended pretraining all the stimuli in the chamber were relevant (all predictors of reinforcement), then subsequent S-S learning to the moving bars could be retarded, that is, contextual blocking could occur. Experiment 4 was a test of this explanation.

Contextual Blocking by Extended Preliminary Training: A Possible Confound? (Experiment 4)

In order to answer the question of whether the extra pretraining given females prevented or retarded their acquisition of the demonstrated response the number of food-only presentations must be systematically varied. But this variable is not under experimenter control with females; therefore, males were employed in this experiment. Sixteen male rats were assigned to four treatment groups (N s $= 4$). Each group received a different number of US only (food-only) trials during pretraining (1-US only, 5-US only, 35-US only, 100-US only). The food-only trials were scheduled according to a Poisson distribution of intertrial intervals, with a 10-sec mean and a 1- to 60-sec range. Except for the rat facing away from the food tray, food was presented independently of behavior in the tunnel. Observational training began in the session following the food-only session and continued until the discrimination criterion was met. All animals were in the C-TBR condition without reversal.

The mean number of trials to criterion on the original go/no-go discrimination for Groups 1, 5, 35, and 100, respectively, was 287.5, 291.3, 304.8, and 235.5 trials. A Kruskal-Wallis one-way analysis indicated that the number of food only trials did not significantly affect the number of trials to criterion in the go/no-go discrimination, H (3) $= 1.936$, $p > .25$. As can be seen in Figure 10.2, however, performance on the S+ and S− trials (CS+ and CS− in Figure 10.2) did differ as a function of the number of pretraining trials. All subjects in Groups 1, 5, and 35 were responding reliably ($> 70\%$ correct) on S+ trials within 80 trials, as compared with Group 100. Clearly, conditioning to S+ was retarded during the observational phase in Group 100. Group 100 also showed a great deal of inhibition to S− on early trial blocks. Both sets of data are consistent with a contextual blocking interpretation. Evidence of blocking is camouflaged when the overall discrimination criterion is used because Groups 1, 5, and 35 take many trials to inhibit to S−.

Figure 10.3 shows that the number of pretraining trials was an important factor in test trial performance. As a result of pretraining trials 1–35, performance increased monotonically, as shown by a significant positive correlation between the logarithm of the number of pretraining trials and the number of correct responses, r (10) $= .48$, $p < .05$, one-sided. One hundred trials produced a significant retarding effect when compared with 35 pretraining trials, $p < .01$. To our knowledge this finding of contextual blocking is the first reported evidence of blocking in observational learning and is especially interesting since it is a decidedly robust effect.

From the results, it seems unlikely that the TBR females' failure to show S-S learning can be explained by contextual blocking for even the most difficult females received fewer than 35 food-only trials during pretraining. In fact,

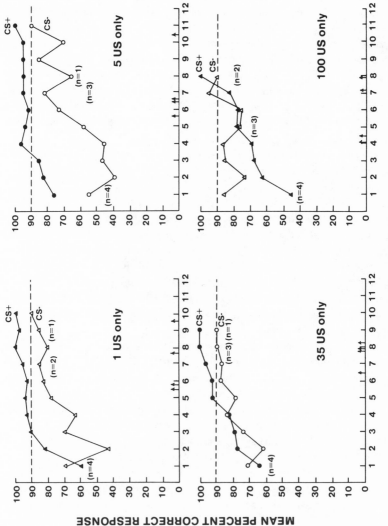

216

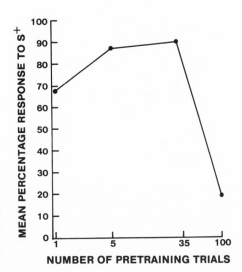

Figure 10.3. Mean percentage correct response on test as a function of the number of pretraining food-only trials. Note abscissa is plotted on a logarithmic basis.

according to the present data females should have performed better on test because of the extra pretraining.

Noise Reduction During Bar Movement: A Possible Solution to the Female Dilemma (Experiment 5)

Because of Andrew's (1975) suggestion that testosterone enhances sustained attention we attempted to test the hypothesis that gonadal hormones account for the males' superiority on our task. Consistently negative results were obtained (Clos & Denny, 1983). In the course of this research, however, we discovered that female subjects had a strong preference to press the right bar even when it was S−. This suggested an explanation for the females' inferior performance on test trials. When the left bar hit the floor of the test chamber it produced a sharp click. The pronounced click may have been selectively aversive to the females, resulting in avoidance of the left bar and poor test performance (adult human females have less tolerance for loud sounds than males [McGuinness, 1972]).

To test this hypothesis, we reduced the noise associated with the operation of the left bar by taping a thick foam pad under the left bar. Also, care was taken

---

Figure 10.2. Mean percentage response on CS+ and CS− (S+ and S−) trials for each of the four groups in Experiment 4. The n represents the number of subjects used in calculating the mean percentage correct for that block. The arrows indicate when subjects reached overall criterion. Subjects reaching criterion within a 40-trial block were included in calculating the mean for that block.

to reduce the force with which the bar struck the pad. The right bar retained the faint click from the microswitch. Six female rats were run under TBR conditions with half trained with the left bar as S+ and half trained with the right bar as S+.

With the reduction of noise from the left bar, responding to it clearly improved. Female TBR subjects pressed the S+ bar an average of 81.6% of the 10 test trials and continued to press this bar 75% of the test trials following reversal training. The median latency to barpress was 34 sec, and 5 out of 6 subjects pressed the S+ bar on the initial test trial. For the first time TBR females as a group (regardless of which bar was S+) showed good evidence of observational learning.

The aversive click of the left bar seems to be largely responsible for the gender difference found earlier. Presumably, if females are given sufficient habituation to the training procedures, the noise of the activated left bar will no longer be aversive and performance on test will be facilitated. Thus, group RBT from the initial female study with approximately 400 more trials than group TBR before initial test readily approached the left bar and pressed it when it was S+ and therefore as a group performed more similarly to the males.

ENHANCEMENT OR SOMETHING MORE?

That an animal comes to behave like another, or in this case comes to make the demonstrated response, may or may not involve copying of the demonstrated response (e.g., Bullock & Neuringer, 1977; Galef, 1971). Indeed perceptual factors alone may lead to the observer's making the target response. For instance, Spence (1937) suggested that the actions of the model bring the attention of the observer to the relevant stimulus features of the experimental problem (stimulus enhancement).

Essentially, then, stimulus enhancement is a matter of place discrimination rather than response discrimination. Thorpe referred to it as local enhancement and defined it as an "apparent imitation resulting from directing the animal's attention to a particular object or to a particular part of the environment" (Thorpe, 1963, p. 134). Local enhancement in the present context refers to the possibility that the rats will approach and manipulate the left or right bar after observational training because their test responses are largely limited to the enhanced region, and any topographic similarity between the rat's pressing the bar and the prior depression of the bar is spurious.

It appears critical, then, to show that subjects have not simply been approaching an attractive place and accidentally making an S+ response that has a relatively high operant level but have indeed learned to execute the appropriate S+ movement. It should be noted that observation of the rats' behavior indicated there was nothing accidental about the responding. Learned responses appeared full-blown with short latencies on the initial test. But more direct tests were in order.

Are Moving Bars Necessary?
(Experiment 6)

If, as we have been asserting, the nature of the to-be-learned response is specified by the moving bars, then a control that eliminates bar depression during training should attenuate responding on test and argue against an enhancement interpretation. The following experiment provided this control (Denny et al., 1983). Six male rats were trained in the tunnel on the go/no-go discrimination to the same criterion as previously used but without bars moving. For 3 rats the light going on above the right bar and the faint sound of a microswitch click was the S+ and the S− was a sharp blow (click) on the back panel behind the point where the tip of the left bar would ordinarily strike the floor. For the other 3 rats, S+ and S− were reversed. The test trial was ended and the subject removed if the subject did not press either bar within 5 min after entry to the test chamber.

The bar movement controls learned the go/no-go discrimination in a mean of 212.5 trials, in about the same number as subjects previously trained with moving bars. But their test trial behavior was markedly different. For the first time on test trials, including the initial one, male rats often failed to respond within 5 min after entry to the test chamber, and the latencies when barpressing did occur were long (median was 136 sec). Also, when both a failure to respond and an S− barpress were counted as errors, exactly 50% of the test trials were incorrect. Thus, it appears that moving bars contributed considerably to the observational learning of pressing the S+ bar in previous experiments.

The possibility remains, however, that poor performance on test was due to the failure to localize auditory cues used during observational training. Had the stimuli been more localizable, the subjects might have approached the positive region on test and made the correct response by chance. Thus, local enhancement may still remain a tenable hypothesis.

Observation of a Directional Response
(Experiment 7)

Experiment 7 involved a more rigorous test of whether moving bars lead to a response discrimination or a place discrimination. If two topographically improbable responses are demonstrated during the observational phase at the same location during both positive and negative trials then simply approach to an enhanced area should not result in either response predominating on test (chance performance). Whereas, if the S+ response predominates, then true observational learning has occurred and local enhancement has been ruled out. Eight male rats were run under TBR conditions without reversal. The apparatus was modified in the following ways. One straight cylindrical black bar (.79 cm diameter) was centered on the front panel (7.3 cm above the floor of the chamber and 25.5 cm from either side) and protruded 8.6 cm into the test chamber. The bar could be easily pivoted right or left of the neutral center position. Half of the subjects were assigned to a TBR-R group with bar movement to the right for S+ trials and to the left for S− trials. The other 4 subjects, TBR-L group, observed just the opposite movement for S+ and S−. Subjects never observed the bar return to the neutral position so as to ensure that bar movement occurred exclusively in one direction for both S+ and S−. After both S+ and S− trials, the bar was returned to the neutral position when the subject had turned to check the food tray or, in the case of a failure to turn, after all room lighting had been extinguished. These blackout periods were on the order of a few seconds and occurred roughly equally often after S+ and S− trials because subjects frequently did not inhibit more than 12 sec. Because of the difficulty of the task, a less stringent discrimination criterion was used. The criterion was (a) inhibiting on 8 of 10 S− trials by continuing to face the test chamber for at least 10 sec after the S− bar moved, and (b) leaving the tunnel door for the food tray in less than 10 sec on 9 of 10 S+ trials of a block. Subjects were tested until 10 tests had been given on which a barpress response occurred. A response was counted as a barpress if the bar had an excursion of at least 2.5 cm from the neutral position. Subjects were removed from the test chamber if no barpress response was made within 8 min of entry to the chamber. Other than these specified modifications, the procedure was the same as for the earlier experiments.

Learning the go/no-go discrimination from bar movement to the right or left was a very difficult task for the subjects. Two of the 8 subjects failed to reach the discrimination criterion even after 1,100 trials and as nonlearners were excluded from further analysis. The other 6 subjects learned the go/no-go discrimination in a mean of 483.3 trials. On test, subjects showed good evidence of having learned the directional response, with 5 of 6 subjects pressing the bar in the S+ direction on the initial test trial. Furthermore, the 6 subjects pressed the bar in the S+ direction (no significant difference between TBR-L and TBR-R, $p > .35$) an average of 81.7% of the first 10 trials on which a response occurred. Anywhere from 10 to 15 test trials were required for the subjects to produce 10 measurable barpresses. The use of only one manipulandum for both the positive and negative bar movement may very well have resulted in conflicting response tendencies of approach and avoidance and led to the occasional failure to respond on test and to the long latencies when barpressing did occur (the median was 96 sec for 60 trials). Support comes from the informal observation that subjects often approached and then left the bar several times before pressing it.

Although the results of this final experiment could have been more conclusive, the test data are not really that discrepant from the two-bar data when the following points are taken into account: (a) the necessarily less stringent learning criterion used for the go/no-go discrimination in the single bar situation; and (b) the question of whether typical laboratory rats are likely to have well-developed push-right and push-left responses in their repertoire—or means-end readiness as Tolman would put it. The data from Experiments 6 and 7, taken together, suggest that something other than local enhancement has been operating in the observational learning of a demonstrated response. Indeed, it is hard to interpret these data "noncognitively." Subjects appear to attend closely to the bar movement and appropriately operate on the environment when given the opportunity to do so. The necessary condition for the appropriate barpress appears to be the actual bar movement, that is, the response demonstration. In other words, the topographic similarity between the rat's test response and the movement of the bar during training is not just spurious.

CONCLUDING REMARKS

Clearly, if there are important contingencies associated with certain external events, the observing animal makes the positive event occur when this becomes possible, even in the absence of both a responding model and subsequent reinforcement of the appropriate tested response, and does so in a full-blown fashion on initial test. Furthermore, once an appropriate response consistently occurs, then even though the value of the external event may change via the go/no-go reversal, the original barpress response continues to be made. Making a consistent response, whether overt as in the test chamber, or covert as when the go/no-go discrimination is learned (perceptual or attentional), leads to relevant learning—consistent with the tenets of elicitation theory (Denny 1971, 1986). This basic finding holds for both males and females, and cannot be explained by overlearning or enhancement effects.

The S-R association predominates over the S-S reversal association even though the S-S association involves many more learning trials than the S-R association. This is expected according to the elicitation position because the S-R habit is not extinguished by the opposite S-S learning that occurs in a very different stimulus context (i.e., observing through the tunnel door). That is, no competing response is pitted against the overt barpress response of the S-R habit in the stimulus context in which the S-R habit was established, namely, in the test chamber. Thus the S-R association is protected from extinction. As such, the intact S-R habit does not appear to impede the development of a reversed S-S association during observational training (trials to reversal criterion are about the same in TBR and RBT groups). The S-R habit appears to compete effectively with the new S-S association only in the test situation.

One final note: When the rat presses the S+ bar, it does *not* attempt to get back in the tunnel to obtain a food pellet; the rat presses the bar rather "deliberately" and just stays there, often hanging onto the bar. This last point invites the speculation that the rat is acting as if it were commenting on the environment, telling us in its own way that this is the S+ bar. Tolman would certainly have appreciated our rats' behavior.

REFERENCES

Adler, H. E. (1955). Some factors of observational learning in cats. *Journal of Genetic Psychology, 86,* 159–177.

Andrew, R. J. (1975). Effects of testosterone on the behaviour of the domestic chick II. Effects present in both sexes. *Animal Behavior, 23,* 156–168.

Bandura, A. (1965). Vicarious processes: A case of no-trial learning. In L. Berkowitz (Ed.), *Advances in experimental social psychology* (Vol. 2, pp. 1–55). New York: Academic Press.

Browne, M. P. (1976). The role of primary reinforcement and overt movements in autoshaping in the pigeon. *Animal Learning and Behavior, 4,* 287–292.

Bullock, D., & Neuringer, A. (1977). Social learning by following: An analysis. *Journal of Experimental Analysis of Behavior, 25,* 127–135.

Clos, C. F., & Denny, M. R. (1983, November). *Learning of a non-performed response by observation of two-choice contingencies.* Paper presented at the meeting of the Psychonomic Society, San Diego, CA.

Corson, J. A. (1967). Observational learning of a lever pressing response. *Psychonomic Science, 7,* 197–198.

Del Russo, J. (1971). Observational learning in hooded rats. *Psychonomic Science, 24,* 37–38.

Denny, M. R. (1971). A theory of experimental extinction and its relation to a general theory. In H. H. Kendler & J. T. Spence (Eds.), *Essays in neobehaviorism: A memorial volume to Kenneth W. Spence* (pp. 43–67). New York: Appleton-Century-Crofts.

Denny, M. R. (1986). "Retention" of S-R in the midst of the cognitive invasion. In D. F. Kendrick, M. E. Rilling, & M. R. Denny (Eds.), *Theories of animal memory* (pp. 35–50). Hillsdale, NJ: Lawrence Erlbaum Associates.

Denny, M. R., & Adelman, H. M. (1955). Elicitation theory: I. An analysis of two typical learning situations. *Psychological Review, 62,* 290–296.

Denny, M. R., Bell, R. C., & Clos, C. F. (1983). Two-choice, observational learning and reversal in the rat: S-S versus S-R effects. *Animal Learning and Behavior, 11.* 223–228.

Galef, B. G. (1971). Social effects in the weaning of domestic rat pups. *Journal of Comparative and Physiological Psychology, 75,* 358–362.

Gardner, E. L., & Engel, D. R. (1971). Imitational and social facilitatory aspects of observational learning in the laboratory rat. *Psychonomic Science, 25,* 5–6.

Grice, G. R. (1948). An experimental test of the expectation theory of learning. *Journal of Comparative and Physiological Psychology, 41,* 137–143.

Groesbeck, R. W., & Duerfeldt, P. H. (1971). Some relevant variables in observational learning of the rat. *Psychonomic Science, 22,* 41–43.

Huang, I., Koski, C. A., & DeQuardo, J. R. (1983). Observational learning of a bar-press by rats. *Journal of General Psychology, 108,* 103–111.

Jacobson, J. M., & Sisemore, D. A. (1976). Observational learning of a lever pressing task. *Southern Journal of Educational Research, 10,* 59–73.

Jacoby, K. E., & Dawson, M. E. (1969). Observation and shaping learning: A comparison using Long Evans rats. *Psychonomic Science, 16,* 257–258.

Kendler, H. H. (1947). An investigation of latent learning in a T-maze. *Journal of Comparative and Physiological Psychology, 40,* 265–270.

McGuinness, D. (1972). Hearing: Individual differences in perceiving. *Perception, 1,* 465–473.

Oldfield-Box, H. (1970). Comments on two preliminary studies of "observation" learning in the rat. *Journal of Genetic Psychology, 116,* 45–51.

Powell, R. W. (1968). Observational learning vs shaping: A replication. *Psychonomic Science, 10,* 263–264.

Spence, K. W. (1937). Experimental studies of learning and the higher mental processes in infra-human primates. *Psychological Bulletin, 34,* 806–850.

Spence, K. W., & Lippitt, R. (1946). An experimental test of the sign-Gestalt theory of trial and error learning. *Journal of Experimental Psychology, 36,* 491–502.

Strobel, M. G. (1972). Social facilitation of operant behavior in satiated rats. *Journal of Comparative and Physiological Psychology, 80,* 502–508.

Suboski, M. D., & Bartashunas, C. (1984). Mechanisms for social transmission of pecking preferences to neonatal chicks. *Journal of Experimental Psychology: Animal Behavior Processes, 10,* 182–194.

Thorndike, E. L. (1898). Animal intelligence: An experimental study of the associative processes in animals. *Psychological Monograph, 2,* (4, Whole No. 8).

Thorpe, W. H. (1963). *Learning and instinct in animals.* Cambridge: Harvard University Press.

Tolman, E. C. (1932). *Purposive behavior in animals and men.* New York: Appleton-Century-Crofts.

Tolman, E. C. (1959). Principles of purposive behavior. In S. Koch (Ed.), *Psychology: A study of a science* (Vol. 2, pp. 92–157). New York: McGraw-Hill.

Zentall, T. R., & Levine, J. M. (1972). Observational learning and social facilitation in the rat. *Science, 178,* 1220–1221.

Learned Imitation
by Pigeons

David E. Hogan
Northern Kentucky University

INTRODUCTION

A number of recent observational learning experiments with pigeons suggest that arbitrary stimuli that control a demonstrator's learned response can quickly gain control over topographically similar behavior in observers. Some examples include learning through observation to peck at a hedonically neutral object such as a plastic disk (Epstein, 1984; Zentall & Hogan, 1976), a Ping-Pong ball (Epstein, 1984) or a loop of rope (Epstein, 1984), or to peck discriminatively at a disk illuminated by different wavelengths of light (Edwards, Hogan, & Zentall, 1980; Hogan, 1986).

Most of the prior research with pigeons has focused on demonstrating the mere existence of learned imitative behavior and only limited research has analyzed how the behavioral match is achieved without explicit shaping (e.g., Miller & Dollard, 1941; Skinner, 1962). The present chapter examines the discriminative and motivational determinants of pigeons' observational learning of simple and complex responses.

DEFINITIONS OF IMITATIVE BEHAVIOR

There are several processes by which imitative behavior may be socially transmitted among conspecifics (Thorpe, 1963). Social facilitation, or contagion, is a process in which the behavior of a conspecific acts as a social releaser of identical, instinctive behavior in an observing conspecific. For example, the sight of one bird feeding may stimulate a conspecific to commence feeding (Tolman & Wilson, 1965); and the sight of a bird taking flight from a predator may elicit similar escape behavior in a conspecific that did not see the predator. Since contagion is an elicitation process, the imitative behavior of the observer may cease to occur when the releaser is removed and recur when the releaser reappears.

Imitative behavior might also result from stimulus (or local) enhancement. Stimulus enhancement is a process in which a demonstrator's action focuses a conspecific's attention on important environmental stimuli that otherwise may be overlooked (Spence, 1937). For example, an operant response may be learned relatively quickly through trial and error if the observer is attracted to the demonstrator's manipulandum, perhaps by noticing a reinforcer in that vicinity. The behavioral similarity of the two subjects is a result of a reinforcement contingency shaping similar responses to the manipulandum.

Stimulus valence transformation may also underlie a learned form of imitative behavior in birds (Bullock & Neuringer, 1977). Although similar to stimulus enhancement, the valence transformation hypothesis holds that a demonstrator's behavior may function as an "instructional" stimulus that focuses the observer's attention on a predictive relationship between a hedonically neutral stimulus and a biologically significant event (i.e., a Pavlovian stimulus-reinforcement contingency). For example, it is well known that if a pigeon is exposed to pairings of a visual signal and food reinforcement (autoshaping), it is likely to approach and peck the signaling stimulus (Brown & Jenkins, 1968; Hearst & Jenkins, 1974). If an observer watches a demonstrator's peck response controlled by an autoshaping contingency, the observer may acquire an association between the object and the reinforcer and eventually peck that object when it becomes accessible (Browne, 1976; Zentall & Hogan, 1975). Imitative behavior may become directed toward the signaling stimulus because both birds are influenced by qualitatively similar conditional and unconditional stimulus sequences (e.g., Johnson, Hamm, & Leahey, 1986).

The instructional process does not imply a covert intention of the demonstrator to teach the observer where to look or what to do with the stimuli that it contacts. Instead, the demonstrator's overt action is functional in causing the observer to learn about a stimulus-reinforcer contingency that otherwise might be discovered independently by the observer (see Zentall & Hogan, 1976, Group 10).

True imitation, or inferential imitation, involves acquisition of a relatively improbable response topography through observation (Thorpe, 1963). Perhaps the distinguishing features of true imitation are that the imitative response depends on (a) the particular response topography of the demonstrator rather than by an observed reinforcer or a predictive relationship between a signaling stimulus and a reinforcer and (b) learning of the response topography rather than elicitation of an instinctive response. If an organism is capable of true imitation, it should be possible to show that the observer can learn to match a variety of topographically different responses emitted by a conspecific, but that are unpredictable from the mechanisms of contagion, valence transformation, or stimulus enhancement.

Although true imitation is a relatively rare phenomenon in nonprimates (Davis, 1973), there appears to be evidence for response copying in cats (Chesler, 1969; John, Chesler, Bartlett, & Victor, 1968) rats (Zentall & Levine, 1972) and various bird species (Cronhelm, 1970; Dawson & Foss, 1965; Lefebvre, see this volume).

ACQUISITION OF SIMPLE RESPONSES

In almost all observation experiments employing pigeon subjects, experimenters have tried to determine whether the peck response of an observer can become associated with a relatively neutral stationary object as a result of simple observation of a well-trained conspecific pecking the appropriate object and consuming food. The observer may be tested for its tendency to peck the object in question either at the same time that the demonstrator is pecking the object (a simultaneous observation/test procedure) or during a post-observation test period when the demonstrator is absent (deferred procedure).

Research by Epstein (1984, Experiments 1 & 3) and Zentall and Hogan (1976) employed a simultaneous observation/test procedure and reported that an observer learned to peck an object (such as a disk) as it watched a demonstrator peck the appropriate object and consume food. Observing either an experimentally naive pigeon (mere presence control) or no demonstrator resulted in significantly less object-directed pecking (cf. Gardner & Engel, 1971; Zajonc, 1965). Although local enhancement was precluded by testing the observer with a manipulandum in its own compartment, neither experiment provides clear evidence of imitative response learning or imitative stimulus sequence learning that cannot be explained more parsimoniously in terms of contagious pecking.

There is stronger evidence of a learned form of imitative behavior when contagion is controlled using a deferred test procedure (Epstein, 1984, Experiment 1 Test 2 & Experiment 2). Epstein (1984, Experiment 2) first exposed an observer to a demonstrator that pecked a Ping-Pong ball for several sessions. He then administered a series of test sessions during which a similar object was placed in the observer's compartment while the demonstrator was absent. The observer pecked the ball more frequently during test sessions (the first of which commenced 24 hr after the last observation session) than it did during adaptation sessions (i.e., before the observer saw the demonstrator peck the object). Thus, the observer's object-directed pecking appeared to depend on having seen the demonstrator peck the object and probably was not "elicited" by the object per se.

Interestingly, seeing the demonstrator consume food reinforcement was not necessary for imitative responding, because the demonstrator's reinforcer was apparently not visible to the observer, and the observer was not trained to eat from the magazine before observation sessions. Nevertheless, the valence of the object may have been augmented by observing the demonstrator pecking the object with the response topography used to consume food (Jenkins & Moore, 1973). Because pigeons forage in groups throughout most of their lives, an individual bird has numerous opportunities to learn by observation the relation between a conspecific's characteristic consummatory response and edible (or drinkable) substances. Actually, it would be higher order conditioning because the sight of food would be a conditional reinforcer. Further research is needed to determine if a pigeon can learn the reinforcement significance of a signal by observing the signal control fragments of a demonstrator's consummatory response.

RECOVERY OF EXTINGUISHED RESPONSES

An alternative line of observational research with pigeons has questioned whether the specific action of a demonstrator can induce imitation of a response that had been weakened through extinction training in the observer. Such research provides a potentially sensitive assessment of a condition under which pigeons are likely to behave imitatively because it is probably easier to copy a response that it already "knows" how to perform than to actually acquire a novel response by mere observation.

Epstein (1984, p. 352) suggested that if an uncommon response, such as treadle pressing in pigeons, is strengthened through reinforcement and is later extinguished, the response may recover in the presence of a demonstrator that is treadle pressing. However, no data were reported and the procedural details of the experiment were not described.

We assessed the generality of Epstein's conclusion in a pilot study on socially induced recovery of an extinguished chain pull response (Hogan & Fry, 1986). The subjects were Carneaux pigeons that had participated in a variety of experiments, including one on observational learning of key pecking (Hogan, 1986). The test chamber consisted of two compartments that were separated by a transparent partition. Each contained a houselight and a grain feeder. The chain (a short wire) was attached to a switch mounted near the top of the partition. A small metal ring that the bird could grasp with its beak and pull for food reinforcement was tied to the free end of the "chain."

During Phase 1, the observer pigeons were first trained through successive approximations to pull the chain for food reinforcement. The response was then extinguished to a preconditioned operant level. Following extinction, the birds observed either a demonstrator receive response contingent reinforcement (variable interval 20 sec) for chain pulling (Group Pre OP), or a "mere presence" demonstrator receive noncontingent reinforcement (variable time 20 sec).

Each of 10 observation periods (10 min duration) was followed immediately by a test session (10 min) during which the demonstrator was removed from its compartment and the chain was positioned in a corresponding location in the observer's compartment. Chain pull responses by the observers were recorded but not reinforced during the test periods.

There was little evidence that the specific action of the demonstrator was necessary to produce recovery of the chain pull response. As may be seen in Table 11.1 (Phase 1), the mean number of chain pull responses (pooled over the 10 test sessions) was actually less for Group Pre OP, though not significantly so. However, both groups responded more during the test periods than they did on the last session of extinction training.

Since the response output was low in Phase 1, the procedure was repeated in Phase 2 except that noncontingent food reinforcement was presented to the observer when the demonstrator was reinforced during the observation period. (Noncontingent reinforcement for the observer was expected to increase arousal and increased arousal might lead to a differential increase in response output during the test period.) Performance did in fact increase differentially during Phase 2 (see Table 11.1), but again the difference between groups was not statistically significant.

Our pilot experiment also included two additional groups of subjects (so-called Groups OP and ON) that were exposed to a similar regimen of observation and testing during Phases 1 and 2, with the exception that the observers were not pretrained to pull the chain. The question was whether observer pigeons of Group OP would learn to pull the chain more quickly than a mere presence control (Group ON). During the 10 test sessions of Phase 1 (noncontingent reinforcement during the observation period was not presented to the observers) the difference in response output was comparable for the two groups (Group OP: mean = 3.4; Group ON: mean = 3.8). However, during Phase 2 (noncontingent reinforcement presented to the observers) Group OP (mean = 13.8) pulled the chain significantly more often than Group ON (mean = 3.2) (Mann-Whitney U test, $p < .05$).

The results of the nonpretrained groups suggest that learning of the chain pull response in Group OP depended on observation of the relevant response and explicit reinforcement. The significant difference between the nonpretrained

Table 11.1
Mean Number of Responses of Each Group Pooled
Over Ten Test Sessions of Phases 1 and 2

| | Groups | | | |
Phase	Pre OP	Pre ON	OP	ON
1	8.0	12.2	3.4	3.8
2	35.4	27.2	13.8	3.2

groups during Phase 2 must be interpreted with caution, however, because the response output during Phase 2 was low in both groups (there were several test sessions during which some Group OP birds made no responses at all, and the between-subject variability was quite large). With the appropriate caution in mind, however, the pilot experiment suggests that the specific action of the demonstrator might be less critical in producing recovery of stimulus-directed pecking than in causing learning of a new stimulus-reinforcer (or stimulus-response) contingency.

DETERMINANTS OF OBSERVATION

Looking at an object that the demonstrator pecks with its beak is a precursor to learning the reinforcement significance of the object by an observing pigeon. In most studies, little is done to establish control over the test subject's observing response by the demonstrator's actions. Instead, the observer is rather passively exposed to a well-trained demonstrator, and then is tested for learning. The results of an experiment by Neuringer and Neuringer (1974; see also Bullock & Neuringer, 1977), however, suggest a learning mechanism by which the peck response of a demonstrator pigeon may control a conspecific's observing response to environmental stimuli.

In Neuringer and Neuringer's experiment, observer pigeons (approx-imately 2 months of age) were fed mixed grain from a cup held in the experiment-er's hand, then learned to follow the hand as it moved toward a disk and "finger-pecked" it. A food hopper was then raised, and the experimenter "pecked" at the available grain as the observer pigeon looked on. On test trials (hand absent) the birds quickly approached and pecked the disk on their own. Birds that were only hand fed (but did not follow the hand to the disk) failed to learn, as did pigeons that only observed the disk "finger-pecked" (but were not initially fed by hand).

Bullock and Neuringer (1977) also demonstrated acquisition of a two-link response chain (approaching and pecking keys in different locations) by following a hand, which had been associated with food, to the different key locations. The results suggest that a young bird might learn to discover new places to feed by following an experienced subject (conspecific or nonconspecific) that had led it to food on an earlier occasion (see also Church, 1957; Galef & Clark, 1971; Wortis, 1969).

Skinner (1962) described a cooperation procedure that also appears to bring the observing response of a follower pigeon under stimulus control of a leader pigeon's behavior (see also Hake, Donaldson, & Hyten, 1983; Hogan, 1986). A pair of birds was trained in compartments divided by a transparent partition. In each compartment a column of three pecking keys was mounted on the intel-ligence panel next to the partition. On each trial, both columns of keys were illuminated simultaneously, and one pair of horizontally adjacent keys (one in each bird's compartment) was arbitrarily designated as correct. Both birds were rewarded when they pecked the correct pair within .5 sec of one another.

Because the correct keys were unsignaled and changed randomly from trial to trial, the pigeons learned to coordinate their pecks to each pair of keys until the correct pair was located. The "leader" pigeon (the hungrier of the two birds) pecked each of its own keys in a roughly random order, whereas the follower appeared to systematically peck the adjacent key. The following behavior also generalized to other stimuli and locations although the cooperation contingency did not require such following (i.e., the pigeons oriented to corresponding areas of the apparatus and both drank from dishes of water at nearly the same time).

Although the cooperative reinforcement contingency (Skinner, 1962) and hand feeding (Bullock & Neuringer, 1977; Neuringer & Neuringer, 1974) are nominally different operations, both appear to strengthen the follower's tendency to approach and peck objects contacted by the demonstrator and may be useful pretraining procedures for examining the pigeon's ability to learn more complex stimulus-reinforcer or stimulus-response relationships through observation (see also Denny, Bell, & Clos, 1983, for an alternative procedure for establishing and maintaining an observing response to relevant environmental stimuli).

ACQUISITION OF DISCRIMINATION PROBLEMS

Pigeons appear able to learn discrimination problems through observation (Biederman, Robertson, & Vanayan, 1986; Edwards, Hogan, & Zentall, 1980) and such learning can be facilitated if the demonstrator's peck response is explicitly established as an instructional stimulus (Hogan, 1986; Millard, 1979; Weist, 1969).

Edwards et al. (1980) exposed observers to a well-trained demonstrator that pecked repeatedly at a key illuminated by red light and withheld pecks when the key was illuminated by green light. On test trials, observers exposed to the same discrimination (red positive, green negative) learned faster than observers exposed to the reverse discrimination (green positive and red negative). Because the observers performed discriminatively on early test trials, and had been tested in a different compartment than the one in which the demonstrator performed, contagion (indiscriminant pecking) and local enhancement are not viable explanations of the results.

The stimulus valence transformation and true imitation (response copying) theories are both viable explanations of the results reported by Edwards et al., however. The valence transformation position would hold that because the observer had been trained to eat mixed grain from a feeder before the observation trials commenced, it may well have learned about the differential correlation between the demonstrator's discriminative stimuli and feeder cues through differential (higher order) autoshaping (Browne, 1976; Johnson et al., 1986; Zentall &

Hogan, 1975). It is also plausible, however, that the observer learned what to do with the discriminative stimuli (i.e., peck differentially) as a result of seeing the demonstrator pecking in the presence of S+, and not pecking S−. The design of the Edwards et al. experiment, however, was not sophisticated enough to distinguish between the response copying and stimulus sequence learning mechanisms, or whether both mechanisms were involved.

A recent study in my laboratory also demonstrated that observer pigeons learned to respond discriminatively to different hues as a result of watching a demonstrator perform the hue discrimination (Hogan, 1986). In this study, however, instructional control was first established by training the observer and demonstrator in a cooperation task similar to that of Skinner (1962).

The test panel used was a 2 × 2 matrix of pecking keys, rather than a 2 × 3 matrix used by Skinner (1962). (Most of the birds, Carneaux pigeons, were experienced in discrimination problems involving red and green hues, but none had learned a discrimination similar to the one described below and their history was counterbalanced over conditions.) The dyads of Group Same (4 pairs) were trained as were the pair in Skinner's experiment. At the start of a trial, the keys comprising both rows of the matrix were illuminated by white light (see Figure 11.1).

The top and bottom row were each designated correct on half of the trials (randomly selected). The correct row was unsignaled, however. The trial ended and both birds were rewarded with mixed grain when they pecked the correct pair of keys within .5 sec of one another.

Group Different dyads (4 pairs) were required to peck keys on different rows (i.e., the upper left and lower right locations on some trials and the lower left and upper right locations on others) within .5 sec of one another.

Group Mixed dyads (4 pairs) received a random mixture of the trials

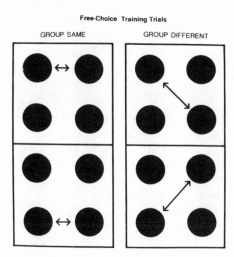

Free-Choice Training Trials

GROUP SAME   GROUP DIFFERENT

Figure 11.1. Trial types presented to Groups Same and Different during cooperation training. The arrows indicate the correct pair of keys on a trial.

presented to Groups Same and Different within each session. Thus the spatial choice of the leader pigeon did not provide the follower with consistent information about the potentially correct location to peck.

Following training, Groups Same and Different were transferred to the mixed-row problem for six sessions to assess whether the spatial choice of one bird systematically controlled the spatial choice of the other. The dependent measure of performance was the mean time to terminate a trial with reinforcement.

As may be seen in Figure 11.2, Group Same dyads terminated the familiar same-row test trials more quickly than the novel different-row test trials. The disruption on different-row trials presumably reflects the dyads' tendency to persistently peck keys on the same row of the matrix (or to avoid pecking keys on different rows of the matrix). Similarly, the behavior of Group Different was disrupted on novel "same-row" test trials, reflecting the dyads' tendency to peck keys on different rows of the matrix (or to avoid pecking adjacent keys).

The performance of Group Mixed indicates that there was no particular bias to respond on the same row of the matrix (or a different row) during test sessions (and no particular preference was observed during acquisition).

Following the stimulus control test, one bird of each pair (the demon-

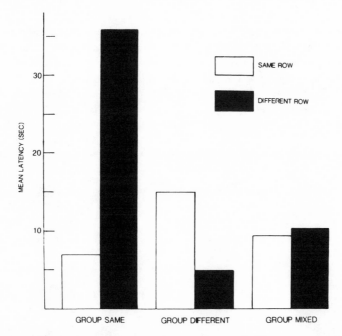

Figure 11.2. Mean latency to terminate same-row and different-row trials for Groups Same, Different, and Mixed. Performance was averaged over six sessions (from Hogan, 1986).

strator) was trained on a hue discrimination, summarized in Figure 11.3. The demonstrator was arbitrarily selected as the bird that had performed in the right-hand compartment during cooperation sessions. We would have assigned the "leader" to the role of demonstrator, but we could not readily discern from our data which of the two birds was a leader throughout training. Because all birds were maintained at equivalent motivational levels, it is quite likely that birds in each dyad "took turns" leading (Skinner, 1962).

When the demonstrator's keys were both red, the top location was correct, and when both keys were green the bottom location was correct. Five pecks were required to terminate the trial and the location of the fifth peck determined the trial outcome (either reinforcement plus a 10 sec intertrial interval, ITI, or only the ITI).

During observation training, the demonstrator performed the discrimination almost errorlessly as the observer watched. The observer's keys were dark on observation trials but in order to maintain attention to the demonstrator's discriminative performance, the observer received reinforcement when the demonstrator emitted the correct response. Six sessions of observation (each session involved 24 trials, 12 red and 12 green) preceded the first test session to ensure adequate exposure to the relation between the discriminative stimuli and reinforcement. Each test session after the first was immediately preceded by a single observation session.

On test sessions, the observers were required to learn the discrimination that was performed by the demonstrator (i.e., the observers were reinforced if the fifth peck occurred to the top key on red trials, etc.). During test trials, the demonstrator remained in the box but the keys were dark.

As may be seen in Figure 11.4, each group learned the discrimination rapidly, perhaps reflecting their previous history of learning discriminations

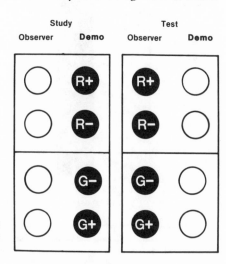

Study   **Test**

Observer   **Demo**   Observer   **Demo**

Figure 11.3. Discrimination trial types presented during the observation phase (left panels) and test phase (right panels).

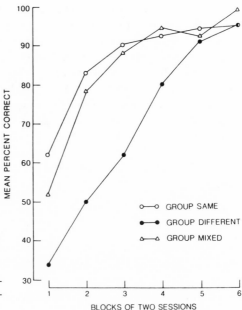

Figure 11.4. Discrimination performance of observers of Groups Same, Different, and Mixed (from Hogan, 1986).

involving red and green hues. However, the groups differed markedly in behavior on early sessions. On the first block of two sessions, one-tailed *t* tests indicated that Group Same was significantly superior to Group Different, but equivalent to Group Mixed. Group Different was also significantly inferior to Group Mixed.

It is possible to explain the early-session effect in terms of valence transformation of the discriminative stimuli. Above-chance performance of Group Same observers suggests that an association between reinforcement and the correct discriminative stimuli (i.e., red in the top location and green in the bottom location) may have been acquired during the observation sessions as they watched the demonstrator peck those discriminative stimuli. The reason they looked selectively at the demonstrator's correct stimuli was presumably a result of cooperation training, in which the observer was reinforced for looking and pecking at a stimulus location close to the key pecked by its partner.

Similarly, the initial below-chance performance of Group Different suggests that on observation trials, the observer looked at a key above or below the one that the demonstrator pecked. Consequently, they may have associated reinforcement with the incorrect stimulus.

The failure to obtain a significant difference between Groups Same and Mixed is puzzling, but the result may indicate either that instructional control was not established effectively in all of the Group Same dyads, or that Group Mixed attended to the keys pecked by the demonstrator despite the fact that the earlier cooperation contingency did not require it.

An alternative explanation for the early session effect (i.e., Group Same vs. Group Different) is that the demonstrator may have continued to instruct the observer where to peck by orienting discriminatively to the observer's keys on red and green test trials. For example, if a Group Same demonstrator saw the observer's keys illuminated red, it may have raised its head toward the observer's top key with an attempt to peck it, which could have caused the observer to orient to, and spontaneously peck the top key (correct location). If the demonstrators of Group Different behaved similarly on say "red trials," the observers may have oriented to and pecked the bottom key (incorrect location). Further research is needed to determine whether the observers of Groups Same and Different would transfer differentially when instructional control is prevented by using a deferred test procedure.

SUMMARY

The mechanisms that can produce imitative behavior in pigeons range from simple elicitation of pecking by a feeding conspecific to copying of a response pattern that is arbitrarily related to an observed consequence. However, it appears that the most complex mechanism of imitative behavior that can be identified in pigeons is stimulus valence transformation. Valence transformation theory holds that the observer's response topography is determined by the learned association involving the manipulandum (predictive stimulus) and the reinforcer, rather than by a perception of the demonstrator's response topography per se. Although some experimenters have confounded response copying effects with instructional effects (Edwards et al., 1980; Hogan, 1986; Hogan & Fry, 1986; Zentall & Hogan, 1976), valence transformation theory can explain more parsimoniously why the observers pecked the manipulandum since (a) the observer's peck response was not arbitrarily related to the observed reinforcer cues and (b) key pecking by pigeons can be learned rapidly when the "instructional" stimulus is a nonconspecific's action (Neuringer & Neuringer, 1974; see also Groesbeck & Duerfeldt, 1971).

It is notable that a clear and reliable experimental demonstration of copying an arbitrary response in pigeons remains to be documented. Despite the fact that some experimenters have established conditions in which response copying could have occurred it did not. Epstein (1984, Experiment 3), for example, included a control condition in which an observer was permitted to watch a demonstrator that had been conditioned to turn circles, presumably for food reinforcement. The condition was included to test for the presence of spontaneous imitation of the circling response, but none was seen. Instead, the observer pecked the object (a ball) at a relatively high frequency. This pecking was probably induced by the general activity of the demonstrator (Zajonc, 1965).

I have also casually looked for evidence of response copying and saw none. A pair of pigeons trained to cooperate by simultaneously pecking adjacent key locations failed to subsequently imitate a circling response emitted occasionally by one of the pair-mates during the intertrial interval. Of course, it is possible that evidence for copying might have emerged if a more sensitive index of learning were used, or if the demonstrator's response involved a simpler topography and was exhibited at a high rate, and so forth. Thus a strong negative conclusion regarding the response-copying ability of the pigeon may be premature. However, the bulk of published evidence to date seems to suggest that the pigeons' observational learning capacity might be limited to learning Pavlovian stimulus contingencies.

REFERENCES

Biederman, G. B., Robertson, A., & Vanayan, M. (1986). Observational learning of two visual discriminations by pigeons: A within-subjects design. *Journal of the Experimental Analysis of Behavior, 46,* 45–49.

Brown, P. L., & Jenkins, H. M. (1968). Autoshaping of the pigeon's key-peck. *Journal of the Experimental Analysis of Behavior, 11,* 1–8.

Browne, M. P. (1976). The role of primary reinforcement and overt movements in autoshaping in the pigeon. *Animal Learning & Behavior, 4,* 287–292.

Bullock, D., & Neuringer, A. (1977). Social learning by following: An analysis. *Journal of the Experimental Analysis of Behavior, 25,* 127–135.

Chesler, P. (1969). Maternal influence in learning by observation in kittens. *Science, 166,* 901–903.

Church, R. M. (1957). Transmission of learned behavior between rats. *Journal of Abnormal and Social Psychology, 54,* 163–165.

Cronhelm, E. (1970). Perceptual factors and observational learning in the behavioural development of young chicks: In J. H. Crook (Ed.), *Social behavior in birds and mammals: Essays on the social ethology of animals and man* (pp. 393–439). New York: Academic Press.

Davis, J. M. (1973). Imitation: A review and critique. In P. P. G. Bateson & P. H. Klopfer (Eds.), *Perspectives in ethology* (pp. 43–72). New York: Plenum.

Dawson, B. V., & Foss, B. M. (1965). Observational learning in Budgerigars. *Animal Behaviour, 13,* 470–474.

Denny, M. R., Bell, R. C., & Clos, C. (1983). Two choice, observational learning and reversal in the rat: S-S versus S-R effects. *Animal Learning & Behavior, 11,* 223–228.

Edwards, C. A., Hogan, D. E., & Zentall, T. R. (1980). Imitation of an appetitive discrimination by pigeons. *Bird Behaviour, 2,* 87–92.

Epstein, R. (1984). Spontaneous and deferred imitation by pigeons. *Behavioural Processes, 9,* 347–354.

Galef, B. G. Jr., & Clark, M. M. (1971). Social factors in the poison avoidance and feeding behavior of wild and domestic rat pups. *Journal of Comparative and Physiological Psychology, 75,* 341–362.

Gardner, E. L., & Engel, D. R. (1971). Imitational and social facilitatory aspects of observational learning in the laboratory rat. *Psychonomic Science 25,* 5–6.

Groesbeck, R. W., & Duerfeldt, P. H. (1971). Some relevant variables in observational learning of the rat. *Psychonomic Science, 22,* 41–43.

Hake, D. F., Donaldson, T., & Hyten, C. (1983). Analysis of discriminative control by social behavioral stimuli. *Journal of the Experimental Analysis of Behavior, 39,* 7–24.

Hearst, E., & Jenkins, H. M. (1974). *Sign-tracking: The stimulus reinforcer relation and directed action.* Austin, TX: Psychonomic Society.

Hogan, D. E. (1986). Observational learning of a conditional hue discrimination in pigeons. *Learning and Motivation, 17,* 40–58.

Hogan, D. E., & Fry, G. (1986). *Observational learning of a chain pull response in pigeons: Dual control by instructional and Pavlovian stimulation.* Unpublished manuscript.

Jenkins, H. M., & Moore, B. R. (1973). The form of the autoshaped response with food and water reinforcers. *Journal of the Experimental Analysis of Behavior, 20,* 163–181.

John, E. R., Chesler, P., Bartlett, F., & Victor, I. (1968). Observational learning in cats. *Science, 159,* 1489–1491.

Johnson, S. B., Hamm, R. J., & Leahey, T. H. (1986). Observational learning in *Gallus gallus domesticus* with and without a conspecific model. *Bulletin of the Psychonomic Society, 24,* 237–239.

Millard, W. J. (1979). Stimulus properties of conspecific behavior. *Journal of the Experimental Analysis of Behavior, 32,* 283–295.

Miller, N. E., & Dollard, J. (1941). *Social learning and imitation.* New York: McGraw-Hill.

Neuringer, A., & Neuringer, M. (1974). Learning by following a food source. *Science, 184,* 1005–1008.

Skinner, B. F. (1962). Two "synthetic social relations." *Journal of the Experimental Analysis of Behavior, 5,* 531–533.

Spence, K. W. (1937). Experimental studies of learning and the higher mental processes in infra-human primates. *Psychological Bulletin, 34,* 806–850.

Thorpe, W. H. (1963). *Learning and instinct in animals* (2nd ed.). Cambridge, MA: Harvard University Press.

Tolman, C. W., & Wilson, G. F. (1965). Social feeding in domestic chicks. *Animal Behaviour, 13,* 134–142.

Weist, W. M. (1969). Socially mediated stimulus control in pigeons. *Psychological Reports, 25,* 139–148.

Wortis, R. P. (1969). The transition from dependent to independent feeding in the young ring dove. *Animal Behaviour Monographs, 2,* 1–54.

Zajonc, R. B. (1965). Social facilitation. *Science, 149,* 269–274.

Zentall, T. R., & Hogan, D. E. (1975). Key pecking in pigeons produced by pairing keylight with inaccessible grain. *Journal of the Experimental Analysis of Behavior, 23,* 199–206.

Zentall, T. R., & Hogan, D. E. (1976). Imitation and social facilitation in the pigeon. *Animal Learning and Behavior, 4,* 427–430.

Zentall, T. R., & Levine, J. M. (1972). Observational learning and social facilitation in the rat. *Science, 178,* 1220–1221.

Culture and Genetics
in the House Mouse

Danilo Mainardi
Marisa Mainardi
University of Parma, Italy

INTRODUCTION: THE HOUSE MOUSE AS A MODEL SPECIES
FOR THE STUDY OF SOCIAL TRANSMISSION

In present day taxonomy, the original species of the house mouse has been divided into seven species, one of which, *Mus domesticus,* this chapter concerns (Marshall & Sage, 1981). To a varying extent, laboratory interfertility of the species (Hunt & Selander, 1973) has probably contributed to the genetic pool of laboratory mice. Nevertheless it can be claimed that the latter is derived from *Mus domesticus* (Berry, 1981a). The tendency of modern research to use inbred strains has created animals with marked differences both between one strain and another and differences from the wild species (Festing & Lovell, 1981). It appears however that outbred laboratory strains, particularly the Swiss Webster, are sufficiently genetically similar to the wild species to be used as a model for the species (O'Brien & Rice, 1979). We have therefore adopted a Swiss outbred strain for the first part of this research. The house mouse in fact presents a series of characteristics that make it particularly suitable for an investigation into the social transmission of information.

A brief glance at the geographical distribution of *Mus* shows its extraordi-

---

[1]Supported by Italian C.N.R. and M.P.I.

nary colonizing capacity, in that it is possible to find populations in the most diverse habitats—coral reefs, temperate farmlands, at altitudes up to 4000 m in the Andes, as well as in man's habitat in the widest sense of the word. This is the first and most concrete proof of the mouse's exceptional ability to adapt. Furthermore, most of these habitats undergo radical transformations from time to time, with enormous variations in the quantity of food supplies and nesting sites available—cultivated land may serve as an example of this. In these situations the mouse is able to adopt reproductive strategies of the r type with considerable fluctuations (Newsome, 1969). A whole population can often derive from a small number of founders, which in turn comes from a highly variable genetic pool. The population then becomes genetically differentiated by drift. This continuous reconstitution of population, often in habitats that have provisionally become unfavorable, has made it essential for the mouse to be able to mold its behaviour and to adapt rapidly to the changed circumstances (Southwood, 1977). In order to do so, the species has certainly been helped by the fact that in a single population a vast number of different genetic combinations exist side by side. Indeed as Berry reported (1981b), the mouse, with a mean heterozygosity of 7% is numbered among the mammals with the highest variability both in comparison with rodents as a whole, which have a mean heterozygosity of 5.6%, and with mammals as a whole, which have a mean heterozygosity of 3.6% (Nevo, 1978; Selander & Kaufman, 1973).

The socio-sexual characteristics of the species may also produce and maintain genetic variability, namely, the tendency towards heterogamy. For example using two inbred strains C57 BL/Ibg and DBA/Ibg, it has been demonstrated that females of both strains prefer to mate and spend their time with the males of the opposite strain rather than with those of the same strain (Yanai & McClearn, 1972a). The same authors (1972b) also report data in support of the idea that mice have evolved behavioral mechanisms to avoid inbreeding. The same phenomenon has been observed by Mainardi (1964) for the Swiss and C57 BL/6 strains: this type of mechanism, based on the female's sexual choice involving olfactory stimuli, is strongly affected by early learning of the parents' characteristics (Mainardi, Marsan, & Pasquali, 1965).

The exteroceptive block of pregnancy in the laboratory mouse, observed by Bruce (1959), may be interpreted as a system to promote exogamy (Bruce & Parrot, 1960). For further discussion of this interpretation, see Schwagmeyer (1979) and Labov (1981). See also studies by Berry (1970) and Van Oortmerssen (1970) with regard to mechanisms that reduce genetic isolation in mice.

A further behavioral element that enables one to predict systems of social transmission of information concerns the presence of a strong exploratory tendency (Barnett & Cowan, 1976; Mackintosh, 1981). This tendency has been shown by Brant and Kavanau (1964) to be independent of rewards. These characteristics can be combined with the fact that the species has, as is well known, a considerable degree of social organization affecting population density (Lidicker, 1976;

Southwick, 1955). This social organization appears, for example, in the presence and importance of a hierarchy (Oakeshott, 1974), in the strong tendency to adopt an outsider's offspring (Favoriti & Mainardi, 1976), and in the habit of making collective nests, in which every female suckles and protects every pup regardless of its parentage (Sayler & Salmon, 1971).

The capacity for social transmission of information would be quite appropriate for a species of this kind, because it offers considerable adaptive advantage, particularly in the early phases of the conquest of new environments, even before genetic adaptations become established. Social transmission of information has been demonstrated in some, if not very many, contexts (see Mainardi, Mainardi & Pasquali, 1986; Mainardi & Pasquali, 1968; Manusia & Pasquali, 1969; Pallaud, 1969; Sanavio & Savardi, 1980; Valzelli, 1973).

Apparatus and Method

In the experiments that follow, we used a small apparatus which required the mouse to solve a problem. The apparatus consisted of a suspended cylindrical container that could be opened by rotating a small round door counter-clockwise. About fifty turns were needed to open the door wide enough for a mouse to get into the cylinder. On experimental trials, sunflower seeds were placed in the cylinder (Figure 12.1). Although the door fit the cylinder closely, the mice were still likely to smell the seeds. The difficulty in opening the door was adjusted such that in a population of mice a small number of individuals would be capable of solving the problem spontaneously. A trial consisted of placing a mouse in a Plexiglas container 55 × 35 × 18 cm together with the apparatus (with sunflower seeds) for 24 hrs. Food and water were provided ad libitum. The cylinder of the apparatus was positioned so that if the small round door were rotated clockwise, the door would shut more tightly. One can thus discriminate between random and correct rotation.

If the mouse opened the cylinder door a "+" was recorded, if it failed to turn the door in the proper direction a "−" was recorded, and if it partially opened the door an "i" was recorded. A complete test consisted of 3 trials, carried out on three successive days.

Five hundred 2−3 month old mice (Swiss, random bred strain) were given a preliminary test (Mainardi, Mainardi, & Pasquali, 1986). Of these only 24 mice (4.8%) managed to open the cylinder on all three trials (+ + +); 176 animals (35.2%) failed completely (− − −), and 300 mice opened the cylinder either once or twice, or rotated the small door an insufficient number of times to open it. Each time the cylinder was opened wide enough for the mouse to get inside, it was allowed to eat some of the sunflower seeds on the floor of the cylinder.

Thus the animals tested can be classified as positive, negative, or intermediate. The intermediate category was, however, strongly heterogeneous be-

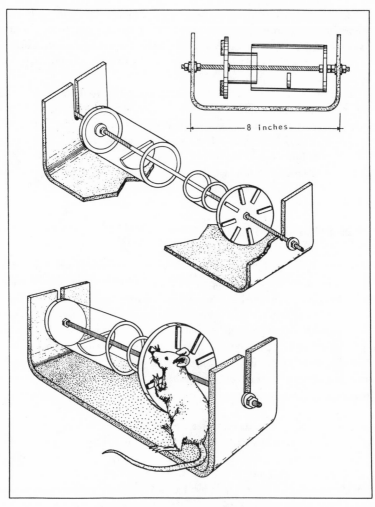

Figure 12.1 Experimental apparatus.

cause it consisted of individuals that had, for example, recorded a $++i$ result, that is they had opened the door on two trials and had attempted to do so on one trial, as well as individuals that had attempted to open the door without succeeding on only one trial. In order to discriminate among individuals that gave an intermediate response on the test, each animal received a score from 9 ($+++$) to 0 ($---$) according to the following scheme:

$+++$	$++i$	$++-$	$+ii$	$+i-$	$+--$	iii	ii-	i--	---
9	8	7	6	5	4	3	2	1	0

Experiment 1:
The Role of Genetic Make-Up and Experience on the Capacity to Open a Rotating Door

Our first experiment (Mainardi, Mainardi, & Pasquali, 1986) was designed in such a way as to extract information with regard to: a) whether the mice's capacity to solve the problem could be non-genetically transmitted from one individual to another; b) how genetic make-up affects the capacity to solve or to socially learn to solve the problem.

In successive tests we selected from a Swiss outbred population positive animals (P), capable of solving the problem consistently, and negative animals (N) which never succeeded in solving it. Pairs were then formed within the two categories in order to obtain offspring from positive (P) parents and offspring from negative (N) parents.

The offspring were then further subdivided according to whether they had been raised in a container with (Yes) or without (No) the apparatus inside it.

Once they became adults it was then possible to compare the behavior of four groups with about 75 individuals in each, together with a control group, thus labelled:

P -Yes = individuals with experience with the problem and offspring of parents able to solve it spontaneously;

P -No = individuals with no experience with the problem and offspring of parents able to solve it spontaneously;

N -Yes = individuals with experience with the problem and offspring of parents incapable of solving it;

Table 12.1

Mean Scores and Frequencies According to the Different Types of Solution Adopted by the Groups in the First Experiment (from Mainardi, Mainardi & Pasquali, 1986)

	Type of solution	P-Yes	P-No	N-Yes	N-No	Controls	
% frequencies	+++	32.3	15.1	13.3	3.9	1.3	
	---	12.3	30.1	21.3	42.1	46.2	$\chi^2 = 51.66$
	intermediate						df = 8
	results	55.4	54.8	64.4	53.9	42.5	P<.001
	number of individuals tested	65	73	75	76	80	
	mean scores	4.85	2.79	2.90	1.59	1.04	Fisher F = 18.17 P<.001

N -No = individuals with no experience with the problem and offspring of parents incapable of solving it.

The results, summarized in Table 12.1, showed significant differences in solution frequency both between the offspring of P and N individuals (which testifies to a genetic effect on the capacity to solve a given problem), and likewise between individuals that during growth had had experience with the problem and those that had none. Genetic and experiential effects in the experimental situation were of comparable magnitude. In the P - No and the N - Yes categories the percentages of animals that solved the problem during the test were 15.1% and 13.3% respectively. Likewise the average scores were comparable (2.79 and 2.90 respectively).

Experiment 2:
Social Transmission from Adult to Adult

Experiment 2 involved the same Swiss outbred strain and the same apparatus as Experiment 1. In Experiment 2, we investigated factors involved in the non-genetic transfer of information. We particularly wanted to investigate whether information can be passed from one adult male to other unrelated younger adult males. There were four social conditions: A, A1, B, B1.

In A a 5-month-old demonstrator mouse, with successful experience in solving the problem, was put into a clean container with an unrelated 2.5 month old observer. The type of social relationship established between them was recorded. The stability of this relationship was checked over the next few days. The demonstrators were always dominant. Once the social relation had been defined, the cylinder was placed in the container, and for 10 days the aperture of the doorway was examined every morning. The observer was then transferred to another container with no cylinder inside it for 3 to 4 days. The observers were then tested as in Experiment 1. In situation A1 (control) the conditions were the same as in A, except the older mouse was a pseudo-demonstrator (i.e., it was incapable of opening the door).

In conditions B and B1 three observers were placed in the containers with each demonstrator mouse (B) or with each pseudo-demonstrator mouse (B1, control).

The frequency of positive, negative, and intermediate tests for the four experimental groups and statistical comparisons are presented in Table 12.2. There was a statistically significant difference in frequency of solution between the groups of individuals which lived with demonstrators (B) and the control groups (B1). None of the other comparisons yielded significant differences, however.

Mean scores obtained by subjects in the four experimental conditions of Experiment 2 are reported in Table 12.3 together with analysis of variance. These

Table 12.2
Frequencies and Comparisons Between the Different Types of Solution
in the Second Experiment

Type of solution	A freq.	A %	A_1 freq.	A_1 %	B freq.	B %	B_1 freq.	B_1 %
+++	6	8.6	3	6.7	11	12.8	3	3.5
− − −	42	60.0	26	57.8	44	51.2	65	74.7
Intermediate results	22	31.4	16	35.5	31	36.0	19	21.8
Total	70		45		86		87	

Comparisons	A vs. A_1	B vs. B_1	A vs. B	A_1 vs. B_1
χ^2	0.291	11.492	1.419	4.014
df	2	2	2	2
P	>.05	<.01.	>.05	>.05

scores take into account variability in the intermediate category, and the analysis considers the two variables (efficient or inefficient demonstrator and one or more observers) independently. The analysis indicates that the demonstrator's presence is important, whereas the number of observers seems not to matter.

Experiment 3:
Comparison Between Inbred Strains

In Experiment 3 we compared the performance of two inbred strains, C57 BL6 and DBA2, on the door opening task (both spontaneous opening and social learning of the opening response). As this experiment is still in progress, we shall

Table 12.3
Mean Scores and Comparisons Between the Different Types of Solution
in the Second Experiment

Experimental situation	A	A_1	B	B_1
Mean scores	1.58	1.31	2.10	0.76
Number of animals	70	45	86	87

Factorial comparisons 2x2	omnibus	$(A+A_1)$ vs. $(B+B_1)$	$(A+B)$ vs. (A_1+B_1)	interaction
F	3.84	0.03	8.77	2.73
df	3/284	1/284	1/284	1/284
P	<.01	n.s.	<.01	n.s.

Table 12.4

Frequencies and Mean Scores for the Different Types of
Solution in the Two Inbred Strains

	DBA		C57	
Type of solution	freq.	%	freq.	%
+ + +	5	14.7	0	0
− − −	10	29.4	28	46.7
Intermediate results	19	55.9	32	53.3
Number of individuals tested	34		60	
Mean scores	2.85		0.71	

report here only some preliminary data and the relative methodology. Why these particular strains were chosen will be discussed later.

Forty-eight C57 BL6 and eighty-three DBA2 strain males and females from 4 to 6 months old were tested. These animals had had no previous experience with the apparatus. Of the animals from the first strain only one (2%) showed a totally positive result, whereas 3 (3.6%) from the second strain did so. Mean scores were 2.1 and 1.3, respectively. Data are only suggestive, because the sample was small.

We then tested animals from both strains reared, in the presence of the apparatus until they were 25 days old, by a mother that opened the door each day. To control for the rearing experience of the two strains, pups of the two strains were fostered by Swiss adoptive mothers as soon as they were three days old. By mixing litters we produced 34 C57 BL6 and 60 DBA2 mice that had experience with the apparatus. For the two groups of experimental animals the apparatus was removed from the container when the animals were 25 days old and the complete test was performed 15 days later. The results of this part of the experiment are reported in Table 12.4.

It should be emphasized that in this initial part of the experiment the animals acquired their experience at a very early age. We are presently investigating the effects of the same experience at a later age.

GENERAL DISCUSSION

The experiments reported here are only a few of many possible experiments that analyze the factors involved in non-genetic transmission of specific information, where the behavior studied spontaneously compounds the repertoire of a small minority of the population. Our first concern was to create a task that would present a potential problem for the mouse, and that would in some way resemble a situation a *Mus* might encounter in the wild. Experiments of this type can obviously be criticised for their excessive artificiality, thus making it impossible to generalize to more natural contexts. In our case the apparatus simulates searching for food as well as escape. And indeed a large number of informal trials carried out while the device was being tested showed that an animal able to open the door does so even when the food (sunflower seeds) is removed. It does so day after day and even several times a day and can repeat the performance after a lengthy retention interval (sometimes as long as six months). Moreover, the door to the cylinder could be opened after being manipulated in a way which is quite spontaneous in this species, whose tendency to explore the minutest details of an environment is well known (Barnett & Cowan, 1976; Poirel, 1968).

The results of the first experiment show that although the Swiss outbred population only includes a small number of individuals capable of solving the problem rapidly and spontaneously (4.8%), it also includes a continuum of individuals who make some attempt to operate the aperture (35.2%). An hypothesis at this point could be that a demonstrator is likely to have the greatest effect on mice that already have some inclination to perform the task. We are probably faced here with a case of local enhancement of the type observed by Hinde and Fisher (1951) in tits. The term is used here in the sense proposed by Thorpe (1963): "Local enhancement is when a model animal succeeds in directing the attention of an observer towards some salient environmental feature, thus accelerating learning."

It will be necessary, however, to determine whether finding the door of the apparatus open (allowing access to the sunflower seeds) does in itself affect learning, as it does in the case of *Parus atricapillus* reported by Sherry & Galef (1984).

The variability found in the experimental data are in agreement with the hypothesis that in a species like the mouse, which is programmed to adapt rapidly to changing environments, it is advantageous if there is a certain number of individuals capable of solving an unfamiliar problem, the solution of which can be learned rapidly at the same time by a sufficient number of individuals genetically inclined towards social learning. That there is some genetic control over the capacity to learn how to open the door of our device, is demonstrated by the data in Table 12.1.

In the second experiment, the relation between demonstrator and observer changes: the solution of the problem is no longer shown by the mother to her young but by one adult to another. It is known that in different species information does not spread haphazardly through populations, but follows "pathways of least resistance." It has been shown for primates that non-genetic transmission of information is affected by sex, age, kinship, ties of affection, and social status (Frish, 1968; Jolly, 1972; Kawai, 1965; Kawamura, 1963; Menzel, Davenport,

& Rodgers, 1972; Strayer, 1976). In the porpoise *Tursiops truncatus* it is the young who imitate the movements of adults (Bondarchuk, Matisheva & Skibnevsky, 1976).

In *Lemur fulvus* observational learning passes more easily from the mother to her children than vice versa (Feldman & Klopfer, 1972). In the cat, kittens learn to press a lever much faster if they have observed their mother doing so rather than a stranger (Chesler, 1969). If however a social tie of affection is created between the kitten and the stranger, the latter becomes an effective demonstrator. With regard to this case, however, it should be emphasized that in cats demonstrators may assume the function of a teacher. According to Barnett (1968) a demonstrator may display behavior specifically tending to simulate the behavior of the learner and the demonstrator gears its own behavior to that of the learner. This is not the case with our mice, where a demonstrator simply acts in the presence of an observer and presents information in this way.

The data from our second experiment (see Table 12.3) show that not only the mother—as demonstrated before—but also a stranger is an effective demonstrator. The data show, moreover, that information passes not only from an adult to its young but also from one adult to another. If once again we refer to the ecological characteristics of the species, it is fair to expect what has, in fact, been seen, namely nonrigid mechanisms that enable new information to be spread so as to allow equally rapid behavioral changes in the population (Mainardi, 1980).

The adaptive value of the cultural transmission of information encourages a more detailed genetic analysis in this species. As was true of the data from the first experiment, there were significantly more totally positive individuals in the groups selected for parents' ability than there were in the descendents of incapable parents. The results indicate the importance that genetic inheritance has on the type of performance examined. It was for this reason that we undertook additional experiments, not on Swiss outbred animals, but using inbred strains which are less variable and better defined genetically (Oliverio, 1983; Oliverio, Castellano, & Puglisi-Allegra, 1979).

Two strains in particular, the C57 BL/6 and the DBA/J2 seemed suitable for our purposes. DBA mice learn rapidly to get through a maze whereas C57 mice do so with greater difficulty (Bovet, Bovet-Nitti, & Oliverio, 1969). The fact that DBA mice are "rapid learners" whereas C57 mice are "slow learners" has received further confirmation from pharmacological investigations by Castellano (1978; 1981).

Preliminary results of the third experiment (still ongoing), in which we used two strains, appear clear enough to extract some information. As can be seen in Table 12.3, not one of the 60 C57 mice yielded a totally positive result, whereas of the 34 DBA mice, five solved the problem three times. The number of totally negative animals was also different for the two strains; 46.6% of the C57 as compared with 24.4% of the DBA strain. Although we need to increase the numbers in the DBA group, these preliminary data, as well as the comparison of average scores (0.71 in the C57 strain as against 2.85 in the DBA), seem to be indicative of a difference between the two strains. It is possible that this difference is also related to a different level of maturity at birth in the two strains, a characteristic that would be reflected in a greater capacity for moulding behaviour, that is, in a tendency for learning in the strain which was more immature at birth as compared with the one which was more mature. Oliverio et al. (1979) discussed this capacity for moulding behavior or the lack of it as characteristics of generalist and specialist species, respectively. Differences in behavioral mutability can be found in different strains within a species, as is the case, though perhaps a unique one, in the mouse.

The hypothesis, already partly confirmed by the data, is that we are faced with an innovative form of non-genetic transmission of information, not linked to critical periods, to preferential pathways within the population, or to forms of crystalization of what has already been learned. In these cases, one would expect the new information acquired by individuals to have a time limited survival value related to the changeability of the environmental conditions. One thus gets an idea of why a tradition might be installed, a "culture" in the broadest sense of the word, as a habit socially transmitted within a population. One population can be distinguished from others living in different environments with different problems to face or which have produced individuals capable of solving the same problem but in a different way (Mainardi, 1980). To return for the last time to the ecology of the species, one might suggest, and it would indeed be of considerable interest to check the hypothesis, that in very numerous, small natural populations that are constantly renewed, and which descend from one or a few founders, one can easily find cases of these "lightening cultures" that are rapidly formed and which equally rapidly disappear.

REFERENCES

Barnett, S. A. (1968) . The "instinct to teach". *Nature, 222,* 747–749.

Barnett, S. A. & Cowan, P. E. (1976) . Activity, exploration, curiosity and fear—an ethological study. *Interdisciplinary Sciences Reviews, 1,* 43–62.

Berry, R. J. (1970). Covert and overt variation, as exemplified by British mouse populations. *Symposia of the Zoological Society of London No.26,* 3–26.

Berry, R. J. (1981a). Town mouse, country mouse: adaptation and adaptability in *Mus domesticus (M. musculus domesticus). Mammal Review, 11* (3), 91–136.

Berry, R. J. (1981b). Population dynamics of the house mouse. *Symposia of the Zoological Society of London No.47,* 395–425.

Bondarchuk, L. S., Matisheva, S. K. & Skibnevsky, R. N. (1976). Development of behaviour in young *Tursiops truncatus. Zoologichesky Zhurnal, 55* 276–281.

Bovet, D., Bovet-Nitti, F. & Oliverio, A. (1969). Genetic aspects of learning and memory in mice. *Science, 163,* 139–149.

Brant, D. H. & Kavanau, J. L. (1964). "Unrewarded" exploration and learning of complex mazes by wild and domestic mice. *Nature. 204*, 267–269.

Bruce, H. M. (1959). An exteroceptive block to pregnancy in the mouse. *Nature, 184*, 105.

Bruce, H. M. & Parrot, D. M. V. (1960). Role of olfactory sense in pregnancy block by strange males. *Science, 131*, 1526.

Castellano, C. (1978). Effects of mescaline and psilocin on acquisition, consolidation, and performance of light-dark discrimination in two inbred strains of mice. *Psychopharmacology, 59*, 129–137.

Castellano, C. (1981). Strain-dependent effects of naloxone on discrimination learning in mice. *Psychopharmacology, 73*, 152–156.

Chesler, P. (1969). Maternal influence in learning by observation in kittens. *Science, 166*, 901–903.

Favoriti, M. P. & Mainardi, D. (1976). Assenza di discriminazione tra figli ed estranei nell'ambito dell'adozione nel topo. *Acta Naturalia, 12*, 259–269.

Feldman, D. W. & Klopfer, P. H. (1972). A study of observational learning in lemurs. *Zeitschrift für Tierpsychologie, 30*, 297–304.

Festing, M. F. W. & Lovell, D. P. (1981). Domestication and development of the mouse as a laboratory animal. *Symposia of the Zoological Society of London No.47*, 15–25.

Frish, J. E. (1968). Individual behaviour and intertroop variability in Japanese macaques. In P. Jay (ed.), *Primates: Studies in adaptation and variability* (pp. 243–252). New York: Holt, Rinehart and Winston.

Hinde, R. A. & Fisher, J. (1951). Further observations on the opening of milk bottles by birds. *British Birds, 44*, 393–396.

Hunt, W. G. & Selander, R. K. (1973). Biochemical genetics of hybridisation in European house mice. *Heredity, 31*, 11–33.

Jolly, A. (1972). *The evolution of primate behaviour.* Collier-MacMillan, London.

Kawai, M. (1965). Newly acquired pre-cultural behaviour of the natural troop of Japanese monkeys of Koshima islet. *Primates, 3*, 45–60.

Kawamura, S. (1963). The process of sub-cultural propagation among Japanese macaques. In C. Southwich (ed.), *Primate Social Behavior.* Toronto: Van Nostrand.

Labov, J. B. (1981). Pregnancy blocking in rodents: adaptive advantages for females. *The American Naturalist, 118*, 361–371.

Lidicker, W. Z. (1976). Social behaviour and density regulation in house mice living in large enclosures. *Journal of Animal Ecology, 45*, 677–697.

Mackintosh, J. H. (1981). Behaviour of the house mouse. *Symposia of the Zoological Society of London No.47*, 337–365.

Mainardi, D. (1964). Relations between early experience and sexual preferences in female mice. *Atti Associazione Genetica Italiana, 9*, 141–145.

Mainardi, D. (1980). Tradition and the social transmission of behavior in animals. In G. B. Barlow & J. Silverberg (eds.). *Sociobiology: beyond nature/nurture?* (pp. 227–255). Boulder, Colorado: Westview Press.

Mainardi, D., Mainardi, M. & Pasquali, A. (1986). Genetic and experiential features in a case of cultural transmission in the house mouse (*Mus musculus*). *Ethology, 72*, 191–198.

Mainardi, D., Marsan, M. & Pasquali, A. (1965). Causation of sexual preferences in the house mouse. The behavior of mice reared by parents whose odor was artificially altered. *Atti della Società Italiana di Scienze Naturali, 104,* 325–338.

Mainardi, D. & Pasquali, A. (1968). Cultural transmission in the house mouse. *Atti della Societá Italiana di Scienze Naturali, 107,* 147–152.

Manusia, M. & Pasquali, A. (1969). A new case of imitation in the house mouse. *Atti della Societá Italiana di Scienze Naturali, 109,* 457–462.

Marshall, J. T. & Sage, R. D. (1981). Taxonomy of the house mouse. *Symposia of the Zoological Society of London No.47,* 15–25.

Menzel, E. W., Jr., Davenport, R. K. & Rodgers, C. M. (1972). Protocultural aspects of chimpanzees' responsiveness to novel objects. *Folia Primatologica, 17,* 161–170.

Nevo, E. (1978). Genetic variation in natural populations: patterns and theory. *Theoretical population Biology, 13,* 121–177.

Newsome, A. E. (1969). A population study of house-mice temporarily inhabiting a South Australian wheatfield. *Journal of Animal Ecology, 38,* 341–359.

Oakeshott, J. G. (1974). Social dominance, aggressiveness and mating success among male house mice (*Mus musculus*). *Oecologia, 15,* 143–158.

O'Brien, S. J. & Rice, M. C. (1979). Genetic aspects of carcinogenesis and carcinogen testing. *Journal of Toxicology and Environmental Health, 5,* 69–82.

Oliverio, A. (1983). Genes and behavior: An evolutionary perspective. *Advances in the Study of Behavior, 13,* 191–217.

Oliverio, A., Castellano, C., & Puglisi-Allegra, S. (1979). A genetic approach to behavioral plasticity and rigidity. In J. R. Royce & M. P. Leendert (eds.), *Theoretical advances in behavior genetics.* Germantown, Maryland: Sijthoff and Noordhoff.

Pallaud, B. (1969) Mise en évidence d'un comportement d'imitation chez la souris. *Revue du Comportement Animal, 3.* 28–36.

Poirel, C. (1968). Variations temporelles du comportement d'exploration chez la souris. *Comptes Rendus des Séances de la Société de Biologie et de ses Filiales, 162,* 2312–2316.

Sanavio, E. & Savardi, U. (1980). Sex and response of models in observational learning in mice. *Bulletin of Psychonomic Society, 15,* 291–292.

Sayler, A. & Salmon, M. (1971). An ethological analysis of communal nursing in the house mouse. *Behaviour, 40,* 62–85.

Schwagmeyer, P. L. (1979). The Bruce effect: an evaluation of male/female advantages. *The American Naturalist, 114,* 932–938.

Selander, R. K. & Kaufman, D. W. (1973). Genic variability and strategies of adaptation in animals. *Proceedings of the National Academy of Sciences U.S.A., 70,* 1875–1877.

Sherry, D. F. & Galef, B. G. (1984). Cultural transmission without imitation: Milk bottle opening by birds. *Animal Behaviour, 32,* 937–938.

Southwick, C. H. (1955). Regulatory mechanisms of house mouse populations: social behaviour affecting litter survival. *Ecology, 36,* 627–634.

Southwood, T. R. E. (1977). Habitat, the templet for ecological strategies? *Journal of Animal Ecology, 46,* 337–369.

Strayer, F. F. (1976). Learning and imitation as a function of social status in macaque monkeys (*Macaca nemestrina*). *Animal Behaviour, 24,* 835–848.

Thorpe, W. H. (1963). Learning and instinct in animals. (3rd ed.). London: Methuen.

Valzelli, L. (1973). The "isolation syndrome" in mice. *Psychopharmacologia, 31,* 305–320.

Van Oortmerssen, G. A. (1970). Biological significance, genetics and evolutionary origin of variability in behaviour within and between inbred strains of mice. *Behaviour, 38,* 1–92.

Yanai, J. & McClearn, G. E. (1972a). Assortative mating in mice. I.Female mating preference. *Behavior Genetics, 2,* 173–183.

Yanai, J. & McClearn, G. E. (1972b). Assortative mating in mice and the incest taboo. *Nature, 238,* 281–282.

PART V

Social Influences
on Communication

13

The Role of Social Factors
in White-Crowned Sparrow
Song Development

Lewis Petrinovich
University of California, Riverside

I review evidence suggesting the importance of social factors in song learning by birds, and develop implications this evidence has for analysis of the behavioral and physiological mechanisms by which song is learned. I first discuss in detail song learning in white-crowned sparrows (*Zonotrichia leucophrys*). Current conceptions of avian song development utilize data obtained from white-crowned sparrows, and I discuss and evaluate these conceptions, especially those pertaining to sensitive periods, sensory templates, and sensory gating mechanisms, in the light of current evidence. I then outline a model of white-crowned sparrow song learning based on orientation and its habituation, and discuss the implications of orientation processes for understanding the possible physiological processes involved in song learning.

OVERVIEW

Many species of song bird learn their songs from older conspecifics (Kroodsma & Baylis, 1982). Song dialects have been described for many passerine birds, and all known species with local dialects learn their songs from older birds, often after the age of dispersal (e.g., Baptista & Petrinovich, 1984, 1986; Bertram, 1970; Jenkins, 1978; Kroodsma, 1974; Kroodsma & Pickert, 1984a; Marler, 1970; Payne, 1981b, 1983; Petrinovich, 1985; Petrinovich & Baptista, 1987).

Theory and research in the area of song acquisition have been concerned both with proximate mechanisms regulating song learning and production, and with the ultimate, evolutionary significance of the song-learning process. Particular attention has focused on song development in white-crowned sparrows, especially on the acquisition of learned dialects by the sedentary *nuttalli* subspecies.

The song system of the white-crowned sparrow is simple enough to support detailed examination of the physiological mechanisms involved in its development. Most adults have a single 2-sec-long song, and the physical elements of the song are organized into a relatively few phrases. The dominant theory of song learning hypothesizes the existence of an auditory template and an auditory sensory-gating mechanism that function during a critical developmental period (e.g., Baptista & Petrinovich, 1984; see Kroodsma, 1982; Marler, 1976). Because of the centrality of these constructs for models of song development, their possible operating characteristics are discussed below.

THE RESEARCH EVIDENCE

Marler (1970) reported data acquired from 10, individually isolated white-crowned sparrows. Two birds raised in complete acoustic isolation developed only undifferentiated whistle songs without syllabic structure. One bird, tutored with a local dialect during days 3 to 8, and 2 tutored during days 50 to 70 developed similar isolate songs, as did 3 birds tutored on days 7–28 with song sparrow song. One bird tape-tutored with a local song on days 8–28, and another treated similarly on days 35–56, both learned complex, species typical song. These last 2 birds were also tutored with either the song of the Harris sparrow (*Z. querula*) or the song sparrow (*Melospiza melodia*) alternating in 2-min periods with a white-crowned sparrow song. The final song patterns of these two tape-tutored sparrows were copies of the white-crowned sparrow song with no trace of alien song. Marler concluded (a) that the critical period for song acquisition in white-crowned sparrows occurs during 10–50 days of age, because birds not exposed to song during that time developed abnormal songs; and (b) that exposure to song of alien species had no effect on song development.

I reported data (Petrinovich, 1985) from 40 tape-tutored male birds of the *nuttalli* subspecies of white-crowned sparrows that essentially replicated Marler's findings, but questioned the generalization that there is a sensory gate that rejects the song of alien species. Six total isolates all sang abnormal songs with no consistent overall pattern of frequency change for the different birds. Two birds tutored with *Z. l. nuttalli* song during 10 to 50 days of age reproduced the tutor song, and *nuttalli* students copied either of two alien subspecies songs (*Z. l. pugetensis* and *Z. l. gambelii*). An additional 4 birds were tutored with two different local dialects alternating: 2 sang only one of the songs, and 2 were bilingual, singing hybrid songs (as has been reported on the contact zone of various dialects by Baptista, 1975, and Petrinovich & Baptista, 1984).

To investigate the number of song inputs sufficient to instill a song, birds were tutored with either 1, 3, 6, or 12 songs a day either throughout the 10–50-day sensitive phase, during an early portion of the sensitive phase, or during a later portion of the sensitive phase. No bird presented with fewer than a total of 120 songs sang the tutor song; 1 bird tutored with 126 songs copied the song, as did 2 tutored with 252 songs. Overall, there was some indication that birds tutored early in the 10–50-day sensitive phase produced better copies than those tutored late.

These results indicated there is a necessary number of song inputs (about 120), given the conditions of the experiment. There also may be an interaction between the total number of songs presented and song density on a given day. A bird presented with 126 tape-recorded songs at a rate of 6 per day for 21 days copied the tutor song, whereas 1 presented with 123 songs at a rate of 3 per day for 41 days did not. If these results are reliable, they would have implications for the nature of the physiological mechanisms involved in establishing the engram for song. Perhaps the effects of a song stimulus must be reactivated a number of times on a single session for the engram to become consolidated.

Three additional white-crowned sparrows were tutored with the song of the allospecific Mexican junco (*Junco phaeonotus*). All 3 sang complex white-crowned sparrow songs with syllabic structure. (Marler's birds tutored with song sparrow song produced only simple isolate songs.) Two of the 3 copied elements of the junco song. The reason these birds copied elements of an alien species song, and Marler's did not, could have been that I presented over 11,000 tutor songs, whereas Marler presented only 1,056 songs. Because I found as few as 120 *Z. l. nuttalli* tape-recorded songs to be effective in the laboratory (Petrinovich, 1985), it could be that many more repetitions are required to learn allospecific as compared to conspecific song. Perhaps a different learning process was involved. In any case, it is clear that it is *possible* for tape-tutored birds to learn at least elements of an alien species song.

The results of this first experiment support Marler's conclusions regarding the length of the sensitive phase and the effects of experience with conspecific song when tape tutoring is used. There seems to be an increased sensitivity to song stimulation during days 10 to 30, and it is possible for white-crowned sparrows to learn elements of the song of alien species.

Baptista and Petrinovich (1984) exposed each of six 50-day-old male white-crowned sparrows to an allospecific live tutor, and all 6 copied the song of the alien tutor, even though the tutor was singing the song of the strawberry finch (*Amandava amandava*); the birds learned either from a real strawberry finch tutor or from a white-crowned sparrow that had learned "strawberry finch." Thus, with a live tutor, the sensitive phase is longer than 50 days, and it is possible for birds to learn an allospecific song, even though, in the present experiment, student birds could hear a dozen adult conspecifics loudly singing white-crowned sparrow song in the laboratory.

Given the effectiveness of live tutoring, another study was conducted comparing live and tape tutoring of both males and females on song learning (Baptista & Petrinovich, 1986), and yet another to determine whether it was possible to modify a song learned between 10 and 50 days using live tutoring after 50 days of age (Petrinovich & Baptista, 1987). The pertinent results of the Baptista and Petrinovich (1984, 1986), Petrinovich (1985), and Petrinovich and Baptista (1987) papers are summarized in Tables 13.1 and 13.2. Table 13.1 contains the results of the tutoring of 53 Z. l. nuttalli students with songs of the Z. l. nuttalli subspecies.

With tape tutoring using nuttalli song on days 10–50, 12 of 15 males (0.80) copied the nuttalli song (Cunningham and Baker, 1983, reported that 8 of 11 males [0.73] copied, and Marler, 1970, that 2 of 2 males [1.0] copied). Two males were live tutored on days 10–50 and both copied. One of 5 similarly treated females (0.20) copied the tutor song. With tape tutoring of birds more than 50 days of age, none of 4 males or 7 females copied (Marler reported that neither of 2 tape-tutored males [50–71] copied). Thus, most males (14 of 17; 0.82) copied the tutor song of either a tape or live tutor during days 10–50, and none of 4 copied with tape tutoring after 50 days. Most important, as can be seen in Table 13.1, 9 of 11 (0.82) copied with live tutoring after reaching 50 days of age.

Almost no females (2 of 21; 0.10) copied with either tape or live tutoring; the only copies produced were partial ones by one female live-tutored after 50 days, and another tape-tutored on days 10–50.

Forty-six white-crowned sparrow students of the nuttalli subspecies were exposed to the song of either an alien subspecies or species (Table 13.2). Four males were tape tutored (10–50) with song of the Z. l. gambelii subspecies: 2 copied and 2 had isolate songs. Two were tutored with song of the Z. l. pugetensis

Table 13.1
Birds Tutored With Nuttall Song

Sex	Males				Females			
Tutoring	Tape		Live		Tape		Live	
Days	10–50	50+	10–50	50+	10–50	50+	10–50	50+
Copy	10	0	1	5	0	0	0	0
Partial	2	0	1	4	1	0	0	1
Complex Isol.	2	1	0	2	3	6	2	6
Simple Isol.	1	3	0	0	1	1	0	0
Total	15	4	2	11	5	7	2	7
Copy+Partial	12/15	0/4	2/2	9/11	1/5	0/7	0/2	1/7
Proportion	0.80	0.0	1.0	0.82	0.20	0.0	0.0	0.14

Table 13.2
Birds Tutored With Alien Subspecies and Species Song

Sex	Males				Females			
Tutoring	Tape		Live		Tape		Live	
Days	10–50	50+	10–50	50+	10–50	50+	10–50	50+
	Alien Subspecies							
Copy	G,G,P	—	P	G	—	—	—	—
Isolate	G,G	G,G	—	G,G,G	G	G	—	G,G,G,G[4]
	Alien Species							
Copy	J,J	—	S[1],S[2],S[2], S[2],S[2],J J[3]	A,A,A, A,A,A	—	—	—	A,S[2],J
Isolate	J,MS3	A,A A,A	J	A	—	A	—	A,S[2]

Symbols: G=gambel; P=pugetensis; J=junco; A=strawberry finch; S=song sparrow;
MS3=Marler's three song sparrows
[1]tutoring started at 30 days of age
[2]tutoring started at 40–42 days of age
[3]tutoring started at 23 days of age
[4]acquired strawberry finch song in second year

subspecies and both learned: 1 was tape and 1 live tutored (10–50). Three males tape-tutored (50+) with *Z. l. gambelii* song did not copy it, and 1 other live-tutored male (50+) copied *gambelli* song. Two females were tape tutored (one 10–50 and the other 50+) with the *Z. l. gambelii* song, 4 were live tutored (50+), and none copied.

Four males were tape tutored (50+) with the strawberry finch song and none copied, but 6 of 7 live-tutored males (50+) copied the song. One live-tutored female (50+) copied the strawberry finch song and another did not. Thus, both males and females greater than 50 days of age can learn the strawberry finch song, but only if live-tutored.

It could be argued that there was no sensory gating mechanism to reject the strawberry finch song because the strawberry finch is not sympatric with the white-crowned sparrow. To evaluate the plausibility of this argument 7 white-crowned sparrow students were exposed to live song sparrow tutors when the students were almost 50 days of age (Baptista & Petrinovich, 1987). Song sparrow songs are quite complex, consisting of many syllable types, some of which are shared by neighboring males (Eberhardt & Baptista, 1977; Harris & Lemon, 1972), and can be heard in the regions of the San Francisco Bay area in which white-crowned sparrows breed. All 5 of the male white-crowned sparrows were judged to have copied song sparrow syllable types, 1 female copied, and 1 did not (Table 13.2). (Marler reported that none of 3 tape-tutored males copied song sparrow song.)

The junco is another sympatric species and as noted earlier, it was found that 2 tape-tutored (10–50) males learned elements of the song but 1 did not. When exposed to a live tutor (23+) 1 male learned, as did another male and female whose tutoring started at 50 days. (These results are summarized in Table 13.2).

Thus, it was possible for males to learn the song of the local subspecies, an alien subspecies, or an alien species when 10–50 days old with either a tape or live tutor. However, when 50+ days old, the males learned only with a live tutor. Only 5 of 32 females (0.16) copied a tutor song.

There is a suggestion in the data that some songs were more likely to be copied than others. For example, the Z. l. gambelii song was copied by only 2 of 4 tape-tutored (10-50) and 1 of 4 live-tutored (50+) nuttalli males, whereas the A. amandava song was copied by 6 of 7 live-tutored (50+) nuttalli males and 1 of 2 live-tutored (50+) nuttalli females. It is possible that characteristics of the A. amandava song make it easier to copy than that of the Z. l. gambelii. Because students learn the song as readily from either A. amandava males or white-crowned sparrows that had learned A. amandava song, it does not appear that the higher incidence of copying is the result of some behavioral characteristics of the male A. amandava.

Another study was conducted (Petrinovich & Baptista, 1987) to determine if learned song could be modified after white-crowned sparrows were 50 days of age, the age by which they would have dispersed from their natal territory (Blanchard, 1941). It was found that 8 of 13 males altered a learned song when exposed to a live tutor after 50 days of age, whereas none of 10 females did. Three of 7 males, trapped in their natal area when they were about 40 days old and exposed to a live tutor singing a song different from the natal dialect, after they were 50 days old, altered the song they had learned in the natal area. Only 1 of 5 field-tutored females altered a learned song. It is, therefore, possible to modify a song learned either in the field or the laboratory if students are exposed to a live tutor when over 50 days old.

There is reason to believe that acquisition of song by white-crowned sparrows that are greater than 50 days of age is not simply a laboratory artifact. White-crowned sparrows have been observed to change their song, either within or between breeding seasons (Baptista & Petrinovich, 1984; DeWolfe, Baptista, & Petrinovich, in preparation). In some instances, it has been documented that an initial song was changed to match the song of neighboring males. These observations, reported by Petrinovich and Baptista (1984) and Baptista and Morton (1982), suggest that males (but not females) can modify their natal song after dispersal to a breeding territory, and indicate that the song-learning mechanism for males in nature, as in the laboratory, is more plastic than previously proposed.

In another study (Petrinovich & Baptista, 1987) 4 students, 2 males and 2 females, were held in group isolation until they were 100 days old and then exposed to a live tutor. None of these birds copied the tutor song. All of the male students were singing an isolate song prior to tutoring, and this isolate song persisted.

SENSORY TEMPLATE THEORY

The sensory template has been described by Marler (1976) as follows: "Sensory templates provide a structural base for the perceptual analyses of arrays of stimuli that is both plastic and yet constrained" (p 328). These templates are considered both to explain some of the complexities of vocal learning and to guide the development of motor behavior. Exposure to song between 10 and 50 days of age is considered to create an engram if the song has the characteristics (unspecified) of the species. If the song is not appropriate, the stimulus is rendered ineffective by a sensory-gating mechanism. Thus, alien song is rejected, the song-learning mechanism is closed after 50 days of age, and crystallized song is the result of matching vocal output to the dictates of the auditory template.

These views originate from two major conceptual sources. One is analysis of physiological control systems, with special reference to optomotor adjustments of insects (e.g., von Holst, 1954; Mittelstaedt, 1964), which provides the concept of the *Sollwert,* or target value. The second source is the classic ethological literature on imprinting (Lorenz, 1935/1970).

Thorpe (1961, pp. 78–80) applied these ideas to song learning in the chaffinch: [Chaffinch have an] "inborn pattern which, although genetically coded, . . . need[s] the trigger-like stimulation of competitive singing to enable them to emerge into the actuality of performance." Thorpe considered chaffinch to be "endowed by nature with a number of vocal motor mechanisms which enable them to alter a variety of sounds, then whenever one of these is set in action the animal hears its own voice uttering a corresponding sound. The sound [of a bird uttering the same sound] will have the same effect, namely it will already have been associated with the vocal motor mechanism." And later he writes "whatever song or songs an individual Chaffinch has learnt by the time it is about thirteen months old, they remain its song or songs for the rest of its life," and "once the song learning period is over it cannot—so far as we know—be renewed. In these respects it resembles imprinting of young chickens during the following response."

Thorpe outlined what is, essentially, the current view of the song template theory: There is an inborn system organized in such a way that it accepts only certain stimulus inputs during an early restricted ontogenetic period. The system is irreversible and permanent once it has closed, and motor aspects of self-vocalization are involved in the realization of song.

The theory, as Marler (e.g., 1976) has developed it for the white-crowned sparrow, has been widely accepted and is discussed in most leading textbooks on animal behavior, ethology, and psychology (e.g., Alcock, 1984; Barnett, 1981; Brown, 1975; Dewsbury, 1978; Fantino & Logan, 1979; Gould, 1982; Manning, 1979). This theory is, in summary:

1. There is an inborn, species-specific, auditory template that imposes constraints on processes of vocal learning by focusing attention on sounds that meet the innate specifications of the template. This template has both a sensory-gating mechanism located in the auditory neural pathways, and a centrally located template that holds both innate and experiential information.

2. Effective sounds are stored in long-term memory.

3. Storage occurs only during an early critical period, and Marler (1970) has identified this to be between days 10 and 50.

4. The stored trace is irreversible.

5. The store is matched to vocal output during development of song by a process of attrition of elements not matching precisely to those stored in the template. The process of overproduction and attrition occurs each year as birds come into song, and the onset of song is hormonally triggered.

Because the research with white-crowned sparrows on which these principles are based used only tape tutoring, there is an implicit auxiliary assumption that taped song provides an adequate stimulus to explore characteristics of the mechanisms by which the template operates. Marler (1976) writes that "restrictions on the type of sound that is most readily learned are not attributable to contextual influences, such as the social situation, since they are manifest in a bird making a selection from sounds coming through a loudspeaker" (p. 320).

STATUS OF THE SONG TEMPLATE THEORY

The results summarized above concerning song acquisition by white-crowned sparrows pose a series of problems for the song template theory.

The sensory template: Only sounds that meet the requirements of an inborn template effectively influence the template. As Marler (1976) has phrased it, "it may serve as a kind of filter for external auditory stimuli . . . and is subsequently involved in motor development" (p. 325). This assumption involves the idea of both a central template and an auditory sensory-gating mechanism. The sensory-gating mechanism was suggested because there is little interspecific song copying in the field (although such copying has been reported for a number of species; see Baptista, 1972, 1974, 1977; Baptista & Morton, 1981; Baptista & Wells, 1975; Cooper & Murphy, 1985; Kroodsma, 1973; Lemaire, 1977) and the song of the alien song sparrow was not copied by Marler's birds in the laboratory. The results summarized above indicate that the song of alien species can be learned readily from live tutors. It has been reported that several other avian species can, and do, learn the song of alien species in the laboratory, some with greater ease than found for white-crowned sparrows (see Kroodsma & Baylis, 1982, for a survey of the literature).

Marler and Sherman (1983, 1985) inquired into the nature of the auditory template by taking eggs of two sparrow species, the swamp sparrow, *melospiza georgiana*, and song sparrow, placing them under foster parents of a different species, and rearing the young to maturity under identical conditions. They reported that there were species-specific differences in the characteristics of the adult songs of the two species, and the songs developed by isolate birds tended to have characteristics similar to those that distinguish the natural songs of the two species.

Marler and Sherman (1985) concluded that "many of the differences between normal swamp and song sparrow songs are innate, developing as a consequence of genotypic differences between the two species" (p. 68). Marler and Sherman's program of research takes a promising comparative approach toward achieving an understanding of the nature of genotypic differences in song systems and will make it possible to identify those physical stimuli that are effective song stimuli from those that are not. However, the program is moot in terms of identifying the behavioral and physical processes that enable some songs to be learned easily in the field, and others with great difficulty.

As mentioned above, interspecific copying in the field has been reported, but it occurs relatively seldom. Interspecific copying can be obtained in the laboratory with no difficulty with live rather than tape tutoring, even at a late developmental age. The identification of the processes regulating such vocal learning is the concern of the revised theory developed below.

The nature of the auditory template has not been specified although the concept has been in use for many years: The anatomical locus, physiological properties, and operating characteristics remain unspecified, and there is no a priori specification of the range of effective stimuli based on any physiological criteria or ecological considerations, except that conspecific stimuli should be acceptable but allospecific should not. The nature and functional properties of the template must be specified if the template concept is to have explanatory value.

The auditory-gating mechanism leads to the expectation that inappropriate stimuli either are prevented from influencing song learning centers, or seldom do so. This implies there is a sensory filter separate from the central song template. A major difficulty in understanding the construct of a sensory template is that the construct is used to account for two different processes[1] and to refer to events at two different levels of discourse. One set of processes are those involved in the

---

[1] I wish to thank Mark Konishi who helped clarify this issue for me. He was careful in his original definition of the concept (Konishi, 1965) to distinguish between the processes of acquisition of song and vocal motor development.

acquisition and storage of song. These processes involve presumed innate tuning, an input to the innate "blueprint," and a long-term storage of the engram. The second set of processes are those involved in the retrieval of the engram (or a match-to-sample) involved in vocal production.

Marler (1976) speaks of auditory templates lying in the auditory pathways that have the capacity to guide motor development: "as the young male begins to sing he strikes a progressively closer match between his vocal output and the dictates of the auditory template," and "The male thus sings from memory. He must be able to hear his own voice to translate into song this remembered 'engram' of the song, learned earlier in life" (pp. 320–321).

It confuses the issue to use the construct of a template variously as a sensory filter, a genetic blueprint "to focus the learning bird's attention upon conspecific song models" (Marler, 1970, p. 323), a long-term memory system, and the model in a match-to-sample process. One advantage of the revised theory I propose is that it conceptually separates these different processes.

The other problem is that in some contexts the template concept is used as merely a shorthand description of data, and at others to refer to underlying physiological processes. Shifting back and forth from the level of shorthand expressions ("intervening variables") to a level of real physiological processes ("hypothetical constructs"; see MacCorquodale & Meehl, 1948) serves to obscure issues and makes it difficult to bring appropriate lines of evidence to bear.

It is generally agreed that there are no simple feature detectors operating at the level of sensory receptors. Capranica (1983) suggested that "detection of a complex sensory stimulus resides at the level of populations of cells" (p. 8). Marler (1983) pointed out that it is unlikely there is "a single anatomically discrete filter somewhere in the brain through which sensory song information is obliged to pass if learning is to occur" (p. 30). He suggested there is a "neural system with the properties of a modifiable sensory template as the basis of oscine song learning." I suggest, below, that it is not necessary to postulate a sensory template in any sense other than that of an organized memory system.

Long-term memory: "Effective songs are stored in long-term memory," but not with great fidelity to the model. The results of isolation studies (Baptista & Petrinovich, 1986; Marler, 1970; Petrinovich, 1985) indicate that although students often produce good copies of their tutor's song there are both improvisations and copying errors evident in many of the songs (see Marler, 1983; Petrinovich, in press).

Critical Period: "Storage occurs only during an early critical period, between 10 and 50 days of age." The results discussed above indicate this is true only with tape tutoring. There seems to be a differentially sensitive phase for initial song learning that varies across age. There was some suggestion that birds were more sensitive from days 10 to 30 than days 30 to 50 (Petrinovich, 1985), and only live tutoring was effective after 50 days of age. It seems that initial learning does not take place after 100 days of age in the laboratory, although such learning has been reported in the field (DeWolfe, Baptista, & Petrinovich, in preparation).

Cunningham and Baker (1983) reported that white-crowned sparrows will accept taped songs as models for imitation during the first 50 days of life. They agree with Marler's conclusion that social factors are unimportant in song learning by white-crowned sparrows because only 3 of 11 birds in their study showed any alteration of learned song when a live tutor was introduced after the students were 50 days of age. The difference between their results and those discussed above (Petrinovich & Baptista, 1987) is probably due to differences in experimental procedure: Each of our subjects could interact with only one adult through a screen, whereas Cunningham and Baker's subjects were free-flying in an aviary, permitting the juveniles to interact freely with one another, but to interact only to a limited extent with the adult male caged in the middle of the aviary. Examination of song types indicates that some juveniles in their experiment appear to have learned from each other.

The increased effectiveness of live tutors found with white-crowned sparrows is compatible with results for several other species (e.g., creeper, *Certhia* spp., Thielcke, 1970; zebra finch, *Poephila gutata,* Price, 1979; indigo bunting, *Passerina cyanea,* Rice & Thompson, 1968, and Payne, 1981a, 1982; marsh wren, *Cistothorus palustris,* Kroodsma, 1982). The mechanism suggested below for song learning by white-crowned sparrows may, therefore, be more generally applicable to other avian song-learning systems.

The irreversible trace: "The stored trace is irreversible." The results of the studies discussed above, as well as field data, indicate that irreversibility is not the case. It is clear that songs learned during the first 50 days (when white-crowned sparrows are in the natal area) can be altered, and there is suggestive evidence that some alteration of learned song can occur between seasons. The word irreversible is probably unfortunate, as Bischoff (1985) has pointed out when discussing imprinting: "it does not mean that the animal is restricted in its reaction to the one object acquired during the sensitive period, but that it prefers this object in a choice situation" (p. 174). The degree of modifiability of song has not been explored, but there is evidence that at the least, whole phrases of song can be substituted one for another. Birds might well acquire a second song, yet have the ability to sing either of the two songs, and might prefer one or the other. Most research designs do not permit one to address this issue.

Matching the store: "The store is matched to vocal output during development of song, through a process of overproduction of song elements followed by a gradual attrition." This assumption may not be correct. There are recordings of birds as young as 50 days old singing almost crystallized full song in the field (DeWolfe, Baptista, & Petrinovich, in preparation), and this singing continues throughout the birds' first year. Numerous instances have been observed in which adult birds were observed spontaneously singing only subsong or plastic song in the fall or winter, and, when presented with song playback, sang one or two strong and complete songs. Thus, the lack of performance may not be due to lack of a mature memory or a difficulty with a match-to-sample, but be a motivationally based performance process.

REVISED THEORY

1. There are innately tuned sensory systems whose sensitivity can be influenced through centrifugal influences on sensory pathways, as well as through memory mechanisms.

There is abundant evidence for differentially sensitive processing systems, generally, and in the white-crowned sparrow, specifically. Ratliff (1980) has argued that parallel processing systems characterize visual sensory systems in a large number of species, and that these systems are characterized by divergence of local retinal activity to several separate cells at higher levels. Capranica (1983) concluded that "A fundamental characteristic of every vertebrate sensory system studied to date points to an increasing complexity in response selectivity as one ascends the central nervous system" (p. 5).

There is abundant evidence that there are differentially tuned sensory systems adequate to cope with encoding and decoding of stimuli similar to those involved in bird song (e.g., Capranica, 1983; Ewert, 1985). In addition, several studies have identified neurones of the white-crowned sparrow that are selectively responsive to song stimuli (e.g., Leppelsack, 1983; Margoliash, 1983; McCasland & Konishi, 1981).

Kroodsma and Pickert (1984b) studied vocal learning in marsh wrens and found stimulus specificity to be important in song learning. The young birds selectively learned conspecific song syllables, especially when the syllables were associated with the introductory or concluding section of a conspecific song. This tutoring study, those with white-crowned sparrows, as well as neurophysiological evidence, support the idea that tuned sensory systems are involved in song learning.

Is the concept of a genetically tuned sensory system significantly different from, or any improvement over, the idea of a sensory template? I believe it is. The concept of a sensory template has resisted specification regarding its operating characteristics. Lacking any clear statement of input-output relationships the concept has little theoretical explanatory value. Lacking specification of its physiological mechanisms it has little value as a realistic entity as well.

Genetically tuned sensory systems have been identified in a wide range of animal species and in all sensory systems investigated. The operating characteristics of such tuned systems have been studied, the physiological systems explored, and their relationship to ecological factors have been examined. When we consider criteria by which we judge theoretical progress, the conception of a tuned sensory system represents an advance over the sensory template conception.

The change in language is more than a mere preference for one descriptive language over another; the change is supported by a body of research that can direct physiological investigations should initial behavioral testing prove fruitful.

2. Stimuli have a differential power to evoke an orienting response, and this power is both genetically and experimentally influenced. The rate of habituation of the orienting response is also related to both genetic and experiential factors.

Novel, salient, or behaviorally significant stimuli cause an organism to perform an orienting response, and this orienting response wanes as a function of repeated trials not involving positive or negative consequences. Petrinovich (1973), Peeke (1984), and Shalter (1984) have reviewed evidence that a number of species have an innate tendency to take avoiding or self-protective action in response to a range of stimuli, and that the rate of habituation to these stimuli varies in relation to their adaptive significance. Patterson, et al. (1980) reported that white-crowned sparrows were differentially responsive to stimuli that had different adaptive significance at different stages of the reproductive cycle of the female.

Schlenoff (1985) studied the startle response of blue jays (*Cyanocitta cristata*) to moth prey models. She found that the jays exhibited an initial startle to novel, odd, conspicuous, or anomalous wing patterns, but that these responses habituated. The habituation was specific to the pattern presented and Schlenoff suggested that habituation regulates the responsiveness of bird predators to moths with different wing patterns in a manner that could provide insight into an adaptive basis for the hindwing diversity observed among moths in nature. This experiment provides another general instance of the importance of orientation and habituation in the regulation of behavior.

I have, in a series of six field experiments (see Petrinovich, 1984, for a summary), investigated response levels and their changes to the playback of male song to territorial pairs of white-covered sparrows. There seem to be two basic processes, habituation and sensitization, that influence response patterns, and each of these processes can be characterized by two underlying factors: relative stimulus specificity and relative permanence. The pattern of behavior of members of the pairs in these experiments can be understood in terms of the biological relevance of the stimuli considered in the context of adaptation to demands of the environment (Petrinovich & Patterson, 1979). Bischoff (1985) found strong indications in the literature that the design of an experiment has a large influence on the time course of the sensitive period, and that this course is somewhat dependent on the naturalness of the stimulus.

The results of these field experiments with white-crowned sparrows indicate that response levels and their patterns of change, as described by the above two-factor, dual-process theory, are involved in the maintenance of territorial integrity, and regulate responsiveness to the presentation of songs in the natural environment.

There are several studies of avian behavior indicating that stimulus preferences do not develop simply as the result of passive stimulus presentation. Ten Cate, Los, and Schilperoord (1984) studied species recognition in zebra finch males and concluded that "The result that behavioral interactions seem to be important in developing sexual preferences leads to the conclusion that more attention must be given to the behaviour of animals used as stimulus objects in imprinting studies" (p. 860).

Ten Cate (1984) raised zebra finch young with mixed pairs of zebra and Bengalese finch parents. He found that the preference of the young for their own species was due to characteristics of the parental behavior of the zebra finch parent, and that this preference could be eliminated if social contact with the zebra finch parent was reduced. He concluded that "the influence of early experience in the development of species recognition in [zebra finch] males is not the result of exposure to a (moving) object only, but that behavioral interactions must have played a role" (p. 281).

Lickliter and Gottlieb (1985) studied maternal preferences in ducklings (*Anas platyrhynchos*) and found a visual preference for conspecifics only if the ducklings were reared in conditions that allowed unrestricted social interaction with siblings, as would normally occur in nature. There was no preference if the birds were raised in social isolation but could see and hear a sibling, were reared with only one sibling duckling, or were reared in a group situation without the opportunity for direct social interaction. Although the work of Lickliter and Gottlieb and of ten Cate does not involve song learning, the findings indicate that social factors can be of primary importance in behavioral development. These social factors are of the type that enhance orientation and would be expected to habituate slowly.

Several studies indicate that young acquire their song by copying from a live tutor, and that interaction between a tutor and a young bird is more important than merely hearing a tutor or tape recording (zebra finch: Böhner, 1983; Immelmann, 1969; Price, 1979), chaffinch (Slater, 1983), canary (Waser & Marler, 1977), indigo bunting (Payne, 1981a), and nightingale (Todt, Hultsch, & Weihe, 1979). There is, then, abundant evidence to support Assumption 2 based on research with many different species in a wide range of laboratory and field conditions and with the white-crowned sparrow, in particular.

3. The frequency with which the orienting response is evoked is related to the probability of forming an engram representing stimuli that are present; the state of activity of the nervous system influences the probability that presentation of a stimulus will result in a permanent engram that is later translated into adult song.

The assumed processes are similar to those postulated in synaptic models of learning and memory based on Hebb's cell assembly model (e.g., Hebb, 1949, 1955; Goddard, 1980; Milner, 1957). As Margoliash (1983) pointed out, song specific auditory units are found in an area (HVc) in which motor activity is specifically related to song production. Neurones of HVc project to other areas, such as area X, and these other (association) areas could be the level at which the different elements of the entire song are integrated, as for Hebb's phase sequences. Nottebohm (e.g., 1984, p. 234) presented evidence that the development of brain networks for song control in several avian species may be involved in song learning, and he suggested that HVc neurones could be related to perceptual learning. The research and conceptions of Nottebohm, as well as those of Margoliash, are consistent with the assumption that the frequency of orienting toward a stimulus is related to the probability of forming an engram representing that stimulus. Engrams may be established in the motor control nuclei (such as HVc) and these could be stable across years (as for white-crowned sparrows; Baker, Bottjer, & Arnold, 1984), or could degenerate and be reformed each year, as for the canary (*Serinus canaria*) and zebra finch (Nottebohm, 1981).

The manner in which avian neural systems function in song learning is speculative at present. The HVc might serve as a perceptual-motor filter, it might serve as a short or intermediate term buffer, or it might serve as the functional system during the acquisition phase of song learning. Research directed toward understanding these mechanisms could provide an exciting breakthrough regarding natural memory systems.

The possibility that, for birds, orientation is an important process affecting the probability of engram formation has been strengthened by several studies of observational learning. Food preferences and aversions were easily acquired when redwing blackbirds (*Agelaius phoeniceus*) observed conspecifics either eating foods, or being made sick by foods of different color (Mason & Reidinger, 1982). Both grackles (*Quiscalus quiscula*) and redwing blackbirds exhibited observational learning, both of the behavior of conspecifics and of the other species (Mason, Arzt, & Reidinger, 1984).

Sasvári (1985) investigated the importance of observational learning by birds required to secure food presented in novel ways. He investigated tits (*Parus major, P. caeruleus, P. palustris*) and thrushes (*Turdus merula, T. philomelos*), and found that all exhibited strong observational learning. The *P. major* were better observational learners than were the *P. caeruleus* or *P. palustris*, although the original learning of the tutors was not different for the three species.

Palameta and Lefebvre (1985) studied pigeons and found, as did Mason and Reidinger, that the birds found food more easily using observational learning than by trial and error learning. The strength of the effects in these studies indicated that observational learning of the kind postulated to be important in song learning can be a powerful factor influencing avian behavior.

Pepperberg (1986, this volume) extensively examined the literature on avian and human vocal learning and argued "that social modeling theory, with its emphasis on the efficacy of live, interacting social tutors, is well suited for analyzing the factors involved in the development of a wide range of avian vocal behaviors". The essential argument is similar to that of the present Assumption 3:

Live tutoring enhances the probability of learning, and can be effective at developmental periods beyond the usual sensitive phase. Although Pepperberg does not delineate the processes that are involved in the enhanced effectiveness of live tutors, she concludes that human studies suggest an important factor might be the degree of emotional arousal of participants. Such enhanced arousal (as indexed by orientation) has been suggested as one of the processes driving song learning in the conceptions offered here.

There is, then, abundant evidence for the particulars of Assumption 3. The appropriate physiological entities exist, and their proposed modes of functioning are those that have stood the test of time for synaptic models. There is evidence that observational learning, of the kind proposed here for song learning, is a potent force in other kinds of avian and human learning.

4. The efficiency of the central processing system decreases with time after 10 days of age.

Marler (1970) has shown that birds do not learn tape-tutored songs prior to 10 days of age. There was a suggestion that tape-tutored birds learn songs more readily when 10–30 days of age than when 30–50 days (Petrinovich, 1985). Baptista and Petrinovich (1986) found that tape tutoring was effective when birds were 10–50 days of age, but not when over 50 days, whereas live tutoring was effective after 50 days of age. It was possible to alter learned song using a live tutor after 50 days of age (Petrinovich & Baptista, 1987).

Eales (1985) studied song learning in zebra finches by raising them with their father until they were 35, 50, or 65 days old. If the young were removed from the father and placed with another adult, a song developed that was a hybrid between the father's and the new adult's song. If there was no song model during the juvenile phase, an abnormal song was produced until a model was made available, at which time a normal song developed. The results indicated that the sensitive phase is not strictly age dependent, but is strongly influenced by the quality of experience, as Bischoff (1985) concluded, above. All of the results summarized in this section can be interpreted to mean that sensitivity to song stimuli may diminish, not due to a lack of capacity to learn, but to what Bateson (1981) calls a "lack of willingness," making it easier to learn at some stages of development than others.

I suggest that decrease in willingness to learn is the result of habituation to auditory stimuli presented by tape recording only. The use of a live tutor provides a continually changing visual stimulus context and impedes the course of habituation to the auditory stimuli.

The greater early sensitivity could also be due to a greater capacity for neural changes. Rosenzweig (1984) reported that the percentage differences in weights and RNA content of the brains of rats raised in an enriched environment over brains of isolate controls were greater when the enrichment was early in life than later. It was also found that with longer periods of exposure, cerebral responses to differential experience could be induced at advanced ages in the rat.

These results are all compatible with those reported here for the white-crowned sparrow.

5. If the system is not activated it loses its storage capacity: There is an initial equipotentiality and a subsequent loss of plasticity, using Lashley's (1949) terminology.

It has long been known that, in humans, there is plasticity such that trauma to areas of the brain that are important in adult language function have little effect if the trauma occurs at an early age. However, the same trauma occurring at a later age has a pronounced functional effect (see Petrinovich, 1972, for a review of these data). With white-crowned sparrows, a loss of plasticity was found when nestlings were isolated until they were 100 days old and then placed with a live tutor. All of these 100-day-old birds already had developed a full isolate song, and none showed any evidence of song learning as the result of live-tutoring (Petrinovich & Baptista, 1987). These data indicate that plasticity is lost and development proceeds in a different direction from that of the normal. It should be indicated, however, that some older birds have been found to alter their songs in both the field (Baptista & Petrinovich, 1984; DeWolfe, Baptista, & Petrinovich, in prep.), and the laboratory (Baptista & Petrinovich, 1986), although it is not a common phenomenon.

I assume that the key factor triggering the loss of plasticity is a hormonal one. At about 100 days of age the juveniles will have undergone the prejuvenile moult, and the striped breast of the fledgling will have changed to the clear breast of the yearling. At this age, total isolates sing a fully crystallized isolate song. One bit of evidence indicating that the loss of plasticity can be hormonally regulated has been provided by Nottebohm (1968) who studied song development in a castrated male chaffinch (*Fringilla coelebs*). The castrated male showed no evidence of having learned a song during the first year, when young of the species normally acquire song. However, when injected with testosterone in the spring of the second year, a time when song learning does not normally occur, the bird acquired tutor themes. This observation suggests that hormonal levels regulate the plasticity of the song learning mechanism.

6. The engram system is hormonally activated each year; coming into song is a performance event, motivationally driven, and not a memory event involving match-to-sample.

Baker et al. (1984) studied the volume of HVc and RA in the white-crowned sparrow and found that both of these nuclei were larger in the male than in the female, but that there were no differences between males held on summer as compared to winter photoperiods. White-crowned sparrows sing less in winter than in summer, seldom learn new song elements each year, and are able to sing perfect full songs at any time of the year (DeWolfe, Petrinovich, & Baptista, in prep.). Nottebohm (1981) found a change in the size of HVc and RA of the canary to be related to androgen level and amount of singing. Because the canary does learn new songs each season, Baker et al. (1984) concluded, "Thus, our data on white-crowned sparrows are consistent with the hypothesis that seasonal changes in volume of HVc and RA may be specifically related to the capacity for learning" (p. 88). The fact that we observed young white-crowned sparrows, as well as adults, that are singing sub- and plastic-song, producing clear full song when stimulated to do so, suggests that the memory system remains intact throughout the year.

If the development of song each year for white-crowned sparrows involved the reinstatement of a sensorimotor memory trace, then a gradual development would be expected. Because the birds are capable of singing a full song at any time, provided the proper stimulation occurs, the lack of singing during some months could well be due to a lack of hormonal support to activate song engrams. The effect of these changes in hormonal levels would be to change the threshold for song production: With low titers of testosterone the elicitation threshold is high, and with high titers the threshold is low.

CONCLUSIONS

The revised theory outlined here involves a set of assumptions that are based on, and do not contradict, well-accepted observations and principles. The assumptions avoid the postulation of a sensory-gating mechanism as currently conceived, or of an auditory template; only genetically biased and differentially tuned sensory systems sensitive to combinations of song components are involved. Effective song stimuli, then, are those that fire receptor units, perhaps in HVc, and which, in turn, stimulate activity in an association area. The differential ease of learning various types of song is the result of the differential frequency of neural firing in association areas. In this view, genetic tuning of receptors is a threshold-adjusting mechanism and does not involve gating—anything that evokes a sensory response often enough, and with the proper timing, can be effective. Once the song engram is established the major factor determining its ease of retrieval is hormonal state. This state could regulate both the threshold of access to the system and the likelihood of vocalization occurring. Konishi (1985) has demonstrated that such self-produced vocalization is a critical factor in the development of song. I believe these assumptions, if favored with more supportive evidence, can remove some of the mystery surrounding models that evoke comparators, or which involve some unspecified template to match.

The proposed theory resolves the anomalies produced by the research results. Live tutoring would be expected to be more effective than tape tutoring because in the tape-tutoring experiments birds are exposed to the repeated and stereotyped presentation of a song. This repetitious stereotype would produce a maximum amount of habituation, and the student should make fewer orienting responses. A live tutor would provide a constantly changing stimulus milieu that would make it difficult for habituation to develop, and would maintain a constant level of short-term sensitization (Shalter, 1984; Petrinovich, 1984). In this way the song of a live tutor is likely to evoke orienting responses more often, and the probability of an association between song stimuli present at the same time will be enhanced: the outcome will be an engram for the song elements present during the orientation. Live tutoring is more effective than tape tutoring, and live tutoring is effective whether or not, for example, the tutor is the very small strawberry finch, or a relatively large white-crowned sparrow singing strawberry finch song. Thus, the effective stimulus event seems not to be some specific visual quality of the white-crowned sparrow.

Tests of predictions based on this model are now underway. These tests involve analyses of the behavior of students and tutors to determine the amount of orientation and rate of habituation to songs of different types that are presented in different ways. Such experiments provide a severe test of the proposed behavioral mechanisms involved in song learning. Even if the proposed mechanisms turn out to be incorrect, analysis of the behavior of students and tutors should provide an approach to understanding the large individual variability found in tutoring studies. Although suggestions can often be made of the kinds of factors producing individual differences, it usually is a mystery why different birds treated the same way differ so markedly. Kroodsma and Pickert (1984a) suggested that "This variation must represent real individual differences in how the young males responded to the social situation we provided in the laboratory" (p. 393). They concluded that an understanding of the causes of these individual differences will contribute to an understanding of their importance in determining the fitness and general behavior of individuals.

Although the evidence and critical factors spelled out for the proposed model are behavioral, I have considered the possible physiological events that might be involved. Only by framing behavioral theory in terms of probable physiological mechanisms will we be able to generate unified theories that adequately traverse both the physiological and behavioral landscape. In addition, careful attention to the processes at one level can produce insights into the workings at the other, to the enrichment of each of the several disciplines involved.

ACKNOWLEDGMENTS

The original research discussed here was supported by grants from the University of California, the National Institutes of Health (HD-04343 and MH-38782), and the National Science Foundation (BNS-7914126 and BNS-8004540).

REFERENCES

Alcock, J. (1984). *Animal behavior: An evolutionary approach,* (3rd ed.). Sunderland, MA: Sinauer.
Baker, M. C., Bottjer, S. W., & Arnold, A. P. (1984). Sexual dimorphism and lack of

seasonal changes in vocal control regions of the white-crowned sparrow brain. *Brain Research, 295*, 85–89.

Baptista, L. F. (1972). Wild house finch sings white-crowned sparrow song. *Zeitschrift für Tierpsychologie, 30*, 266–270.

Baptista, L. F. (1974). The effects of song wintering white-crowned sparrows on song development in sedentary populations of the species. *Zeitschrift für Tierpsychologie, 34*, 147–171.

Baptista, L. F. (1975). Song dialects and demes in sedentary populations of the white-crowned sparrow (*Zonotrichia leucophrys nuttalli*). *University of California Publications in Zoology, 105*, 1–52.

Baptista, L. F. (1977). Geographic variation in song and dialects of the Puget Sound white-crowned sparrow. *Condor, 79*, 356–370.

Baptista, L. F., & Morton, M. L. (1981). Interspecific song acquisition by a white-crowned sparrow. *Auk, 98*, 383–385.

Baptista, L. F., & Morton, M. L. (1982). Song dialects and mate selection in montane white-crowned sparrows. *Auk, 99*, 537–547.

Baptista, L. F., & Petrinovich, L. (1984). Social interaction, sensitive phases and the song template hypothesis in the white-crowned sparrow. *Animal Behaviour, 32*, 172–181.

Baptista, L. F., & Petrinovich, L. (1986). Song development in the white-crowned sparrow: Social factors and sex differences. *Animal Behaviour, 34*, 1359–1371.

Baptista, L. F., & Wells, H. (1975). Additional evidence of song-misimprinting in the white-crowned sparrow. *Bird Banding, 46*, 269–272.

Barnett, S. A. (1981). *Modern ethology: The science of animal behavior*. New York: Oxford University Press.

Bateson, P. (1981). Control of sensitivity to the environment during development. In K. Immelmann, G. W. Barlow, L. Petrinovich, & M. Main (Eds.), *Behavioral development* (pp. 432–453). New York: Cambridge University Press.

Bertram, B. (1970). The vocal behaviour of the Indian hill mynah, *Gracula religiosa. Animal Behaviour Monographs, 3(2)*, 81–192.

Bischoff, H.-J. (1985). Environmental influences on early development: A comparison of imprinting and cortical plasticity. In P. P. G. Bateson & P. H. Klopfer (Eds.), *Perspectives in ethology* (Vol. 6, pp. 169–217). New York: Plenum.

Blanchard, B. D. (1941). The white-crowned sparrows (*Zonotrichia leucophrys*) of the Pacific seaboard: Environment and annual cycle. *University of California Publications in Zoology, 46*, 1–178.

Böhner, J. (1983). Song learning in the zebra finch. (*Taeniophygia guttata*): Selectivity in the choice of a tutor and accuracy of song copies. *Animal Behaviour, 31*, 231–237.

Brown, J. L. (1975). *The evolution of behavior*. New York: Norton.

Capranica, R. R. (1983). Sensory processing of key stimuli. In J.-P. Ewert, R. R. Capranica, D. J. Ingle (Eds.), *Advances in vertebrate neuroethology* (pp. 3–6). New York: Plenum.

Cate, C. ten. (1984). The influence of social relations on the development of species recognition in zebra finch males. *Behaviour, 91*, 263–285.

Cate, C. ten, Los, L., & Schilperoord, L. (1984). The influence of differences in social experience on the development of species recognition in zebra finch males. *Animal Behaviour, 32*, 852–860.

Cooper, B. A., & Murphy, E. C. (1985). Savannah sparrow sings a white-crowned sparrow song. *Animal Behaviour, 33,* 330–331.

Cunningham, M. A., & Baker, M. C. (1983). Vocal learning in white-crowned sparrows: Sensitive phase and song dialects. *Behavioral Ecology & Sociobiology, 13,* 259–269.

DeWolfe, B. B., Baptista, L. F., & Petrinovich, L. (in preparation) Song development and territory establishment in free-living white-crowned sparrows.

DeWolfe, B. B., Petrinovich, L., & Baptista, L. F. (in preparation) Circannual song cycle in sedentary white-crowned sparrows.

Dewsbury, D. A. (1978). *Comparative animal behavior.* New York: McGraw-Hill.

Eales, L. A. (1985). Song learning in zebra finches: Some effects of song model availability on what is learnt and when. *Animal Behaviour, 33,* 1293–1300.

Eberhardt, C., &, Baptista, L. F. (1977). Intraspecific and interspecific song mimesis in California song sparrows. *Bird Banding, 48,* 193–205.

Ewert, J.-P. (1985). Concepts in vertebrate neuroethology. *Animal Behaviour, 33,* 1–29.

Fantino, E. J., & Logan, C. A. (1979). *The experimental analysis of behavior: A biological perspective.* San Francisco: W. H. Freeman.

Goddard, G. V. (1980). Component properties of the memory machine: Hebb revisited. In P. W. Jusczyk & R. M. Klein (Eds.), *The nature of thought* (pp. 231–247). Hillsdale, NJ: Lawrence Erlbaum Associates.

Gould, J. L. (1982). *Ethology: The mechanisms and evolution of behavior.* New York: Norton.

Harris, M. A., & Lemon, R. E. (1972). Songs of song sparrows (*Melospiza melodia*): Individual variation and dialects. *Canadian Journal of Zoology, 50,* 301–309.

Hebb, D. O. (1949). *The organization of behavior.* New York: Wiley.

Hebb, D. O. (1955). Drives and the CNS (conceptual nervous system). *Psychological Review, 62,* 243–254.

Holst, E. von. (1954). Relations between the central nervous system and the peripheral organs. *British Journal of Animal Behaviour, 2,* 89–94.

Immelmann, K. (1969). Song development in the zebra finch and other estrildid finches. In R. A. Hinde (Ed.), *Bird vocalizations* (pp. 61–74). New York: Oxford University Press.

Jenkins, P. F. (1978). Cultural transmission of song patterns and dialect development in a free-living bird population *Animal Behaviour, 25,* 50–78.

Konishi, J. (1965). The role of auditory feedback in the control of vocalization in the white-crowned sparrow. *Zeitschrift für Tierpsychologie, 22,* 770–783.

Konishi, M. (1985). Birdsong: From behavior to neuron. *Annual Review of Neurosciences, 8,* 125–170.

Kroodsma, D. (1973). Coexistence of Bewick's wrens and house wrens in Oregon. *Auk, 90,* 342–352.

Kroodsma, D. (1974). Song learning, dialects and dispersal in the Bewick's wren. *Zeitschrift für Tierpsychologie, 35,* 352–380.

Kroodsma, D. E. (1982). Learning and the ontogeny of sound signals in birds. In D. E. Kroodsma & E. G. Miller (Eds.), *Acoustic communication in birds: II. Song learning and its consequences* (pp. 1–23). New York: Academic Press.

Kroodsma, D. E., & Baylis, J. R. (1982). Appendix: A world survey of evidence for vocal learning in birds. In D. E. Kroodsma & E. G. Miller (Eds.), *Acoustic communication in birds: II. Song learning and its consequences,* (pp. 311–337). New York: Academic Press.

Kroodsma, D. E., & Pickert, R. (1984a). Sensitive phases for song learning: Effects of social interaction and individual variation. *Animal Behaviour, 32,* 389–394.

Kroodsma, D. E., & Pickert, R. (1984b). Repertoire size, auditory templates, and selective vocal learning in songbirds. *Animal Behaviour, 32,* 395–399.

Lashley, K. S. (1949). Persistent problems in the evolution of mind. *Quarterly Review of Biology, 24,* 28–42.

Lemaire, F. (1977). Mixed song, interspecific competition and hybridization in the reed and marsh warblers (*Acrocephalus scirpaceus* and *palustris*). *Behaviour, 63,* 215–240.

Leppelsack, J.-J. (1983). Analysis of song in the auditory pathway of song birds. In J.-P. Ewert, R. R. Capranica, & D. J. Ingle (Eds.), *Advances in vertebrate neuroethology* (pp. 783–799). New York: Plenum.

Lickliter, R., & Gottlieb, G. (1985). Social interaction with siblings is necessary for visual imprinting of species-specific maternal preferences in ducklings (*Anas platyrhynchos*). *Journal of Comparative Psychology, 99,* 371–379.

Lorenz, K. (1935/1970). Companions as factors in the bird's environment. *Studies in animal and human behaviour* (Vol. 1, pp. 101–258). Cambridge, MA: Harvard University Press.

MacCorquodale, K., & Meehl, P. E. (1948). On a distinction between hypothetical constructs and intervening variables. *Psychological Review, 55,* 95–107.

Manning, A. (1979). *An introduction to animal behaviour* (3rd ed.). Reading, MA: Addison-Wesley.

Margoliash, D. (1983). Acoustic parameters underlying the responses of song-specific neurons in the white-crowned sparrow. *Journal of Neuroscience, 3,* 1039–1057.

Marler, P. (1970). A comparative approach to vocal learning: song development in white-crowned sparrows. *Journal of Comparative and Physiological Psychology, 71,* 1–25.

Marler, P. (1976). Sensory templates in species-specific behavior. In J. C. Fentress (Ed.), *Simpler networks and behavior* (pp. 314–329). Sunderland, MA: Sinauer.

Marler, P. (1983). Some ethological implications for neuroethology: the ontogeny of birdsong. In J.-P. Ewert, R. R. Capranica, & D. J. Ingle (Eds.), *Advances in neuroethology* (pp. 21–52). New York: Plenum.

Marler, P., & Sherman, V. (1983). Song structure without auditory feedback: Emendations of the auditory template hypothesis. *Journal of Neuroscience, 3,* 517–531.

Marler, P., & Sherman, V. (1985). Innate differences in singing behaviour of sparrows reared in isolation from adult conspecific song. *Animal Behaviour, 33,* 57–71.

Mason, J. R., Arzt, A. H., & Reidinger, R. F. (1984). Comparative assessment of food preferences and aversions acquired by blackbirds via observational learning. *Auk, 101,* 796–803.

Mason, J. R., & Reidinger, R. F. (1982). Observational learning of food aversions in red-winged blackbirds (*Agelaius phoeniceus*). *Auk, 99,* 548–554.

McCasland, J. S., & Konishi, M. (1981). Interaction between auditory and motor activities in an avian song control nucleus. *Proceedings of the National Academy Science, USA, 78,* 7815–7819.

Milner, P. M. (1957). The cell assembly: Mark II. *Psychological Review, 64,* 242–252.

Mittlestaedt, H. (1964). Basic control patterns of orientational homeostasis. *Symposium of the Society for Experimental Biology, 18*, 365–386.

Nottebohm, F. (1968). Auditory experience and song development in the chaffinch (*Fringilla coelebs*). *Ibis, 110*, 549–568.

Nottebohm, F. (1981). A brain for all seasons: Cyclical anatomical changes in song control nuclei of the canary brain. *Science, 214*, 1368–1370.

Nottebohm, F. (1984). Birdsong as a model in which to study brain processes related to learning. *Condor, 86*, 227–236.

Palameta, B., & Lefebvre, L. (1985). The social transmission of a food-finding technique in pigeons: what is learned? *Animal Behaviour, 33*, 892–896.

Patterson, T. L., Petrinovich, L., & James, D. K. (1980). Reproductive value and appropriateness of response to predators by white-crowned sparrows. *Behavioral Ecology and Sociobiology, 7*, 227–231.

Payne, R. B. (1981a). Song learning and social interaction in indigo buntings. *Animal Behaviour, 29*, 688–697.

Payne, R. B. (1981b). Population structure and social behavior: models for testing the ecological significance of song dialects in birds. In R. D. Alexander & D. W. Tinkle (Eds.), *Natural selection and social behavior: Recent research and new theory* (pp. 108–120). New York: Chiron Press.

Payne, R. B. (1982). Ecological consequences of song matching: breeding success and intraspecific song mimicry in indigo buntings. *Ecology, 63*, 401–411.

Payne, R. B. (1983). The social context of song mimicry: Song-matching dialects in indigo buntings. (*Passerina cyanea*). *Animal Behaviour, 31*, 788–805.

Peeke, H. V. S. (1984). Habituation and the maintenance of territorial boundaries. In H. V. S. Peeke & L. Petrinovich (Eds.), *Habituation, sensitization, and behavior* (pp. 393–421). New York: Academic Press.

Pepperberg, I. M. (1986). Social modeling theory: A possible framework for understanding avian learning. *Auk, 102*, 854–864.

Petrinovich, L. (1972). Psychobiological mechanisms in language development. In G. Newton & A. H. Riesen (Eds.), *Advances in psychobiology* (*Vol. 1*, pp. 259–285). New York: Wiley.

Petrinovich, L. (1973). A species-meaningful analysis of habituation. In H. V. S. Peeke & M. J. Herz (Eds.), *Habituation: Behavioral studies* (pp. 141–162). New York: Academic Press.

Petrinovich, L. (1984). A two-factor dual-process theory of habituation and sensitization. In H. V. S. Peeke & L. Petrinovich (Eds.), *Habituation, sensitization, and behavior* (pp. 17–55). New York: Academic Press.

Petrinovich, L. (1985). Factors influencing song development in the white-crowned sparrow (*Zonotrichia leucophrys*). *Journal of Comparative Psychology, 99*, 15–29.

Petrinovich, L. (in press). Cultural transmission of song in white-crowned sparrows (*Zonotrichia leucophrys nuttalli*). *Acta XIX Congressus Internationalis Ornithologicus.*

Petrinovich, L., & Baptista, L. F. (1984). Song dialects, mate selection, and breeding success in white-crowned sparrows. *Animal Behaviour, 32*, 1078–1088.

Petrinovich, L., & Baptista, L. F. (1987). Song development in the white-crowned sparrow: Modification of learned song. *Animal Behaviour, 35*, 961–974.

Petrinovich, L., & Patterson, T. L. (1979). Field studies of habituation: I. The effects of reproductive condition, number of trials, and different delay intervals on the responses of the white-crowned sparrow. *Journal of Comparative and Physiological Psychology, 93*, 337–350.

Price, P. H. (1979). Developmental determinants of structure in zebra finch song. *Journal of Comparative and Physiological Psychology, 93*, 260–277.

Ratliff, F. (1980). Form and function: Linear and nonlinear analyses of neural networks in the visual system. In D. McFadden (Ed.), *Neural mechanisms in behavior* (pp. 73–142). New York: Springer-Verlag.

Rice, J. O., & Thompson, W. L. (1968). Song development in the indigo bunting. *Animal Behaviour, 16*, 462–469.

Rosenzweig, M. R. (1984). Experience, memory, and the brain. *American Psychologist, 39*, 365–376.

Sasvári, L. (1985). Different observational learning capacity in juvenile and adult individuals of congeneric bird species. *Zeitschrift für Tierpsychologie, 69*, 293–304.

Schlenoff, D. H. (1985). The startle responses of blue jays to *Catocala* (Lepidoptera: Noctuidae) prey models. *Animal Behaviour, 33*, 1057–1067.

Shalter, M. D. (1984). Predator-prey behavior and habituation. *In* H. V. S. Peeke & L. Petrinovich (Eds.), *Habituation, sensitization, and behavior* (pp. 349–391). New York: Academic Press.

Slater, P. J. B. (1983). Chaffinch imitates canary song elements and aspects of organization. *Auk, 100*, 493–495.

Thielcke, G. (1970). Lernen von Gesang als moglicher Schrittmacher der Evolution. *Zeitschrift für Systematik Evolutionsforschung, 8*, 309–320.

Thorpe, W. H. (1961). *Bird-Song.* Cambridge: Cambridge University Press.

Todt, D., Hultsch, H., & Weihe, D. (1979). Conditions affecting song acquisition in nightingales (*Luscinia megarhynchos L.*). *Zeitschrift für Tierpsychologie, 51*, 23–35.

Verner, J. (1976). Complex song repertoire of male Long-billed Marsh Wrens in eastern Washington. *Living Bird, 14*, 263–300.

Waser, M. S., & Marler, P. (1977). Song learning in canaries. *Journal of Comparative and Physiological Psychology, 91*, 1–7.

The Importance of Social Interaction and Observation in the Acquisition of Communicative Competence: Possible Parallels Between Avian and Human Learning

Irene M. Pepperberg
Northwestern University

INTRODUCTION

A persistent problem in behavioral research involves understanding the processes by which humans and nonhumans acquire information about their environment and about how to interact with that environment, including other organisms. Language often mediates acquisition of such knowledge in humans. Numerous studies suggest that related, albeit less complex, communication processes similarly mediate information transfer in animals (for example: Beer, 1982; Cheney & Seyfarth, 1985; Kroodsma, 1982; S. Robinson, 1981; Snowdon, 1982; cf. Macphail, 1982, 1985). Understanding the factors that influence how organisms acquire competence in a communication code is of fundamental importance in understanding how they use this code. Information gathered from the study of one species may lead to important insights into understanding the processes in another. Such appears to be true for the study of avian and human communication, where parallels exist not only in the functions but also in the mechanisms for acquisition of communication codes (Marler, 1970; Petrinovich, 1972; Payne, Thompson, Fiala, & Sweany, 1981), particularly with respect to the roles of observation, learning, and social interaction (Pepperberg, 1985, 1986a).

Although researchers disagree about the extent to which human language acquisition and development can be influenced either by observation or by social interaction (Collis, 1981; Furrow & Nelson, 1986; Gleitman, Newport, & Gleitman, 1984; Lieberman, 1984; Shatz, 1982; Snow, 1979), all acknowledge that human communicative competence cannot arise in a social vacuum. Similarly, although the extent of vocal learning varies considerably among avian species (e.g., Kroodsma, 1981, 1984, 1985), acquisition of avian communicative competence can often be attributed to the quality and quantity of the social interactions with adult conspecifics (see Baptista & Petrinovich, 1984, 1986; Kroodsma, 1978, 1981; Kroodsma & Pickert, 1984a, 1984b; Nottebohm 1970; Payne, 1981, 1982, 1983; Payne et al., 1981; Petrinovich, 1985, this volume; Todt, Hultsch, & Heike, 1979; West & King, 1985a, 1985b). Thus, for both humans and birds, understanding the mechanisms by which communication skills are acquired necessitates investigating the effects of amount and type of social input on all aspects of the acquisition process. Researchers must examine not only *what* is acquired, but also both *how* it is acquired and how organisms learn appropriate *use* of what is acquired; i.e., the development of not only the semantic and syntactic but also the pragmatic aspects of the communication code (Beer, 1982; King & West, 1984).

Human social psychologists (e.g., Bandura, 1971, 1977) have derived a theory comprising a set of principles that delineate the effects of social input and context on learning. I have previously suggested that this social modeling theory may provide insights into the development of communication processes in birds, particularly those communicative behaviors considered *exceptional* (Pepperberg, 1985, 1986b). *Exceptional* communication is usually characterized by vocal learning that, in the normal course of development, is thought unlikely to occur: (a) use of nonspecies-specific (*allospecific*) vocalizations by subjects generally expected to acquire functional use of only conspecific vocalizations (e.g., contextual use of song of unrelated species; see Baptista & Petrinovich, 1984), and (b) age-independent acquisition of vocalizations in species generally recognized as having a limited *sensitive phase* for vocal learning (Baptista & Morton, 1982; Petrinovich, this volume; see also Marler, 1970). In this chapter I discuss how human social modeling theory provides a theoretical framework for understanding a particular instance of exceptional avian learning: referential interspecies communication and concept acquisition in the African Grey parrot (*Psittacus erithacus*). I also discuss (1) the importance of training protocols using social interaction and observation for the development of this referential interspecies communication, (2) data on avian conceptual abilities gathered via this communication system, (3) data on a particular communicative behavior that had been otherwise difficult to train in animal subjects, and (4) the relation of my results to field and laboratory work on song acquisition. First, however, I describe those aspects of social modeling theory that are germane to this discussion.

SOCIAL MODELING:
OBSERVATION, INTERACTION, CONTEXT, AND LEARNING

Some Principles of Social Modeling

Social modeling theory developed from an analysis of the mechanisms that enabled human subjects to overcome strong inhibitions or phobias (e.g., fear of dogs, Bandura, 1971). Subsequent studies examined the relevance of these principles for tasks involving human communicative competence (e.g., I. Brown, 1976; Snow & Hoefnagle-Höhle, 1978). The principles relevant to exceptional avian vocal learning are as follows (summarized from Bandura, 1971, quoted from Pepperberg, 1986b): (1) Changes in behavior are most likely to occur if the targeted behavior is carefully demonstrated by a live tutor who adjusts the demonstration to the responses of the observer. (2) Learning is most effective when observers see and practice the targeted behavior under conditions similar to those they face in their regular environment; thus a demonstration must be *contextually relevant*. A corollary is that the modeled behavior is more likely to be acquired if it has functional value for the observer, and this functionality, i.e., *referentiality*, is also demonstrated. (3) The more intense the contact between the observer and the model, the more likely is the observer to learn the targeted behavior. (4) The more resistance the observer has toward acquiring the targeted behavior—whatever the reason—the more intense must be the interaction between the observer and the model, and the more referential and contextually relevant must be the demonstration. Thus, in cases where minor inhibitions or no inhibitions exist, audiotaped demonstration of the behavior or verbal instruction on how to perform without explicit demonstration may be sufficient (Bandura & Walters, 1965). Teaching a strongly inhibited behavior or one for which the subject is not developmentally ready, however, requires intense interaction with a live tutor who is performing in a contextually applicable, referential manner (Bandura, 1977).

Social Modeling and Exceptional Avian Communication

Social modeling theory therefore suggests why extensive exposure to a live, interacting tutor (contextual observation of a tutor, referential interaction with a tutor, and deliberate modeling of behaviors) appears crucial for inception of exceptional communication.

If exceptional avian learning is considered an inhibited behavior, regulated, as ornithologists have proposed, by (a) limited sensitive phases during which learning capacities are maximal and (b) sensory templates that act to restrict attention to a subset of the auditory environment (Marler, 1970, 1984), then the procedures for circumventing inhibitory mechanisms in humans may be equally effective in birds. That is, for birds predisposed to acquire species-specific communication systems, learning to use allospecific vocalizations in a referential manner might require a live tutor that interacts in appropriate ways. Recent research on acquisition of avian communicative competence suggests that this is indeed the case (see reviews in Pepperberg 1985, 1986a; Petrinovich, this volume). Social modeling theory does not suggest that exceptional learning is "unexceptional"; social modeling theory is merely a device for analyzing the mechanisms and conditions that engender certain behaviors, which, albeit uncommon, have been observed (Pepperberg, 1985, 1986b).

EXCEPTIONAL LEARNING IN THE AFRICAN GREY PARROT: REFERENTIAL USE OF ENGLISH SPEECH

Although the African Grey parrot is well known for its ability to reproduce allospecific vocal patterns (e.g., Amsler, 1947; Baldwin, 1914; Boosey, 1947, 1956; Hensley, 1980), this mimetic ability has usually been considered synonymous with contextually and referentially nonsensical vocal repetition (Fromkin & Rodman, 1974; Lenneberg, 1967). Because several attempts at establishing referential communication with parrots and other mimids in laboratory settings achieved little success (e.g., Gossette, 1969; Grosslight & Zaynor, 1967; Grosslight, Zaynor, & Lively, 1964; Mowrer, 1950, 1952, 1954, 1958), such studies reinforced the view that these birds were unable to attach meaning to acquired human vocalizations.

However, for the past 10 years I have been studying the communicative competence and cognitive abilities of the African Grey parrot through a system of two-way, referential interspecies communication; the modality is English speech. The significantly different results of my research as compared with previous efforts came, I believe, from recognition that acquisition of allospecific communicative competence by a parrot is an exceptional form of learning. That is, it is an inhibited behavior, which, in order to occur, requires intense social interaction and referential, contextually relevant modeling (Pepperberg, 1986a). A brief review of the unsuccessful methods of earlier projects from the standpoint of social modeling theory might provide reasons for their failures.

Early Attempts at Avian-Human Intercommunication

As early as the 1940s, various scientists had reasoned that the vocal ability of mimetic birds, coupled with their considerable intelligence (e.g., Koehler, 1943), should enable them to engage in two-way communication with humans.

Mowrer (1950) was one of the first to investigate such a possibility. He used the standard psychological techniques of the day, including extrinsic (noncontextual, nonreferential) rewards: i.e., a single reinforcer, generally a favorite food, which directly related neither to the task being taught nor to the skill being targeted. Mowrer did not employ modeling, and rarely demonstrated a clear connection between a label and its referent. An example of Mowrer's training protocol demonstrates how his procedure was actually likely to delay acquisition by confounding the label of the object or action to be taught with that of the unrelated food reward (see Pepperberg, 1978, 1981; also Bruner, 1978; Greenfield, 1978; Miles, 1983).

If the bird did replicate any of several targeted sounds produced by the trainer, whether the label of a food, a nonfood object (e.g., various toys), or a conversational phrase ("How are you?"), the bird was rewarded with a nut for each different replication. The researchers did not expect the bird to connect the reproduction of the various sounds with the inevitable appearance of the nut (a salient object to a hungry bird) rather than with their actual referents (for example, "Hello" and the appearance of the trainer). The bird's subsequent inappropriate vocalizations of "Hello" when the trainer was already in place would fail to produce a nut, and thus production of the strange sound ("Hello") would be extinguished. This technique made it difficult for the avian subject to realize that appearance of the trainer was the controlling variable, especially as the nut (the discriminative stimulus) was likely to be more important than the trainer to the subject. Although such procedures are unlikely to be a straightforward means of teaching the connection between action or object and label, they are still the ones most commonly used (e.g., Terrace, 1979), even for projects designed to teach communication skills to language-deficient humans (see Levine & Fasnacht, 1974; comments in Bandura, 1971, and Pepperberg, in press-a, in press-b).

Mowrer (1950, 1954) did attempt to socialize his birds, but only in the sense of acquainting them with, and making them dependent upon, human keepers. Learning tasks were not referentially related to socialization, and Mowrer's birds acquired few human vocalizations (1952, 1954, 1958). Although Ginsburg (1960) and Gramza (1970) were able to place some vocalizations of budgerigars (*Melopsittacus undulatus*) under stimulus control, they never obtained referential, two-way communication with their subjects. Other researchers (Gossette, 1969; Grosslight & Zaynor, 1967; Grosslight et al., 1964; see also Ginsburg, 1963) played recordings of human vocalizations to mynahs (*Gracula religiosa*) in nonsocial, nonreferential settings; their birds also failed to acquire much in the way of trained, allospecific vocalizations. The puzzling aspect of these failures was why these birds, which were so vocal in the wild and learned allospecific vocalizations so readily in the informal setting of a home (e.g., Amsler, 1947; Boosey, 1947; Hensley, 1980), were incapable of significant vocal learning in well-controlled laboratory settings.

The answer had to await reports by ornithologists of some details of the ontogeny of the vocal behavior of mimetic birds in the wild (Bertram, 1970; Nottebohm, 1970; Nottebohm & Nottebohm, 1969); for the work of Todt (1975), who was able to construct the first model for this behavior in the laboratory; and for research by social psychologists (e.g., Bandura, 1971) whose schemata provided a theoretical framework for the ornithologists' data.

Communication between Mimetic Birds in a Natural Environment

Nottebohm found that orange-winged Amazon parrots (*Amazona amazonica*) nesting within audible range of one another in Trinidad often shared calls, whereas colonies of the same species that lived in different habitats had completely different dialects. The dialects were so different as to suggest initially that the areas were inhabited by different species (Nottebohm & Nottebohm, 1969). At about the same time, Bertram (1970) showed that mynahs in the wild predominantly shared calls with and appeared to learn vocalizations from nearby mynahs and, on occasion, other animals in their habitat (see Tenaza, 1976). Nottebohm (1970), combining these data with evidence for song learning in several passerine species, proposed that the parrots learned their vocalizations through social interactions with their parents, flock members, and other organisms. Recent studies have shown that auditory exposure also produces allospecific imitation in another mimid, the starling, if presented in conjunction with social interaction (West, Straud, & King, 1983). Wickler (1976, 1980) has even suggested that the extensive duetting behavior often observed in mated pairs of parrots is the result of a complex socialization process, wherein both individuals synergistically adapt and adjust their repertoire (see also Mebes, 1978).

Laboratory Investigations on Social Interaction and Vocal Learning in Parrots

To determine optimal conditions for acquisition of communication skills in mimids, Todt (1975) investigated the effects of social interaction on vocal learning in the African Grey parrot. He developed the original version of the model/ rival, or M/R technique, in which humans assume the roles played by psittacine peers in the wild. Humans thus demonstrate to the parrots the types of interactive vocalizations to be learned. In Todt's procedure, one human acts exclusively as a principal trainer for each parrot, asking questions and providing increased visual and vocal attention for appropriate responses. Another human acts exclusively as a model for the parrot's behavior and as a rival of the parrot for the attention of the principal trainer. So, for example, the trainer would say "What's your name?" and the human M/R would respond "My name is Lora." This human duetting behavior is quite similar to the duetting behavior observed to occur between parrots in large aviary settings (see Mebes, 1978).

Todt's parrots would learn their parts of the duet often in less than a day. Although the rapidity with which these birds acquired targeted vocalizations was impressive (compare Grosslight et al., 1964; Grosslight & Zaynor, 1967), there was no evidence that the vocalizations had acquired referential or contextual meaning. That is, Todt's birds might not have learned more than a human-imposed form of antiphonal duetting (see Thorpe, 1974; Thorpe & North, 1965) or a simple conditioned response (e.g., Lenneberg, 1971, 1973): Todt's parrots would engage in vocal interactions solely with their particular trainer, and the sentences employed did not test the parrots on either contextual or referential content. Todt's intent, however, had not been to examine contextual meaning, but only to determine optimal conditions for acquisition of vocalizations.

My students and I, using as our subject an African Grey parrot named Alex, have taken Todt's work somewhat further. We adapted the M/R procedure and incorporated the findings of Bandura (1971, 1977) and some later work of Mowrer (1966) to counter what we saw as an inhibition against the acquisition of *functional* allospecific vocalizations. Our intent was to establish an interactive, referential form of communication with our bird. To that end, we frequently exchanged roles of principal trainer and M/R, and used the technique to emphasize and demonstrate referential and contextual use of labels for observable objects, qualifiers, quantifiers, and actions. Alex did not simply hear stepwise human vocal duets, but rather observed such communication as part of an interactive process that (a) involved reciprocity and (b) could be a source of information. One person was never exclusively the interrogator and the other the respondent. Rather, an exchange of roles demonstrated that the code could be employed by either individual—in other words, that this form of communication was to be a "two-way street."

We consistently emphasized training of labels for objects (or actions) that themselves aroused Alex's interest, so that there was the closest possible connection between the object (or action) and the label to be learned. For example, we began by determining which objects Alex preferred to manipulate. Each of those objects (e.g., cork, paper, wood) was employed in our training technique. The human temporarily acting as trainer would hold up such an object and ask the M/R "What's this?" A correct answer would be rewarded by praise and the object itself. The M/R would also make errors that replicated those being made by the bird at the time. The trainer would respond to such errors by scolding and briefly removing the object from view. Alex quickly learned which novel vocalizations controlled the transfer of desired objects between the human experimenters, and would attempt these vocalizations himself, often within 72 hr of initiation of training (Pepperberg, 1981).

In addition, when Alex experimented with sounds in his repertoire and combined them in novel ways, we would use the M/R technique to associate these novel vocalizations with novel objects. For example, after learning the label *grey*, Alex produced—in the absence of any object—grate, grape, grain, chain, and cane. Upon hearing each of these vocalizations, we would present him with, and use the M/R technique to discuss, respectively, a nutmeg grater (which could be used to trim his beak), the appropriate fruit, some parakeet treat, and a connected series of paper clips. We were unable to come up with an appropriate referent for *cane*. All but "cane" remained in his repertoire and have subsequently become referential vocalizations (Pepperberg, 1983a).

Thus our procedures, by adapting psychological techniques so that they recreated, at least to some extent, the natural learning environment, solved the problem of facilitating referential vocal learning in the laboratory. To summarize briefly: (a) Communication among parrots in both wild and aviary settings appears largely to be in the vocal mode and learned through social interaction, so that our training demands were closely related to naturally occurring tasks; (b) conversational turn taking resembles natural duetting behavior, so that Alex was exposed to, and required to participate in, behaviors similar to those in which parrots engage in the wild; that is, our subject did not need to learn a response technique outside of his normal range of behaviors; (c) to facilitate exceptional learning, all training procedures involved referential, contextually applicable situations; and (d) vocal innovation, which is likely in the wild, was encouraged and incorporated into the procedure, and enabled us to expand the range of Alex's vocal responses.

INTERSPECIES COMMUNICATION AS A TOOL FOR ASSESSING CONCEPTUAL ABILITIES

Using the M/R technique over the course of several years, we have taught Alex tasks that were once thought beyond the capability of all but humans or, possibly, certain nonhuman primates (see Premack, 1978). Alex has learned labels for more than 30 different objects: paper, key, wood, hide (rawhide chips), grain, peg wood (clothes pins), cork, corn, nut, walnut, showah (shower), wheat, banana, pasta, gym, cracker, scraper (a nail file), chain, shoulder, rock (lava stone beak conditioner), carrot, gravel, back, chair, water, grape, cup, grate, treat, cherry, popcorn, citrus, and banerry (apple). We have tentative evidence for labels such as box, chalk, and jacks. He has functional use of "no," phrases such as "come here," "I want X" and "Wanna go Y" where X and Y are appropriate labels for objects or locations; incorrect responses to his requests by a trainer (e.g., substitution of something other than what he requested) generally results (~75% of the time) in his saying "No" and repeating the initial request (Pepperberg, in press-a). He has learned labels for six colors: rose (red), green, blue, yellow, orange, and grey; he is presently learning purple. He identifies five different shapes by labeling them as two-, three-, four-, five-, or six-cornered objects. He uses the labels "two," "three," "four," "five," and "sih" (six) to distinguish quantities of objects up to six, including collections made up of novel objects, heterogeneous sets of objects, and sets in which the objects are placed in random arrays (Pepperberg, 1984, 1987). He combines all the vocal labels to identify proficiently, request, refuse, categorize, and quantify more than 80 different objects, including those that vary somewhat from training exemplars. His accuracy has averaged ~80% when tested on these abilities (Pepperberg, 1981, 1984, 1987, in press-a).

We have also examined Alex's capabilities on tasks such as categorical concept formation that are of direct interest to psychologists and of indirect interest to ethologists (see Kroodsma et al., 1984-a). We have been able to demonstrate not only that Alex can recognize what is or is not *green* (or any one of the other color labels in his repertoire), but that *green* is a particular instance of the category *color*. For example, we have shown that, for a particularly colored *and* shaped object, "green" and "three-corner" represent different categories of markable attributes of this single exemplar. Thus Alex has learned to categorize objects having both color and shape with respect to either category based on our vocal query of "What color?" or "What shape?" (Pepperberg, 1983b). Because the same exemplar is often categorized with respect to shape at one time and color at another, the task involves flexibility in changing the basis for classification. Such flexibility, or aptitude for *reclassification,* is thought to indicate the presence of *abstract aptitude* (Hayes & Nissen, 1956/1971).

Alex is also currently learning abstract concepts of *same* and *different,* a faculty once thought beyond the capacity of an avian subject (Premack, 1978; but see Zentall, Hogan, & Edwards, 1984). When presented with two objects that vary with respect to color, shape, or material, Alex can respond with the appropriate *category* label as to which category is "same" or "different" for any combination. For example, if shown a green wooden triangle and a blue wooden triangle and questioned as to "What's different?" he will respond "color"; if queried "What's same?" he will respond either "shape" or "mah-mah" (matter). Transfers to instances involving objects, colors, shapes, and materials not used in training, including those for which he has no labels, appears to be successful. Preliminary analysis of the data indicates an accuracy between 70% and 80%. Alex seems not to be responding only to variations in the attributes of the objects, but rather to the questions as well, because his responses are still above chance levels when the correct answer is either of two of the three possible categories (Pepperberg, 1986c, in press-c).

The fact that one particular parrot can do all this is *not* the point of this chapter. Findings of researchers such as Braun (1952), Koehler (1943, 1950), Lögler (1959), and Krushinskii (1960) suggested these avian capabilities decades ago. My point is that social modeling and observational learning techniques provided the means to elicit and substantiate these abilities. Our training protocols, which demonstrate contextual applicability and referentiality, and use live tutors who interact consistently with the subject and thus provide opportunities for observational learning, have engendered the type of communication we use as an analytic tool.

IMPLICATIONS FOR RELATED STUDIES
ON INTERSPECIES COMMUNICATION:
SEPARATION OF "REQUESTING" AND "LABELING"

The efficacy of our modeling technique was particularly apparent while training Alex to separate functional *requesting* and *labeling*. Alex, unlike chimpanzees exposed to traditional nonmodeling techniques, very quickly learned to signal these communicative intentions (Pepperberg, in press-b).

Because Alex was initially trained to employ exemplar labels for both naming and requesting any object, in a manner not unlike that of children in the one-word stage (R. Brown, 1973) or other animals in interspecies communication projects (e.g., Savage-Rumbaugh, Rumbaugh, Smith, & Lawson, 1980b), at first we had no way to distinguish Alex's discussions about, identifications of, or requests for particular items. Similarly, we were unable, except through contextual evidence, to learn if Alex's utterances might be comments upon or requests for an object not in view. Acquisition of verbal skills that demonstrate that a subject can make such discriminations is eventual in the normal course of human development (R. Brown, 1973; de Villiers & de Villiers, 1978). The ability to train such behavior in a nonhuman species would be a significant step in establishing its communicative competence (Savage-Rumbaugh, Rumbaugh, & Boysen, 1980a). We therefore began training Alex to preface all requests for objects with the vocalization "Want" (Pepperberg, in press-b).

We employed the M/R technique described above. Training sessions were held once a week, for periods that ranged from 5 min to 2 hr, depending upon Alex's attention span during a session. During sessions, Alex observed the following interactions: the trainer held two of the bird's favored toys (e.g., paper and cork; two objects were used so that Alex would be less likely to assume that "want" was a particular attribute of either object). The human model produced phrases such as "Want cork!" with the emphasis on the word "want." The trainer gave the cork to the model. This was repeated with the paper, and then roles of model and trainer were reversed. If the model produced only the label, the trainer would say something like "Yes, this is a cork. . . . Do you *want* it?" Alex, who had already learned that names of objects were sufficient for acquisition, often called "paper" or "cork" during these exchanges. Such vocalizations were rewarded at first, as we did not wish to extinguish Alex's learned associations. However, responses to the one-word vocalizations were gradually phased out, and

Alex was then treated just as the human models when they employed one-word vocalizations. Also, after every correct identification of a particular object, X, in training or testing, we asked "Do you *want* X?" After affirmative responses the object was transferred as usual. Alex's negative replies were countered with the query "What do you want?" Alex would then have to respond "Want Y," if Y was a more favored object. Evidence exists (see Fig. 1, from Pepperberg, in press-a) that Alex actually does want what is requested. He generally refuses substitute items offered by his trainers, and eats or manipulates the requested objects. Transcripts from taping sessions (Pepperberg, in press-b) show that use of "want," "wanna" or "I want" to preface possible requests increased from 0% before training, to 38% after 2 months of instruction, to 70%–75% after 7 months. Use of "want" was generalized, without additional training, to new lexical items (Pepperberg, in press-b). At no time was there a decrease in Alex's accuracy on labeling tasks, although certain behaviors (e.g., holding on to objects he did obtain for significantly longer periods) suggested that the procedure engendered some frustration.

It is interesting that one of the procedures used to teach chimpanzees to separate requesting from labeling (Savage-Rumbaugh, 1984) actually led to a temporary breakdown in food-symbol correlations (i.e., short-term loss of labeling ability). Savage-Rumbaugh's procedure for chimpanzees did not use a modeling technique. Instead, the experimenter indicated that labeling rather than requesting was expected by providing a single, nonreferential (extrinsic) reward for the animals' correct responses to any displayed object. Recovering previous levels of accuracy in the chimpanzees required a series of steps, including presentation of both the intrinsic and extrinsic reward, fading out the intrinsic reward, and use of an iconic gestural marker (within a system otherwise based on non-iconic symbols) to denote whether the experimenter was demanding labeling or requesting (Savage-Rumbaugh, 1984).

IMPLICATIONS FOR OTHER STUDIES OF AVIAN VOCAL BEHAVIOR

It appears, from the material presented above, that previous laboratory failures to inculcate allospecific, referential vocalizations in mimetic birds might have been closely connected to choice of training procedure and not due to inherent limitations in avian capabilities (Pepperberg, 1981, 1985). As is often the case with human learning (Bandura, 1977), some forms of avian learning may require social, referential models that actively demonstrate the interactive responses to be acquired (Baptista & Petrinovich, 1984, 1986; Kroodsma & Pickert, 1984a, 1984b; Petrinovich, 1985, this volume; West et al., 1983). Such findings may be relevant to the study of mimetic and nonmimetic birds inside and outside the laboratory.

Recent Studies of Mimetic Birds in Nature

Although researchers disagree on the extent to which direct social interactions play a role in vocal learning in mimetic birds in the wild, some data suggest that such birds may be incapable of significant vocal learning in social isolation (see Hatch, 1967). In addition to findings on the importance of social interaction for vocal learning in starlings (West et al., 1983) and parrots (see above), there is evidence that certain allospecific vocalizations of mockingbirds may be learned during aggressive interactions with other species (Glase, as discussed by Brenowitz, 1982; Hatch, 1967; also Baylis, 1982), and that much of the observed vocal mimicry of lyrebirds and bowerbirds may be of aggressive or predatory allospecifics (Robinson, 1975; see review by Klump & Shalter, 1984). The exact advantage of imitation of allospecific competitors and predators is not entirely clear, although Morton (1982, 1986) has suggested some interesting possibilities: because the acoustic features of song change, or degrade, as they propagate through the habitat (e.g., trees and bushes deflect or absorb the sound), a bird may obtain reliable information as to the whereabouts of a sympatric allospecific by matching the undegraded song he has learned to sing during close encounters to the degree of degradation in the song he later hears at a distance. A bird may thereby avoid wasting energy in responding to another bird that is not close enough to be a threat to its resources. Furthermore, production of neighbors' territorial songs is most likely to cause interruption of their foraging or mating. If resources are limited, these behaviors could be critical for survival.

Studies of Nonmimetic Birds

Although some avian species actually appear incapable of significant learning without live tutors (Price, 1979; Thielcke, 1970, 1972; see also Slater, 1983), in most cases song of a live tutor is merely a more effective stimulus than that presented via audiotape. Certain birds have been shown to learn more from live tutors than from tapes, and some birds preferentially learn songs of live tutors over those presented by tapes (Kroodsma, 1978, 1981; Payne, 1981; Todt et al., 1979; Waser & Marler, 1977). In these cases, social interaction may merely facilitate normal learning rather than significantly alter the course of development.

The effectiveness of social tutoring may also depend upon the social status of the tutor. High status makes for an effective model in humans (Bandura, 1977; Mischel & Liebert, 1967), and the same may be true of birds. Some birds appear to choose from whom to learn their song, and it is interesting to note which birds are chosen to serve as vocal models in the wild. Quality and quantity of avian vocalization may provide an indication of the relative "vigor" or "fitness" of the various possible models in an area (Catchpole, 1980; Kroodsma, 1976, 1979; McGregor, Krebs, & Perrins, 1981; Yasukawa, 1981; cf. Searcy, McArthur, & Yasukawa, 1985), and there is evidence that for some species, a "strong" or "respected" male (as demonstrated by age or quality of his territory) is more likely to be a model than a "subordinate" male (Baptista & Morton, 1982; McGregor & Krebs, 1984; Mundinger, 1979; Payne, 1978, 1982, 1983, 1985; Payne & Payne, 1977; Snow & Snow, 1983). Conceivably, a bird that reproduces the sounds of a high-status male may himself achieve a significant degree of status and peer acceptance. Such status might be useful in defending territory and attracting a mate.

If, however, no single model is dominant, human social modeling theory predicts (Bandura, 1971, 1977), and avian research shows evidence for, behavioral innovation. Birds that normally have large repertoires, when equally exposed to many models during their learning period, exhibit considerable vocal innovation or invention (see Marler & Peters, 1982, for the distinction between these terms). Thus, some birds will not copy specific songs, but rather develop subtle individual variations on their species-specific themes. For example, they may develop new temporal arrangements or inclusions of novel syllables (Kroodsma & Pickert, 1984a, 1984b; Marler & Peters, 1982; Todt et al., 1979).

One of the principles of social modeling discussed above involves the degree of referentiality and contextual applicability of the modeled act. Under certain conditions, strong referentiality may compensate for a model that is not strongly interactive. This seems consistent with the ability of some avian species to acquire allospecific features of territorial songs but not of courtship songs from tape (i.e., in the absence of social interaction). Thus, for certain North American warblers (*Parulinae, Muscicapidae*) thought to use different songs in different contexts (Ficken & Ficken, 1967; Morse, 1970; Kroodsma, 1981; Kroodsma, Whitlock, & VanderHaegen, 1984b; cf. Lein, 1978), referentiality in conjunction with the presence or absence of a live tutor may differentially affect learning of different songs. Experiments have shown that when hand-raised chestnut-sided warblers (*Dendroica pensylvanica*) were tutored with tapes of allospecific vocalizations, the songs they developed were classified as territorial (Kroodsma, Meservey, & Pickert, 1983), but a wild chestnut-sided warbler that acquired song from a live indigo bunting (*Passerina cyanea*) appeared to use this vocalization in courtship (Payne, Payne, & Doehlert, 1984). If territorial defense is indeed enhanced by matching the song of a competitor (Kroodsma, 1979), then there may be a selective advantage for birds to learn allospecific components of territorial song in the absence of a live tutor. A competitor need not be observed to be perceived as a threat, and therefore an isolation chamber can be considered a territory worth defending against the possible incursions of a taped competitor. Only under the effects of intense social interaction, however, would the ostensibly maladaptive behavior of learning allospecific courtship song occur.

CONCLUSIONS

Clearly, differences exist in the degree of plasticity of learning in different avian species, and the particular features of social interaction crucial for exceptional learning are likely to vary. My point has simply been to suggest that scientific investigations, whether they occur in the field or laboratory, should examine the possible significance of social interaction, observation, and referentiality on various forms of learning, and carefully monitor the *extent* to which social interaction, observation, and referentiality can affect or effect change.

With respect to avian vocal learning, social modeling theory provides a framework for understanding the significance of social interaction and observational learning for the acquisition of exceptional communication codes. The idea that a close and individual relationship may be necessary to effect learning probably has much wider application; that is, it is unlikely that the application of social modeling theory is limited to communicative behaviors. Future investigations should therefore examine the degree to which this theory can be applied to understanding the mechanisms underlying other animal behaviors.

ACKNOWLEDGMENTS

This research was supported by National Science Foundation grants BNS 7912945, 8014329, 8414483, and the Harry Frank Guggenheim Foundation. I thank Denise Neapolitan, Jeff Galef, and Tom Zentall for critical comments on an earlier version of this manuscript.

REFERENCES

Amsler, M. (1947). An almost human Grey parrot. *Aviculture Magazine, 53,* 68–69.
Baldwin, J. M. (1914). Deferred imitation in West African Grey parrots. *IXth International Congress of Zoology,* Monaco, 536.
Bandura, A. (1971). Analysis of modeling processes. In A. Bandura (Ed.), *Psychological modeling* (pp. 1–62). Chicago: Aldine-Atherton.
Bandura, A. (1977). *Social modeling theory.* Chicago: Aldine-Atherton.
Bandura, A., & Walters, R. H. (1965). *Social learning and personality development.* New York: Holt, Rinehart & Winston.
Baptista, L. F., & Morton, M. L. (1982). Song dialects and mate selection in montane white-crowned sparrows. *Auk, 92,* 537–547.
Baptista, L. F., & Petrinovich, L. (1984). Social interaction, sensitive phases, and the song template hypothesis in the white-crowned sparrow. *Animal Behaviour, 32,* 172–181.
Baptista, L. F., & Petrinovich, L. (1986). Song development in the white-crowned sparrow: Social factors and sex differences. *Animal Behaviour, 34* 1359–1371.
Baylis, J. R. (1982). Avian vocal mimicry: its function and evolution. In D. E.

Kroodsma & E. H. Miller (Eds.), *Acoustic communication in birds: Vol. 2. Song learning and its consequences* (pp. 51–83). New York: Academic Press.

Beer, C. G. (1982). Conceptual issues in the study of communication. In D. E. Kroodsma & E. H. Miller (Eds.), *Acoustic communication in birds: Vol. 2. Song learning and its consequences* (pp. 279–310). New York: Academic Press.

Bertram, B. C. R. (1970). The vocal behavior of the Indian Hill mynah, *Gracula religiosa*. *Animal Behaviour Monograph, 3*, 79–192.

Boosey, E. J. (1947). The African Grey parrot. *Aviculture Magazine, 53*, 39–40.

Boosey, E. J. (1956). *Foreign Bird Keeping*. London: Iliffe Books, Ltd.

Braun, H. (1952). Uber das Unterscheidungsvermögen unbenannter Anzahlen bei Papageien. *Zeitschrift für Tierpsychologie, 9*, 40–91.

Brenowitz, E. A. (1982). Aggressive response of Red-winged Blackbirds to mockingbird song imitations. *Auk, 99*, 584–586.

Brown, I. (1976). Role of referent concreteness in the acquisition of passive sentence comprehension through abstract modeling. *Journal of Experimental Child Psychology, 22*, 185–199.

Brown, R. (1973). *A first language: The early stages*. Cambridge, MA: Harvard University Press.

Bruner, J. S. (1978). Learning how to do things with words. In J. S. Bruner & A. Garton (Eds.), *Human growth and development* (pp. 62–84). Oxford: Oxford University Press.

Catchpole, C. K. (1980). Sexual selection and the evolution of complex songs among European warblers of the genus *Acrocephalus*. *Behaviour, 74*, 477–482.

Cheney, D. L., & Seyfarth, R. M. (1985). Social and non-social knowledge in vervet monkeys. In L. Weiskrantz (Ed.), *Animal intelligence* (pp. 187–201). Oxford: Clarendon Press.

Collis, G. M. (1981). Social interaction with objects: a perspective on human infancy. In K. Immelmann, G. W. Barlow, L. Petrinovich, & M. Main (Eds.), *Behavioral development* (pp. 603–620). Cambridge: Cambridge University Press.

de Villiers, J. G., & de Villiers, P. A. (1978). *Language acquisition*. Cambridge, MA: Harvard University Press.

Ficken, M. S., & Ficken, R. W. (1967). Singing behavior of the Blue-winged and Golden-winged warblers and their hybrids. *Behaviour, 28*, 149–181.

Fromkin, V., & Rodman, P. (1974). *An introduction to language*. New York: Holt, Rinehart & Winston.

Furrow, D., & Nelson, K. (1986). A further look at the motherese hypothesis: A reply to Gleitman, Newport & Gleitman. *Journal of Child Language, 13*, 163–176.

Ginsburg, N. (1960). Conditioned vocalization in the budgerigar. *Journal of Comparative and Physiological Psychology, 53*, 183–186.

Ginsburg, N. (1963). Conditioned vocalization in the mynah bird. *Journal of Comparative and Physiological Psychology, 56*, 1061–1063.

Gleitman, L. R., Newport, E. L., & Gleitman, H. (1984). The current status of the motherese hypothesis. *Journal of Child Language, 11*, 43–79.

Gossette, R. L. (1969). Personal communication to O. H. Mowrer, 1980: *Psychology of language and learning* (pp. 105–106). New York: Plenum.

Gramza, A. F. (1970). Vocal mimicry in captive budgerigars (*Melopsittacus undulatus*). *Zeitschrift für Tierpsychologie, 27*, 971–983.

Greenfield, P. M. (1978). Developmental processes in the language learning of child and chimp. *Behavioral and Brain Sciences, 4,* 573–574.

Grosslight, J. H., & Zaynor, W. C. (1967). Vocal behavior of the mynah bird. In K. Salzinger & S. Salzinger (Eds.), *Research in verbal behavior and some neurophysiological implications* (pp. 5–9). New York: Academic Press.

Grosslight, J. H., Zaynor, W. C., & Lively, B. L. (1964). Speech as a stimulus for differential vocal behavior in the mynah bird (*Gracula religiosa*). *Psychonomic Science, 1,* 7–8.

Hatch, J. J. (1967). *Diversity of the song of Mockingbirds (Mimus polyglottos) reared in different auditory environments.* Unpublished doctoral dissertation, Duke University, Durham, NC.

Hayes, K. J., & Nissen, C. H. (1956/1971). Higher mental functions of a home-raised chimpanzee. In A. M. Schrier & F. Stollnitz (Eds.), *Behavior of nonhuman primates* (Vol. 4, pp. 60–115). New York: Academic Press.

Hensley, G. (1980). Encounters with a hookbill—II. *American Cage Bird Magazine, 52,* 11–12, 59.

King, A. P., & West, M. J. (1984). Social metrics of song learning. *Learning and Motivation, 15,* 441–458.

Klump, G. M. & Shalter, M. D. (1984). Acoustic behavior of birds and mammals in the predator context. *Zeitschrift für Tierpsychologie, 66,* 189–226.

Koehler, O. (1943). 'Zähl'-Versuche an einem Kolkraben und Vergleichsversuche an Menschen. *Zeitschrift für Tierpsychologie, 5,* 575–712.

Koehler, O. (1950). The ability of birds to 'count.' *Bulletin of the Animal Behaviour Society, 9,* 41–45.

Kroodsma, D. E. (1976). Reproductive development in a female songbird: differential stimulation by quality of male song. *Science, 192,* 574–575.

Kroodsma, D. E. (1978). Aspects of learning in the ontogeny of bird song: Where, from whom, when, how many, which, and how accurately? In G. Burghardt & M. Bekoff (Eds.), *The development of behavior: Comparative and evolutionary aspects* (pp. 215–230). New York: Garland STPM Press.

Kroodsma, D. E. (1979). Vocal dueling among male marsh wrens: evidence for ritualized expressions of dominance/subordinance. *Auk, 96,* 506–515.

Kroodsma, D. E. (1981). Ontogeny of bird song. In K. Immelmann, G. W. Barlow, L. Petrinovich, & M. Main (Eds.), *Behavioral development* (pp. 518–532). Cambridge: Cambridge University Press.

Kroodsma, D. E. (1982). Learning and the ontogeny of sound signals in birds. In D. E. Kroodsma & E. H. Miller (Eds.), *Acoustic communication in birds: Vol. 2. Song learning and its consequences* (pp. 1–23). New York: Academic Press.

Kroodsma, D. E. (1984). Songs of the alder flycatcher (*Empidonax alnorum*) and willow flycatcher (*Empidonax traillii*) are innate. *Auk, 101,* 13–24.

Kroodsma, D. E. (1985). Development and use of two song forms by the Eastern phoebe. *Wilson Bulletin, 97,* 21–29.

Kroodsma, D. E., & Pickert, R. (1984a). Sensitive periods for song learning: effects of social interaction and individual variation. *Animal Behaviour, 32,* 389–394.

Kroodsma, D. E., & Pickert, R. (1984b). Repertoire size, auditory templates, and selective vocal learning in songbirds. *Animal Behaviour, 32,* 395–399.

Kroodsma, D. E., Meservey, W. R., & Pickert, R. (1983). Vocal learning in the Parulinae. *Wilson Bulletin, 95,* 138–140.

Kroodsma, D. E. (rapporteur), Bateson, P. P. G., Bischoff, H-J., Delius, J. D., Hearst, E., Hollis, K. L., Immelmann, K., Jenkins, H. M., Konishi, M., Lea, S. E. A., Marler, P., & Staddon, J. E. R. (1984a). Biology of learning in nonmammalian vertebrates: Group report. In P. Marler & H. S. Terrace (Eds.), *The biology of learning* (pp. 399–418). Berlin: Springer-Verlag.

Kroodsma, D. E., Whitlock, A. L., VanderHaegen, W. M. (1984b). Blue-winged warblers (*Vermivora pinus*) "recognize" dialects in type II but not type I songs. *Behavioral Ecology and Sociobiology, 15,* 127–131.

Krushinskii, L. V. (1960). *Animal behavior: Its normal and abnormal development.* New York: Consultants Bureau.

Lein, M. R. (1978). Song variation in a population of Chestnut-sided Warblers (*Dendroica pensylvanica*): Its nature and suggested significance. *Canadian Journal of Zoology, 56,* 1266–1283.

Lenneberg, E. (1967). *Biological foundations of language.* New York: Wiley.

Lenneberg, E. (1971). Of language, knowledge, apes, and brains. *Journal of Psycholinguistic Research, 1,* 1–29.

Lenneberg, E. (1973). Biological aspects of language. In G. A. Miller (Ed.), *Communication, language, and meaning* (pp. 49–60). New York: Basic Books.

Levine, F., & Fasnacht, G. (1974). Token rewards may lead to token learning. *American Psychologist, 29,* 816–820.

Lieberman, P. (1984). *The biology and evolution of language.* Cambridge, MA: Harvard University Press.

Lögler, P. (1959). Versuche zur Frage des 'Zahl'-Vermögens an einen Graupapagei und Vergleichsversuche an Menschen. *Zeitschrift für Tierpsychologie, 16,* 179–217.

Macphail, E. M. (1982). *Brain and intelligence in vertebrates.* Oxford: Clarendon Press.

Macphail, E. M. (1985). Vertebrate intelligence: The null hypothesis. In L. Weiskrantz (Ed.), *Animal intelligence* (pp. 37–50). Oxford: Clarendon Press.

Marler, P. (1970). A comparative approach to vocal learning: Song development in white-crowned sparrows. *Journal of Comparative and Physiological Psychology, 71,* 1–25.

Marler, P. (1984). Song learning: innate species differences in the learning process. In P. Marler & H. S. Terrace (Eds.), *The biology of learning* (pp. 289–309). Berlin: Springer-Verlag.

Marler, P., & Peters, S. (1982). Subsong and plastic song: their role in the vocal learning process. In D. E. Kroodsma & E. H. Miller (Eds.), *Acoustic communication in birds: Vol. 2. Song learning and its consequences* (pp. 25–50). New York: Academic Press.

McGregor, P. K., & Krebs, J. R. (1984). Song learning and deceptive mimicry. *Animal Behaviour, 32,* 280–287.

McGregor, P. K., Krebs, J. R., & Perrins, C. M. (1981). Song repertoires and lifetime reproductive success in the Great Tit (*Parus major*). *American Naturalist, 118,* 149–159.

Mebes, H. D. (1978). Pair-specific duetting in the peach-faced lovebird, *Agapornis roseicollis. Naturwissenshaften, 65,* 66–67.

Miles, H. L. (1983). Apes and language: The search for communicative competence. In J. de Luce & H. T. Wilder (Eds.), *Language in primates* (pp. 43–61). New York: Springer-Verlag.

Mischel, W., & Liebert, R. M. (1967). The role of power in the adoption of self-reward patterns. *Child Development, 38,* 673–683.

Morse, D. H. (1970). Territorial and courtship songs of birds. *Nature, 226,* 659–661.

Morton, E. S. (1982). Grading, discreteness, redundancy, and motivation-structural rules. In D. E. Kroodsma & E. H. Miller (Eds.), *Acoustic communication in birds: Vol. 1. Production, perception, and design features of sound* (pp. 183–212). New York: Academic Press.

Morton, E. S. (1986). Predictions from the ranging hypothesis for the evolution of long distance signals in birds. *Behaviour, 99,* 65–86.

Mowrer, O. H. (1950). *Learning theory and personality dynamics.* New York: Ronald Press.

Mowrer, O. H. (1952). The autism theory of speech development and some clinical applications. *Journal of Speech and Hearing Disorders, 17,* 263–268.

Mowrer, O. H. (1954). A psychologist looks at language. *American Psychologist, 9,* 660–694.

Mowrer, O. H. (1958). Hearing and speaking: An analysis of language learning. *Journal of Speech and Hearing Disorders, 23,* 143–152.

Mowrer, O. H. (1966). The behavior therapies, with special reference to modeling and imitation. *American Journal of Psychotherapy, 20,* 439–461.

Mundinger, P. C. (1979). Call learning in the Carduelinae: ethological and systematic considerations. *Systematic Zoology, 28,* 270–283.

Nottebohm, F. (1970). Ontogeny of bird song. *Science, 167,* 950–956.

Nottebohm, F., & Nottebohm, M. (1969). The parrots of Bush Bush. *Animal Kingdom, 72,* 19–23.

Payne, R. B. (1978). Microgeographic variation in songs of Splendid Sunbirds *Nectarinia coccinigaster:* Population phenetics, habitats, and song dialects. *Behaviour, 65,* 282–308.

Payne, R. B. (1981). Song learning and social interaction in indigo buntings. *Animal Behaviour, 29,* 688–697.

Payne, R. B. (1982). Ecological consequences of song matching: breeding success and intraspecific song mimicry in indigo buntings. *Ecology, 63,* 401–411.

Payne, R. B. (1983). The social context of song mimicry: song matching dialects in indigo buntings (*Passerina cyanea*). *Animal Behaviour, 31,* 788–805.

Payne, R. B. (1985). Behavioral continuity and change in local song populations of village indigobirds *Vidua chalybeata. Zeitschrift für Tierpsychologie, 70,* 1–44.

Payne, R. B., & Payne, K. (1977). Social organization and mating success in local song populations of village indigobirds, *Vidua chalybeata. Zeitschrift für Tierpsychologie, 45,* 113–173.

Payne, R. B., Payne, L. L., & Doehlert, S. M. (1984). Interspecific song learning in a wild Chestnut-sided warbler. *Wilson Bulletin, 96,* 292–294.

Payne, R. B., Thompson, W. L., Fiala, K. L., & Sweany, L. L. (1981). Local song traditions in indigo buntings: Cultural transmission of behavior patterns across generations. *Behaviour, 77(4),* 199–221.

Pepperberg, I. M. (1978, March). *Object identification by an African Grey parrot (Psittacus erithacus*). Paper presented at the meeting of the Midwest Animal Behavior Society, W. Lafayette, IN.

Pepperberg, I. M. (1981). Functional vocalizations of an African Grey parrot (*Psittacus erithacus*). *Zeitschrift für Tierpsychologie, 55,* 139–160.

Pepperberg, I. M. (1983a, June). *Interspecies communication: Innovative vocalizations of the African Grey parrot.* Paper presented at the meeting of the Animal Behavior Society, Lewisburg, PA.

Pepperberg, I. M. (1983b). Cognition in the African Grey parrot: preliminary evidence for auditory/vocal comprehension of the class concept. *Animal Learning & Behavior, 11,* 179–185.

Pepperberg, I. M. (1984, November). *Vocal identification of numerical quantity by an African Grey parrot.* Paper presented at the meeting of the Psychonomic Society, San Antonio, TX.

Pepperberg, I. M. (1985). Social modeling theory: A possible framework for understanding avian vocal learning. *Auk, 102,* 854–864.

Pepperberg, I. M. (1986a). Acquisition of anomalous communicatory systems: Implications for studies on interspecies communication. In R. Schusterman, J. Thomas, & F. Wood (Eds.), *Dolphin behavior and cognition: Comparative and ethological aspects* (pp. 289–302). Hillsdale, NJ: Lawrence Erlbaum Associates.

Pepperberg, I. M. (1986b). Sensitive periods, social interaction, and song acquisition: The dialectics of dialects? *Behavioral and Brain Sciences, 9,* 756–757.

Pepperberg, I. M. (1986c, June) *Categorization and second-order concepts in the African Grey parrot.* Paper presented at the meeting of the International Ornithological Congress, Ottawa.

Pepperberg, I. M. (1987). Evidence for conceptual quantitative abilities in the African Grey parrot (*Psittacus erithacus*): Labeling of cardinal sets. *Ethology, 75,* 37–61.

Pepperberg, I. M. (in press-a). Interspecies communication: A tool for assessing conceptual abilities in the African Grey parrot (*Psittacus erithacus*). In G. Greenberg & E. Tobach (Eds.), *Language, cognition, and consciousness: Integrative levels.* Hillsdale, NJ: Lawrence Erlbaum Associates.

Pepperberg, I. M. (in press-b). An interactive modeling technique for acquisition of communication skills: Separation of "labeling" and "requesting" in a psittacine subject. Applied Psycholinguistics

Pepperberg, I. M. (in press-c). Acquisition of the same/different concept by an African Grey parrot (*Psittacus erithacus*): Learning with respect to categories of color, shape, and material. *Animal Learning & Behavior.*

Petrinovich, L. (1972). Psychobiological mechanisms in language development. In G. Newton & A. H. Riesen (Eds.), *Advances in psychobiology* (Vol. 1, pp. 259–285). New York: Wiley-Interscience.

Petrinovich, L. (1985). Factors influencing song development in the white-crowned sparrow (*Zonotrichia leucophrys*). *Journal of Comparative Psychology, 99,* 15–29.

Premack, D. (1978). On the abstractness of human concepts: Why it would be difficult to talk to a pigeon. In S. H. Hulse, H. Fowler, & W. K. Honig (Eds.), *Cognitive processes in animal behavior* (pp. 423–451). Hillsdale, NJ: Lawrence Erlbaum Associates.

Price, P. H. (1979). Developmental determinants of structure in Zebra finch songs. *Journal of Comparative and Physiological Psychology, 93,* 260–277.

Robinson, F. N. (1975). Vocal mimicry and the evolution of bird song. *Emu, 75,* 23–27.

Robinson, S. R. (1981). Alarm communication in Belding's ground squirrels. *Zeitschrift für Tierpsychologie, 59,* 150–168.

Savage-Rumbaugh, E. S. (1984). Verbal behavior at a procedural level in the chimpanzee. *Journal of the Experimental Analysis of Behavior, 41,* 223–250.

Savage-Rumbaugh, E. S., Rumbaugh, D. M., Boysen, S. (1980a). Do apes use language? *American Scientist, 68,* 49–61.

Savage-Rumbaugh, E. S., Rumbaugh, D. M., Smith, S. T., & Lawson, J. (1980b). Reference: The linguistic essential. *Science, 210,* 922–925.

Searcy, W. A., McArthur, P. D., & Yasukawa, K. (1985). Song sparrow repertoire size and male quality in song sparrows. *Condor, 87,* 222–228.

Shatz, M. (1982). On mechanisms of language acquisition: Can features of the communicative environment account for development? In E. Wanner & L. R. Gleitman (Eds.), *Language acquisition: The state of the art* (pp. 102–127). Cambridge: Cambridge University Press.

Slater, P. J. B. (1983). Bird song learning: theme and variations. In A. H. Brush & G. A. Clark, Jr. (Eds.), *Perspectives in ornithology* (pp. 475–499). Cambridge: Cambridge University Press.

Snow, C. E. (1979). The role of social interaction in language acquisition. In W. A. Collins (Ed.), *Children's language and communication* (pp. 157–182). Hillsdale, NJ: Lawrence Erlbaum Associates.

Snow, C. E., & Hoefnagel-Höhle, M. (1978). The critical period for language acquisition: Evidence from second language learning. *Child Development, 49,* 1114–1128.

Snow, D. W., & Snow, B. K. (1983). Territorial song of the Dunnock *Prunella modularis. Bird Study, 30,* 51–56.

Snowdon, C. T. (1982). Linguistic and psycholinguistic approaches to primate communication. In C. T. Snowdon, C. H. Brown, & M. R. Petersen (Eds.), *Primate communication* (pp. 212–238). Cambridge: Cambridge University Press.

Tenaza, R. R. (1976). Wild mynahs mimic wild primates. *Nature, 259,* 561.

Terrace, H. S. (1979). *Nim.* New York: Knopf.

Thielcke, G. (1970). Die sozialen Funktionen der Vogelstimmen. *Vogelwarte, 25,* 204–229.

Thielcke, G. (1972). Waldbaumläufer (*Certhia familiaris*) ahmen artfremdes Signal nach und reagieren darauf. *Journal für Ornithologie, 113,* 287–295.

Thorpe, W. H. (1974). *Animal and human nature.* New York: Anchor Press, Doubleday.

Thorpe, W. H., & North, M. E. W. (1965). Origin and significance of the power of vocal imitation: with special reference to the antiphonal singing of birds. *Nature, 208,* 219–222.

Todt, D. (1975). Social learning of vocal patterns and modes of their applications in Grey parrots. *Zeitschrift für Tierpsychologie, 39,* 178–188.

Todt, D., Hultsch, H., & Heike, D. (1979). Conditions affecting song acquisition in nightingales (*Luscinia megarhynchos* L.). *Zeitschrift für Tierpsychologie, 51,* 23–35.

Waser, M. S., & Marler, P. (1977). Song learning in canaries. *Journal of Comparative and Physiological Psychology, 91,* 1–7.

West, M. J., & King, A. P. (1985a). Learning by performing: An ecological theme for the study of vocal learning. In T. D. Johnston & A. T. Pietrewicz (Eds.), *Issues in the ecological study of learning* (pp. 245–272). Hillsdale, NJ: Lawrence Erlbaum Associates.

West, M. J., & King, A. P. (1985b). Social guidance of vocal learning by female cowbirds: Validating its functional significance. *Zeitschrift für Tierpsychologie, 70,* 225–235.

West, M. J., Straud, A. N., & King, A. P. (1983). Mimicry of the human voice by European starlings: The role of social interaction. *Wilson Bulletin, 95,* 635–640.

Wickler, W. (1976). The ethological analysis of attachment. *Zeitschrift für Tierpsychologie, 42,* 12–28.

Wickler, W. (1980). Vocal duetting and the pairbond: I. Coyness and the partner commitment. *Zeitschrift für Tierpsychologie, 52,* 201–209.

Yasukawa, K. (1981). Song repertoires in the red-winged blackbird (*Agelaius phoeniceus*): A test of the Beau Geste hypothesis. *Animal Behaviour, 29,* 114–125.

Zentall, T., Hogan, D. E., & Edwards, C. A. (1984). Cognitive factors in conditional learning by pigeons. In H. L. Roitblat, T. G. Bever, & H. S. Terrace (Eds.), *Animal cognition* (pp. 389–405). Hillsdale, NJ: Lawrence Erlbaum Associates.

Infants' Imitation of Novel and Familiar Behaviors

Elise Frank Masur
Northern Illinois University

INTRODUCTION

The study of imitation in human infants has proceeded along rather different lines from that of imitation in animals. In research on social learning in animals, a major goal has been to determine whether or not learning can occur through observation of conspecifics (see Galef, this volume; Zentall, this volume). In contrast, because imitation by humans is not in doubt, the goals of research on human infants have been instead to determine when, why, and what infants imitate.

Although these three questions can be considered individually, they are clearly interrelated. The first is a developmental question, asking at what point infants exhibit imitative behavior and whether or not there are rudimentary precursors to true imitation performance. Those concerned with this question have been strongly influenced by the theoretical formulation of Piaget (1962) who conceptualized imitative ability as developing qualitatively during infancy through six stages from mere immediate elicitation of a reflex behavior (such as contagious crying) in newborns to delayed performance of complex and novel behaviors (including nonvisible actions infants cannot see themselves perform, such as eye blinking), by children at the end of the second year of life. The second question addresses the purposes or functions of infants' imitative performance of different kinds of actions at different times in development. Researchers have studied imitation because of the role it may play in infants' cognitive, social, and language development. Imitation has been considered variously as a manifestation of cognitive development (Kuhn, 1973; McCall, 1979; Piaget, 1962), an aspect of and contributor to social interaction (Masur, in press; Pawlby, 1977; Uzgiris, 1981, 1984), or a strategy for acquiring new and complex behaviors from the culture, including language forms and structures (Bandura, 1977; Bloom, Hood, & Lightbown, 1974; Snow, 1981; Uzgiris, 1981). The third is an empirical question, designed to determine the characteristics of behaviors that infants are able or likely to repeat. The kinds of actions infants imitate may change with development, and such changes are likely to affect the functions infants' imitation may serve.

These three questions—when, why, and what infants imitate—have implications as well for researchers' definitions of imitation. As in animal research, definitional controversies exist. Although all investigations of infant imitation start with the infant's matching of a modeled behavior, whether such a behavioral reproduction should be classified as imitation depends on one's operational definition. A definition of imitation reflects the methodological tradition within which a researcher works. Those studying cognitive, social, and language development in human infants frequently employ somewhat different criteria in identifying instances of imitation but all of these criteria depend on judgments about the relationship between the behavior of mimic and model. In determining whether an infant's performance should be described as imitative, four dimensions of the mimic/model relationship are frequently considered: *similarity/dissimilarity, immediacy/delay, contingency/independence,* and *novelty/familiarity* (Masur, in press; Meltzoff & Moore, 1983; Uzgiris, 1984). These dimensions affect judgments of imitation in animals as well (see Galef, this volume; Zentall, this volume).

For researchers of human as well as animal behavior, a replication of behavior must be judged qualitatively *similar* to the modeled behavior to be considered true imitation. The reproduction must be either an exact copy or a close approximation (Masur, in press; Masur & Ritz, 1984; Meltzoff & Moore, 1983; Uzgiris, 1984). Thus, contagion phenomena, such as cases in which an adult's vocalization evokes a different vocal response from the child, although recognized as the beginning of imitation by Piaget (1962), are generally not classified as true imitation (Uzgiris, 1972). However, some researchers have investigated such behavior. For example, McCall, Parke, and Kavanaugh (1977) coded children's responses to modeled behaviors along a continuum from refusal to manipulate the materials to perfect reproduction with an intermediate point for systematic response that did not approximate the target behavior.

The distinction between *immediate* and *delayed* or deferred reproduction is another dimension influencing judgments of imitation. Deferred imitation has been considered an index of the child's attainment of mental representational ability during Piaget's (1962) final stage of sensorimotor development (approximately 18 to 24 months of age). Meltzoff (1985) has recently demonstrated deferred performance of a simple action on an object in 14-month-old infants. McCall et al. (1977) also found that a small proportion of modeled motor acts involving objects were exactly or approximately repeated by some 15-month-olds and even a few 12-month-olds if the objects were presented again at the end of the experimental session. Although practical considerations have limited most research studies to relatively immediate production, the criterion for immediate varies widely. For example, in experimental studies in which both vocal and motor items are presented, a short time interval, such as 15 sec, is typically provided for a response (Abravanel, Levan-Goldschmidt, & Stevenson, 1976; Masur & Ritz, 1984; McCall et al., 1977). However, Uzgiris, Vasek, and Benson (1984) imposed a more stringent limit, counting as imitation only those replications that occurred within 2 sec of the modeled act.

Contingency is a third issue crucial in defining imitation. The production of the specific matching behavior must be contingent upon performance of the particular modeled behavior rather than occurring spontaneously, through a general increase in responding caused by the mere presence of the model (social facilitation; cf. Galef, this volume; Zentall, this volume), or because of the increased salience of stimuli manipulated by the model (local enhancement; cf. Galef, this volume; Zentall, this volume). The last is not an issue when actions without objects are demonstrated. Statistical or experimental procedures can be used to decrease the probability that chance performance of a modeled behavior will be counted as imitation. Such procedures include comparing the performance of an experimental group that saw a behavior modeled with their own performance during a baseline premodeling period or with the performance of a control group that saw either no behavior or a different modeled behavior (e.g., Abravanel et al., 1976; Meltzoff, 1985). Another control strategy is to substitute an alternative behavior for a subject who happens to display the target act shortly before it is to be modeled (e.g., Masur & Ritz, 1984; McCabe & Uzgiris, 1983; McCall et al., 1977).

Another means of ensuring contingency between the observed and modeled behaviors is to model behavior that is *novel* to the observer. Children's reproduction of novel behaviors, those not previously present in their performance repertoires, provides the clearest demonstration of contingency because only the model's act could have elicited that production. Although imitation of novel behaviors is important methodologically, researchers have typically not ascertained whether individual items presented were novel or familiar for the children tested (e.g., Abravanel et al., 1976; McCall et al., 1977).

Infants' replication of novel behaviors is also theoretically important. The ability to repeat novel behaviors marks a transition to a more advanced cognitive level on the way to full symbolic representational capacity (McCall, 1979; Parton, 1976; Piaget, 1962). Furthermore, reproduction of novel actions is one means for acquiring a potentially unlimited number of culturally significant behaviors (cf. Bandura, 1977). For example, language imitation researchers seek to determine whether imitation can serve as a learning mechanism in acquiring new lexical items or morphological and syntactic structures (Bloom et al., 1974; Kuczaj, 1982; Ramer, 1976; Snow, 1981).

Thus, because of its methodological and theoretical significance, infants' performance of novel versus familiar behaviors is the focus of the present chapter. In the next three sections, the developmental, functional, and experimental implications of infants' transition from performance of familiar behaviors only to replication of modeled actions that are novel and familiar is discussed.

PIAGET'S DEVELOPMENTAL THEORY OF IMITATION

Much of the present research on human infant imitation has been stimulated by the developmental progression of imitation delineated by Piaget (1962). Piaget traces the development of infants' imitative ability from its emergence in the immediate repetition of simple, familiar, visible, and audible behaviors to its culmination in the deferred replication of complex, novel, and nonvisible actions.

Piaget (1962) describes the steps in infant development of imitative skill in terms of his six stages of sensorimotor development that chart a progressive differentiation and elaboration via the complementary processes of assimilation and accommodation of infants' schemes, or cognitive structures underlying patterns of action. Assimilation involves the incorporation of environmental stimuli into existing structures, whereas accommodation includes the modification of current structures resulting in their greater correspondence with and adaptation to the environment. Throughout development, imitation is seen not as a passive mirroring of experience, but as an active assimilative and accommodative reconstruction process, with accommodation predominating in later stages. (For a more complete description of sensorimotor development in general and as a framework for considering imitation, see Piaget, 1952, 1962.)

During the first stage of sensorimotor development (approximately the first month of life), infants' repertories of cognitive structures or schemes are limited to reflexive behaviors. Piaget (1962) asserts that at this stage imitation only exists as an evocation of a reflex behavioral response by an external stimulus, as when a newborn cries upon hearing others cry. Recent research by Meltzoff and Moore (1983), however, challenges Piaget's contentions about the limits of newborns' imitative abilities. (See also Meltzoff's chapter in this volume.)

According to Piaget, during the second stage of sensorimotor development (approximately 1–4 months), reflexes become coordinated and primary schemes involving infants' own bodies emerge. The second stage marks the beginning of imitation, although only sporadic imitation of familiar visible and audible behaviors is possible at this point in development. Because of their failure to distinguish others' actions from their own productions, infants can be induced to repeat their own behaviors if they are modeled while the infants are emitting them. Inconsistent imitation of familiar vocalizations can also sometimes be elicited, even when the infants' own sounds have not immediately preceded the models'. Vocal contagion is also evident, but any matching of nonvisible behavior, such as the "apparent imitation of smiling" is dismissed as "imitation through training" or "pseudo-imitation" (Piaget, 1962, p. 18).

In Stage 3 (approximately 4–8 months), secondary schemes involving the infants' actions on external objects appear. Because of the increase in secondary schemes, a variety of modeled behaviors can be imitated through assimilation to these secondary schemes. Thus, infants in the third stage can display systematic imitation of their own familiar sounds and familiar simple primary and secondary schemes, such as waving the hands or scratching objects, even without watching their own performance. However, they are not capable of replicating novel or nonvisible acts or specific movements that are components of secondary schemes, but not yet isolated from them, such as extending and withdrawing the forefinger.

In Stage 4 (approximately 8–12 months), which marks the beginning of differentiation between accommodation and assimilation, infants become able to generalize their secondary schemes to new situations and coordinate them intentionally into means-ends relationships. These achievements make possible infants' imitation of nonvisible behaviors already familiar to them. Children accommodate, gradually through successive approximations, their familiar felt movements to the model's visible actions.

The elaboration and coordination of relationships among schemes during Stage 4 also afford flexible accommodation of individual schemes. This ability makes possible the beginning of imitation of novel audible and visible behaviors. Such imitation first appears shortly after imitation of familiar nonvisible actions. However, imitation of novel behaviors also develops through gradual approximation to the model and is limited to those behaviors that are analogous to sounds and movements already in the infants' repertories. Children are motivated to attempt to reproduce acts that are partially similar to and partially different from their existing schemes.

From Stage 5 (approximately 12–18 months) on, the increasing differentiation between assimilation and accommodation makes possible infants' active experimentation on objects to investigate their properties and the invention of new secondary schemes to serve as means to ends. In Stage 5, imitation of novel behaviors, including nonvisible ones, becomes systematic and exact through trial and error. Thus, even direct imitation of novel nonvisible behaviors becomes possible since the child differentiates and experiments with his current schemes.

In Stage 6 (approximately 18–24 months), the culmination of sensorimotor intelligence, mental representation emerges. Experimentation on and coordination of schemes can take place internally as the schemes have become independent of perception. Similarly, for imitation, because accommodation to the model is interiorized, immediate reproduction of novel and complex behaviors can occur. In addition, deferred imitation, replication of a model even after a considerable intervening delay, becomes evident. "In other words, imitation is no longer dependent on the actual action and the child becomes capable of imitating internally a series of models in the form of images or suggestions of actions. Imitation thus begins to reach the level of representation" (Piaget, 1962, p. 62).

FUNCTIONAL PERSPECTIVES ON IMITATING NOVEL AND FAMILIAR BEHAVIORS

Piaget's theoretical formulation of imitation development and its relation to the progression of sensorimotor intelligence has strongly influenced empirical researchers investigating cognitive development in infancy. A number of researchers adopted his perspective on imitative development as a manifestation of the child's growing mental ability (Kuhn, 1973; McCall, 1979; Uzgiris & Hunt, 1975). Kuhn (1973), for instance, characterized imitation as "an *aspect* of overall cognitive functioning, from which it cannot be strictly separated, rather than a unique *process* of behavior acquisition" (p. 163). In contrast, it is precisely the process of behavior acquisition that Uzgiris (1981) emphasizes. For Uzgiris, one function of imitation is as a cognitive strategy infants can employ in mastering new or incompletely comprehended behaviors. Infants' capacity for replicating novel behaviors of models permits them access to a flexible learning mechanism. As a means of encoding information and representing experience, at first overtly through action and later internally through stored mental images, imitation provides a powerful tool for acquiring a diversity of knowledge from the environment.

In addition to this cognitive function, imitation has a social dimension as well, as it is a component of the interaction between model and imitator (Uzgiris, 1981, 1984). As an aspect of social interaction, imitation "communicat[es] mutuality and shared understanding with another person" (Uzgiris, 1981, p. 1). Mothers' imitation, as well, can be interpreted as a procedure for acknowledging and validating their infants' contributions to the social interchange (Masur, in press; Pawlby, 1977; Uzgiris, 1984). From this interactional perspective, the nature of the behavior reproduced, including its novelty or familiarity, is of less importance than the achievement of a match between the partners' actions (Uzgiris, 1984). In fact, infants' matching of familiar behaviors and their ready participation in familiar games and routines should be characteristic of such an interpersonal function of imitation. Uzgiris's (1981) dual social and cognitive orientation allows performance of familiar and novel behaviors to be viewed not only as representing developmentally ordered levels, but also as expressing concurrent alternative functions, one emphasizing a social interaction and the other an intellectual process.

Infants' imitation of behaviors that are not familiar to them, but instead are previously unknown, innovative, and at the forefront of new competences, marks a significant advance. As discussed above, this accomplishment has implication for several aspects of the study of imitation—for experimental methodology, for theories of developmental progress, and for conceptualizations of the functions imitation serves for infants.

BEHAVIOR CHARACTERISTICS AFFECTING IMITATIVE PERFORMANCE

Much of the empirical research on what behaviors infants are able or likely to imitate has been motivated by a cognitive developmental perspective. Because an infant's imitation is assumed to reflect or distort the modeled act in accordance with his or her cognitive structures (Kuhn, 1973), the kinds of behaviors attempted and the quality of the matching performance can be used as indications of the infant's underlying level of cognitive ability (e.g., McCall, 1979; Uzgiris & Hunt, 1975). This correspondence has provided the impetus for a host of studies of infants' imitation of diverse kinds of behaviors—gestural versus vocal, object related versus body part, individual versus sequenced, sound producing versus silent, immediate versus deferred, and conventional versus counterconventional (e.g., Abravanel et al., 1976; Killen & Uzgiris, 1981; McCabe & Uzgiris, 1983; McCall et al., 1977; Rodgon & Kurdek, 1977). As described above, infants' production of more complex and advanced actions would signal their attainment of higher developmental levels.

These empirical studies have uncovered a set of parameters influencing infants' reproduction of particular behaviors. One factor that influences infants' likelihood of imitating motor actions is the presence or absence of objects. Actions on objects are copied more frequently than actions without objects (Abravanel et al., 1976; Rodgon & Kurdek, 1977). However, this generalization may require modification when other behavioral characteristics are taken into account, because both of these classes of actions (those on objects and those without objects) include heterogeneous subclasses that need to be distinguished. For example, McCall et al. (1977) reported individual differences among children in their repetitions of actions on objects producing sounds and those resulting in a change in form of the object. Actions on objects can also be classified according to their typicality or conventional meaningfulness. Uzgiris and her colleagues (Killen & Uzgiris, 1981; McCabe & Uzgiris, 1983) found that typical actions on conventionally appropriate objects, such as pretending to drink from a cup, were reproduced more readily by 10- to 17-month-olds than the same actions modeled with inappropriate objects (e.g., pretending to drink from a toy car). Only the oldest infants studied, those 22 months of age, systematically reproduced conventional and unconventional behaviors equally often.

Actions without objects are also of diverse kinds, and experimental studies have not adequately differentiated among them. Most surprising, two performance dimensions that deserve particular scrutiny because of their theoretical significance (Piaget, 1962) have received only scant empirical attention—infants' transitions from matching visible to nonvisible behaviors and from matching familiar to novel behaviors. Rodgon and Kurdek (1977) noted more frequent performance of motor behaviors involving objects than of motor behaviors involving body parts, but they did not categorize body-part actions either as to visibility or familiarity. Abravanel et al. (1976) abandoned a planned comparison between infants' repetition of visible and nonvisible acts when they realized that virtually all their visible items involved objects whereas none of their nonvisible ones did so. In addition, Uzgiris and Hunt's (1975) gestural imitation scale, based on Piaget's developmental progression, has items assessing infants' repetition of familiar visible, novel visible, and novel nonvisible actions, but not their replication of familiar nonvisible behaviors. McCall et al. (1977) reported that 12- to 24-month-olds' performance of nonvisible actions, only one of which included an object, was less accurate than their reproduction of several categories of visible acts using objects. However, the novelty or familiarity of the visible and nonvisible behaviors presented was neither ascertained nor controlled, an omission common to other investigations as well (Abravanel et al., 1976; Rodgon & Kurdek, 1977).

The meaningfulness or arbitrariness of modeled actions may further affect the likelihood of infants' reproduction. In the imitation literature, various actions without objects, and even some with objects, have been termed *gestures*. However, for language researchers, gesture refers to a specific class of conventionally meaningful communicative acts (Masur, 1983). Because communicative gestures are socially meaningful and likely to be familiar, even young infants should copy them more readily than comparable arbitrary, novel hand or arm movements. Again, previous research has not examined this contrast for actions without objects.

Thus, another empirical conclusion that warrants reexamination is the statement that infants imitate "gestural" actions more often than vocal behaviors, a result clearly established only in comparisons involving actions on objects (McCall et al., 1977; Rodgon & Kurdek, 1977). In fact, on the basis of results from the study of language development, one should expect to find a correspondence between infants' gestural and vocal performance. Language acquisition researchers have uncovered relations among infants' spontaneous gestural, vocal, and verbal production (e.g., Bates, Benigni, Bretherton, Camaioni, & Volterra, 1979; Masur, 1982; 1983) and associations between spontaneous or elicited imitation and children's development of both communicative gestures and early words (Bates et al., 1979; Bloom et al., 1974; McCall, 1979; Rodgon & Kurdek, 1977). However, a number of experimental studies have failed to find any significant correlations in imitation performance across motor and vocal items for infants younger than 20 months of age (McCall et al., 1977; Rodgon & Kurdek, 1977); in particular, Uzgiris and Hunt (1975) reported a correlation of only .07 between scores on their gestural and vocal imitation scales when age was controlled.

The results of these empirical studies emphasize the need for examining more systematically the various characteristics or dimensions of behaviors that influence imitation performance. These dimensions include the presence or absence of objects, the meaningfulness or arbitrariness of the behaviors, the familiarity or novelty of the acts, and their visibility or nonvisibility. Despite previous research denying cross-category consistency in infants' imitation, we predicted that if these dimensions were taken into account coherent patterns of relationships among infants' performance on diverse categories of behaviors would nonetheless appear.

INFANTS' MATCHING OF NOVEL AND FAMILIAR BEHAVIORS

With the above goal in mind, we undertook an investigation to examine infants' imitation of motor, vocal, and verbal behaviors selected to vary systematically on dimensions of presence/absence of objects, meaningfulness/arbitrariness, visibility/nonvisibility, and familiarity/novelty (Masur & Ritz, 1984). Our subjects were 10- to 16-month-old infants. The age range was chosen to encompass imitative levels from approximately early Stage 4 through late Stage 5 (Piaget, 1962) as well as to span a range of communicative abilities from the emergence of gestures through the acquisition of first words. We studied 42 first-born children divided among five age groups (10–11, 12, 13, 14, and 15–16 months of age) each composed of equal numbers of girls and boys: There were 8 children in each group, except the 14-month-old group, which had 10. The children were recruited from DeKalb, Illinois, the surrounding suburbs, small towns, and rural areas for a "naturalistic study of infants' interactions with people and objects in their environments." Although mother-infant dyads were videotaped in natural interactions the preceding week, no mention was made of infants' imitating or repeating their mothers' behaviors until the experimental sessions.

During the experiment, mothers in their own homes presented their infants with 21 behaviors to imitate. Mothers served as models after careful instruction by the experimenter. The mothers attracted the children's attention, performed the behaviors, and paused for about 15 sec for responses. Mothers were instructed both to refrain from saying anything while carrying out actions and not to react to their children's responses.

Four categories of motor behavior and two categories of verbal behaviors were modeled by each mother for her infant. The motor behaviors included four conventional communicative gestures (e.g., waving, pointing); four hand and arm actions chosen to be similar to the communicative gestures in difficulty and configuration but without communicative meaning (e.g., raising the arm, extending and withdrawing the index finger); two nonvisible items (touching the top of the head, following a gaze to the ceiling); and three object-related actions (e.g., hitting two blocks together). The two vocal categories included four vocalizations, two designated "easy" (*ma-ma-ma, ba-ba-ba*) and two "difficult" (*eeee, zzzz*), and four words, two designated "easy" (*car, book*) and two "difficult" (*chalk, gnome*), on the basis of the expected familiarity of the items. The actual familiarity of the modeled behaviors was determined at the end of the session when each mother was asked whether each gesture, action, vocalization, word, and nonvisible item was new to her child or a behavior the child already did on his or her own.

The experimenter controlled item presentations by handing an index card listing a behavior that was to be modeled to the mother only when the child was neither distracted nor fretting. A few times, when a child was spontaneously engaged in the action on the next card, the following item was substituted. To maximize the likelihood of performance of more difficult behaviors, the battery was presented in two counterbalanced halves with each half containing behaviors from each category in an order designed to have predicted easier items precede more difficult ones. The infants' responses were videotaped for later coding as "exact imitation," "close approximation," or "no imitation." Each infant's best response for each item was later compared to the experimenter's notes of the best response recorded during the session. Interobserver agreement for transcription and for coding averaged 95% or better.

The numbers of behaviors that infants exactly or approximately imitated were evaluated by a mixed analysis of variance with age group, sex, and behavior category (with scores for nonvisible and object-related actions adjusted for differing numbers of items) as the factors. The analysis yielded significant main effects for age and sex and an age by sex interaction. Performance in the two youngest age groups was low for both boys and girls; the mean numbers of items imitated ranged between 5.67 and 7.50 out of an adjusted total of 24. Imitative performance increased for the older children, especially the girls. Tests of simple main effects for sex showed differences between girls and boys only for the 13- and 14-month age groups, where the girls' production ($Ms = 14.50$ and 11.00) outstripped the boys' ($Ms = 6.34$ and 5.07). In the oldest age group, however, the scores of the girls ($M = 14.34$) and boys ($M = 8.25$) did not differ significantly from each other. Individual children's performance varied widely. For example, two children (a 12-month-old girl and a 14-month-old boy) copied only one behavior each, whereas one 15-month-old girl matched all but 3 of the 21 items (two arbitrary actions and one object-related behavior).

The analysis also revealed marked differences in infants' reproduction of different categories of behavior. The arbitrary actions and the words elicited the fewest replications, with means of only 0.71 and 0.95 out of 4.00 possible. Post hoc tests showed that the mean for imitation of actions, but not words, differed significantly from mean production rates for vocalizations ($M = 1.31$), gestures ($M = 1.43$), and nonvisible items (adjusted $M = 1.43$). In keeping with previous research, object-related actions were copied significantly more frequently than any other type of behavior (adjusted $M = 2.64$).

These findings demonstrate the value in studies of imitation of considering the characteristics of the behaviors presented. Overall, meaningful communicative gestures were matched more readily than comparable but arbitrary hand and arm movements. Moreover, gestures were not more frequently imitated than vocalizations, words, or nonvisible behaviors. In fact, contrary to previous conclusions in the literature, vocalizations were produced more often than arbitrary actions, as, to our surprise, were nonvisible items.

It is most likely that our findings were influenced by the familiarity or novelty of particular items for individual children. Results from separate analyses of performance of items within certain behavior categories strongly suggested such a conclusion. Analysis of performance of arbitrary visible actions, for instance, besides producing an age by sex interaction, revealed a main effect for items and an age by items interaction that approached significance ($p < .09$). The behavior of raising an arm was copied more frequently ($M = 0.64$) than any other action ($Ms = 0.05-0.45$). Production of arm raising was more frequent, especially among younger children, than performance of any other action. Furthermore, all but one of the children who raised their arms were reported to have this action as a familiar behavior, many as part of the imitation routine, "So Big." On the other hand, virtually all repetitions of other items were instances of novel action imitation, performed only by infants at least 13 months old.

The effect of the novelty of a modeled behavior on probability of imitation was also indicated in our analysis of imitation of words. Production of words was significantly related to age. Only 3 of the 16 youngest children repeated a word. In contrast, 60%–75% of the infants at each of the three oldest ages imitated at least one word; 7 of these 26 children matched three or four words. There was also a significant age by word-level (easy or difficult) interaction which is displayed in Table 15.1. The 13- and 14-month-olds reproduced more easy than difficult words; but the opposite pattern characterized the oldest group's performance. The 15- and 16-month-olds replicated more difficult words, which were all novel (except in the case of one 16-month-old who could say *chalk*). If we examine infants' matching performance in terms of the actual rather than expected novelty of the items, however, we see a different picture: Three of the five easy words repeated by the oldest group were determined by maternal reports to be familiar, but the majority (8 of 15) of the easy words copied by the 13- and 14-month-olds were reported by their mothers as novel. Thus, most words reproduced by children at the three older ages (10 of 13, 6 of 10, and 11 of 15, respectively) were not previously present in their productive lexicons.

With the expectation that coherent and interpretable relationships among performance of different items would be revealed when behavioral familiarity was

Table 15.1
Mean Numbers of Easy and Difficult
Words Imitated by Age Group

Age in months	Easy words	Difficult words
10–11	0.12	0.12
12	0.00	0.12
13	1.00	0.68
14	0.70	0.30
15–16	0.68	1.12

Note. The number of imitations includes exact and approximate imitations. There were two easy and two difficult words. Reprinted from "Patterns of gestural, vocal, and verbal imitation performance in infancy," *Merrill-Palmer Quarterly*, Vol. 30, No. 4, 1984, by Elise Frank Masur and Elsbeth G. Ritz by permission of Wayne State University Press. Copyright © 1984 by Wayne State University Press, Detroit, MI 48202.

taken into account, we classified the children in terms of their reproduction of novel behaviors. Distinct patterns of infants' performance on diverse kinds of behaviors emerged when the familiarity or novelty of the individual items that particular children imitated was considered: There was a major contrast between the 14 children who repeated only familiar behaviors—gestures, actions, vocalizations, and sometimes words—and the 27 children who reproduced some novel behaviors as well as familiar acts. As predicted from Piaget's developmental stage theory, a chi-square analysis showed that a higher proportion of older ($\geq$ 13 months; 81%) than younger (38%) infants matched novel behaviors. Of those children who replicated novel behaviors, 13 imitated at least one novel vocalization and/or word, 3 imitated one novel action each, and 11 reproduced one or more novel vocalizations and/or words plus novel actions. Only 2 children failed to match at least one object-related or familiar behavior. The complete distribution of the children's four patterns of performance by age, younger and older, and by sex is presented in Table 15.2.

In an analysis of variance examining quantitative differences in children's performance of familiar behaviors, employing the factors of pattern, age, sex, and familiar behavior category (gestures, actions, vocalizations, and words), we found that the children with the most advanced performance pattern (Pattern 4), who imitated greater numbers and kinds of novel items, also reproduced significantly more familiar behaviors, whereas children who imitated novel actions only (Pattern 3) repeated fewest. Significant differences between the sexes, favoring girls, and among the familiar behavior categories were also evident. A comparison between performance on novel sounds and words by the two pattern groups that produced them disclosed that the group most advanced qualitatively in imitation

Table 15.2

Percentages of Children Imitating and Mean Scores for Production of Object-Related, Familiar, Novel, and Nonvisible Behaviors

	n		Object-Related Behaviors		Familiar Behaviors								Total Familiar	
					Gestures		Actions		Vocalizations		Words			
	Girls	Boys	%	M	%	M	%	M	%	M	%	M	%	M
1. No Novel														
No Familiar	1	0	0	0.00	0	0.00	0	0.00	0	0.00	0	0.00	0	0.00
Younger	1	0	0	0.00	0	0.00	0	0.00	0	0.00	0	0.00	0	0.00
Older	0	0												
Familiar Only	4	10	100	2.00	93	1.64	28	0.36	50	0.79	7	0.07	100	2.79
Younger	3	6	100	2.00	89	1.44	44	0.55	44	0.89	0	0.00	100	2.89
Older	1	4	100	2.00	100	2.00	0	0.00	60	0.60	20	0.20	100	2.60
2. Novel Vocalizations and/or Words	7	6	92	1.85	54	0.92	31	0.31	54	0.62	31	0.38	92	2.23
Younger	3	1	100	2.25	25	0.50	0	0.00	50	0.50	0	0.00	75	1.00
Older	4	5	89	1.67	67	1.11	44	0.44	56	0.67	44	0.56	100	2.78
3. Novel Actions	1	2	67	1.67	67	1.00	0	0.00	0	0.00	0	0.00	67	1.00
Younger	1	0	100	3.00	100	1.00	0	0.00	0	0.00	0	0.00	100	1.00
Older	0	2	50	1.00	50	1.00	0	0.00	0	0.00	0	0.00	50	1.00
4. Novel Vocalizations and/or Words plus Novel Actions	8	3	100	2.36	100	2.00	54	0.54	91	1.54	36	0.45	100	4.54
Younger	0	1	100	2.00	100	2.00	100	1.00	100	1.00	0	0.00	100	4.00
Older	8	2	100	2.40	100	2.00	50	0.50	90	1.60	40	0.50	100	4.60

(Continued)

TABLE 15.2 (Continued)

Pattern	n		Novel Behaviors								Nonvisible Behaviors			
			Vocalizations		Words		Vocalizations and/or words		Actions		Look at ceil-ing	Touch head	Total Nonvisible	
	Girls	Boys	%	M	%	M	%	M	%	M	%	%	%	M
1. No Novel														
No Familiar	1	0	0	0.00	0	0.00	0	0.00	0	0.00	100	0	100	1.00
Younger	1	0	0	0.00	0	0.00	0	0.00	0	0.00	100	0	100	1.00
Older	0	0												
Familiar Only	4	10	0	0.00	0	0.00	0	0.00	0	0.00	28	7	36	0.36
Younger	3	6	0	0.00	0	0.00	0	0.00	0	0.00	33	11	44	0.44
Older	1	4	0	0.00	0	0.00	0	0.00	0	0.00	20	0	20	0.20
2. Novel Vocalizations and/or Words	7	6	62	0.69	77	0.92	100	1.62	0	0.00	62	8	69	0.69
Younger	3	1	50	0.50	50	0.50	100	1.00	0	0.00	0	25	25	0.25
Older	4	5	67	0.78	89	1.11	100	1.89	0	0.00	89	0	89	0.89
3. Novel Actions	1	2	0	0.00	0	0.00	0	0.00	100	1.00	0	33	33	0.33
Younger	1	0	0	0.00	0	0.00	0	0.00	100	1.00	0	100	100	1.00
Older	0	2	0	0.00	0	0.00	0	0.00	100	1.00	0	0	0	0.00
4. Novel Vocalizations and/or Words plus Novel Actions	8	3	73	0.91	91	1.54	100	2.45	100	1.09	64	64	91	1.27
Younger	0	1	100	1.00	100	1.00	100	2.00	100	1.00	100	0	100	1.00
Older	8	2	70	0.90	90	1.60	100	2.50	100	1.10	60	70	90	1.30

Reprinted from "Patterns of gestural, vocal, and verbal imitation performance in infancy," *Merrill-Palmer Quarterly*, Vol. 30, No. 4, 1984, by Elise Frank Masur and Elsbeth G. Ritz by permission of Wayne State University Press. Copyright © 1984 by Wayne State University Press, Detroit, MI 48202 of novel behaviors (Pattern 4) was also more productive quantitatively in performance of novel vocal acts.

When the analysis of familiar behavior performance was recalculated substituting proportions, arcsine transformed, of familiar gestures, actions, and vocalizations presented that were performed by children in the four pattern groups, the differences by pattern were again demonstrated, F (3, 25) = 4.73, p = .01. Children in Pattern 4 replicated an average of 52% of modeled behaviors familiar to them, whereas those in the other patterns copied only from 5% to 33% of familiar modeled behaviors. However, the effects of sex and items no longer reached the .05 level of significance (ps = .11 and .06, respectively). Challenging previous conclusions that "gestures" are imitated more than vocal behaviors (McCall et al., 1977), this analysis shows that when the availability of familiar items is controlled, performance of familiar motor and vocal behaviors does not differ significantly.

Further analyses were motivated by the question of consistency in infants' production of diverse behaviors: Is there in fact a general tendency to imitate a variety of both vocal and nonvocal behaviors? Although previous studies have found no significant associations in performance across motor, vocal, and verbal items in infants of the age range we studied, we uncovered relationships among performance of these kinds of behaviors when familiar and novel actions were analyzed separately. Intercorrelations, with age controlled, were significant for infants' frequencies of imitation of familiar gestures, actions, and vocalizations. Similar correlations, employing proportions of familiar behaviors presented that were performed, revealed the same associations (rs = .41 − .44, ps < .01). In parallel fashion, infants' production of nonvisible items was related to their matching of novel acts. For example, with age controlled, imitation of following a gaze and of novel vocalizations and novel words was correlated. Production of patting the head and of novel actions was related as well. Analogous correlations, employing proportions of novel behaviors presented that were imitated, produced the same results (rs = .41 and .51, respectively, ps < .01). In addition, there was an association between performance of head patting and the proportion of novel vocalizations and words reproduced (p = .30, p < .05).

Corroborating evidence for some of these results is provided by a recent study that examined in greater detail imitation performance by 14- to 18-month-old infants of familiar and novel motor behaviors that were either visible or nonvisible (Ashley, 1986; Ashley & Masur, in preparation). When infants were classified into groups according to their highest level of performance, it was found that children who imitated the most difficult novel, nonvisible behaviors also imitated the greatest proportion of familiar behaviors. In addition, partial correlations, controlling for age, between proportions of familiar visible and nonvisible and of novel visible and nonvisible behaviors reproduced were significant, rs = .56 and .62, respectively, ps < .01 (Ashley, 1986).

In sum, meaningful patterns of relationships among children's imitation of diverse kinds of actions emerged when the familiarity or novelty of individual behaviors was taken into account. We found cross-category consistency in infants' imitation of a variety of novel and familiar acts, a finding others have failed to produce.

There were also striking individual differences in both quantitative and qualitative performance. Some children imitated only familiar items; others matched novel behaviors in either the vocal or action domain or both, a cognitively more demanding feat (Piaget, 1962). Regarding infants' imitation of familiar behaviors not only as a reflection of their cognitive capacity (or limitation), but also as an aspect of their social interactions (cf. Uzgiris, 1981, 1984), we surmise that the procedures in this study maximized the children's social involvement by employing mothers as models in their own homes. Virtually all the children imitated some familiar behaviors. A few infants even interpreted our items in terms of their familiar social routines. For example, a 10-month-old girl touched her mother's nose as she copied the sound *eeee*. Her mother explained that they had a game in which they "beeped" each other's noses.

In reproducing novel behaviors, imitation can serve as a cognitive strategy for mastering new experiences (cf. Uzgiris, 1981). Twenty of the children imitated words they had never before produced and, in many cases, imitated words they had never previously heard. It is interesting to note that the 13- and 14-month-olds reproduced more novel easy words, which were probably receptively though not productively familiar, than difficult words that were wholly unknown to them. This finding illustrates the challenge of behaviors just beyond one's competence. It is reminiscent of Piaget's (1962) comments on infants' motivation to attempt actions analogous to existing schemes, both partially similar and partially discrepant. The finding also suggests that receptive, as well as productive, familiarity should be taken into account in future investigations.

If we view children's performance of familiar gestures, actions, and sounds as an aspect of social interaction and children's attempts to replicate novel verbal and motor behaviors as an adoption of a cognitive strategy, we can ask whether and how these two functions might be related. In the present study we found that children who replicated more novel acts also matched more familiar behaviors. Uzgiris (1984; McCabe & Uzgiris, 1983) also reported that 22-month-olds who repeated complex and counterconventional actions continued to match simple, conventional, presumably familiar behaviors. We need also to examine both the causes and consequences of infants' imitation of familiar and novel behaviors. We have seen here and in other studies (e.g., Masur, 1980; in press) that imitation is part of mother-infant interaction. Some mothers may actively encourage their infants to imitate through either demonstration or explicit suggestion (Masur, in press). We should, therefore, consider the possibility that young children who frequently reproduce their mothers' familiar behaviors are more likely later to recruit this social procedure as a cognitive strategy for mastering new and challenging behaviors, including language. Such questions should inspire future explorations of infant imitation.

REFERENCES

Abravanel, E., Levan-Goldschmidt, E., & Stevenson, M. B. (1976). Action imitation: The early phase of infancy. *Child Development, 47,* 1032–1044.

Ashley, D. R. (1986). *Imitation performance of 14- to 18-month old children: The effects of item visibility and familiarity.* Unpublished master's thesis, Northern Illinois University.

Ashley, D. R., & Masur, E. F. (in preparation). Infants' imitation of familiar and novel visible and nonvisible behaviors.

Bandura, A. (1977). *Social learning theory.* Englewood Cliffs, NJ: Prentice-Hall.

Bates, E., Benigni, L., Bretherton, I., Camaioni, L., & Volterra, V. (1979). *The emergence of symbols: Cognition and communication in infancy.* New York: Academic Press.

Bloom, L., Hood, L., & Lightbown, P. (1974). Imitation in language development: If, when, and why. *Cognitive Psychology, 76,* 380–420.

Killen, M., & Uzgiris, I. C. (1981). Imitation of actions with objects: The role of social meaning. *Journal of Genetic Psychology, 138,* 219–229.

Kuczaj, S. A., II. (1982). Language play and language acquisition. In H. W. Reese (Ed.), *Advances in child development and behavior,* (Vol. 17, pp. 197–232). New York: Academic Press.

Kuhn, D. (1973). Imitation theory and research from a cognitive perspective. *Human Development, 16,* 157–180.

Masur, E. F. (1980). The development of communicative gestures in mother-infant interactions. *Papers and Reports on Child Language Development,* No. 19. 121–128.

Masur, E. F. (1982). Mothers' responses to infants' object-related gestures: Influences on lexical development. *Journal of Child Language, 9,* 23–30.

Masur, E. F. (1983). Gestural development, dual-directional signaling, and the transition to words. *Journal of Psycholinguistic Research, 12,* 93–109.

Masur, E. F. (in press). Imitative interchanges in a social context: Mother-infant matching behavior at the beginning of the second year. *Merrill-Palmer Quarterly.*

Masur, E. F., & Ritz, E. G. (1984). Patterns of gestural, vocal, and verbal imitation performance in infancy. *Merrill-Palmer Quarterly, 30,* 369–392.

McCabe, M., & Uzgiris, I. C. (1983). Effects of model and action on imitation in infancy. *Merrill-Palmer Quarterly, 29,* 69–82.

McCall, R. B. (1979). Qualitative transitions in behavioral development in the first two years of life. In M. H. Bornstein & W. Kessen (Eds.), *Psychological development from infancy: Image to intention* (pp. 183–224). Hillsdale, NJ: Lawrence Erlbaum Associates.

McCall, R. B., Parke, R. D., & Kavanaugh, R. D. (1977). Imitation of live and televised models by children one to three years of age. *Monographs of the Society for Research in Child Development, 42* (5, Serial No. 173).

Meltzoff, A. N. (1985). Immediate and deferred imitation in fourteen- and twenty-four-month-old infants. *Child Development, 56,* 62–72.

Meltzoff, A. N., & Moore, M. K. (1983). The origins of imitation in infancy: Paradigm, phenomena, and theories. In L. P. Lipsitt & C. K. Rovee-Collier (Eds.), *Advances in infancy research,* (Vol. 2, pp. 266–301). Norwood, NJ: Ablex.

Parton, D. A. (1976). Learning to imitate in infancy. *Child Development, 47,* 14–31.

Pawlby, S. J. (1977). Imitative interaction. In H. R. Schaffer (Ed.), *Studies in mother-infant interaction* (pp. 203–224). New York: Academic Press.

Piaget, J. (1952). *Origins of intelligence in children.* New York: International Universities Press.

Piaget, J. (1962). *Play, dreams and imitation in childhood.* New York: Norton.

Ramer, A. (1976). The function of imitation in child language. *Journal of Speech and Hearing Research, 19,* 700–717.

Rodgon, M. M., & Kurdek, L. A. (1977). Vocal and gestural imitation in 8-, 14-, and 20-month-old children. *Journal of Genetic Psychology, 131,* 115–123.

Snow, C. E. (1981). The uses of imitation. *Journal of Child Language, 8,* 205–212.

Uzgiris, I. C. (1972). Patterns of vocal and gestural imitation in infants. In F. J. Monks, W. W. Hartup, & J. deWit (Eds.), *Determinants of behavioral development* (pp. 467–471). New York: Academic Press.

Uzgiris, I. C. (1981). Two functions of imitation during infancy. *International Journal of Behavioral Development, 4,* 1–12.

Uzgiris, I. C. (1984). Imitation in infancy: Its interpersonal aspects. In M. Perlmutter (Ed.), *Minnesota Symposium on Child Psychology* (Vol. 17, pp. 1–32). Hillsdale, NJ: Lawrence Erlbaum Associates.

Uzgiris, I. C., & Hunt, J. McV. (1975). *Assessment in infancy.* Urbana: University of Illinois Press.

Uzgiris, I. C., Vasek, M. E., & Benson, J. B. (1984). *A longitudinal study of matching activity in mother-infant interaction.* Paper presented at the Fourth Biennial International Conference on Infant Studies, New York City.

The Human Infant
as Homo Imitans

Andrew N. Meltzoff
University of Washington

INTRODUCTION

A central goal of this book is to bring together essays on social learning and imitation in animals and man. This goal builds upon a long-standing question asked at least as far back as Aristotle. Aristotle (1941) was quite decisive in his evaluation of the comparative imitative capacities of man and animals: "Imitation is natural to man from childhood, one of his advantages over the lower animals being this, that he is the most imitative creature in the world, and learns at first by imitation" (p. 448b).

Before evaluating this statement in the light of modern-day experiments, we might inquire why human beings' putative imitative prowess would put them at an advantage over lower animals. What is the use of imitation? What Aristotle recognized, it seems, is that imitation is a vehicle for the transmission of culture from one generation to the next. It provides a mechanism for a kind of Lamarckian evolutionary change in humans. Imitation provides an efficient channel through which acquired behaviors, skills, customs, and traditions may be incorporated by the young.

Bona fide instances of the transmission of acquired behavior patterns in animals are rare enough to be noteworthy. Such examples become celebrated cases in the literature. Animal behavior texts highlight the role of imitation in the acquisition of song in certain passerine birds (Marler & Tamura, 1964). Similarly Kawamura's (1959) work has been widely cited for the observation that members of a troop of Japanese macaques began washing their sweet potatoes in the sea after watching a few juveniles who invented this technique.

In contrast, even the most casual observer of human behavior sees numerous instances of imitation in young children—the imitation of parental postures, facial expressions, and tool use. It is commonly observed that a little boy will lather his smooth face and pretend to shave with a stick, or sit in front of his father's word-processor and studiously poke at the keys with his fingers. Imita-

a

b

Figure 16.1. Balinese infants between 10 and 12 months of age engaging in object play. (Photographs from Mead & Macgregor, 1951.)

tion even plays a role during early infancy, well before linguistic instruction could mediate such activity. This is graphically illustrated by one of Margaret Mead's studies.

Mead published a series of photographs from her 1936–1939 research of the Balinese people in Indonesia (Mead & Macgregor, 1951). One cannot be certain of the events surrounding each photograph, and her research notes did not focus on imitation. Nonetheless, Mead's plates provide snapshots of behavior that may be partly attributable to imitation. Figure 16.1a shows an infant just over 10 months old who, barely able to stand, is poking at a wooden table with a knife. In Figure 16.1b a 1-year-old boy is playing a *tjoengklik,* a bamboo xylophone, and according to Mead, is "crossing his mallets in a highly professional manner" (p. 146).

Figures 16.2a–d show infants between 14 and 20 months of age squatting

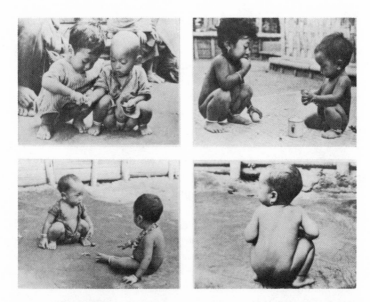

Figure 16.2. Balinese infants between 14 and 20 months sitting in a low squat position. Most Western-raised infants of this age do not position themselves in this fashion. The Balinese infants may have picked up this body posture from observing the adults in their culture. (Photographs from Mead & Macgregor, 1951.)

quite stably, often while using their hands for manipulation. Western infants, at least those tested in my laboratory in Seattle, are not commonly seen in such low, stable squats at this young age. Although one cannot rule out differential carrying postures as the root of this behavioral difference, one intriguing possibility is that the young Balinese infants are copying the low squat position of their Balinese elders, for whom it is a common form.

A classic experiment by the Kelloggs (1933) also bears on man's comparative imitative prowess. Ironically, their goal was to downplay the genetic bases of behavioral differences between man and apes. They sought to attribute behavioral differences to differential rearing conditions. The Kelloggs raised an infant chimpanzee contemporaneously with their infant son, providing them with environments as identical as possible. Both were diapered, talked to while playing on the Kelloggs' laps, hugged, and so on. Of course the infant chimp never grew to be very human-like, much to the Kelloggs' disappointment. But what of the child? A close reading of the report reveals behavior patterns that are atypical for human young. For example, the little boy was reported to scrape paint off walls with his teeth, as engaging in certain "mauling" play tactics, and perhaps most dramatically, as spontaneously duplicating the food barks and grunts of the chimp when he saw the chimp's favorite food. It seems likely that these behaviors were performed by the human child in imitation of the ape—a direction of transmission that had not been anticipated by the Kelloggs.

There is no compelling reason to disagree with at least two of Aristotle's points—that man is indeed the most imitative creature in the world, and that this accords him several advantages. But what of Aristotle's third point, that imitation is "natural" to man? If we take this to mean that very young human infants are highly proficient imitators, or even more literally that there is some innate ability to imitate, then findings from modern developmental psychology would seem to diverge from this view. If a consensus can be discerned among psychologists, it is that the imitative proficiency of the older child is only very gradually acquired during the first two years of infancy.

Piaget's (1962) stage-developmental theory is the most widely accepted view of the origins and development of imitation in human infancy. His theory is based on naturalistic observations of the development of his own three children. The central idea in the theory is that there are cognitive constraints that severely delimit the imitative competence of infants. Just as infants are thought to progress through stages of cognitive development, so too are they thought to progress through different stages of imitative skill.

Piaget's theory postulates six stages of imitative ability between birth and two years of age. These can be collapsed into three general levels of imitative skill. Level 1 is said to last from approximately birth to 8 or 12 months of age. During this phase infants are thought to be limited to imitating simple vocal and manual maneuvers. In Piaget's own work he reports numerous instances of vocal imitation (repeating vowel sounds or syllables) and manual gestures (hand opening or finger movements) during the first year. The key, according to Piaget, is that in these types of behavior infants can perceive both the model's and their own responses in the same sensory modality. Infants can hear both an adult's vocalizations and their own. By comparing their own auditory output to the model's, they can alter their performance to bring it into line with that of an adult. A similar matching process can underlie manual imitation. Here the infant can see both his own hand movements and those of an adult. Again an intramodal process, albeit visual-visual (versus auditory-auditory for vocal imitation) can underlie manual imitation.

According to Piaget, level 2 imitation first becomes possible at about 1 year of age. The hallmark of level 2 is the onset of imitation of facial gestures, such as mouth opening/closing or tongue protrusion/withdrawal. Piaget notes that simple intramodal matching processes are not sufficient for facial imitation. Although the infant can see an adult's face, he cannot see his own. If the infant is young enough, he will never even have seen his own reflection in a mirror. Visual-visual matching is ruled out. The ability of infants to match gestures they see with actions of their own to which they have no visual access seems to require some form of cross-modal matching. According to standard developmental theories, the human infant lacks the ability to recognize cross-modal matches, that is to detect correspondences between information picked up by separate sensory modalities, until about 1 year old. Thus, Piaget predicted that younger infants could not perform untrained facial imitation.

It is crucial to note that Piaget's theory is concerned only with spontaneous, untrained imitation. The theory by no means holds that young infants could not be conditioned to respond to an adult tongue protrusion with one of their own. Research has shown that young infants can be conditioned to respond differentially to certain signals and not others (e.g., Lipsitt & Werner, 1981). There is no reason to doubt that they could also be conditioned to perform motor movements to certain visual displays. The claim, then, is not that young infants cannot be conditioned to respond to a particular facial display with a matching one. Rather the claim is that without any such training facial imitation is impossible before about 1 year. After that age, Piaget reports numerous observations of such spontaneous facial imitation.

Finally, level 3 of imitative development emerges at about 18–24 months. The developmental milestone associated with level 3 is the onset of untrained deferred imitation, that is the spontaneous duplication of observed acts long after the target has disappeared from view. Piaget's observations revealed that young infants could duplicate acts immediately, or with a short delay, but there were no indications of deferred imitation until level 3. Again, cognitive/memory deficits were thought to restrict imitative performance.

In summary, Piaget resisted the notion that human infants begin life with highly developed imitative faculties. His observations indicated that infants are constrained to imitating only certain things at certain ages. The theory postulated a progression in imitation from behaviors that could be directly compared within the same perceptual modality (vocal and manual imitation), to behaviors that required a cross-modal comparison (facial imitation), to behaviors that could not be directly compared to anything in the perceptual field (deferred imitation).

Recent research has challenged this now-standard developmental account. Research conducted in both my laboratory and others' over the past 10 years has revealed a more advanced imitative competence than Piaget and other traditional theories of child development have ascribed to the human infant. In this sense the recent history of research on infant imitation reverses that of animal imitation, at least as that history is described by Galef (this volume). Galef suggests that the early naturalistic observations of animals led to an overestimation of their imitative abilities; more careful laboratory experiments now show that this ability is rare. In contrast, Piaget's naturalistic work with humans greatly underestimated what can be established in carefully controlled laboratory studies. In the case of humans, recent laboratory studies have uncovered a surprising imitative facility in infants that could not have been predicted on the basis of earlier home observations.

IMITATION IN 1- TO 2-YEAR-OLD INFANTS

Studies in our laboratory were designed to investigate imitation in the second year of human infancy. The aims of the studies were twofold: (a) to develop a methodologically sound procedure for assessing imitation in the second year, one that eliminates the potential confounds described both in the animal literature (Galef, this volume; Zentall, this volume), and in the human literature (Meltzoff & Moore, 1983a); and (b) to assess both immediate and deferred imitation in 14- and 24-month-old infants under these laboratory conditions.

Most previous experimental studies of infant imitation have focused on immediate imitation. Yet it is interesting, both for cognitive and social-developmental theory, to investigate deferred imitation, the onset of imitation after a significant delay. From a cognitive perspective, deferred imitation indicates an ability to act on the basis of some stored memory of the modeled act, and thus provides a technique for investigating the development of infant memory. Deferred imitation is also relevant to social theory because imitation can play only a limited role in the acquisition of behavior traits and culturally specific customs if the infant is restricted to imitating in the presence of the model and cannot yet delay his imitation. If an infant were constrained to "resonating" to actions of his conspecifics, copying them on-line, but could not yet delay such imitations for a significant time, imitation would have far less generality and utility than it does in later human development.

Our work on object-directed imitation included two age groups, 14- and 24-month-olds (Meltzoff, 1985a). Traditional developmental theory predicted success on both immediate and deferred imitation tasks in the older group, and success on the immediate, but not the deferred task, in the younger group.

Experiment 1 involved 2-year-old infants. A total of 60 normal infants were recruited from the Seattle area and tested in the university laboratory. We tested whether infants would imitate a simple action with a novel toy. The object used during the experiment was specially constructed so that it could be pulled apart and put back together again. It consisted of two 1-in. wooden cubes, each with a piece of rigid tubing mounted to it. The tubing attached to one cube was of slightly larger diameter than that attached to the other so the two pieces fit snugly together. When assembled the object looked like a one-piece dumbbell-shaped toy. The object could be separated by grasping the two wooden cubes and pulling outward.

Each infant was randomly assigned to either the immediate ($N = 30$) or deferred ($N = 30$) group. Within each group, infants were randomly assigned to either the imitation condition or one of two control conditions. In the imitation condition, the experimenter simply picked up the toy and pulled it apart with a very definite movement. He then reassembled it and repeated the act two more times. These three demonstrations took place within a 20-sec stimulus-presentation period. The toy was then placed on the table and a 20-sec response period was initiated from the time the infant first touched the toy.

Two control conditions were used: baseline and activity control. In the baseline-control condition, the adult did not demonstrate the target action, but simply placed the toy on the table and the 20-sec response period was initiated from the time the infant first touched the toy. We noted, however, that this baseline condition alone is not a sufficient control for establishing true imitation. Infants in the imitation condition see the experimenter pick up and manipulate the toy, and this might prompt them to engage in nonspecific manual exploration of it. This exploration could in turn result in chance discovery that the object could be pulled apart. Thus more of the target behavior (toy pulling) would be found in the imitation condition than in the baseline condition. Nonetheless, such elevated target behavior would not be uniquely attributable to imitation of the adult's act and could be explained in terms of local enhancement (Meltzoff, 1985a; Galef, this volume).

For a rigorous test of imitation one also should compare performance of the infants in the imitation group with infants who had been shown a different attention-getting action with the same toy, rather than simply to compare the imitation group's performance with that of baseline control. Ideally one would want the same experimenter using the same toy to perform an action slightly different from the target action. If the infants perform more of the target behavior after seeing it demonstrated than after seeing a comparable control action performed with the same toy, by the same experimenter, at the same rate of movement, then the inference of imitation would be warranted.

Such an activity-control condition was included in the study. For this control group infants saw the adult pick up the object and move it in a small circle during the stimulus-presentation period. The diameter of the circle was similar to the linear movement used in pulling the toy apart. The rate of action was also controlled; the experimenter traced three circles in the same 20-sec demonstration period. As in the imitation group, the object was then placed on the table and a 20-sec response period was timed.

The deferred group were exposed to the same three test conditions as were subjects in the immediate group. The only difference was that a 24-hr delay was imposed between the stimulus-presentation and response periods.

The results supported the hypothesis of imitation. Using all 60 2-year-olds, the data showed that the production of the target action significantly varied as a function of test condition, with a greater proportion of infants in the imitation condition (75%) producing the target behavior than in either the baseline (25%) or activity (20%) controls, $\chi^2(2) = 15.42$, $p < .001$. The two control conditions did not differ ($p > .50$). A further subdivision of these data showed that infants successfully imitated regardless of delay. In the immediate group 80% of the imitation infants produced the target behavior in contrast to

20% of the controls ($p < .01$). In the deferred group, 70% of the imitation infants duplicated the target in contrast to 25% in the controls ($p < .05$).

A second study was undertaken to assess the imitative performance of 14-month-olds. The procedure, test object, and experimental room were all identical to that described above. The subjects were 120 14-month-old infants. Infants were randomly assigned to either the immediate ($N = 60$) or deferred ($N = 60$) group. Within each group three test conditions were used, as previously described. A 24-hr delay was again imposed for the deferred group. An overall test using all 120 subjects showed that infants' performances significantly varied as a function of test condition, with more infants producing the target in the imitation condition (60%) than in either the baseline (12.5%) or the activity (15%) controls, $\chi^2(2) = 27.67$, $p < .001$. Again the two control conditions did not differ ($P > .50$). A further breakdown of the data provided evidence for both immediate ($p < .001$) and deferred imitation ($p < .01$).

Figure 16.3 depicts the imitative effect across both studies combined ($N = 180$). Fully 65% of the infants in the imitation condition produced the target behavior as compared to 17% of the controls. Moreover, differences in the latency to produce the target response reveal an interesting aspect of the imitation effect. Those few infants in the control conditions who pulled the toy seemed to stumble onto this activity when manipulating the object. Indeed the probability among controls of producing the target behavior in the first 5 sec was virtually zero. Yet, 52% of the infants in the imitation condition did so. This quantitative measure captures what one observes during the test period. Infants who produced the target behavior in the imitation condition did not engage in extended trial and error behavior with the toy when it was presented. They often produced the target behavior immediately. Even the youngest infants initiated the target behavior quickly after a 24-hr delay (mean latency to pull = 5.02 sec).

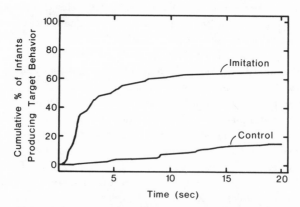

Figure 16.3.   Cumulative percentage of infants in the imitation ($N = 60$) and control ($N = 120$) conditions producing the target behavior as a function of time.

These studies provide a strong test of deferred imitation. The infants were not allowed to handle the object on Day 1. They were merely exposed to the adult demonstration without any chance to copy it at the time. Had the infants been allowed to imitate on Day 1, their performance on Day 2 would have involved merely a retention of their own previous imitative action over the delay period, rather than a memory for the perceptual display per se. Developmental theory (e.g., Piaget, 1954, 1962) would predict the former to be easier than the latter. Nonetheless, the data show that infants, at least by 14 months of age, can perform deferred imitation under these stringent conditions. Evidently a brief, 20-sec demonstration by an unfamiliar adult on one day can have a lasting effect on the subsequent behavior of infants.

At the conclusion of this experiment, we sought to investigate further the basis of infants' performance on these tasks. Is it possible that these strong effects might be at least partly attributable to the fact that infants in the imitation condition saw the test object in two pieces, and neither the baseline nor activity control infants saw this? To check this possibility we tested an additional 40 14-month-olds, 20 immediately and 20 after a 1-day delay, using the procedure as previously described. For this test the infants were simply shown the toy in its already pulled-apart state. The adult held both halves in his hands as he had after pulling them apart. He then moved them in a linear up-down movement three times in the 20-sec stimulus-presentation period to match the horizontal movements of the toy in the imitation condition.

The results of this condition were very similar to the other two controls that had been used in the study (baseline and activity control). Out of the 40 subjects only 15% produced the target behavior with the same number doing so immediately as in the delayed test. Evidently the probability of infants spontaneously producing the target behavior in the absence of the model is fairly stable over a variety of control procedures. Thus, if one now considers all 160 of the 14-month-olds tested, the results show that 60% of the infants in the imitation condition produce the target behavior in contrast to 12.5% in the baseline, 15% in the activity control, and 15% in this new control, $\chi^2(3) = 33.15, p < .0001$. This provides strong support for the hypothesis of imitation.

IMITATION OF OBJECT-MANIPULATION IN 9-MONTH-OLD INFANTS UNDER CONDITIONS OF IMMEDIATE AND DELAYED TESTING

One purpose of the next experiment was to test for imitation, particularly deferred imitation, in still younger infants. A second question concerns the generality of the imitation effect. The previous work assessed imitation of a single act. Can imitation of a range of fairly arbitrarily chosen actions be demonstrated?

To investigate these questions we tested 120 9-month-old infants (Meltzoff, in press). Testing took place at the university laboratory. Three actions on objects were used to assess imitation; all were chosen to be within the motor capability of a 9-month-old, but were fairly arbitrary in nature. Task 1 consisted of shaking a small, plastic egg-shaped object. Task 2 involved closing a vertically mounted flap of wood that was hinged to a baseplate. Task 3 consisted of pushing a small button mounted on the face of a black rectangular box. The button activated a beeper housed inside the box.

Sixty infants were tested for immediate and sixty for deferred imitation, the latter by using a 24-hr delay imposed between the stimulus-presentation and response periods. Other than the delay, the procedure was the same for both tests. Within each test group, 24 infants were assigned to the imitation condition and 36 were assigned to the control conditions.

For the imitation conditions, the experimenter demonstrated each of the three target actions with a repeated-measures procedure. Each of the target actions was presented three times in a 20-sec stimulus-presentation period while the infants watched from across a table. For the immediate imitation test, after all three actions were demonstrated, each object was placed on the table for a 20-sec response period. For the deferred imitation test, a 24-hr delay was interposed between the stimulus-display and the response periods.

The control infants were subjected to the same general procedure as infants in the imitation conditions, except that they did not see the target actions modeled. Again, half were tested immediately and half over a 24-hr delay. To approximate different aspects of the display, three different control groups were used: a baseline, an adult-touching, and an adult-manipulation control.

For the baseline condition, the modeling periods were simply omitted and the infants were timed for the three sequential 20-sec response periods; all else was identical to the imitation condition. For the adult-touching condition, infants saw the adult reach out and hold each object three times in the modeling periods, but they were not shown the particular target actions. These modeling periods were followed by a series of three 20-sec response periods, as in the imitation condition. This adult-touching condition controls for the possibility that infants would produce the target actions if they saw the adult approach and touch the object, even if the exact target action were not modeled. The adult-manipulation control was conducted to mimic further aspects of the target display without demonstrating the critical target action. Infants who see that movement of objects can have consequences, that they beep or rattle, may be more motivated to manipulate them. The adult-manipulation condition demonstrated such consequences without demonstrating the target actions. For example, infants were exposed to the beeping sound made by the black box during the modeling period (as were infants in the imitation group); however, this sound was produced by having the experimenter place both his hands on the sides of the box and surreptitiously use his thumb to activate a small switch in the back of the box, which was invisible to the child. Similarly, infants were exposed to the rattling sound made by the egg during the modeling period; however, this was accomplished by having the adult use one finger to spin the egg in place so that it made the sound. Finally, regarding the third object, infants were shown that the small flap could move relative to the wooden base. This was accomplished by showing a toy similar to that shown to the imitation group but without the metal hinge screwed on. Infants saw the object with the flap already placed in a horizontal position (the "end state" for the flap shown to the imitation group). The flap was then moved toward the infant and back while being held between the experimenter's thumb and forefinger. The forward and backward movement approximated the distance traversed by the arc of the flap in the imitation condition.

The results support the hypothesis of imitation. Each infant in each condition could produce up to three target behaviors. The obtained means and standard deviations are displayed in Table 16.1. The results can be analyzed using a Condition (4) × Delay (2) ANOVA. The main effect for Condition was significant, $F(3,112) = 10.39, p < .001$. A follow-up Neuman-Keuls test showed that infants in the imitation condition produced more target behaviors than did infants in each of the three control conditions (all p's $< .05$), and that the number of target behaviors infants produced in each of the control conditions did not differ significantly from one another. There was no main effect of Delay ($F < 1$) and no Condition × Delay interaction ($F < 1$), indicating that the imitation effect was not significantly reduced due to the 24-hr delay.

The strength of the imitation effect can be further illustrated by considering just the extreme cases, those in which all three target actions were produced. It is striking that nearly 20% of the subjects (9 of 48) in the imitation condition duplicated all three of the events they were shown, whereas none of the 72 control infants produced all three targets (this difference in performance between the imitation group and the control group was significant, $p < .001$, Fisher exact test). Once again, there is no effect of delay on this performance. Five of the 24 infants in the deferred test reproduced all three behaviors and 4 of the 24 infants in the immediate test did so.

Table 16.1
Infants' Test Scores as a Function of Delay and Experimental Condition

| | Delay | | | | | |
| | Immediate | | Deferred | | Combined | |
Condition	Mean	SD	Mean	SD	Mean	SD
Baseline Control	1.00	.74	1.17	.72	1.08	.72
Adult-Touching Control	.75	.45	.58	.67	.67	.57
Adult-Manipulation Control	.50	.52	.83	.72	.67	.64
Imitation	1.54	.93	1.58	.97	1.56	.94

Note: Maximum score = 3.

Finally, the generality of the effect is demonstrated by the evidence that each of the three actions was imitated when each was considered individually. For those infants who saw the shaking action demonstrated, 35.4% produced the target action, in contrast to only 16.7% of the control infants ($\chi^2(1) = 4.55, p <$ .05). Similarly, there was evidence for imitation of the button-pushing act, with 56.3% of the infants in the imitation condition and 25% of the controls producing this behavior ($\chi^2(1) = 10.70, p < .01$). There was also evidence that infants duplicated the hinge-close behavior, with 64.6% of the imitation infants and 33.3% of the control infants producing the target behavior ($\chi^2(1) = 10.10, p <$ .01).

This experiment shows that infants as young as 9 months of age are proficient at copying simple actions demonstrated by an adult. The results indicate that there is some generality to the imitative effect, for there was evidence for imitation of each action. Yet none of the actions can be thought of as innate motor programs or as having great biological significance. They were purposely chosen to be rather arbitrary, and the results showed that it was highly improbable (0% probability in this sample) that individual infants would spontaneously engage in all three of these actions. Nonetheless, about 20% of the infants in the imitation group remembered and reproduced all three actions even after the 24-hr delay.

FACIAL AND MANUAL IMITATION IN 2- TO 3-WEEK-OLD INFANTS

Our previous research assessed imitation of object-directed behaviors. A different type of imitation is the copying of pure body movements without objects, for example the imitation of facial gestures. For such imitation the subjects must translate the body transformations they see into body movements of their own with no external object, beyond the movement pattern itself, playing a role. Developmental theory predicts that gestural imitation is highly constrained in infancy. The onset of spontaneous facial imitation is predicted to occur at about 1 year of age. Before this age, infants are thought to be unable to match a gesture they see with one of their own that they cannot see, unless specifically trained to perform such tasks. For a variety of reasons we were led to doubt this prediction, and in 1977 we conducted two studies of facial imitation in 2- to 3-week-old infants (Meltzoff & Moore, 1977).

Assessing imitation in infants 2 to 3 weeks of age raises interesting methodological problems. The chief concern is to distinguish true imitation from a general arousal response. (This is related to the social facilitation and contagion issues in the animal literature.) For example, suppose an experiment were designed with a baseline period in which a neutral face (or no face at all) were presented, and this was followed by a tongue-protrusion demonstration by an adult experimenter. Further suppose that there were significantly more infant tongue protrusions to the adult tongue display than during the baseline condition. Such results would not permit the inference of infant imitation. Infants could be aroused at the sight of a moving human face, and infant oral movements including tonguing could be part of this general arousal response.

To address this problem we developed a cross-target comparison technique (Meltzoff & Moore, 1977, 1983a), in which infants are shown several gestures (targets) in a repeated-measures design and their response across these different targets is monitored. For example, we show an infant both a mouth-opening display and a tongue-protrusion display. If infants respond with more mouth openings to the mouth display than to the tongue display, and conversely respond with more tongue protrusions to the tongue display than to the mouth display, this cannot be due to a general arousal. Both gestures are presented by the same experimenter, at the same distance, and at the same rate of movement. The differential matching response to both displays cannot be explained by a general arousal response.

Another methodological issue is that young infants' oral movements are fairly fine motor behaviors. Machine recording of these actions is still beyond existing technology, and this opens the possibility of scorer bias in counting infants' responses. Therefore we videotaped the experiment using a close-up picture of the infant to facilitate scoring these fine-grained behaviors. There was no record of the adult's gesture on the videotape and thus the behaviors were scored by observers who were blind to the treatment.

Two studies of imitation in human neonates were conducted. The first study tested four different body actions: lip protrusion, mouth opening, tongue protrusion, and sequential finger movement. A repeated measures design was used in which each infant was exposed to each display. The results provided clear support for the imitation hypothesis; infants differentially copied all four gestures. These results were informative because the four gestures were carefully chosen to evaluate both the generality and specificity of the imitative response. As for generality, the gestures assessed both manual and facial imitation, showing that imitation was not limited to only one body region, such as the mouth. The specificity of the behavior was also demonstrated because infants responded differentially to two types of lip movements (mouth opening vs. lip protrusion) and two types of protrusion actions (lip protrusion vs. tongue protrusion). In other words, the results showed that when the body part was precisely controlled—when lips were used to perform two subtly different movements—infants still responded differentially. Moreover, the results showed that when the same movement pattern was demonstrated (protrusion) but with two different body parts (lip vs. tongue protrusion), they also responded differentially. This is imitation that far outstrips that predicted by standard theories.

In the present study infants were allowed to begin their response in the presence of the adult's display. We thought that very young infants might be limited to some form of motor resonance in which fleeting matching responses were elicited by salient present events, and that these imitative responses might be easily disrupted by temporal delay or competing motor interference.

Another study was designed to address this point. Again a repeated-measures design was used in which each infant served as his own control. The target displays were mouth opening and tongue protrusion. In this study, we developed a "pacifier technique." The pacifier was put in infants' mouths as they watched the displays so that they could only observe but not duplicate the gestures online. The technique was quite effective. Infants' sucking reflex ensured that they sucked actively on the pacifier during the stimulus-presentation periods. Infants did not tend to open their mouths and let the pacifier drop out during the mouth display; nor did they tend to push the pacifier away with their tongues during the tongue display. After the pacifier was removed the infant was given a 150-sec response period during which the experimenter maintained a passive face pose. The experiment was videotaped using a close-up picture of the infant's face, and the videotape was subsequently scored by an observer who was kept blind to the treatment.

Even with this pacifier technique, the infants imitated the two displays. The results showed significantly more infant mouth opening after the mouth display than after a baseline period ($p < .05$) or after the tongue display ($p < .05$). Similarly there were more infant tongue protrusions in response to the adult tongue display than after a baseline period ($p < .005$) or the ault mouth display ($p < .005$).

These two experiments show that very young human infants can imitate simple body movements presented by adult models, a finding that has now been replicated in several independent laboratories (see Meltzoff, 1985b, for a review). What might underlie this unexpected infant competence? The simplest answer might be that infants had learned to copy these displays during the elaborate mother-infant interaction that occurs in the first postnatal weeks. Developmental studies have emphasized the rich, nonverbal "dialogues" that occur, often in *en face* position, between mothers and their young infants, and the similarly rich experience of early feeding episodes. Dedicated empiricists might propose that infants had somehow learned to imitate by the time we tested them at 2 to 3 weeks of age. The goal of the next study was to test this view.

IMITATION IN NEWBORN INFANTS

If the early imitation we reported depends upon contingencies learned during early feeding and other early interactions, then newborn infants in the first hours of postnatal life should fail at these tasks. A test was designed involving 40 newborns with a mean age of 32 hr (Meltzoff & Moore, 1983b). The youngest subject was only 42 min old at the time of test.

The infants were tested in a laboratory located within a newborn nursery in a large Seattle hospital. Following the logic of the cross-target comparison, infants acted as their own controls, and each was presented with both a mouth-opening and a tongue-protrusion gesture in a repeated measures design, counterbalanced for order of presentation. We used two 4-min test periods in which the experimenter alternately demonstrated the gesture (for 20 sec), then assumed the passive-face pose (for 20 sec), and so on. At the end of this first 4-min period, the experimenter switched gestures and alternating 20 sec periods of demonstration and passive face continued. Thus, the test followed a fixed stimulus-presentation format, regardless of the infant's response. The overall test duration of 8 min fit within the span of attention that pilot studies showed could be expected at this early age. Pilot studies also revealed that certain features of the test environment would help to foster newborns' attention and alertness, and the test room was designed to capitalize on these things. Testing took place in a darkened room; the only lighting was a dim spotlight focused directly on the experimenter's face. Behind the experimenter was a black curtain. The experimenter's face was thus the brightest object in an otherwise black, homogeneous surround. Under these dim lighting conditions the newborns tended to open their eyes and fixate on the face. Again, the experiment was videotaped and subsequently scored by an observer who was blind to the modeled behavior.

The results supported the hypothesis of imitation. There were significantly more infant mouth openings in response to the mouth display than to the tongue display ($Z = 2.26$, $p < .05$, Wilcoxon matched-pairs signed-ranks test). Conversely, the frequency of infant tongue protrusions was greater to the tongue display than to the mouth display ($Z = 3.31$, $p < .001$).

The results for individual subjects were noteworthy. Each infant can produce a greater frequency of mouth openings to the adult mouth-opening display than to the tongue-protrusion display ($+$), a greater frequency of mouth openings to the adult tongue-protrusion display ($-$), or an equal frequency of mouth openings to both displays (0). Similarly, each infant can produce a greater frequency of tongue protrusion to the tongue display ($+$) or to the mouth display ($-$), or have an equal frequency to both (0). In Table 16.2 all 40 subjects are categorized in terms of their responses to both displays considered simultaneously. These data can be analyzed using a one-sample chi-square test. The results are significant, $\chi^2 = 38.70$, $df = 7$, $p < .001$.

The hypothesis of infant imitation can be most stringently examined by comparing the number of infants falling into the two most extreme cells ($++$ vs. $--$). The infants in the $++$ cell can be classified as imitators, consistently matching both gestures. The infants in the $--$ cell can be classified as anti-imitators, consistently mismatching both gestures. Under the null hypothesis, there is an equal probability of infants falling into one or the other of these two response types. The results identify 16 infants with the $++$ pattern and only one with the $--$ pattern, thus supporting imitation. Statistical tests were also conducted to assess the correlation between imitative performance and hours since

Table 16.2
Number of Infants Displaying Each of
Eight Response Types.

Response Type	Number of Infants
+ +	16
+ 0	5
0 +	1
+ −	5
− +	9
0 −	1
− 0	2
− −	1
Total N	40

Note: The response patterns are shown as ordered pairs depicting the two infant behaviors in the order: mouth openings, tongue protrusions. (+) indicates a greater frequency of an infant behavior to the matching adult display than to the mismatching display; (−) indicates a greater frequency of an infant behavior to the mismatching display than to the matching display; (0) indicates an equal frequency of an infant behavior to both displays.

birth. While recognizing that there was only a narrow age range tested (.7–72 hr), it is still of interest that no such correlation was found.

The results show that human infants in the first 72 hr of life can imitate at least two facial displays performed by their conspecifics. The study established that some basic imitative ability is present at birth in the human infant.

CONCLUSIONS

The history of research on imitation is replete with controversies over how best to isolate imitative responding from other nonimitative production of the target. Imitation is not a particular behavior. Poking out the tongue is a particular behavior, but it may be imitative or not depending upon whether it is based on the perception of this very same action in another. Pulling apart an object is a particular behavior. It may be performed spontaneously in the course of exploring the object, in which case it is not imitative. Alternatively, it may be performed on the basis of perceiving another perform this same act, in which case it qualifies as imitation. In short, simply counting the performances of a particular target behavior tells you that the behavior occurs, but the raw existence of the particular target behavior does not indicate that it was produced imitatively. This problem is at the root of many definitional and methodological debates about establishing imitation, especially in the animal literature.

Although there are many suggestions in the animal literature as to the proper experimental procedures for isolating imitation (Galef, this volume), the literature on human infancy has a somewhat different history. Piaget sought to avoid methodological and definitional debate in studying infant imitation by adopting the same approach used by Supreme Court Justice Potter Stewart in his decision on pornography. Justice Stewart admitted that he could not define pornography precisely and to everyone's satisfaction—"But," he insisted, "I know it when I see it" (*Jacobellis v. Ohio,* 1964). In some ways this is not a bad way to start in studying imitation in human infancy, because the issue in human development is surely not, as in animals, whether or not imitation can be demonstrated. There is near-universal acceptance of the notion that humans at some age can imitate actions demonstrated by their conspecifics.

Although there can be no debate about the existence of imitation in humans, there is disagreement about how early in development such behavior can be demonstrated. By two years? Young children are speaking by that age and surely the words they use (if not, as Chomsky has persuasively argued, the underlying grammatical rules), such as "hat" versus "chapeau," are learned, at least in part, by imitation. Moreover, dialects, accents, and intonation patterns are also learned in part by imitation of the surrounding adult milieu. One would not mistake the language of a Brooklyn 2-year-old for a Chinese or French 2-year-old, and probably not even for the sound of a Texan 2-year-old. Thus, there can be little debate over the presence of true imitation in humans even as young as 2 years old.

Piaget's naturalistic observations helped establish that imitation of vocalizations and actions takes place in young human infants. However he also proposed that this imitative skill emerged in stages. Only certain types of imitation were possible at certain ages. At this point Justice Stewart's approach to science begins to have some weaknesses. "Knowing it when you see it" can lead to both overestimations and underestimations of infants' imitative abilities.

An important problem in infant studies is distinguishing imitation from spontaneous behaviors that may happen to match the target behavior. Following Piaget's observational research style, most of the early studies of infant imitation did not include the controls necessary to make this distinction (e.g., Mehrabian & Williams, 1971; Paraskevopoulos & Hunt, 1971; Rodgon & Kurdek, 1977; Uzgiris & Hunt, 1975). In these studies, various models were presented and infants were scored according to whether or not they performed similar behaviors during a given response period. Imitation was inferred if the infant produced a behavior that matched the adult's. Imitative development was inferred if older infants produced more behavior matching the target than did younger infants.

Such designs do not allow inferences about the existence of imitation and its development. First, they do not provide conclusive evidence for imitation, because control conditions were not used to assess the spontaneous production of the target behaviors in absence of exposure to the model. The demonstration of imitation requires more than showing that infants produce behaviors that match adult target behaviors. It also requires that the infants' productions are above the spontaneous rate to be observed when infants have not been exposed to the target behavior. Lack of proper controls tends to *overestimate* the true imitative abilities of infants.

Second, inferences about imitative development cannot be drawn from data showing that older infants produce more target behaviors than do younger infants. For some of the behaviors under study, it is likely that older infants have a higher spontaneous rate of the target behavior than do younger infants. Imitative development is not assessed simply by testing whether the rate of the target behavior increases as a function of age, but by testing whether there is a differential increase as a function of age in the rate of the target behavior in modeling versus the control conditions. Without such comparisons, there will be a tendency to *underestimate* the imitative powers of younger infants relative to older ones, because the younger groups will tend to have a lower base rate of emitting many target actions.

Our research on infant imitation was designed both to address these methodological concerns and to test aspects of developmental theory, as discussed sequentially below.

On Distinguishing Infant Imitation
From Social Facilitation, Contagion,
and Local Enhancement

All studies in our laboratory included controls to distinguish imitative from nonimitative production of target behaviors. Some involved independent groups and some repeated-measures designs with each infant acting as his own control. Regardless of design, the core logic in these studies was to use a cross-target comparison. The infants in the imitation condition were exposed to the target behavior. Infants in the control condition were exposed to a highly similar behavior performed by the same experimenter, at the same distance, at the same rate of movement, and using the same object (if one was involved). This comparison addresses the chief dilemma in studies of infant imitation—to distinguish imitation from a spontaneous production of the target behaviors and production of target behaviors due to increased excitement or arousal. This approach also addressed the problems most often raised in animal studies, i.e., distinguishing imitation from its cousins social facilitation, contagion, and local enhancement.

The imitation results we reported are not reducible to "social facilitation," that is, an increase in production of target behaviors due to the mere presence of the conspecific rather than observation of the behavior itself. Because a cross-target comparison was used, if infants had a tendency to increase the target behavior due to the mere presence of the experimenter, such increase would have been obtained in both the imitation and control conditions (same experimenter present).

Similarly, the imitation results we reported are not easily reducible to "contagion," that is, an increase in an instinctual behavior pattern upon observing a like pattern by a conspecific (such as inducing "eating" by seeing eating). There are three arguments against applying the contagion label to the phenomena reported here. First, the control actions we have used resemble the target action so closely that it is difficult to see how simple contagion could be involved. If it had merely been the case that adult "oral movements" activated infant "oral movements," then it would be possible to account for the results within the contagion framework. However, the results were more specific than that. The adult tongue-protrusion display elicited more infant tongue protrusion than did the adult mouth-opening display. Conversely, the adult mouth-opening display elicited more infant mouth opening than did adult tongue protrusion. Yet both adult displays were oral movements.

Second, many of the tests involved a significant delay with intervening motor activity. Infants were not permitted to imitate on-line. It is difficult to invoke the classic contagion concept when the demonstration is no longer perceptually present and the response begins only after it has long disappeared from view. It stretches the concept considerably to say that the occurrence of a target action after a forced 24-hr delay is somehow "contagious" induction.

Third, many of the actions we tested cannot be considered instinctual motor programs, which is usually a criterion for invoking contagion. For example, it is difficult to consider the duplication of seeing an adult close a hinged flap, or shake an object, or pull a toy apart as an induction of an instinctual behavior pattern.

Finally, the results of infant imitation we reported are also not explicable by "local or stimulus enhancement." There are two reasons for this. First, the cross-target control procedure addresses this possibility, because the adult manipulates the same object in both the experimental and control conditions. The infant's attention is drawn to the same toy in both cases. For example, the adult pulls apart the toy in the imitation condition, but he picks up the same toy and moves it in a circle or holds it in two already pulled-apart pieces in the control conditions. The toy was "enhanced" in both cases, and indeed the procedure was successful in drawing the infants' attention to the toy in that all the infants in the control groups did in fact pick up the toy themselves; they simply were significantly less likely to produce the target behavior (Meltzoff, 1985a). The same points can be made with regard to the 9-month-old study, which tested the actions of egg shaking, hinge closing, and button pushing. Again, the controls included conditions in which the adult picked up and manipulated the test object in various ways.

Second, the local enhancement objection does not apply to the imitation of pure body-actions, such as mouth opening and tongue protrusion. Local enhancement is classically involved in cases of object manipulation, but it has not been applied to cases in which a body movement is copied in the absence of any external object at all.

On Using Infant Imitation
To Address Developmental Theory

Standard theories of infancy propose several important changes in infant imitation between birth and two years of age. Two milestones, deferred imitation and facial imitation, have been singled out in nearly all developmental texts, and they are often included in batteries assessing infant "intelligence." According to the standard theories the onset of facial imitation occurs at about 1 year of age, and the earliest deferred imitation is said to occur at about 18–24 months.

The present research suggests that standard theories have underestimated infants' abilities. The results show that 24-month-olds can perform deferred imitation after a 1-day delay, which confirms the standard view. However, the work also shows that 14-month-olds can delay their imitation. A more recent study established deferred imitation of three actions in infants as young as 9 months.

The other developmental milestone, that infants first perform untrained facial imitation at about 1 year, also profoundly underestimated infants' imitative prowess. In research reported here there was evidence for both facial and manual imitation in 2- to 3-week-old infants. Moreover, imitation was not so fragile as to be blocked by interfering motor activity (sucking on a pacifier) and short delays.

What mechanism might underlie this precocious facial imitation? The first, most obvious answer is that human infants learn to imitate in early interactions with their parents. Although the data from the 2- to 3-week-olds are not decisive evidence against this view, the results from the newborns, the youngest of whom was 42 min old at the time of test, indicate that postnatal learning is not a necessary condition for facial imitation. Apparently some primitive capacity to imitate is available at birth and does not require extensive interactive experience, mirror experience, or reinforcement history.

On the basis of these results it is possible to suggest that imitation is part of a basic human biological endowment. Our tentative working hypothesis is that infants can, at some level, apprehend the isomorphism between body transformations they see and those they feel themselves make. They use this as the fundamental basis for generating imitative responses. By this account, imitation— even newborn imitation—involves active matching to an environmentally provided target. In the case of facial imitation we have suggested that infants are comparing the proprioceptive information from their own unseen facial movements to the visual information from the adult's display (Meltzoff & Moore, 1977). The key point is that imitation, even in newborns, is mediated by a detection and utilization of equivalence between an act seen and an act done. (For a more elaborated statement of this account, see Meltzoff, 1985b; Meltzoff & Moore, 1983a, 1983b.)

What about imitative development? In one sense it is clear that a neonate is not as good an imitator as a 1-year-old. Everyone agrees that something changes. The relevant questions are whether the development represents changes in (a) simple motor skill, (b) underlying mechanism, (c) the types of actions that can be copied, (d) the motivation to imitate, (e) the meaning the imitative exchange has to the infant, (f) the function imitation subserves, or (g) some combination of the above. At the present time there is no reason to assume that the observable shifts in imitative performance are attributable to one rather than another of these possibilities. Alternatives can be distinguished experimentally, but so far the relevant developmental studies have not been conducted. There is a pressing need, not only for more research, but especially for more theoretically motivated experiments.

The Infant as *Homo imitans*

The human animal, like others, has evolved a reciprocal relationship between the adult and infant members of the species. It has been postulated that humans have a unique drive toward instruction (Barnett, 1973), that we, more than any other animal, instruct our young in behavioral skills and culturally relevant rituals and customs. As might be expected in such a species, there is a complementary deeply rooted capacity for the young to imitate. Imitation is not an isolated phenomenon in humans. A wide range of acts can be imitated, even by preverbal infants, including pure motor acts (Meltzoff & Moore, 1977, 1983b), the manipulation of objects (Meltzoff, 1985a, in press), and vocal maneuvers (Kuhl & Meltzoff, 1982; Kuhl & Meltzoff, 1988). The human parents' propensity for instruction is richly complemented by the human infant's proclivity for imitation.

This chapter began with a citation from Aristotle in which he claimed that humans are the most imitative creatures in the world, and that imitation was "natural" to them. The first part of this claim should be evaluated by the readers after taking into account the recent studies of nonhuman animals reported elsewhere in this book. As for the second claim, imitation indeed appears to come "naturally" to man, for it is present at birth prior to postnatal training. It is widely celebrated that our species manifests creativity and thought (*Homo sapiens*). Evidently this is coupled, especially during our early period of rapid psychological growth, with a powerful complementary proclivity for re-creation and imitation (*Homo imitans*).

ACKNOWLEDGMENTS

The preparation of this chapter was supported by grants from NICHD (HD-22514) and the MacArthur Foundation. I thank M. K. Moore, Craig Harris, and Calle Fisher for help on all phases of this research, and Patricia Kuhl for comments on a draft of this chapter.

REFERENCES

Aristotle (1941). In R. McKeon (Ed.), *The basic works of Aristotle*. New York: Random House.

Barnett, S. A. (1973). Homo docens. *Journal of Biosocial Science, 5,* 393–403.

Jacobellis v. The State of Ohio (1964). 378 U.S. 197.

Kawamura, S. (1959). The process of sub-culture propagation among Japanese macaques. *Primates, 2,* 43–60.

Kellogg, W. N., & Kellogg, L. A. (1933). *The ape and the child*. New York: McGraw-Hill.

Kuhl, P. K., & Meltzoff, A. N. (1982). The bimodal perception of speech in infancy. *Science, 218,* 1138–1141.

Kuhl, P. K., & Meltzoff, A. N. (1988). Speech as an intermodal object of perception. In A. Yonas (Ed.), *Perceptual development in infancy: Minnesota symposia on child psychology* (Vol. 20, 235–266). Hillsdale, NJ: Erlbaum.

Lipsitt, L. P., & Werner, J. S. (1981). The infancy of human learning processes. In E. S. Gollin (Ed.), *Developmental plasticity* (pp. 101–133). New York: Academic Press.

Marler, P., & Tamura, M. (1964). Culturally transmitted patterns of vocal behavior in sparrows. *Science, 146,* 1483–1486.

Mead, M., & Macgregor, F. C. (1951). *Growth and culture*. New York: G. P. Putnam's.

Mehrabian, A., & Williams, M. (1971). Piagetian measures of cognitive development for children up to age two. *Journal of Psycholinguistic Research, 1,* 113–126.

Meltzoff, A. N. (1985a). Immediate and deferred imitation in fourteen- and twenty-four-month-old infants. *Child Development, 56,* 62–72.

Meltzoff, A. N. (1985b). The roots of social and cognitive development: Models of man's original nature. In T. M. Field & N. Fox (Eds.), *Social perception in infants.* (pp. 1–30). Norwood, NJ: Albex.

Meltzoff, A. N. (in press). Infant imitation and memory: Imitation by nine-month-olds in immediate and deferred tests. *Child Development, 59.*

Meltzoff, A. N., & Moore, M. K. (1977). Imitation of facial and manual gestures by human neonates. *Science, 198,* 75–78.

Meltzoff, A. N., & Moore, M. K. (1983a). The origins of imitation in infancy: Paradigm, phenomena, and theories. In L. P. Lipsitt (Ed.), *Advances in infancy research* (Vol. 2, pp. 265–301). Norwood, NJ: Albex.

Meltzoff, A. N., & Moore, M. K. (1983b). Newborn infants imitate adult facial gestures. *Child Development, 54,* 702–709.

Paraskevopoulos, J., & Hunt, J. McV. (1971). Object construction and imitation under differing conditions of rearing. *Journal of Genetic Psychology, 119,* 301–321.

Piaget, J. (1954). *The construction of reality in the child*. New York: Basic Books.

Piaget, J. (1962). *Play, dreams and imitation in childhood*. New York: W. W. Norton.

Rodgon, M. M., & Kurdek, L. A. (1977). Vocal and gestural imitation in 8-, 14-, and 20-month-old children. *Journal of Genetic Psychology, 131,* 115–123.

Uzgiris, I. C., & Hunt, J. McV. (1975). *Assessment in infancy: Ordinal scales of psychological development*. Urbana, Ill: University of Illinois Press.

Author Index

Subject Index

A

Abstract concepts,
  different, 287
  same, 287
Accommodation, 304, 305
Allelomimetic behavior, 11, 17
Allospecific song, 257
Anorexia,
  social determinants, 166
Antipredator response, 84
Anxiety reduction, 20
Arousal-producing cues, 198
Assimilation, 304, 305
Assortive mating, 169
Attention,
  socially enhanced, 15
Auditory,
  cues, 198
  feedback, 20
  sensory-gating, 256
  template, 256, 261, 272
Automaintenance, 203
Autoshaping, 208, 226, 231
Avoidance,
  discriminated, 198
  generalization, 99
  learning, 100
  observationally acquired, 112
  predator, 51, 53, 69, 75
  snake, 51
  socially acquired, 112
  vicarious, 99, 104, 112, 113
  visually mediated, 108, 113

B

Baboons, 51
Blackbirds, 75–97, 99–115, 155, 200, 269
Budgerigars, 283
Buntings,
  indigo, 265, 268, 291
Butterflies,
  Monarch, 101, 112
  Viceroy, 101

C

Canaries, 268
Cats, 141, 227
Chaffinches, 88, 100, 261, 268, 271
Chickadees, 109, 146
Chickens, 146
Chimpanzees, 51, 52, 76, 289, 321
Classical conditioning, 19, 21, 53, 66, 69
Classification concept, 287
Coaction, 12

353